SURVIVING KATYŃ

SURVIVING KATYŃ

*Stalin's Polish Massacre
and the Search for Truth*

Jane Rogoyska

ONEWORLD

A Oneworld Book

First published by Oneworld Publications in 2021

Copyright © Jane Rogoyska 2021

The moral right of Jane Rogoyska to be identified as the Author of this work has been
asserted by her in accordance with the Copyright, Designs, and Patents Act 1988

ISBN 978–1–78607–892–6
eISBN 978–1–78607–893–3

Illustration credits: Hitler invades Poland, International Medical Commission at Katyń,
Krivovertsov talks to International Medical Commission © Imperial War Museum. Bronisław
Młynarski, General Jerzy Wołkowicki, General Wacław Przezdziecki, Ambassador Stanisław Kot,
General Anders with Colonel Okulicki, Ferdynand Goetel, Joseph Goebbels, Józef Czapski with
General Anders courtesy of Polish National Digital Archives. Major Sobiesław Zaleski, Adam
Sołtan, Maksymilian Łabędź, sketch from Starobelsk, wooden cigarette box © Muzeum Katyńskie.
Sketch of Griazovets, Wołkowicki's notes © Polish Museum and Sikorski Institute London. Zygmunt
Berling with Wanda Wasilewska © Wojskowe Biuro Historyczne. Stanisław Swianiewicz courtesy
of Maria Swianiewicz–Nagięć. Zdzisław Peszkowski courtesy of Muzeum Historyczne w Sanoku.
Sketch of Kozelsk by Dr Salomon Słowes, courtesy of United States Holocaust Memorial Museum
gift of Salomon Słowes. Dr Marian Wodziński courtesy of a private collection. Józef Czapski
older, Father Zdzisław Peszkowski © Polish Press Agency. Katyń 1943: graves, priest, hands, skull,
POW delegation from Amtlichtes Material zum Massenmord im Katyn. Józef Czapski © Historic
Collection / Alamy Stock Photo. Lavrenty Beria © Granger Historical Picture Archive / Alamy
Stock Photo. Narcyz Łopianowski © UtCon Collection / Alamy Stock Photo. Sikorski-Maisky
signing © Granger Historical Picture Archive / Alamy Stock Photo. Burdenko Commission ©
SPUTNIK / Alamy Stock Photo. Yalta Conference © Photo 12 / Alamy Stock Photo. Jan Bober
from Gazeta Administracji i Policji Państwowej nr 33 1925, courtesy of Dr Krzysztof Halicki.

Set in Minion and Nocturne by Tetragon, London. Nocturne, designed by
Mateusz Machalski, was inspired by the lettering on stone tablets commemorating
the victims of World War II and pre-war Jewish shop signage.

Printed and bound in Great Britain by Clays Ltd, Elcograf S.p.A.

Oneworld Publications
10 Bloomsbury Street
London WC1B 3SR
England

MIX
Paper from
responsible sources
FSC® C018072

'The struggle of man against power is
the struggle of memory against forgetting.'

MILAN KUNDERA

Contents

PART IV: THE FOREST 1943-44

PART V: COLD WAR 1945-

Note

MANY PEOPLE UNDERSTANDABLY ASSUME THAT THE TERM 'KATYŃ' or 'Katyń Massacre' refers to a single event. In fact, it is an umbrella term used to designate the murder of nearly 22,000 Polish prisoners of war, mainly but not uniquely officers of the Polish army, who were killed by the NKVD in different locations around the Soviet Union between April and May 1940 as a consequence of a direct order signed off by Stalin on 5 March 1940. In April 1943, the German army discovered the bodies of just over 4,000 of these prisoners in the Katyń Forest near Smolensk in Russia, giving rise to the name.

NOTE ON PLACE NAMES

Many of the place names featured in this book have changed several times over the course of recent history. For places featuring frequently in the text I have used the names used by the Poles during the period in which events occurred, thus present-day Lviv is Lwów, Vilnius is Wilno. Others I have updated.

NOTE ON POLISH PRONUNCIATION

Polish names present a considerable challenge to the English reader, an embarrassment of consonants guaranteed to strike fear into the non-linguist's heart. In fact, Polish is a logical language and once the rules are understood pronunciation is (relatively) simple. In the hope of easing the reader's passage through this text I have included a basic phonetic guide to names that appear frequently:

J = y   e.g. Jan = Yan, Józef = Yoosef

W = v   e.g. Zbigniew = Zbigniev, Godlewski = Godlevski

Ł = w   e.g. Młynarski = Mwynarski, Bronisław = Broniswav,
           Stanisław = Staniswav, Władysław = Vwadyswav

Cz = ch   e.g. Czapski = Chapski

Sz = sh   e.g. Peszkowski = Peshkovski, Szczypiorski =
           Shchypiorski

Dz = dj   (+ i or e) e.g. Zdzisław = Zdjeeswav

Rz = zh   e.g. Jerzy = Yezhy

Ck = tsk   e.g. Wołkowicki = Vowkovitski

Preface

IMAGINE, IF YOU WILL, SEVERAL THOUSAND MEN WHO HAVE recently experienced a crushing defeat in battle. Of these, approximately half are professional soldiers; the others are reservists, officers who until only weeks ago were busily engaged in civilian professions as lawyers, engineers, teachers, politicians, journalists, scientists, writers, doctors, priests. All are men accustomed to be in control of their lives. Now bemused and bewildered, woefully – tragically – out of their depth, they face a new and inscrutable enemy: not soldiers with guns but officers of the NKVD, highly-trained professionals whose methods of operation are mystifying, whose special skill is the control of a population through terror.

The barest of facts about the 1940 Katyń Massacre are easily summarised: on 17 September 1939, just two weeks after Britain and France declared war on Nazi Germany following its invasion of Poland from the west, the Red Army invaded from the east. No declaration of war was made. Thousands of members of the Polish armed forces were captured as they retreated from the German onslaught, then taken to prison camps across the Soviet Union. After several weeks the enlisted men and NCOs were sent home, leaving behind some 14,800 officers, police and border guards imprisoned in three special NKVD-run prisoner of war camps at Kozelsk, near Smolensk in Russia; Starobelsk, near Kharkov (Kharkiv) in Ukraine; and Ostashkov, near Kalinin (now Tver) in Russia. For seven months the men were questioned by NKVD interrogators, their loyalties probed, their susceptibility to communist conversion tested.

In April–May 1940 all but 395 of these men were murdered in the strictest secrecy on the direct orders of the head of the NKVD, Lavrenty Beria, signed off by Stalin. It was not until April 1943, when the USSR and Germany were no longer allies and the German army had advanced into Soviet territory, that the Nazis discovered mass graves in the Katyń Forest near Smolensk. The bodies were those of 4,000 Polish officers previously held in Kozelsk camp.

This shocking revelation led to one of the most bitterly-fought propaganda battles of World War II. While the Nazis sought to divide the Allies with evidence of 'Bolshevik bestiality', the Soviets pointed the finger at Hitler's 'fascist hangmen', claiming the massacre had taken place not in 1940 but 1941, when the Smolensk area was under Nazi control. Given the Allied position of dependence on Stalin to win the war against Hitler, neither Britain nor the US dared challenge the Soviet version of events. So the story was allowed to stand: the Katyń Massacre officially became a Nazi crime, complete with fake dates and fake monuments. The fate and whereabouts of the missing prisoners of Starobelsk and Ostashkov camps remained a mystery until the collapse of communism in 1990, when Soviet president Mikhail Gorbachev finally acknowledged Katyń as a Stalinist crime and handed over relevant NKVD documents to the Polish president, General Wojciech Jaruzelski. The bodies of the prisoners of Starobelsk camp were revealed to be buried in Piatykhatky Park near Kharkov, those of the prisoners of Ostashkov in Mednoye, near Tver. Researchers have subsequently increased the total number of victims to nearly 22,000 (21,857 to be precise), including 7,300 Polish officers who were held in prisons in Ukraine and Belorussia and murdered under the same order.

Knowledge of the Katyń Massacre in the West is fading fast. Many people have never heard of it; those who have are often familiar only with the basic outlines of the story. In Poland, by contrast, Katyń remains deeply controversial, a source of national pain and a continuing bone of contention between Russia and Poland in which politics plays a prominent role. Nazi crimes have been examined and laid bare in all their brutal detail; apologies and reparations made and paid. By contrast, the decades of enforced silence on the subject of Soviet misdeeds have left this period of history 'live' and incomplete. There are still gaps to be filled in, scores to be settled. The legacy of resentment and mistrust continues to play out across eastern Europe.

So why should we care about Katyń now? As the British Permanent Undersecretary for Foreign Affairs, Sir Alexander Cadogan, pointed out in 1943, the death of a few thousand Poles at the hands of the NKVD is a drop in the ocean compared to the millions of Soviet citizens murdered by Stalin. Indeed, the number of Polish citizens who died as a result of the Soviet deportations of 1940–41 was infinitely greater, in the hundreds rather than the tens of thousands. Among the many crimes of the Stalinist era one might question why Katyń has come to hold such symbolic importance.

The methods employed by the Stalinist state to dispose of its enemies were many and various: show trials, executions, labour camps – take your pick, the list is long. But even by those brutal standards the organised murder of thousands of foreign nationals held not as criminals but as prisoners of war was unusual. The NKVD might dispatch foreign individuals to the Gulag, they might assassinate them, but they did not generally deliberately eliminate them *en masse* (that was a fate reserved for Soviet citizens). The men in question belonged to Poland's elite. Their loss wiped out a generation of thinkers, politicians, soldiers, artists. The massacre formed part of a wider Stalinist strategy aimed at removing anyone who might conceivably pose a threat to the imposition of future Soviet rule in Poland – a decapitation of Polish society strikingly similar to Nazi policy in occupied Poland at the same time. The symbolism of their deaths is powerful enough, memorable and disturbing. But what really makes Katyń stand out from other, equally murderous, crimes, and what makes it so relevant today, is what we might call 'the lie'.

For over four decades the Soviet state maintained the fiction of Katyń as a Nazi crime, an achievement made possible by the unparalleled dedication of the Soviet (and communist Polish) security services in controlling the 'story'. The deceit began in 1940 with rumours deliberately cultivated to make the prisoners believe they were going home. The effect was so complete that for a long time the men who survived were convinced they were the ones who had been 'left behind'. It continued with a series of often dramatic interventions designed to silence and intimidate those who would speak out as the NKVD (later the KGB, the UB and SB) worked tirelessly to reshape the facts into their desired form, from planting documents on dead bodies to pursuing a truck full of evidence across Europe, destroying records, or staging 'accidents' in European capitals. The people who paid the highest price for this elaborately-constructed edifice of deceit were those who could or would call into question the official version of events.

Only 395 men survived the Katyń Massacre. For many of them, their role as unwitting witnesses to a crime that officially never happened brought them exile, persecution, arrest. Most powerfully, it brought them a twin mystery that would haunt them for the remainder of their lives: 'Why were our comrades killed, and not us?' And its mirror image: 'Why were we saved, and not them?'

London, 1 September 1939. Evening newspapers announce Germany's invasion of Poland.

Introduction

CAPTURE

The news of this stab in the back was like the sensation one feels in the theatre when a crime which has long been impending is finally perpetrated.[1]

NAZI GERMANY'S INVASION OF POLAND ON 1 SEPTEMBER 1939 IS one of the twentieth century's most familiar dates, followed two days later by a declaration of war by Britain and France. The next few months of military inactivity, dubbed variously the 'phoney war', 'twilight war', *'drôle de guerre'* (funny war) or *'sitzkrieg'* (sitting war), fills barely a page in most Western history books. Britain slowly mobilised while France and Germany glared at each other from behind the seemingly impregnable safety of the Maginot and Siegfried Lines. For the Polish protagonists of this book, by contrast, the eight months between September and April 1940 mark the tragic opening act in a drama which has not yet fully played itself out today. For them, the significant date comes barely two weeks after the war's official start. Whereas Hitler's actions surprised no one, the arrival of half a million Red Army soldiers at Poland's eastern borders on 17 September 1939 was so unexpected that Polish forces, caught up in a chaotic retreat from the German onslaught, did not at first know whether to greet them as enemies or friends.

The Soviet action was a direct consequence of the Molotov–Ribbentrop Pact, signed in Moscow on 23 August 1939 by Soviet Commissar for Foreign Affairs Vyacheslav Molotov and German Foreign Minister Joachim von Ribbentrop. This unlikely last-minute alliance had emerged on the tail of a series of slow-moving and unconvincing efforts by Great Britain and France over the early summer of 1939 to cooperate with the Soviet Union in facing down German aggression. The talks had left Soviet leader Joseph Stalin frustrated, insulted and, finally, open to the idea of collaboration with

Hitler. The benefit of the Molotov–Ribbentrop Pact to Hitler was obvious: it gave him *carte blanche* to invade Poland, safe in the knowledge that her great eastern neighbour would not intervene. The advantage to Stalin was concealed in a Secret Supplementary Protocol which envisaged the future disposition of territories of interest to both sides, setting out Soviet and German spheres of influence in the Baltic states and Romania and drawing a line down Poland, dividing it in half. It also included a trade deal highly beneficial to both parties. Neither Germany nor the Soviet Union had been reconciled to the territorial losses resulting from the rebirth of Poland at the end of World War I. Since 1772, when Russia, Austria and Prussia first subjugated the once-great commonwealth of Poland-Lithuania, the country had been partitioned three times between these three great powers, finally ceasing to exist as an independent state in the third partition of 1795. For Hitler, Poland was the 'unreal creation' of the 1919 Treaty of Versailles, for Molotov it was its 'ugly offspring'.[2] The pact presented an opportunity to reacquire these territories while avoiding conflict with one another.

> The weather is superb, the sun is shining, the summer is dry. The river levels are low. The German tanks encounter no obstacles. A splendid visibility favours the enemy planes. Ours, unfortunately, no longer exist.[3]

The *Blitzkrieg* unleashed by the Nazis on Poland represented a new and devastating form of warfare for which no army could have been fully prepared: tanks rolled over harvest-ready fields, aircraft rained bombs and bullets on military and civilian targets alike. The popular image of the Polish army as a band of valiant but doomed knights fighting a modern war with last century's weapons is far from reality, but their 900,000 men could not hope to match the 1.5 million-strong Wehrmacht. Faced with an enemy numerically superior and infinitely better equipped, Polish forces retreated east in the hope that help would arrive from their Western allies, allowing them time to regroup and launch a counter-attack. Polish faith in Allied action was admirable but misplaced. At this stage neither the French nor the British were able or prepared to offer Poland anything except warm words. Left to fight alone, the Polish army was soon overwhelmed. As the Germans advanced on Warsaw the Polish government and High Command fled east to the town of Brest-Litovsk (now Brest in Belarus).

Then, on 17 September 1939, in defiance of all former Soviet–Polish non-aggression pacts, the Red Army crossed Poland's eastern border. In Poland they called it the 'stab in the back'.

In the early hours of the morning of 17 September the Soviet Deputy Commissar for Foreign Affairs, Vladimir Potemkin, summoned Poland's ambassador, Wacław Grzybowski, to his office in Moscow and attempted to hand him a note from the Soviet government. One glance at the text convinced Grzybowski to refuse to accept it.

> The Polish Government has collapsed and shows no signs of life. This means that the Polish state and its government have, in fact, ceased to exist… Therefore, the agreements concluded between the USSR and Poland have ceased to operate. Left to its own devices and bereft of leadership, Poland has become a fertile field for all kinds of accidents and surprises, which could pose a threat to the USSR. Therefore, the Soviet government, which has been neutral until now, can no longer maintain a neutral attitude toward these facts.
>
> Nor can the Soviet Government remain indifferent to the fact that its kindred Ukrainian and Belorussian peoples, living on Polish territory, are abandoned to their fate and left unprotected.
>
> In view of this state of affairs, the Soviet government has directed the High Command of the Red Army to order troops to cross the frontier and to take under their protection the lives and property of the population of Western Ukraine and Western Belorussia.
>
> At the same time, the Soviet government intends to take all measures to liberate the Polish people from the disastrous war into which they have been dragged by their unwise leaders and to give them the opportunity to live a peaceful life.[4]

In refusing the note Grzybowski pointed out that the Polish army fought on and its government was still in existence. Potemkin eventually prevailed upon him to communicate its contents to the Polish government. Molotov, meanwhile, copied it to all ambassadors in Moscow, reassuring them of Soviet 'neutrality'. A public broadcast repeated the information.

Ambassador Grzybowski could also legitimately have asked Potemkin: from whom or what is the valiant Soviet army protecting the Ukrainians and Belorussians living in Poland's eastern territories? What are the 'accidents and surprises' that could harm the USSR, since the Germans were allied to the Soviets and therefore posed no threat? Rogue Poles? Bandits? The ambassador would doubtless also have noticed the ominous reference to Poland's eastern territories as Western Ukraine and Western Belorussia.

The region in question – known in Polish as *kresy*, or borderlands – did indeed contain substantial Ukrainian and Belorussian minorities, as well as Jews (who were not, it seems, in such urgent need of Soviet protection). The multi-cultural nature of the population reflected both the broad make-up of pre-war Poland and the historically fluid nature of borders in this region. In the ferment following the 1917 Russian revolution both Ukraine and Belorussia had declared, fought for and lost their independence, their eastern territories eventually going to the Soviet Union and the remaining western areas to Poland. Poland's re-emergence as an independent nation had presented numerous challenges (not least that of uniting the three separate legal and educational systems, currencies and even railway gauges produced by over a century of Russian, Austrian and German rule). The task had been met by successive Polish governments with the same varying levels of inspiration, incompetence and misjudgement to be found in any European country during the 1920s and 30s. That is to say, their policies, combined with the role of prejudice, snobbery and nationalism, could provide many good reasons why sections of Poland's minorities might be discontented and might even welcome the Soviet invasion, at least at first.

From the outset Stalin had a precise goal: he wanted permanent control of this region, joining the 'defenceless' Ukrainians and Belorussians with their brethren in the neighbouring Soviet Socialist Republics of Ukraine and Belorussia. Both of these had recently been divested of large portions of their ethnic Polish population during an operation against 'Polish spies' in which the NKVD executed over 110,000 Soviet Poles during the Great Terror of 1937–38.[5] In a second treaty, signed on 28 September 1939, the Soviet Union and Germany formalised what, in effect, constituted the fourth partition of Poland. A further secret supplementary protocol gave Germany control of the regions around Lublin and Warsaw – previously allotted to the Soviet sphere of interest – in exchange for Soviet control in Lithuania. Despite endless political discussions about Poland's eastern borders during the course of the war, Stalin's ruthlessly effective land grab was eventually rubber-stamped by the Allies at the Yalta conference in February 1945.

BALTIC SEA

LITHUANIA

Dvina

Neman

Königsberg

Danzig

EAST
PRUSSIA

Wilno

Grodno

Białystok

Vistula

Narew

Poznań

Warta

Warsaw

Bug

Pińsk

Pripyat

Łódź

GERMANY

Lublin

Łuck

Równe

Vistula

San

USSR

Kraków

Przemyśl

Lwów

Tarnopol

SLOVAKIA

Dniester

ROMANIA

HUNGARY

0   100   200 km

Occupied by Nazi Germany:

Annexed to the Reich

General Government

|||||| Annexed to the USSR

//// Administered by Lithuania

⌒ Poland's pre-war boundaries

Divided Poland 1939–41.

On the day of the Soviet invasion the Polish president, Ignacy Mościcki, and senior members of his government had reached Kuty, near the Romanian border. When he first heard the news Mościcki was initially unsure how to react, but once Ambassador Grzybowski had communicated the contents of the Soviet diplomatic note, all doubts vanished. The Red Army was advancing rapidly in their direction. A decision had to be made: stay and fall into Soviet hands, or flee. Mościcki decided on the latter course, reasoning it was preferable to continue the fight from abroad than surrender. The Polish government crossed into Romania the same day, followed shortly afterwards by the commander-in-chief, Marshal Edward Rydz-Śmigły, and his staff. Under pressure from Germany the (supposedly) neutral Romanian government promptly interned the president, commander-in-chief and prime minister, along with many other top officials, as a consequence of which new leaders had to be chosen from those who managed to reach France unscathed. Władysław Rackiewicz was made president, General Władysław Sikorski took on the dual role of prime minister and commander-in-chief.

The decision to flee was controversial. Citizens enduring bombardment in Polish cities felt abandoned; many officers viewed the departure of their commander-in-chief while Polish forces were still fighting as shameful. But the decision allowed Polish units to join Allied forces abroad and enabled a sophisticated network of resistance to operate throughout the war in the form of the Polish Underground State and the Home Army (*Armia Krajowa* – AK), formed in 1940 under the direction of the government in exile after it moved from France to London.

If the Soviet invasion came as a complete surprise to the Polish government, it caused utter confusion among forces on the ground: the move east had severely disrupted communications with army High Command. As a consequence, nobody had the slightest idea whether the Red Army was coming to help or to conquer. The confusion was further amplified by an order, issued by Marshal Rydz-Śmigły before he left Poland, instructing Polish troops not to fight the Soviets unless they came under direct attack. The order eventually filtered through just at the moment when the threat from the Red Army was becoming all too evident. Although some Polish units resisted, many others surrendered in response to Rydz-Śmigły's command.

On the morning of 17 September, forty-year-old reserve Second Lieutenant Bronisław Młynarski had reached the town of Dubno, some thirty-five miles from the Soviet border. After reporting to garrison command he was awaiting orders, along with hundreds of other officers converging on the town from all over Poland. Urbane, humorous, warm-hearted, Młynarski was by profession a businessman, deputy director of the government-owned Gdynia-America Shipping Line. But his passion was music. It ran in his family. His father was the eminent composer and conductor Emil Młynarski, his sister Aniela was married to the celebrated pianist Artur Rubinstein. Both Młynarski's sisters lived in the US, where he had spent many years. Like his good friend, the artist Józef Czapski, Bronisław Młynarski belonged to a generation of cultured, cosmopolitan Poles who had come of age in newly independent Poland and seen it flourish. A talented raconteur, he spoke English, French, German and Russian and could hold an audience in all four languages.

Bronisław Młynarski.

Since receiving his call-up papers in the last-minute general mobilisation Młynarski had seen no action, spending the first two weeks of the war travelling ever further eastwards in a largely futile attempt to locate and join his unit. On his circuitous journey from Warsaw he had fallen in with a couple of fellow officers, both reserve lieutenants like him: a towering 35-year-old forester, Zygmunt Kwarciński, and an engineer, Józef Laudański, known as Laud, whose round and friendly face reminded Młynarski of a country vicar. The three were to form the core of a group of friends who would remain inseparable over the next eight months.

Although the war was barely a fortnight old there was already an element of routine in the daily German bomber attacks. With meticulous regularity they passed overhead every morning at 6 a.m., flying from west to east. On the morning of 17 September a change occurred. Nearly one hour after the morning raid a formation of thirty planes approached from the east, flying west. They dropped no bombs. After firing a few salvoes the Polish ack-ack guns fell silent.

> Zygmunt, Laud and I were standing not far from one of our guns. Puzzled by the unusual display we rushed to our anti-aircraft experts who knew the silhouettes of every aircraft by heart. As we were approaching them we saw that they were greatly agitated. With his usual coolness and characteristic drawl Laud said: 'It looks to me as if they are not German planes.'
>
> 'My guess is that they are French or maybe British,' said Zygmunt. 'And they have come from Romania. Things will be fine now, my friends, just you see.'
>
> The experts were not convinced. They looked anxious. 'What sort of planes were they, for Heaven's sake, British or French?' they asked.
>
> More of our companions had now joined us around the battery. A general uproar resulted. Finally, put in a spot, the commanding officer, a young Lieutenant, announced calmly and distinctly: 'Gentlemen, they were neither British nor French, they were Soviet planes.'[6]

As each man put forward his interpretation of the strange event the group grew more excited, speculating in ever more fanciful terms as to the meaning of the strange apparition. After several hours news of the invasion began to filter in from the Polish–Soviet border. The men argued violently about how to interpret the Soviet presence on Polish soil, with 'the blind optimists on one side and the pessimists on the other who had fallen prey to complete despair. The fight was short-lived. As more dismal news came in, the camp of enthusiasts was dwindling fast.'[7]

This scene was repeating itself all over eastern Poland. With the Germans advancing rapidly from the west and the Soviets closing in from the east, it was now abundantly clear there was only one option left: a corridor remained – narrowing by the day – which neither the Germans nor the Soviets had yet reached. Down this the remains of the army hastened, hoping to get out of Poland into Hungary or Romania and from there make their way to France. Around 35,000 members of the Polish armed forces succeeded in escaping in this manner. The rest were not so lucky.

Towards evening on 19 September Bronisław Młynarski and his friends were part of a vast column of men and vehicles slowly heading south. Towards dusk they reached a tiny hamlet named Dolna Kaluska. Here, Młynarski recalled a scene of bucolic peace, with swampy fields to one side, farmyards and peasant cottages on the other. In front of them a large wooden bridge spanned the river. Several cars and trucks had already crossed the bridge, accelerating to climb the steep hill on the other side before swerving sharply round a tight corner and disappearing one after the other in clouds of dust behind a curtain of thick green foliage. 'It was then that a violent burst of bullets spluttered from the opposite bank.'[8]

After a short battle with an invisible enemy silence fell, interrupted by an ominous rumbling sound that suggested the presence of tanks. Then came shouting from the other side of the river. As he waited, crouched in a ditch, staring at the bodies strewn on the road, Młynarski was overcome by a feeling of dread. 'Some dark monstrous spectre seemed to advance gradually, and rhythmically, crushing one by its sheer mass and weight.'[9] A voice called out in Russian: 'Stop firing – you are surrounded. Give your-selves up or else we'll finish everybody off.' For a brief moment Młynarski contemplated the idea of using his brand new gun – never used except to test it – to shoot himself. He had been a student in Moscow during the Russian revolution and witnessed the bloody violence that followed. He was under no illusion about what would await him in Soviet captivity.

And so there I was toying with my gun, pressing it against my temple or would it not be better in my mouth? No, with my mouth wide open it looks so stupid. Damn it, no! Dash it all, this would be too easy. At that moment I felt suddenly as if somebody had wanted to snatch my cap from my head. Zygmunt yelled behind my back: 'For God's sake hide your head or you'll lose it.'[10]

A bullet had grazed Młynarski's head. Zygmunt passed him a handkerchief to staunch the blood and the momentary desire to put an end to his life passed. He sat in the ditch with his friends and watched as a young air force lieutenant crossed the bridge carrying a stick with a white scarf fastened to it. After a while the young man returned alone. Then he and a lieutenant-colonel 'walked slowly back again, step-in-step, into the lion's den to discuss the capitulation of the Polish Army'.[11]

Artist and writer Józef Czapski was captured some days later, on 27 September, at Chmielek, not far from the city of Lwów (now Lviv in Ukraine), after days of wandering with two reserve cavalry squadrons without horses and almost without arms. They meandered east, then west, before finally being encircled by Soviet tanks and artillery. For ten days Polish commander General Władysław Langner had managed to defend Lwów against the Germans, but the arrival of the Red Army on 19 September brought the siege to an abrupt end. The German army withdrew, leaving Langner and General Franciszek Sikorski[12] to negotiate the terms of surrender with the Soviets, signed on 22 September. The Soviets gave Langner concrete assurances that privates and NCOs would be allowed to go home; officers would be free to leave Poland and cross into Romania and Hungary to reach France. The promise was broken as soon as the Red Army occupied the city. The officers were arrested and taken to Tarnopol, after which the majority, including General Franciszek Sikorski, were transferred to Starobelsk camp.[13]

The Red Army soldiers charged with taking prisoners were mainly young conscripts, known as *boytzy*, drawn from every corner of the Soviet Union. After rounding up their captives they disarmed them, roughly separating the officers from the enlisted men before relieving them of their valuables. Wedding and signet rings were torn from fingers. Watches, leather belts, map holders, bags. Some even snatched the eagles from the officers' caps and ripped off their epaulettes, all the while insulting them in class terms as *pany* (lords or masters) or *pomyeshchyki* (landowners).

They showed a strange terror, which was further expressed by their senseless shouting and the way in which they searched us, brutally prodding our bodies as though our uniforms concealed bombs... For twenty-two years the authorities had been cramming into their heads the idea that anybody living outside their country was automatically an enemy of the people, of the Soviets, a bandit and a *krovopiytsa*, that is, a man who feeds on the blood of the exploited masses of working-class people or peasants.[14]

Meanwhile, the Soviets dropped leaflets on Polish troops:

Soldiers, turn on your officers and generals! Do not submit to the orders of your officers. Drive them out from your soil. Come to us boldly, to your brothers, to the Red Army. Here you will be cared for, here you will be respected.[15]

Many Polish officers and NCOs, police, civilians and border guards were shot on the spot. But the majority were taken prisoner, along with vast numbers of enlisted men. For days they rode on trucks or marched on foot, weak from hunger and exhaustion, along main roads 'lined with the statues of saints, their crosses broken and knocked over by the Soviet troops', until they reached the border. Here, a vast strip of no man's land enforced by barbed wire served as a physical reminder of the isolation in which the Soviet state kept its people from the outside world. Once over the border, prisoners were greeted by their first sight of a Soviet town. Józef Czapski recalled it vividly:

Another world. Poor, ugly houses which looked as if they had never been repaired. The famous electrification about which so much had been written in luxury print editions: the odd electric bulb blinking with a feeble reddish light, Stalin's profile in red neon in the middle of a miserable little square; that was all.[16]

Between late September and early October 1939 thousands of Polish prisoners of war were brought to wait by railway lines, to be transported to destinations unknown. At some point during this part of the journey prisoners noticed that the frightened young *boytzy* had been replaced by men wearing different uniforms with distinctive red-banded caps. These new arrivals moved calmly among the crowds, answering the endless questions put to them by anxious officers: would their belongings be returned to them, would they be given toothbrushes, razors or soap, would they be able to write to their families, and what about receiving their pay? The questions reflected the expectations of Polish officers captured as prisoners of war according to internationally recognised norms formalised in the 1929 Geneva Convention. To every question the red-capped officers replied with brief, soothing answers.

> '*Da, da, u nas vsyo yest, u nas vsyevo mnogo.*' (Yes there is plenty of every-thing in our country.)
>
> '*Da, konyechno, eto budyet,*' etc (Of course it will be like that. We shall return all your things, and there will be soap too. Tomorrow, the day after tomorrow.)
>
> 'Nothing to worry about. We shall make you feel safe.'[17]

These men were *politruks*, political commissars of the NKVD, the *Narodny Komissariat Vnutreknnykh Del*, the People's Commissariat of Internal Affairs. This was Stalin's internal security service, the precursor to the KGB and the Soviet Union's most efficient organisation. It was run by the pince-nez-wearing industrialist of terror Lavrenty Beria, who had recently taken over the reins from his predecessor and former boss, Nikolai Yezhov. Having presided over Stalin's Great Terror, Yezhov was now in disgrace and would shortly be executed.

When the trains eventually arrived the prisoners were loaded inside, eighty to a wagon, up to a thousand in each transport. There were no seats. Crushed up against one another in the darkness, back to back, legs uncom-fortably intertwined, they had no idea how long their journey would last nor where they were being taken. All they knew was that the direction of travel was east, into the heart of the Soviet Union.

Warsaw held out against the Germans until 27 September 1939. The last Polish fighting unit disbanded on 6 October. Poland was now a wholly occupied country: the Nazis controlled western and central Poland, the Soviets occupied the east.

PART I

Starobelsk, Kozelsk, Ostashkov 1939–40

Sketch of Kozelsk camp by Dr Salomon Słowes, with key. Note the 'Lady's shed' where the only female prisoner, pilot Janina Lewandowska, was held.

I
—
MONASTERIES

In the distance, on the left side of the road, a high long wall glistened white. Silhouetted against the sky behind the wall were the rooftops of a number of buildings dominated by the bulbous outline of a dark blue church cupola. As we approached the wall, we saw that it was reinforced on the outside by a high barbed wire abatis and dotted with many wooden mushroom-shaped towers inside which we saw machine guns and huge searchlights.[1]

Since 17 September the Red Army had captured between 230,000 and 240,000 members of the Polish military, including around 10,000 officers. The army had no expertise in dealing with large numbers of prisoners or in running prison camps, so the task was entrusted to the only Soviet organisation capable of operating on such a vast scale: the NKVD. Within two days of the invasion preparations were in place: on 18 September NKVD Convoy Troops were put on a war footing and instructed to take charge of the reception points to which the Polish prisoners of war were being taken. On 19 September the head of the NKVD, Lavrenty Beria, ordered the establishment of the Administration for Prisoner-of-War Affairs, or UPV (*Upravlenie po Delam Voennoplennykh*), to be run by NKVD Major Pyotr Soprunenko under the supervision of Beria's deputy and close colleague, Vsevolod Merkulov. Regimental Commissar Semyon Nekhoroshev was to act as the UPV's commissar. A total of fourteen prison camps were made ready to receive Polish prisoners of war. Of these, seven were transit camps, four were labour camps and three – Kozelsk, Starobelsk and Ostashkov – were designated as special camps where officers, prominent state and military officials, intelligence agents, counter-intelligence agents, gendarmes, prison guards and police would be held. Each camp was situated in a different region of the Soviet Union: Kozelsk lay 200 miles south-east of Smolensk in Russia, Starobelsk in the eastern part of Soviet Ukraine about 150 miles from Kharkov, Ostashkov lay 150 miles west of the city of Kalinin (now Tver) in Russia's freezing north.

Higher-ranking and staff officers were to be sent to Starobelsk; police and prison guards to Ostashkov; privates from the German part of Poland were to be divided between Kozelsk and Putyvl camp in Ukraine. When it became obvious that Starobelsk could not hold all the officers, several thousand were sent on to Kozelsk, which thus became an officer camp.[2]

Given the sheer number of Polish prisoners captured by the Red Army, the Politburo swiftly decided that privates and non-commissioned officers would be released and sent home. In civilian life these (mainly young) men were labourers, drivers, agricultural or factory workers; they were of no strategic or political interest to the Soviet authorities. Since it was impossible to separate officers from men effectively in the field the process of sorting took place within the camps themselves. As a result, between early October and mid-November thousands of men arrived in the three special camps only to be sent back home again, in some cases returning on the train in which they had just arrived. Residents of the Soviet zone of occupation went first, followed by those whose homes were in German-occupied territory, who were handed over to the German authorities in a prisoner exchange. Others were sent to work on roads and in mines within the Soviet Union. The chaos of those first weeks is hard to overestimate: on 14 October 1939 Starobelsk camp held over 7,000 men, including 4,813 privates and NCOs, 2,232 officers and 155 others. By 1 April 1940 there were 3,893 prisoners, almost all of them officers. In Kozelsk the camp population halved from a total of nearly 9,000, mainly privates, to 4,599, mainly officers. A total of 16,000 men passed through Ostashkov camp: after 9,400 privates and NCOs were released to the Germans and others transferred to work in the mines, the camp population settled at 6,364.[3] It was not until mid-November that camp numbers finally stabilised and a routine was established.

The three camps were housed in former monasteries or convents whose occupants had been massacred during the revolution, their buildings then 'repurposed' for use by the NKVD. The sites bore grim witness to the violence of the recent past: in Starobelsk, formerly an Orthodox clerical seminary, tombs in the old graveyard had been uncovered; prisoners found skulls and bones buried in shallow earth in the grounds; bullet marks scarred the walls. Ostashkov camp occupied the remains of the magnificent Nilova Hermitage on Stolbny Island in Lake Seliger. Prisoners making repairs to the monastery cellars came across bones and scraps of fabric, even part of a gun. Two of the original monks had apparently survived and still worked there; one of them – 'a tall man, with expressionless face and deep-sunken eyes [who] looked like a walking corpse' – never spoke.[4]

Despite the NKVD's fearsome reputation for efficiency, honed in running the vast network of Soviet labour camps known as the Gulag, camp commanders faced a considerable logistical challenge in financing and organising the provision of food, material and medical supplies for so many prisoners of war arriving simultaneously and at such short notice. Transports comprising hundreds of Polish officers and enlisted men streamed daily into camps which, despite hasty preparations, were in no fit state to accommodate them. In Kozelsk, construction of the bunks had only just begun when the first prisoners arrived; there was not enough straw for mattresses and a lack of sheets, blankets and pillows; a chronic shortage of brooms, cloths and bins made cleaning the camp next to impossible; while the toilets (inadequate in number) had no roofs or walls. Food supplies were unevenly distributed, with many essential items missing and an almost total lack of fresh food.

As to the matter of vegetables, the situation is bad indeed. We have enough potatoes for three or four days and now they are not bringing them to the camp, because the region did not complete a supply plan and all the local potatoes are being sent to Moscow. There is no cabbage at all and no hope of obtaining any.[5]

It was dusk when Bronisław Młynarski passed through the gates of Starobelsk, along with a group of around a thousand men. The only order they received on arrival, shouted by a revolver-wielding *politruk* from the steps of the church, was to find themselves somewhere to sleep for the night. Młynarski had managed to stick with his cheerful group of friends and together they went in search of shelter. Every building was already full to bursting, every spare inch of muddy ground occupied by men stretched out on coats or blankets. As darkness fell, bringing with it a penetrating cold, the friends decided to take a look inside the smaller of the two churches. It had already acquired a nickname: 'the Circus' (or, sometimes, 'Shanghai'). Upwards of a thousand men lay on cramped bunks piled up to the ceiling on a precarious metal scaffold. On the floor sleeping men squeezed together like pilchards. The entire space reeked of unwashed bodies and dirt. A young reserve army doctor, Zbigniew Godlewski, arrived in Starobelsk in early October. He found the building so intimidating it was a month before he dared enter it:

> The ranks and ranks of bunks, the darkness, the noise of people swearing and shouting. As soon as I entered some cried out: 'Shut the door!' while others shouted: 'There's no harm in a little fresh air.' Immediately, I was asked whom I had come to visit. As I did not answer immediately, cries went up: 'Look! A stranger's come to spy on us. Something'll go missing, that's for sure. Or maybe he's a sneak.' I was swiftly surrounded by several people. Fortunately, I remembered the name of my acquaintance and they recognised me from chopping wood.[6]

Józef Czapski described the Circus as a strange and intimidating place, to be entered as one would a jungle. His close friend, the engineer Zygmunt Mitera, lived there, as did a lively group of students from the Academy of Arts in Warsaw and an avant-garde poet from Kraków, Lech Piwowar, who had married just a few weeks before the outbreak of war. In the centre of the church was a stage that had apparently been used for party and komsomol [Communist Youth League] meetings. Several prisoners slept underneath it, entering and exiting via the prompter's box. The larger church building remained locked throughout their stay; rumour had it that it was used to store grain which was sent to the front to feed German soldiers. On the summit of its cupola was an Orthodox cross. '[It] did not reach upwards in a proud vertical line. Corroded at its base by the rust of time, it hung crooked and inert.'[7]

In the confusion created by the departure of the enlisted men some officers saw an opportunity. With registration yet to begin, restless young men weighed up their future prospects: was it worth the risk to try to escape?

Dr Zbigniew Godlewski's journey to Starobelsk echoed that of many of the captive officers: after losing contact with his division when it came under German attack near Warsaw, the young doctor had wandered ever further eastward, tending to the wounded as best he could before eventually falling into the hands of the Red Army as he tried to escape home from

Białystok. Separated from his friend and fellow medic, Barć, Godlewski spent his first night in the camp alone, falling fast asleep in a stone trough resembling a coffin, his army rucksack serving as a pillow. The following morning Barć reappeared carrying a bowl of lukewarm porridge which he had somehow – miraculously – managed to obtain from a kitchen some-where within the crowded camp. Godlewski was delighted to be reunited with his friend but noticed Barć seemed agitated, scarcely able to conceal his impatience while Godlewski ate his breakfast. As soon as the porridge was gone Barć spoke. He had a plan, he declared: the enlisted men and NCOs from German-occupied regions of Poland were about to leave. What did Godlewski think about taking the very same train on which they had just arrived and getting out of there? 'My face must have shown such fear he stepped away and went over to a corporal near him who was urging him to leave. After a long while he came back, saying lots of people were going and everyone was telling him to get out of this place as quickly as possible.' Godlewski refused. He thought the risk too great. 'We embraced warmly and I realised I was saying goodbye to a true friend.' Barć left the camp undetected, along with an unspecified number of other officers. There are no records to tell us how many of these men were caught or how many made it back to Poland alive. It was some years before Godlewski discov-ered Barć's fate: he reached Warsaw without incident but was immediately arrested by the Gestapo. As a doctor he was allowed to work in the prison hospital, thus surviving the war.[8]

After the first few days the prisoners were allotted more permanent places in one of the semi-ruined buildings which were gradually growing emptier as the enlisted men moved out. Orders arrived from somewhere – nobody yet knew from whom – instructing officers to be billeted with others of the same rank. In each of the three camps the procedure was identical: buildings were designated as blocks, numbered and segregated by seniority.

Numbers tell a story. Imprisoned in the camps of Starobelsk and Kozelsk were some of Poland's most skilled military leaders. Starobelsk held the highest number of senior and staff officers: 8 generals (Billewicz, Haller, Kowalewski, Orlik-Łukoski, Plisowski, Sikorski, Skierski, Skuratowicz),[9] 181 lieutenant colonels and colonels, 316 majors, 843 captains, 2,527 lieutenants and second lieutenants, 9 other officers, plus a handful of others.[10] When Starobelsk was full, Kozelsk took the overflow: 4 generals (Minkiewicz,

Bohaterewicz, Smorawiński, Wołkowicki), 1 admiral (Czernicki), 98 lieutenant colonels and colonels, 232 majors, 647 captains, 17 naval captains, 8
other officers, 3,480 lieutenants, second lieutenants and cadet officers, 61 state
officials, plus a handful of others. With over 6,000 prisoners Ostashkov was
the largest of the three camps. Police and gendarmes made up the majority,
alongside 200–300 army officers, 200 or so prison workers and a handful
of Polish military settlers, refugees and civilians.

Over half the officers in Kozelsk and Starobelsk were not professional
military men but reservists mobilised shortly before the outbreak of war. In
civilian life they were doctors, dentists, pharmacists, veterinary surgeons,
lawyers, judges, court officials (in Kozelsk there were so many judges they
had their own block), engineers, school teachers, university professors,
journalists, writers, poets, industrialists, politicians, businessmen. The very
youngest were officer cadets in their early twenties; a couple of teenage
boys had even been captured by mistake. The majority of officers came
from the army, a small number from the air force and navy. Kozelsk held
a single female prisoner, Janina Lewandowska, a pilot who had been shot
down in a reconnaissance plane. She was held separately (her accommodation is designated in Dr Słowes's sketch of Kozelsk as 'Lady's shed' – see
page 2). A handful of civilians also found themselves among the military
men, captured by mistake or for reasons unknown. In November 1939
the former major domo to the Polish president appeared in Starobelsk
dressed in a ragged fur coat, minus his teeth, a stocking pulled over his
head against the cold. Major Domo Michalski's illustrious connections
had apparently convinced the NKVD he was in possession of important
intelligence – hence the missing teeth, knocked out during a series of brutal
interrogations. He was housed alongside the majors, whether because the
NKVD misunderstood his official title or not is unclear, but it tickled the
prisoners to call him 'Major Michalski'.[11] Between twenty and twenty-five
clergy of various faiths, mainly military chaplains, were spread across the
three camps.

As desperate diplomatic efforts to avert war continued throughout
August 1939, the British and French had urged the Poles to hold off announcing general mobilisation to the very last minute for fear of provoking Hitler.
As a consequence, when the announcement finally came many officers set
off for war in a hurry. Some, anticipating a short battle, wore light summer

uniforms; others thought ahead to a long campaign and packed winter coats and heavy boots. Warsaw was already under attack when Bronisław Młynarski was called up, but as he hurried to join his unit he had the foresight to pay a last-minute visit to his tailor, acquiring a new cap and a top-quality greatcoat originally destined for a colonel killed on the first day of the war. With the onset of winter these last-minute choices were to prove vitally important, marking the difference between sickness and health. No clothing was ever issued to the prisoners. In April 1940 the victims went to their deaths dressed in the same garments in which they had been captured.[12] The senior Polish officer in Kozelsk was retired 59-year-old General Henryk Minkiewicz. When the Red Army came for him he was working on his allotment, dressed in a shabby brown suit with knickerbocker trousers and a cyclist's cap. He was so ashamed of this undignified garb that he rarely ventured outside in Kozelsk, preferring to issue orders and words of encouragement from the privacy of his quarters.[13]

The NKVD made a point of refusing to acknowledge the rank or status of any prisoner, however important he thought he might be. It was a policy deliberately designed to provoke and humiliate their captives and flew in the face of military custom (as well as the Geneva Convention). Nevertheless, in all three camps senior officers were afforded superior accommodation, a reflection either of Beria's wish to be seen to respect at least some of the conventions of war, or of the fact that high-ranking officers were a more valuable asset to the NKVD. The majority of prisoners in Kozelsk slept on primitive bunks in the freezing church building ('the Indian tomb'). By contrast, the four generals and Admiral Czernicki enjoyed separate quarters furnished with proper beds and tables on which hot meals were served from a kitchen. The same was true of the colonels and lieutenant colonels, who lived in a nearby block nicknamed 'Bristol' (in reference to the luxurious Warsaw hotel, still in operation today, still enviably plush). All prisoners received a ration of 800g of black bread daily, accompanied most often by a cabbage soup known as *shchi* ('foul, sour') and *kasha* (porridge) for lunch and supper. Along with this came a small daily allowance of tea (*czajok*), sugar and *makhorka* (a kind of ersatz tobacco made from ground vegetables), which was handed out to all prisoners regardless of whether they smoked, leading to a lively trade in which the non-smokers were at a distinct advantage. Senior officers received more generous rations.

The eight generals in Starobelsk ranged in age from their forties to their seventies; over half were living in retirement at the outbreak of war. On arrival in Starobelsk they were separated from the other officers and taken to a house in town. Seven of them lived on Volodarskaia Street. The eighth, the leader of the defence of Lwów, General Franciszek Sikorski, lived with his staff at 19 Lenin Street. Around a hundred colonels and lieutenant colonels occupied a house at 32 Kirov Street.[14] We know nothing of the generals' lives since none survived. They lived in isolation and for much of their captivity the officers in the main camp were unaware of their presence nearby. Lieutenant Colonel (later General) Zygmunt Berling describes the colonels' house on Kirov Street as a large, single-storey dwelling, probably once a school, standing directly on the street, its windows barred. The colonels lived in relative comfort: they slept on bunks, ten or twelve to a room with a wood-burning stove. They prepared their own food in an indoor kitchen. A guard lived on site in a smaller room.[15] It is reasonable to assume the generals enjoyed similar or slightly better conditions.

The majority of the officers in Kozelsk came from the German-occupied zone of Poland. They lived in the main monastery complex, along with prisoners from Lithuania, either in the church building or one of the blocks scattered around the camp known by various ironic nicknames – 'Chinese Grove', 'Monkey Grove', or 'Louse Hotel' on 'Destitution Square'. The remaining quarter of the camp's population, around a thousand men, was made up of officers whose homes were in the Soviet zone of occupation. They were held separately in the 'skit', formerly a refuge for hermit monks where Gogol, Dostoevsky and Tolstoy sought inspiration and Rasputin was once rumoured to have stayed. Surrounded by a pleasant forest of pine, spruce, beech and oak, the skit was nearly half a mile from the main camp. Although it was sometimes possible to communicate with the help of Russian workers, the officers here were relatively isolated. For 22-year-old cavalry cadet officer Zdzisław Peszkowski, visiting the monastery – 'Greater Kozelsk' – was a highlight of otherwise dull days, offering a rare opportunity to obtain news and information.

In Ostashkov, prisoners lived in twenty-two blocks scattered around the former monastery complex. The small number of higher-ranking officers enjoyed superior accommodation in two rooms furnished with beds, blankets, sheets, chairs, cupboards and stools. When visitors came to inspect the camp these were the only two rooms on show. Everyone else slept on damp, cold bunks infested with bed bugs.[16]

Bronisław Młynarski was delighted to find himself billeted with his friends, all reserve second lieutenants or lieutenants like him, in block number 8 in Starobelsk, a small house standing on half-metre posts. Officers slept tightly packed on bunks so short their legs hung over the edges. In the first days, before the privates left, those not lucky enough to grab a bunk had to sleep on the floor, while prisoners who had secured a place on the top tier (where there was just enough room for a man to assume a half-seated position) had to balance this advantage with the fact that the smell of unwashed bodies, mud and dirt rose upwards. A single light bulb remained on throughout the night. Lice lurked everywhere. Many years later Dr Godlewski still recalled his sense of horror at discovering the creatures crawling all over his body.

Arriving in Starobelsk in late October, Józef Czapski initially found himself isolated from the comrades in his unit with whom he had spent the past few weeks. Although at forty-three he was only three years older than Bronisław Młynarski, as a captain he was assigned with a group of

Józef Czapski.

older men to a block known unflatteringly as 'the Morgue', not only because of its high incidence of sickness but because its residents (many of whom, ironically, were doctors) were so bitterly defeatist. Czapski could not bear their company. An equivalent block in Kozelsk inhabited by older majors was dubbed 'the old people's home'.

A devotee of Paul Cézanne and Marcel Proust, Czapski had spent his early career in Paris before returning to Poland in the 1930s to consolidate his reputation as a talented painter and critic. He was a sensitive and deeply private man, accustomed to working in solitude surrounded by books, with a small group of close friends with whom he could discuss his twin passions of art and literature. Now he found himself pitched into a crowd of confused and angry men, crawling with lice, covered in mud, unable to wash and without sufficient food. Worse than the physical discomfort of those early days was the mental anguish as, 'isolated and trapped in [his] grief', each man dwelled on the defeat of the Polish army, the humiliation of their capture and – most painfully – the absence of news from their families. Strung up outside the blocks in every corner of the camp were loudspeakers which churned out propaganda from dawn until late at night: news from the front boasting of the bombardment of Polish towns, endless tales of wealthy capitalists sucking blood from the oppressed Polish workers, all of this intermingled with bursts of music and the latest production figures from local factories and collective farms. Under these circumstances, it is scarcely surprising that some officers initially experienced what Czapski defined as a kind of 'moral collapse'.

> Oh, the mornings when we were awakened abruptly by the sound of quarrels which often broke out over nothing!… There were some sickening scenes sometimes in those first weeks: two high-ranking officers fought with each other, pulling one another by the beard because they each wanted to be first to reach a well surrounded by black ice.[17]

Disputes blew up easily – 'matters of honour', arguments over rank and position. Professional officers, in particular, found the situation hard to bear. The deliberate lack of respect afforded by the NKVD – the refusal of even the most junior guard to salute officers or address them by their rank – was bitterly humiliating. For men whose lives were wholly bound up in the army it was another bewildering insult to add to the despair they felt at their military defeat.

It can be hard to grasp the atmosphere in which these thousands of individuals existed alongside one another. The image of Polish officers incarcerated in a prison camp suggests a mass of like-minded men united in purpose and background. Words like 'elite' or 'the cream of society' convey a similarly deceptive sense of uniformity. But these were human beings, not saints. Quite apart from the differences that defined career soldiers from their reservist comrades, the prisoners represented every conceivable political and social viewpoint, and a complete cross-section of the professions. They were artists, scientists, judges, journalists, doctors, poets, engineers. Teachers of Literature, Physics, Maths and Art. Experts in mining and ballistics, Latin philology and military history. Catholics, Lutherans, atheists, Jews. Snobs and socialists, aristocrats and entrepreneurs, pompous know-it-alls and men of unfailing courage. If we imagine what it might be like to cram several thousand such men into a crumbling, freezing former monastery consisting of ruined buildings and muddy grounds, to leave them unwashed and underfed, isolated from all news of their former lives and families, deprived of recognition of their status and rank, it might be possible to understand the chaos and despair of those early days in captivity. It might also allow us, for a moment, to pause to imagine what the loss of such a group of men might represent to a country and its families.

As camp life settled into something approaching a routine and the departure of the enlisted men created more space, these painful first impressions were gradually replaced by more positive observations. Bronisław Młynarski noted that although their physical suffering was at its worst during these first few weeks, the great majority of prisoners bore their burden with dignity, their optimism buoyed by a set of firm beliefs (later to succumb to the 'dry rot' of uncertainty): 'that Hitler would be overcome, that their conditions would improve, that the Allies would come to Poland's aid, that there was justice in history, that Providence would take care of us....'[18] Czapski, too, observed that those men whom misfortune appeared to have divested of all dignity, and whose only concern was to procure a little more food or a warm corner, were a small but noisy group, soon put in their place by men 'of a firmer character'. Gradually, the prisoners began to discern among the crowds old friends, relatives, colleagues not seen since before the war. New friendships were formed, old ones renewed, a semblance of order established. As they took stock of their surroundings, the outlines of their new existence gradually took shape. The question uppermost in every man's mind concerned the nature of the camps in which they were being held. Most prisoner of war camps were run by the army. There were clear rules and expectations for officers and other ranks. What did it mean to be in the hands of the NKVD? Who was in charge? And what did they want from their Polish captives?

2

NAMES

From our very first day at Starobelsk, it had become clear to us that one figure who on casual observation looked no different from our other guardians exercised supreme authority. In his early forties, with strong semitic features, clean-shaven, ruddy and red-haired, he would stroll about the camp without visible aim, in an insignia-less brown jacket. Only his cap with the red band denoted his membership of the NKVD. Intelligent, clever and self-controlled, he used a friendly tone that was sometimes jesting and sometimes betrayed a note of superiority.... The measure of this little man's authority was the fact that at the sight of him *politruks* and *komandirs* of one rank or another stood to attention, looking into his narrowed eyes with humility and obedience. For this unimpressive-looking fellow in brown leather jacket and red cap was Kirshin, the camp's political commissar.[1]

Ever since the moment when the young Red Army recruits who robbed them of their valuables were replaced by *politruks* wearing the red-banded caps of the NKVD, the prisoners had slowly been realising that the ruined monasteries to which they had been taken were not regular prisoner of war camps. In the succinct words of Kozelsk prisoner Stanisław Swianiewicz: 'Very soon after arriving in Kozelsk, it became obvious that it was mainly an interrogation camp.'[2]

When the UPV (Administration for Prisoner-of-War Affairs) was set up by Beria on 19 September, all camps where Polish POWs were to be taken were assigned a commander in charge of organisational matters, and a commissar who controlled the political side of things. In addition, within each camp a 'Special Section', or OO (*Osoboe Otdelenie*), was responsible for intelligence work. Moscow's orders to the Special Sections were precise

and exacting: on arrival, they were to register and photograph each prisoner before requiring them to fill in a detailed personal questionnaire.
Record files were to be opened on each individual, kept in alphabetical
order and allotted a number. Any prisoners of war found to be conducting
'anti-Soviet work', as well as those belonging to specific political groups,
were to be investigated and a file established on them. The entire officer
contingent was to be included in the category of those under investigation.
On the first of each month the Special Section in each camp was to submit
an operational report to the regional NKVD Special Department, with a
copy sent to Moscow.[3]

Lavrenty Beria's lengthy directive on 'Operational-Cheka' (intelligence)
work, dated 8 October 1939 and addressed to the Special Sections of NKVD
camps across the USSR, sets out in minute detail what the NKVD was looking for. According to this directive, the first task of the OOs was to create
'an agency-informational network to uncover c-r [counter-revolutionary]
groupings among the POWs and to shed light on their moods'. In other
words, he wanted them to use spies and informers to identify and monitor
any prisoners whose political viewpoint could be seen as inimical to the
Soviet system. They were to use the registration process as an opportunity
to familiarise themselves with the prisoners and select suitable candidates
as agents. With this in place they could focus on the job of uncovering and
penetrating a list of organisations so long it begged the question whether
there were any pre-war Polish organisations the NKVD did *not* consider
suspicious.

   a)   individuals who served in the intelligence, police, and security
        organs of former Poland – branch agencies, intelligence posts, state
        security departments in the voivoidships [provinces], police stations,
        intelligence sections attached to military units, intelligence sections
        attached to 'Dovudstvo Okrengovo Korpusnove' [District Corps
        Commands] – prison employees, and those serving in KOP [Polish
        Frontier Protection Corps]
   b)   [secret] agencies of the organs listed above (informants, intelligence
        agents)
   c)   participants in fascist military nationalistic organisations of former
        Poland [*there follows a list of 11 organisations, including the Polish*

> *Military Organisation, Polish Socialist Party, various professional*
> *unions, Zionists and others*]⁴

d) employees of law courts and the prosecutor's office

e) [secret] agencies of other foreign intelligence services

f) participants in foreign White émigré terrorist organisations [*there*
    follows a list of 12 organisations]

g) provocateurs from the former tsarist secret police, and persons who
    served in the police and prison institutions of pre-revolutionary
    Russia

h) provocateurs from secret police in the fraternal communist parties
    of Poland, Western Ukraine and Belorussia

i) kulak and anti-Soviet elements who fled to the former Poland from
    the USSR.⁵

The complexity of the requirements set out by Beria presupposed a level of efficiency not necessarily matched by the competence of available staff in camps located far from Moscow, with large numbers of prisoners to process. The struggle to recruit suitably qualified staff was a constant source of complaint among camp leaders. Inspecting Ostashkov, Commissar Makarov commented scathingly on the workers engaged in creating POW records: 'The majority of those who have been assigned to the job have a very low level of education – they are half-illiterate, as a consequence of which the records are in a mess and do not reflect the real state of affairs.' Not only this: the wrong documents had been sent to German territory, while other papers were left lying around or placed in unlocked cupboards with no regard for their security.⁶ Meanwhile, a power struggle between the commander of the camp, Pavel Borisovets, and the head of the Special Section, Grigory Korytov, had resulted in several thousand police and gendarme registration forms and photographs lying untouched for an entire month because the two men were too busy arguing about who was responsible for filing them.⁷ Worse, the offices allotted by Borisovets to the Special Section were situated in full view of the camp yard: 'All day long policemen, gendarmes, snoopers etc are hanging about in the yard, and they themselves are great specialists in conspiracies and take note of everyone who goes near the special section.' Policing a camp full of policemen was evidently not a straightforward task.

Jan Bober as a young regional Deputy Inspector in 1919.

Commissar Makarov was not alone in noting the gulf between ambition and reality. At the age of forty, Chief Inspector Jan Bober had a long career in the Polish police behind him, much of it spent flushing out Ukrainian nationalists and communist spies in Poland's eastern regions. A fervent patriot with strong opinions he was not shy of sharing, Bober had frequently come into conflict with his superiors (one described him as an 'exceptionally disloyal swine and a plotter') as a consequence of which he had more than once been demoted.[8] Prisoners were photographed several times and, in Ostashkov camp at least, fingerprinted. While the photographs were taken according to international norms – in two poses (straight on and in profile), the prisoner holding a board bearing his personal file number against his chest – Bober thought the quality of the fingerprinting left much to be desired: 'The way they were carried out – it was pitiful! The prints were illegible, Moscow's central administration must have had very little joy from those prints.'[9]

At Starobelsk, dozens of clerks were bussed in from the local town to register the prisoners. The process was initially hampered by a shortage of paper and ink, then rendered chaotic by the fact that most of the clerks knew only the Cyrillic alphabet and could not correctly transliterate the Polish surnames, much to the amusement of the captive officers. The camp commander, Aleksandr Berezhkov, eventually gave up and ordered the senior Polish liaison officer, Major Sobiesław Zaleski, to organise the job instead. When camp numbers eventually stabilised in November, Major Zaleski decided it would be a good idea to create their own list. He duly entrusted Bronisław Młynarski with the task and Młynarski spent much of the autumn diligently compiling a 200-page document containing an alphabetical list of just under 4,000 names, including notes on those who died, or were taken to hospital, or were removed from the camp never to return. The list survived until Młynarski's last day in the camp, when it was found by the Soviet guards during a search. When Józef Czapski was leading the search for the missing officers in 1941 he was forced to compile the records again from scratch.

Enjoyable as it was for the prisoners to observe the bureaucratic stumblings of their captors, their mood swiftly changed when they saw the questionnaires. The forms presented a series of searching questions: What were your military duties? Give the locality and date of your capture by the Red Army. State your political affiliations. Your parents' names. Your job in civilian life. In considering how to respond to these questions the men were chiefly anxious about the possible consequences for their families if they revealed information about them. Nevertheless, most answered truthfully. Prisoners whose homes were in the Soviet zone rightly assumed that whatever they wrote was already known to the NKVD; those from central and western Poland reckoned the NKVD were probably exchanging information with the Gestapo. Besides, guards had confiscated numerous personal documents during their regular searches of the barracks. The NKVD had plenty of ways to cross-check details.

One man did take the risk of concealing his identity. Professor Stanisław Swianiewicz was a forty-year-old economist from the University of Wilno, a reserve lieutenant and prisoner at Kozelsk camp. Swianiewicz's work before the war had resulted in two important books, one on the Soviet economy (*Lenin as an Economist*, his doctoral thesis, published in 1930), the second on the Nazi economic system (*The Economic Policies of Nazi Germany*, 1938). Rightly nervous that revelation of his real name and status would lead the NKVD to take a close interest in him, Swianiewicz slightly changed his surname at registration, declaring himself a civil servant in the Industrial Chamber of Commerce in Warsaw.[10] The consequences of this little act of deception were to be far-reaching.

The rules laid out in the 1929 Geneva Convention regarding the treatment of prisoners of war were familiar to the Polish officers and informed their expectations on capture. When it became clear that many of their rights were being ignored by their captors – most urgently the right to correspond with their families – senior officers submitted written protests to the camp commanders, who assured them that they would be passed on to the appropriate authorities in Moscow. The doctors in Starobelsk, led by Dr Henryk Levittoux, also attempted to contact the Soviet authorities with a request to be released and sent on to neutral countries or allowed home. Such requests either received no answer or were denied. The USSR did not recognise the Geneva Convention, although somewhat paradoxically it claimed to respect its rules. (Indeed, Beria's 19 September 1939 order to set up the UPV – the Administration for Prisoner-of-War Affairs – contains instructions for prisoners to receive food, clothing and pay. Only food was ever supplied. Whether the other orders were ignored or payments siphoned off by local camp officials we do not know.) In response to the doctors' request Starobelsk commander Aleksandr Berezhkov received a sharp reminder from the head of the UPV, Pyotr Soprunenko: his work should be guided not by the Geneva Convention but by the directives of the UPV alone.[11]

If the three camps did not entirely resemble regular POW camps it was also true they were not run like Soviet prisons or labour camps. There was no violence, no torture or beatings. There was a cooler but thus far nobody knew what it was for. Food, if not plentiful, provided just enough energy to keep the men from starvation; extra rations could be earned through work. The camps were supposed to be self-sufficient: prisoners ran their own kitchens, clinic, barber and other facilities, aided by a small number of local civilians who came in to help with certain tasks. Any additional work was supposedly voluntary, at least for officers. Each camp boasted a small hospital, an infirmary, a pharmacy and (in Kozelsk and Ostashkov) baths. In Starobelsk there were only cold-water standpipes until the end of the year, when – thanks to the dedication of the camp's senior liaison officer, Major Zaleski – the restoration of the camp *banya* (baths) was completed. Until then the prisoners were marched every few weeks to the local town baths. The walk back to the camp, through mud and rain, often left them as filthy on their return as when they left.

Soviet doctors, generally considered to be sympathetic towards the prisoners, supervised sanitary arrangements in the camps, while Polish doctors oversaw the day-to-day running of medical matters. There was no shortage of expertise: with supreme disregard for the neutrality of medical personnel, the Soviets had captured over eight hundred medical staff, including some of Poland's finest specialists. Dr Henryk Levittoux ran the little clinic in Starobelsk, along with Dr Jan Kołodziejski, Dr Julian Gruner and other senior doctors. Seriously ill patients were taken to the local hospital (from which most never returned). Junior doctors like Dr Godlewski took on responsibility for hygiene in individual blocks, administering typhus injections and performing other routine tasks. Godlewski fought a constant battle against their filthy living conditions, insisting on rigorous daily lice inspections, showing his fellow prisoners how to search the seams of their underwear and in winter encouraging them to hang their clothes outside, where the cold froze the creatures. In Ostashkov, the small group of doctors took a minor stand against their captors by wearing the Red Cross armband on their sleeve as a symbol of international humanitarianism and their independence.[12]

The senior Polish physician in Kozelsk was the eminent surgeon Professor Bolesław Szarecki. 'Sturdy, erect, clear of mind, and strong of character' despite his age (he was 65), Professor Szarecki exuded a paternal warmth and projected a hearty bedside manner. He also managed to combine an openness to communist ideals (his humble background strongly influenced his beliefs) with unquestioned loyalty to Poland. As a result, he was 'revered by both the POWs and the Soviet command'.[13] Szarecki survived, one of few senior doctors to do so, serving in the Polish army under General Anders as head of army medical services and later returning to Poland where he continued his distinguished career until his death in 1960. Szarecki's job in Kozelsk was to assist the Russian doctor who ran the little hospital, housed in a two-storey wooden structure with a 'miserably equipped clinic' on the ground floor and, upstairs, three rooms with iron beds packed closely together.

Józef Czapski spent several weeks in the similarly ill-equipped clinic at Starobelsk, suffering from a lung infection. Despite the primitive conditions, his stay afforded him not only the luxury of clean sheets and the care of some of Poland's best doctors but that most precious of commodities: silence. When Bronisław Młynarski came to visit Czapski he found his old friend lying with his legs dangling over the end of the tiny bed (although at 6'5" no bed was ever quite long enough), racked with fever but joyfully quoting Baudelaire, Apollinaire, Proust…

> I felt fascinated by that head of his, as if I were seeing it for the first time in my life.… A tremendous skull, elongated, with a high forehead, a bony aquiline nose jutting out of the sunken eye-sockets and the sunken temples. And his greying red hair blending with a several weeks old growth of beard. He looked like a saint.[14]

In Kozelsk, the 'voluntary work' performed by officers consisted primarily in helping the Russian civilian workmen who looked after the camp's central heating and piped-water system; occasionally they would visit the nearby *kolkhoz* (collective farm) to pick beetroot or unload timber. The prisoners of Ostashkov ran the electrical department, lumber mill, carpentry work-shop, blacksmiths, locksmiths, sewing and tailoring workshops, bakery, kitchen, laundry, baths and barbers. Since the majority of prisoners here were not officers work was compulsory, but the small group of officers often chose to join them, either out of solidarity or a desire for increased rations. Ostashkov's island location gave rise to specific tasks: prisoners built a causeway between the mainland and the island; they cleared snow from the roads near the camp. There was also work cutting and transporting ice from the lake: it was sawn into blocks, loaded onto sleighs pulled by humans and stored in an enormous cellar under one of the camp buildings.[15]

Starobelsk appears to have been in a particularly poor state of repair when the officers arrived. The NKVD's cost-effective solution was to task the prisoners with renovating their own prison camp. In this, Commander Berezhkov can have had no inkling of the dedication which Major Zaleski and his 'planning team' would demonstrate in achieving this aim.

Major Sobiesław Zaleski was by profession an engineer. A tall man of enormous energy and enthusiasm, 'strongly built with the face of a bulldog, but with an engaging smile',[16] Zaleski had in the early days of their captivity volunteered to take on 'the job that nobody else wanted' as the officer in charge of liaising with the NKVD on behalf of the prisoners. As he was not the senior Polish officer in the camp Zaleski asked at the outset that everyone agree to his command and had since then evinced a stubborn determination to do his best for his fellow prisoners. In this he was ably

Major Sobiesław Zaleski (1893–1940).

aided by his deputy, Major Walenty Miller, a handsome man of considerable charm and biting wit who managed to find ways to joke even with camp staff. Both men spoke superlative Russian. Like many of the older prisoners, Zaleski and Miller had grown up in a Poland still partitioned between Tsarist Russia, Austria and Germany. Zaleski served in the Russian army during World War I, Miller was born in Russia.

Since there were professionals from every conceivable walk of pre-war Polish society within the camp, Major Zaleski had no problem gathering around him a team of skilled volunteers – architects, engineers, scientists and planners. This group gradually assumed responsibility for routine matters, including the camp kitchen and the construction works. The camp authorities required a daily contingent of 1,000 men, half of whom were taken outside the gate, under escort, to unload logs from railway wagons. The logs were destined for sawmills, to be returned later to the camp as boards for use in the construction of new barracks, designs for which were drawn up by Zaleski and a team of architects who worked in the 'building office' (a tiny room off the Circus). A local builder checked and corrected the construction plans before submitting them to the camp commander for approval. Lengthy arguments would then ensue about the ambitious nature and high cost of Zaleski's plans. Eventually, a compromise would be reached, the supplies would eventually arrive in distorted and inadequate form, and Zaleski and his team would have to make do with what was to hand.

The men who worked outside the camp were generally the younger and fitter of the officers. They volunteered mainly to give themselves something to do. Bronisław Młynarski's friend Zygmunt Kwarciński was by profession a forester, the manager of saw mills in the famous Białowieża Forest. His powerful physique proved a distinct advantage when confronting physical tasks ('Emanating from him was the strength of an oak-tree combined with the slenderness of an ash'[17]), while his professional knowledge enabled the work group to unload enormous logs in icy conditions with little or no equipment. Dr Godlewski also volunteered:

> I liked this work. We would leave the camp and find ourselves among the villagers, who were almost all women (the men were at war), mainly older, dressed in *fufaiki* [padded jackets] and trousers, their heads covered with scarves. They were short and round, and at first glance resembled penguins. The women were very kind, and even gave us things – one of my friends was given a bottle of milk, which gave him the runs, and when one of the women tried to give me one, I refused it, causing her much offence.[18]

Planks and boards soon started arriving in the camp, and building work commenced on the new barracks that the prisoners themselves would later inhabit. Inevitably, the opportunity of working with building materials offered the chance to purloin much-needed items for the prisoners' own use.

> It was so cold that quite often some of the wood that had been used during the day to build the barracks was taken at night to heat them. When Major Zaleski was questioned about this by the camp commander, he explained very calmly that the men were poorly dressed and it was very cold. As they were speaking, two men appeared carrying a huge beam in order to burn it. Zaleski distracted the commander while signalling to the men to get rid of the beam.[19]

Another group of officers worked in the camp itself. The most imperative task was to dig ditches to make latrines. The main ditch in Starobelsk, dubbed 'the Siegfried Line' after the German defensive line (the equivalent ditch in Kozelsk shared the same nickname), was thirty metres in length. Prisoners also mended damaged roofs and panelled walls; they drilled two artesian wells and constructed a new kitchen. The cooks began their painstaking task at dawn, filling huge cauldrons with *kasha* (porridge) which volunteers known as 'gondoliers' stirred patiently for hours. The kitchen at Starobelsk was presided over by a prisoner known simply as Antoni. Once the owner of a jam factory, Antoni was renowned for working wonders with the meagre supplies at his disposal. Weaker men took on minor tasks: Józef Czapski's poor state of health excluded him from hard physical work; instead he cleaned the soup buckets, peeled potatoes or carried boxes and sacks.

For some officers the idea of performing such menial tasks for the Soviets was humiliating, even unpatriotic. But work gave men a purpose, as well as extra food. Forced to get up early in the mornings, at night they slept soundly. Every prisoner was plagued by anxiety about the fate of his family and those who did not work were far more likely to succumb to despair. Dr Godlewski was much preoccupied by this phenomenon:

> Amongst those groups of men who did nothing, who almost never went for a walk, there began to appear more or less defined symptoms of psychosis: weight loss, staring or gazing at the ground without expression, scurrying quickly back to their holes. It pained me to see this and sometimes I tried to talk to these people, to stop them – but they would run off as if terrified.[20]

Józef Czapski, too, was troubled by the often unpredictable ways in which men reacted to their situation, observing how in some it brought out the noblest impulses while others quickly became disheartened. He observed with particular sadness the profound change that had overtaken Dr Kazimierz Dadej, the director of a sanatorium for poor children in Zakopane, a man who before the war had been renowned for his professional dedication and unstinting generosity.

> Out of all of us he found it the hardest to put up with the conditions: the dirt, the disorder, the suspicion towards us shown from the first Soviet soldier we met. Always sad and bitter, aged by ten years, with his face covered in blisters around his eyes and crow's feet at his temples, he was always to be found sitting down, motionless, doing nothing, this Polish 'bourgeois' who in his own country had found a thousand reasons to refuse money from his patients and who was incapable of spending one sole instant without occupation.

Now, swamped by the patter of naive propagandists and interrogated by wily, obtuse interrogators, he could not adapt to this new way of life.[21]

Physical tasks could not keep the men occupied the entire day. There were many hours left to fill and an urgent need to find purposeful activity to fill them. In the first few weeks religious life flourished unchecked. Across the camps over twenty priests had been captured from every denomination belonging to pre-war Polish cultural life: Catholic, Protestant, Jewish, Orthodox, Uniate. Most were military chaplains, the majority were Catholic; among their number in Starobelsk was the chief rabbi of the Polish army, Major Baruch Steinberg, and Major Jan Józef Potocki of the Evangelical-Reform church. The priests conducted improvised services using altars made from wooden boards covered with white cloth; they heard confessions during walks around the camp grounds on the pretext of taking exercise. In Kozelsk, the officers followed the Polish army tradition of evening prayer: at 9 p.m. every evening in the main room of the 'Indian tomb' the order was given: 'We will now observe a three-minute silence.' The silence was observed by all, whatever their religious persuasion.[22] On one occasion an NKVD captain entered the building at just this moment. 'He was taken aback, and asked one of the prisoners for an explanation, and the echoes of his voice (he received no reply) seemed to fill every corner of the building, still further increasing the strange effect.'[23]

Impromptu lectures sprang up almost immediately, initially focused on the recent military defeat as prisoners sought to explain to themselves the catastrophe that had befallen their army and their country. At Starobelsk, General Anders' chief of staff, Major Adam Sołtan, was one of the first to speak on the subject. A highly decorated cavalry officer and professor of military history, Sołtan was careful to avoid the bitter recriminations levelled by many of the officers at their military commanders and their absent government. Instead, he emphasised the heroism shown by many leaders and soldiers during the unequal battle, thereby doing much to improve the morale of his fellow prisoners:

He took advantage of the moments of rest allowed in the camp to talk to the men about the political and social problems of Poland and to discuss each question with honesty and without preconceived notions. He had

Major Adam Sołtan (1898–1940) as a captain.

fought against Piłsudski's coup d'état in 1926 but that did not prevent him from admiring the writings of the marshal, which he had studied deeply.[24]

Poland was everything to Sołtan: he once told Czapski that if he could he would crawl back to Poland on his knees from the end of the world.

Sołtan's measured opinions were in marked contrast to the fervent patriotism expressed by a small group of officers who were determined to encourage a spirit of rebellion. The ringleaders were Major Ludwik Domoń, Captain Mieczysław Ewert and Lieutenant Stanisław Kwolek. So carried away were they in exercising the Polish talent for conspiracy (honed over long years of suppression during the partitions) that they failed to notice they were being observed:

> Comrade Kaganer, an instructor in the Political Section, has established that prisoner of war Mieczysław Ewert, a former captain in the Polish army, organised a group out of the officer contingent – Major Ludwig Domoń, Stanisław Kwolek, and others – with the aim of conducting counter-revolutionary work under the guise of 'cultural enlightenment work' (lectures on hygiene,

foreign language study, [lectures] on technology in capitalist states etc) but in fact during these 'talks' on the above issues, counter-revolutionary activity was conducted against the internal regulations of the camp and the camp administration [using such slogans as] 'Speak only Polish', 'Don't go to your camp jobs', 'The worse it is in the camp, the better for us – this way we will compromise the camp administration and the camp procedures before the international commission that is going to come soon', etc.[25]

This ferment of patriotic and religious feeling came to a head on 11 November, when an attempt was made in Starobelsk to celebrate Poland's Independence Day. The main organiser of the celebration was Lieutenant Kwolek, the unofficial leader of the group of men housed in the Circus. Readings of Polish poetry were followed by a short prayer service involving the serious offence of hanging a cross made from pieces of wood on the wall. Somebody – either a *politruk* or an informer – reported the meeting to Commissar Kirshin. Kirshin ordered a search. The individuals responsible were identified and Ewert, Domoń and Kwolek were removed from the camp, along with several other rebels. The religious services were stopped.[26] In an act of calculated humiliation, on the same day NKVD guards marched the prisoners out of the camp, through Starobelsk town and into the countryside, where they made them stand pointlessly for hours in the cold before marching them back again. This 'fake parade' appears to have been deliberately conceived in reference to Polish Independence Day celebrations.[27]

The prisoners of Starobelsk had no idea where Ewert, Kwolek and Domoń had been taken. The men were simply removed from the camp at night, leaving their comrades to speculate as to their fate. We now know Captain Ewert and Lieutenant Kwolek were taken to an NKVD prison in Kharkov, along with another prisoner, Captain Józef Rytel. They were charged with anti-Soviet activity and sentenced to eight years in a labour camp. Ewert and Rytel survived to join the Polish army in 1941 while Kwolek, who had TB, died in April 1941. Major Domoń was taken to Moscow and interrogated there for several months before rejoining his comrades in Griazovets camp in June 1940. Apparently undeterred by his experience in Moscow's notorious Lubyanka prison, where prisoners of particular interest to the NKVD were brought for investigation and (sometimes) torture, Domoń was later to play a major role in organising 'counter-revolutionary' activities in Griazovets.

Commissar Kirshin's swift actions in clearing out the rebels did not meet with approval in Moscow: a trio of senior NKVD officers (Trofimov, Yefimov and Yegorov), sent to inspect Starobelsk camp, observed that the commissar had handled the discovery of these 'anti-Soviet activities' poorly. Instead of waiting for instructions from his superiors, Kirshin had gone into the barracks on his own initiative and started 'demasking' the rebels, thus revealing what the NKVD knew about them and giving the rebels time to prepare themselves. (He was also accused of compromising himself by 'living together with one of the female medical workers in the camp'.) Their conclusion: 'Commissar Kirshin is not in the right place and is not carrying out the right work for the conditions of Starobelsk camp.' The trio suggested his removal in favour of someone more capable of organising political work with officer POWs.[28] Whether this happened is not clear: a temporary commissar was in post for part of the operational period at Starobelsk but Kirshin appears to have returned in early 1940.

The events of 11 November marked a turning point in Starobelsk. Kirshin summoned senior officers and block representatives to a meeting during which he read out a long list of regulations which prisoners were expected to obey henceforth. Forbidden activities included such heinous crimes as walking in groups of more than two people, moving from one block to another, reading aloud from books, keeping a diary, playing cards, and smoking inside.[29] The removal of Kwolek, Ewert and Domoń came as a profound shock to the prisoners. How naive they had been not to realise that the NKVD was monitoring their actions in minute detail! And how foolish not to suspect that informers – fellow prisoners prepared to shop their comrades in return for favourable treatment – lurked in their midst. These events also marked their first experience of a mysterious and terrifying ritual, when a guard appeared by a prisoner's bunk at night and uttered the words, 'Come along now, get ready and bring your things', before leading the man away to an unknown destination.

Bronisław Młynarski identified this as a test period:

The Soviet authorities probably deliberately relaxed their reins and made it a point not to oppose a mass demonstration of the patriotic and religious feelings that had welled up within us. Such a policy afforded them an excellent opportunity to gauge our frame of mind and draw appropriate conclusions.[30]

Młynarski's interpretation was essentially correct: the first few weeks of their captivity marked a period of transition not just for the prisoners but for their captors. And although there was no equivalent dramatic moment in the other two camps, the result was the same. Until now the camp authorities had numerous practical matters to attend to: accommodation to be arranged, food and supplies to be obtained, the enlisted men to be sent home, registration to be carried out. Only once all these tasks were completed could the real work of the Special Sections begin.

3

QUESTIONS

'COME ALONG NOW, GET READY.' WITH THESE WORDS A GUARD would rouse the prisoner before leading him away. At first, every man lay awake all night waiting for his comrade to return, eager to learn what news he would bring of the hitherto mysterious building that housed the Special Section, its windows blanked out with lime. Soon, the men became familiar with the ritual. So long as the command did not contain the four words 'and bring your things' they knew more or less what to expect.

The main wave of interrogations took place in the three camps between late November 1939 and the end of January 1940. Depending on his seniority and status as a person of potential interest to the NKVD, a prisoner would be interviewed either by lower-ranking NKVD officers or by specialists sent from Moscow who enjoyed powers overriding those of the camp commanders and commissars. The former were unsophisticated in their methods, employing crude attempts at blackmail and threats concerning the fate of the prisoner's family: 'Ah, your poor wife, she will never see you again unless you confess that…if you don't promise to…'[1] The specialists from Moscow, by contrast, took a different approach. Kozelsk's Major Zarubin, known as the 'Kombrig' (brigade commander), was rumoured to have been an ambassador in the West before the war.

> The Kombrig was a very agreeable man to talk to. He was an educated man, he knew not only Russia, but the West as well. He spoke fluent French and German and had also some knowledge of English. Usually he asked prisoners their opinion on various social, political and philosophical problems.… And usually he would offer his victim cigarettes of good quality. Sometimes also tea, cakes and even oranges were served.[2]

Zarubin had a small but select library of around five hundred books in Russian, French, English and German, which he allowed officers to borrow. When physicist and mathematician Lieutenant Colonel Tadeusz Felsztyn was called to see Zarubin in early January 1940 he found him to be a man of culture who had evidently travelled widely, observing that his library contained not only works of serious literature (Winston Churchill's sweeping account of World War I, *The World Crisis*, was the most widely borrowed item in his collection) but also popular American novellas written in 'such cowboy slang we couldn't understand them'.[3] According to Felsztyn, Zarubin had brought his seven-year-old son with him to Kozelsk and liked to emphasise, in his conversations with the officers, that 'I too have children'.

Zarubin generally interrogated only the most senior officers, from the rank of lieutenant colonel upwards, sometimes younger officers from well-known regiments or those who had a prominent public profile. Conversations with him tended to be so wide-ranging it was hard to work out 'what he was getting at' and he was sufficiently subtle never to insist where he met with resistance: Felsztyn, for example, was a noted expert on weapons and ballistics; Zarubin once attempted to question him about Polish armaments but, in the face of Felsztyn's clear reluctance to answer, promptly steered the conversation in a different direction. Zarubin's affable persona was not limited to conversation: on several occasions when officers asked him for help – for example, when a relative had been thrown out of their home or was unable to travel for lack of papers – Zarubin's intervention resolved their problems. Everything was geared towards gaining the trust of senior officers, presumably in the hope they would eventually confide some interesting titbit of intelligence or agree to cooperate. 'Whether the Kombrig knew about the fate of those who were taken away I don't know,' mused Felsztyn. 'If he did know, then his farewell to the group of generals, with Minkiewicz at their head, was particularly cynical, because before they left the Kombrig organised a breakfast of blinis before seeing them off personally, wishing them a "*bon voyage*".[4]

While the specialists from Moscow were able to call upon substantial resources in pursuit of their objectives, the functionaries permanently based at the camps had to make do with what was available. In Ostashkov the lack of resources was a perpetual problem, perhaps reflecting the greater strategic importance to the NKVD of officer prisoners over policemen. At one point Commissar Makarov was even prompted to write to the head of the UPV, Pyotr Soprunenko, asking for a new uniform for himself and Commander Borisovets as they were interrogating police officers wearing only lightweight, dirty shirts. 'Apart from anything else, from a purely operational point of view one should be dressed so as to make a decent impression.'[5]

Cadet officer Zdzisław Peszkowski recalled being asked the same basic questions again and again: 'What is my name? Why was my father a capitalist exploiter? What organisations do I belong to? Had I acted against the Soviet Union?'[6] We know from Beria's directive of 8 October that the Special Sections had been tasked with uncovering members of a wide range of political organisations. We also know that one of their primary goals was to identify men with a connection to Poland's pre-war intelligence service, *Oddział II* (the Second Section, unofficially known as *Dwójka* or No. 2). The Second Section had a reputation for effectiveness, with a large network of intelligence officers in Poland and abroad, many within the armed forces. The NKVD historically had something of an obsession with Polish 'spies': former NKVD chief Nikolai Yezhov's paranoid belief that 'they know everything' led to the persecution of vast numbers of Soviet Poles during the Great Terror of 1937–38.[7] Any prisoner plausibly suspected of working for Polish intelligence was usually removed from the camps and taken to Moscow for further interrogation. Here, fates varied depending on an individual's perceived usefulness or willingness to cooperate with the NKVD. The survival of a number of officers with an openly hostile attitude towards the Soviet political system (such as Ludwik Domoń, Józef Lis or Jan Mintowt-Czyż) may be attributed to their background in intelligence as well as, or in addition to, their military skills.[8]

For officers with no involvement either in politics or the intelligence services conversations with their NKVD interrogators often took a surreal turn. Answers to the effect that they had no party affiliation were routinely disbelieved, as if it was incomprehensible to their inquisitors that an intelligent man could have no interest in politics. Trips abroad were commonly interpreted as adventures in espionage. During one interrogation Józef Czapski was asked about the eight years he had spent working in Paris as an artist:

'What orders did you receive from the ministry of foreign affairs when you left for Paris?' asked one of the NKVD men.

I answered that the minister did not even know I had gone to Paris.

'So what did his deputy say?'

'He was also unaware of my departure. I went as a painter, not a spy.'

'You think we don't understand – as a painter you could have drawn a plan of Paris and sent it to the minister in Warsaw.'

I could not make this man understand you could buy a map of Paris for a few pennies on any street corner and Polish painters were not spies who secretly drew plans of cities. Right to the end, my inquisitors refused to believe you could go abroad for reasons other than espionage.[9]

Bronisław Młynarski relates his own interrogation at the hands of an inexperienced young officer in Starobelsk as a scene of Kafka-esque absurdity. Woken late at night by the camp messenger, he was taken across the courtyard to the Special Section. Here, he was subjected to a lengthy wait in the corridor before eventually being admitted to the office of his interrogator. The room was small, illuminated by bare bulbs. On the wall hung the usual triptych of Marx, Lenin and Stalin. A desk and chairs. Młynarski waited.

Suddenly, an inside door camouflaged by wallpaper, which I had failed to notice, swung open and a hatless NKVD officer with curly black hair in a green overblouse entered the room smoking a cigarette.... Without uttering a word, he sat down at the desk, unlocked a drawer, pulled it out a little, removed a big revolver from it, put it on the table, then looked through some papers without taking them out of the drawer. He did not pay the slightest attention to me. Not until he was in the act of lighting another cigarette did he look at me, study me for a moment, then, pointing to the chair opposite the table, curtly invite me to sit down.[10]

Intimidated by the sight of the gun, Młynarski did as he was told. The NKVD officer leaned over the table and proceeded to reel off a list of details concerning Młynarski's background: his parents' names, his occupation, his military position. Młynarski was shocked by the accuracy of the information.

A moment later he again glanced into the drawer and suddenly declared in a high-pitched, angry voice: 'You are of course in the intelligence service.'

'No, I am not in the intelligence service,' I shot back immediately, although I was taken aback by this question.

'*Nu*, we know, we know very well. Why lie, why not admit the truth?' he laughed loudly.

I assured him in a definite and emphatic voice: 'I am a Reserve Officer in the Sappers and have never served in intelligence.' And I added: 'Besides, you know very well that as a prisoner of war I do not have to answer such questions.'

The officer jumped up from his chair, seized his gun and cried out, trembling with rage: 'I advise you not to try to teach me or lay down conditions. You are to answer all questions. I warn you for the last time!'

After this carefully enacted opening scene the young officer became apparently absorbed in writing, leaving Młynarski to watch him, dazzled by the bright light, the smoke from the man's cigarette smarting his eyes. Even taking into account the lapse of time between the event and its narration, and the inevitable liberties taken by an author with a gift for a well-told anecdote, the element of performance is remarkable, a carefully planned sequence of actions specifically designed to weaken the prisoner. After a long silence the young officer posed a series of questions about Młynarski's civilian occupation (he was deputy director of a large government-owned steamship company) which, like Czapski's interview, revealed a startling combination of naivety and paranoia concerning Western life:

'Did you own your own house? How big was it? How many servants did you have? Did you have your own car?'

Młynarski's passport, stamped with dozens of foreign visas, solicited a further series of questions about his 'spying' activities. His attempts to explain his love of travel appeared only to confuse the young interrogator, who abruptly broke off the interview and left the room. For an hour Młynarski waited, a guard administering a sharp kick every time he dozed off. When the interview resumed it followed the same lines as before. This time it was Młynarski's activities in Russia, where he had spent four years as a student, which were the focus of the young NKVD man's interest. In vain did Młynarski attempt to explain that his father had worked regularly with Russian musicians and as a consequence the whole family spent a great deal of time in Russia. The NKVD officer simply could not or chose not to understand. With the interview now into its fourth hour Młynarski was angry and humiliated, his mind clouded with exhaustion. It was at this moment, as he cast around for some way of cutting through the young NKVD officer's impenetrable 'Sovietness' to find the human being within, that he suddenly hit upon a bizarre idea. He would try to connect with the man through the subject he knew best:

'Do you like music? Because, you see, I am a musician at heart, though I am not a professional. I live music, I love it, I've been immersed in it since infancy. And I know that all of you in this country love music. Maybe we can arrive at a human understanding on this score. Do you play any instrument or do you sing? Tell me please, will you?' I said it all in one breath, stubbornly insisting on an answer from him. His facial expression changed somewhat, his ironic smile disappeared, his black eyes looked at me with unconcealed surprise. He muttered reluctantly: 'What has that got to do with anything?'

'Well, please answer me!' I insisted. He was taken off guard and did not quite know how to react. There was no doubt but that our thin papered walls had additional eyes and ears. Finally, pressed into a corner, he stammered in a lowered voice: 'Yes, I like music very much. I play the balalaika and I sing. But what the devil has this got to do with anything?' he added angrily.

Młynarski launched into a long monologue to which the officer listened intently. He spoke of his father's music and all the musicians he had known as a child, rambling on, delirious with exhaustion, forgetting in his urgent desire to tap into his dearest memories that he was talking to a representative of the NKVD. Suddenly, the camouflaged door opened and the senior interrogator, Lebedyev, entered. 'His shirt open, sleepy and dishevelled, he sat down in a chair which creaked under his weight. He yawned audibly and addressed his subordinate in a lazy voice: "What's all this talking about?"'

The interrogation was over. The exhausted prisoner was marched back to his block. When his friend Zygmunt Kwarciński woke him the following morning to ask him how the interrogation had gone Młynarski answered rudely, his mind preoccupied with one thought which whirled insistently round his head: 'The NKVD knows all about me by now.' This sense of shame was a common reaction to the interrogations (known in Russian as *doprosy*), resulting in a widespread taboo around any detailed discussions between comrades of what had passed during their nocturnal visits to the Special Section. Prisoners might exchange information about the type of intelligence sought by their interrogators, but nobody wished to reveal how expertly their personal weaknesses had been exposed.

For the small group of officers who chose to cooperate with the Soviets the interrogations ran along distinctly different lines. Friendly NKVD officers offered them tea or coffee, sometimes fruit or decent cigarettes, before sounding out their willingness to perform various services for the Soviet authorities. Lieutenant Colonel Zygmunt Berling was a well-known and highly skilled senior staff officer whose pre-war military career had been cut short by a personal scandal involving his divorce. Disillusioned both with Polish politics and the military hierarchy, Berling approached Poland's situation with ruthless logic. Although during his captivity he maintained a deliberately ambiguous stance among his fellow colonels (which later led them to regard him with greater hostility than they did openly communist officers such as Captain Rosen-Zawadzki or Lieutenant Imach), Berling had concluded early on that an alliance with the Soviet Union presented the only viable route to Poland's survival as a nation. Upon arrival in Starobelsk he immediately made his views plain to the Soviet authorities. During subsequent conversations with senior NKVD interrogators he was several times offered the opportunity of leaving the camp in exchange for his cooperation in gathering intelligence. Although he declared himself willing to be dropped into German-held territory to report troop and supply movements, Berling refused – on the grounds he was a soldier, not a spy – to undertake any work that involved reporting on civilians.[11]

Another prominent pro-Soviet prisoner was Captain Kazimierz Rosen-Zawadzki. Zawadzki was a highly unusual character: a professional cavalry and tank officer, his interest in Marxist ideology dated from his student days.

Zygmunt Berling with communist activist Wanda Wasilewska in 1943.

Unlike Berling, he never sought to hide his political opinions either from his fellow cavalry officers (a wing of the Polish military more usually associated with highly conservative, nationalistic attitudes) or from other prisoners. When called to interrogation at Starobelsk Rosen-Zawadzki immediately stated unequivocally that he did not support Sikorski's government in France and believed cooperation with the Soviet Union was essential. Having expressed himself in these terms he received an initial proposal to report on what was going on in the camp, which – like Berling – he claims to have refused. However, when offered the chance to go to France, he agreed. 'I began to dream I was going to France, to the army…but in the end it was just dreams.'[12] None of the proposals put to these officers were ever realised; we do not know whether this was for practical reasons or because, as Berling suspected, they were intended more as tests of commitment than practical propositions.

Holding pro-Soviet views was not an automatic passport to the trust of the NKVD authorities. Indeed, members of the pre-war Polish communist party (disbanded by the Comintern in 1938) were viewed with suspicion, featuring in Beria's October 1939 directive listing organisations to be 'uncovered and penetrated'.[13] Lieutenant Roman Imach was taken initially to Ostashkov before being transferred with a group of officers to Kozelsk. Imach noted a 'certain reserve' on the part of his interrogators towards former members of the party and makes no mention of any offer of collaboration from the NKVD.[14] Another communist prisoner, Lieutenant Stanisław Szczypiorski, remarked with bitterness that, despite making his political affiliations clear immediately upon capture, he was taken to the Soviet Union as a prisoner of war along with everyone else.[15] It was not until after the surviving prisoners were transferred to Griazovets camp in the summer of 1940 that pro-Soviet officers were singled out for openly favourable treatment.

Offers of collaboration were not made uniquely to prisoners with pro-Soviet views: many officers received proposals of this nature. Most refused outright. The majority of these were sent on transports in April 1940 and never seen again. A few, those with specialist knowledge or rare skills, were spared. One of these was a young air force observer, Second Lieutenant Jan Mintowt-Czyż, who received several offers to collaborate with the Soviet authorities both in Kozelsk and, later, in Griazovets. This may have been due to the fact that the Soviets had very few airmen in captivity and their skills were in demand, particularly for intelligence work abroad. It is also possible the NKVD suspected Mintowt-Czyż of working for Polish intelligence, a suspicion which in his case was well founded. The young airman refused all offers.[16]

One could argue that for men like Czapski and Młynarski, who had no useful intelligence to offer the NKVD, the interrogations were fruitless. What, after all, did they achieve? As we shall see, the proportion of men willing to collaborate with the Soviet authorities was vanishingly small. What these encounters reveal more than anything is the gulf that existed between Soviet and Western culture. If many of the interrogators found the lives led by Polish artists, teachers, lawyers or doctors incomprehensible, it was in part due to the cultural isolation in which the Soviet Union existed; it also reflected the generally poor level of education of NKVD staff employed to question prisoners considered to be strategically or politically unimportant. (It is a measure of the lack of importance of men like Czapski and Młynarski to the NKVD that in their memoirs neither names the head of the Special Section, Mikhail Yefimov. Młynarski identifies the 'corpulent giant' Lebedyev as the senior interrogating officer, apparently unaware of

Yefimov's existence.) But the incomprehension was mutual, frequently noted by older Polish officers such as Major Zaleski or Dr Levittoux, men who had been educated in Russia, knew Russian culture intimately and spoke the language fluently but for whom '*homo Sovieticus*' was a mystery as impenetrable as a sphinx. They could no more comprehend the motives and mindset of Commissar Kirshin or Commander Berezhkov than the junior NKVD interrogators could understand the cosmopolitan lives led by Józef Czapski or Bronisław Młynarski. Specialists like Major Zarubin, who were familiar with Western culture and able to engage with the officers on equal terms, were rare and often little trusted by their NKVD superiors by virtue of having been 'tainted' by too much contact with the West. How effective Zarubin was in eliciting useful intelligence from his interlocutors we do not know. The personal records kept by the NKVD on individual prisoners were destroyed by the KGB in 1959.[17]

4

LECTURES

IF THE MAIN PURPOSE OF THE INTERROGATIONS WAS TO EXTRACT information from the prisoners, the programme of cultural activities provided by the NKVD was aimed at cramming information into them, educating them about the benefits of the communist system and convincing them of its merits. The programme was similar in all three camps and involved talks, games, films, group discussions, communal newspaper readings and the provision of books, as well as glass cases where educational articles and objects were displayed and 'club rooms' decorated with posters and slogans. There was a choir for 'teaching the songs of the Soviet Union'. There were even performances by visiting theatre companies and schoolchildren.[1] The leaders of this political 'work' were the camp commissars, who spared no detail in their efforts to impress their superiors in their monthly reports to Moscow. Commander Berezhkov and Commissar Kirshin's report on Starobelsk, dated 3 December 1939 states:

> The following work was done in November:
>
> Mass political work was done for 3,907 POWs.
>
> All mass political work among the POWs was organised according to plan, in the fulfilment of which the party and Komsomol [Communist Youth League] organisations took the lead.
>
> The measures foreseen in the plan of party political work among the POWs were carried out for the most part in full.
>
> A. Talks were given on the following topics:
>
>   a) The reasons for the victory of the October Socialist Revolution in the USSR and its international significance

b) The twenty-second anniversary of the Great October Socialist
    Revolution

c) The beginning of the new imperialist war[2] and the foreign policy
    of the Soviet Union

d) What the victory of socialism has given the workers of the USSR

e) The material and cultural welfare of the workers of the USSR

f) What tsarist Russia was and what the USSR has become

g) A discussion was held with the POWs about the film *Lenin v
    Oktiabre* [Lenin in October].

B. Readings were held and explanations conducted of material read in
    newspapers:

1. On the foreign policy of the Soviet Union (report by Comrade
    Molotov of 31 October 1939).

2. The report by Comrade Molotov at the ceremonial plenum
    devoted to the twenty-second anniversary of the Great October
    Socialist Revolution, 6 November 1939.

3. An English magazine on the reasons for Poland's defeat (*Pravda*
    [Truth] 18 November 1939).

4. Materials from the fifth session of the Supreme Soviet of the
    USSR.

5. Twice a week a political information session is held on the topic
    'What's new in the USSR and abroad'.

6. The reading of newspapers out loud has been organised in the
    blocks.

C. Organisational-instructional measures carried out among the POWs:

1. Talks were given in all the blocks on the topic 'Internal Regulations
    in the Camp'.

2. Conversations took place with block commandants and [POW]
    elders groups on the topic 'Internal Regulations in the Blocks'.[3]

3. Explanatory work has been done among the POWs about per-
    mission to write letters.

    a) a conversation took place with the heads of the rayons [districts].

b) a conversation took place with the block commandants and group elders.

4. An organised procedure for answering questions was established and a journal for questions was hung in each block. Each prisoner of war personally receives a reply to a written question from an instructor of the political section in two days.

D. The following films have been shown to the POWs:

1. *Chelovek s Ruzhem* [Man with a Rifle]
2. *Gorny Marsh* [Mountain March]
3. *Povest o Zavoevannom Schaste* [Tale of Happiness Hard-Won]
4. *Lenin v Oktiabre* [Lenin in October]
5. *Sluchai na Polustanke* [Incident at the Stop]
6. *Noch v Sentiabre* [Night in September]
7. *Lenin v 1918 g.* [Lenin in 1918]
8. *Morskoi Post* [The sea post]
9. *Pyotr Pervy* [Peter the first, part one]
10. *Pyotr Pervy* [Peter the first, part two]
11. *Marseleza* [The Marseillaise]
12. *Vragi* [Enemies]
13. *Bogatyri Rodiny* [Heroes of the Homeland]

As many as 30,000 POWs have attended the film shows. The POWs liked each picture and are interested in what the next film will be. Two movie showings were organised at the municipal cinema for the former brigadier generals and colonels, who were also pleased and thanked [the organisers] for the attention [shown them].

E. Glass cases for photocopies of newspapers on the following topics have been installed in the camp:

1. The Difficult Past of our Homeland
2. The USSR – Land of Victorious Socialism
3. The Third Stalinist Five-Year Plan

The camp buildings were decorated with slogans and posters for the twenty-second anniversary of the October Revolution.[4]

This sunny portrait of prisoner engagement is repeated in every report submitted to Moscow, the Polish officers apparently posing eager questions on the rights of Soviet citizens, the functioning of *kolkhozy* or the nature of collective work.[5] However, given the NKVD's general obsession with statistics – we know, for example, that in November alone the Starobelsk authorities purchased 50 chess sets, 143 sets of draughts, 112 sets of dominoes, 4 gramophones, 3 harmonicas, 3 mandolins, 3 guitars and 3 balalaikas for the prisoners' benefit[6] – there is one glaring omission: at no time do we ever learn how many men actually participated in these political activities.

In reality, the vast majority of prisoners showed little interest in the talks and discussions so industriously laid on for their benefit. True, the film screenings were popular; some prisoners even attended on a daily basis, but they did so more from a need to pass the time than out of political engagement. Many of the films were well-known examples of early Soviet cinema; some had considerable artistic merit. Prisoners were also happy to play chess, draughts and dominoes, all sanctioned by the NKVD. In Ostashkov prisoners were granted permission to form a musical group (membership was restricted to non-commissioned police officers – no higher-ranking officers need apply). They managed two performances of Polish folk songs before disbanding when they discovered it was compulsory to include Soviet songs in the repertoire.[7] In truth, for every discussion promoted by the NKVD with joyful themes such as 'Bourgeois or socialist democracy', 'Destroying the difference between intellectual and physical work', or 'The Chinese nation in its fight for national independence',[8] a far greater number of clandestine talks were taking place on subjects as diverse as French literature, fine art, engineering, geology, ancient history, ballistics, medical science, mathematics, politics or history. For every game of chess there were ten of bridge or poker, capitalist 'games of chance' much frowned upon by the camp authorities. At every search guards confiscated dozens of homemade packs of cards, yet the games continued. Zygmunt Berling describes whiling away winter evenings with his fellow colonels playing bridge with cards made out of newspaper stuck together with flour.[9]

Despite the dozens of rules spelled out by Kirshin in his talks on 'Internal Regulations in the Blocks' – which forbade activities such as visiting other blocks, walking in groups or keeping a diary – in practice these were rarely strictly enforced. Marooned for the first three months in 'the Morgue' with companions who showed no interest in anything except their own misery, Józef Czapski took particular pleasure in visiting the room where the majors lived, one of the few places where there was sufficient light to read. Here, he would listen to talks given by Major Adam Sołtan, who had a passion for Henryk Sienkiewicz's *Trilogy*, a classic of Polish literature filled with descriptions of patriotic courage and romantic chivalry. Sołtan knew these books almost by heart and would read aloud from them (two copies had made their way into the camp in someone's pockets and enjoyed enormous popularity). 'When I read of the grand deeds of Skrzetuski and Kmicic,' he confessed to Czapski, 'then I dream of doing something crazy…a cavalry charge, for example, where my death would be certain.'[10] Another book to escape the many searches, *La Femme de Trente Ans* by Honoré de Balzac in a translation by Tadeusz Boy-Żeleński, was divided into sections, five or six people reading it at a time, each urging the next to hurry up and hand on the next chapter. There was even a leather-bound copy of the translated works of William Shakespeare that had somehow evaded scrutiny.

Cavalry cadet Zdzisław Peszkowski shortly before the war.

For 22-year-old officer cadet Zdzisław Peszkowski, leaving the skit to visit 'Greater Kozelsk' was an all-too-rare treat. This was where the majority of senior officers lived, as well as well-known cultural and academic figures. Lectures took place in the main building of the ruined church ('the Indian tomb') as well as communal prayers. Peszkowski only rarely had access to these men, but even in the skit he found plenty of companions to stimulate his enquiring young mind: 'People speaking the most varied selection of languages, travellers, writers, journalists, diplomats, even one lucky fellow who before the war had won a million zloties in the lottery, people with a fantastic range of interests.' Peszkowski was steeped in the culture of scouting which had played and would continue to play a major part in his life. He did his best to act on the advice offered him by his parents and scout masters:

> Try to find someone wiser than you because this is the best way of 'fur-nishing' your mind and your character. So I sought out – first in the skit and later, when our hermitage was emptied, in 'greater Kozelsk' – men who could tell me something – university professors, people with a high level of education, with special passions.[11]

Peszkowski's thirst for learning was echoed throughout the camps as men sought a means of giving shape and meaning to days only partially filled by work and nights spent under the shadow of the *doprosy*. Some officers embarked on ambitious literary or academic projects: Józef Czapski devoted himself to writing about French painting; Edward Ralski, a naturalist and scholar, the author of works on grassland science and a professor at the University of Poznań, began writing a book about grass; the avant-garde poet Lech Piwowar scribbled down verses on cigarette papers which he would read aloud to Czapski, 'standing in the damp snow, at dusk, just outside one of the smoky, crowded barracks, at a moment when we were never farther from being able to transpose into poetry what we had experienced'.[12] There was an acute shortage of paper everywhere in the Soviet Union, so any prisoner not fortunate enough to have been carrying a diary or pocket book when he was captured was forced to pursue his interests in the margins of the Soviet-sponsored newspapers handed out in all the barracks – the *Lwów Red Banner* or the *Soviet Voice* – or to use cigarette papers as miniature notepads.

Artists took commissions for portraits and sketches, using pencil stubs or burnt match-heads to draw onto 'canvases' of yellowed paper picked up around the camp offices or the propaganda sheets handed out by the *politruks*. According to Kozelsk prisoner Dr Salomon Słowes, pamphlets containing the Soviet constitution and the history of the Russian Communist Party were especially popular for this purpose. Other prisoners sculpted chess pieces or religious symbols from pieces of wood found lying around, using nails as improvised tools which they smoothed and sharpened on flagstones, hiding them out of sight during searches. 'Exquisite carved reproductions of Mary and Jesus in various sizes, pipes for smoking, and cigarette cases with delicate artistic covers. The camp commander paid 2,000 roubles for a splendid, complete chess set.'[13] One officer patiently created a model of the Belvedere Palace in Warsaw, constructing the grand palace and its surrounding gardens out of used matches and bits of wood stuck together with bread dough.

Sketch made in Starobelsk camp with a dedication 'To a good friend and companion in misery', signed Eugeniusz Maj.

This clandestine cultural life was harder to organise in Ostashkov than in Kozelsk and Starobelsk because in each block a Russian supervisor lived with the prisoners. Nevertheless they, too, wrote diaries, poetry and stories, carefully concealed from the camp authorities and their spies. Sculptors here had at their disposal not just wood but marble from the ruined churches; sometimes they even used human bones.[14]

Apart from lectures inside the barracks it was common practice to combine a walk around the camp with a talk of some kind, discussing history, politics, poetry or economics. One of Dr Godlewski's friends in Starobelsk was a former classmate from school and university in Wilno, Józef Marcinkiewicz. Marcinkiewicz was a precociously brilliant mathematician who, at the age of twenty-eight, had already achieved considerable recognition in his field and had been due to take up a chair of mathematics at the University of Poznań when war broke out. In April 1939 Marcinkiewicz travelled to England at the invitation of University College, London. He was still in London when general mobilisation was announced in Poland and could have opted to remain abroad. Despite the entreaties of his British friends not to leave, Marcinkiewicz felt it would be disloyal not to answer the call to fight for his country and returned to Poland. After taking part in the defence of Lwów the mathematician was captured by the Red Army. On the way to Starobelsk he was once again offered the chance of escape when a friend urged him to jump with him from the train. Again he refused. Like other distinguished figures in the camps Marcinkiewicz received a proposal to collaborate with the NKVD, and he was said to have written to his family asking them to send him some of his mathematics books and a copy of his PhD certificate, but he declined the offer.[15] Dr Godlewski was delighted to discover his old school friend in Starobelsk and often took him out for walks, but their companionship was frequently disrupted by enthusiastic supporters besieging the eminent scholar and Godlewski soon found himself sidelined by the crowds of adoring acolytes.[16]

Even the loudspeakers, which woke the prisoners at dawn with a rendition of the 'Internationale' and the words *Zdraztvuytye, tovarishchy!* ('Good morning, Comrades!'), played a vital, if not always welcome, role in their lives. They were inescapable. By early December in Starobelsk a total of forty-five speakers had been installed inside and outside the camp buildings, with a further eight envisaged for delivery later in the year. The

December report from Starobelsk to Moscow notes brightly, 'The prisoners are able to take advantage of the radio daily from 6 a.m. to 11 p.m.',
observing that a large group of prisoners particularly enjoyed listening to
Stalin deliver a lecture on the Soviet constitution.[17] Once again, we must
take this description with a substantial pinch of salt. Some speakers were
installed in the bunk rooms where the men slept, placed high up out of
reach, with securely fixed cables and no knobs, making it impossible to turn
them off. The prisoners were not alone in enduring the constant barrage
of state-sponsored propaganda: every village square throughout the Soviet
Union, every railway station, canteen or other public building boasted a
similar set of loudspeakers broadcasting remorselessly to its citizens.

Despite the propagandic slant of the hourly news bulletins the prisoners paid great attention to them, setting up rotas to monitor events so that
nothing of importance would be missed in the progress of the war. Kozelsk
never received its full quota of loudspeakers so they were not installed inside
the barracks. Instead, volunteers stood outside in the cold to listen to the
news (the same procedure was followed in Starobelsk until the arrival of
the extra speakers in late November). Every evening a select group of men
would 'broadcast' a digested version of the news secretly in each block,
along with jokes and humorous sketches. Chief among these 'broadcasters'
was Naval Captain Julian Ginsbert. The author of popular westerns which
he wrote under the pen name Jim Poker, Ginsbert was celebrated among
his fellow prisoners for his uncanny ability to imitate the Soviet style of
delivery. The NKVD were concerned at the influence of these 'anti-Soviet
elements' over other prisoners[18] and for his actions, as well as for editing a
camp magazine and giving public talks, Ginsbert was arrested and spent
ten days in the camp cooler.[19]

Occasionally, the loudspeakers offered a refuge. Hidden among the
propaganda and the endless exhortations to increase productivity were
concerts of classical music. Even via the poor-quality equipment, they
slaked the thirst of music-lovers like Bronisław Młynarski:

Hunched on my upper-tiered bunk I would push myself as near as possible
to the speaker in order not to miss a single bar. It was not easy to secure
silence even during the most interesting musical programme. Down below,
the place was always full of conversation, debate and bouts of forced,

morbid gaiety. Even in the concert hall or at my home there were endless distractions to the music. Here, in the darkness of my bunk, there was none of all this: no one would ask me to the dining room, the telephone would not ring and there was no conductor in his tails. I succeeded in alienating myself completely from reality and learned to attain a maximum capacity for concentration. I drank in the sounds of music as a lost traveller in a desert oasis would drink cool refreshing water.[20]

Although the names of the performers were rarely announced, one evening Młynarski was deeply moved to hear the announcer declare that Chopin's 'Piano Concerto in A-Flat' was to be played by his brother-in-law, the renowned Polish pianist Artur Rubinstein, accompanied by an unnamed orchestra. It is possible, although not verifiable, that Młynarski survived because of his connection to the great musician.

A mobile shop (*lavotchka*) appeared in the camp at regular intervals. Run by civilians, it was officially supposed to stock the kind of essential items every prisoner might need – toothpaste, safety pins, boot polish, *makhorka*, thread, soap, boiled sweets. The reality was somewhat different. Conforming to the Soviet model of supply and demand, the shop supplied many things for which there was no demand and failed to supply those for which there was a need: if there were pencils there was no paper, if there was thread there were no needles. But the men greeted its arrival with an enthusiasm they would doubtless have found laughable in their previous lives. It broke up the monotony of camp existence and offered a tiny, if inadequate, reminder of the everyday normality of shopping. What qualified as 'essential' varied enormously from week to week, and men would queue up patiently to purchase items which they could not yet see (since the shop did not display goods but kept them on shelves behind a counter presided over by a stern female 'sales representative'), only to arrive at the front of the queue to be confronted by an assortment of lipsticks, boxes of scented powder, or bottles of perfume.[21]

The presence of such feminine items was initially puzzling until it became clear the mobile shop was a source of supply not just to the prisoners but to camp staff and locals too. Despite the commonly-repeated mantra that in the Soviet Union there was 'plenty of everything', in reality, even for privileged NKVD officials shortages were commonplace. Items purchased from the mobile shop at official rates could be taken home to families or sold on for a profit. Consignments of various goods would appear in large quantities, sometimes in response to a need previously agreed with the camp authorities, at other times apparently at random. On one occasion Major Zaleski had petitioned the camp commander in Starobelsk to supply galoshes to protect the officers' boots, which were being rapidly destroyed by the mud and snow. When the galoshes eventually arrived most disappeared before the prisoners caught sight of them, while those remaining proved to be of dubious quality. When a freezing Bronisław Młynarski eventually reached the front of a lengthy queue he discovered the only galoshes left were for women, complete with pointed toes and rubber heels. Undeterred, he bought a pair. Since they would not stretch over his boots he wore them directly on his feet, stuffing the heels and toes with paper and tying them on with shoelaces, much to his friends' amusement. Ridiculous and imperfect as they were, the night guard offered him 150 roubles for them. Similarly, a local carpenter arrived in Kozelsk one day having heard the shop would be selling shoes. When he eventually reached the counter and discovered only indoor plimsolls on sale his fury was so great he momentarily threw caution aside and held forth on everything he hated about the Soviet system and its economy. 'I remember how that man went back in a foul temper,' recalled Zdzisław Peszkowski.

For Peszkowski and his friends in the skit the arrival of the *lavotchka* offered the chance to visit 'greater Kozelsk', even though he had no money to spend. Most prisoners possessed only Polish zloties, many of them in large quantities, but payment had to be made in roubles. The problem was resolved in the somewhat bizarre form of a Soviet government commission known as the *Glaviuvelirtog* (Main Jewellery Trade Administration), which duly appeared in each of the camps and purchased from the prisoners objects such as watches, pens, cigarette cases and other valuables which had survived the frequent searches. After an official exchange rate was established a row of civilians inspected the items for sale, weighing them, checking (in the case of watches) that the mechanism was working, and offering a (non-negotiable) price for them. Each prisoner was entitled to no more than fifty roubles per month; any sums above this were to be kept in trust by the camp authorities and paid out as required.[22]

This process led inevitably to a thriving illicit trade as those in possession of valuable items they did not need exchanged or sold them for something they did. Middlemen sprang up to act as brokers, acquiring an array of tempting goods from one prisoner which they then offered to others at a profit. Speculators were not large in number. Once identified, they were either removed from the camp or 'persuaded' to act as informers. Speculation was not limited to the prisoners: many staff members engaged in illegal transactions, buying much-coveted watches or other items from prisoners, later spotted sported ostentatiously on the wrists of camp guards. Ostashkov in particular had a continual problem with workers entering into business arrangements with prisoners to buy valuable items or help them send 'illegal' letters.[23] If discovered, staff members found guilty of such transgressions were swiftly removed and replaced by 'sturdier' comrades. And yet it was a widely known fact among the local workers – who in turn told the prisoners – that supplies sent to the camps were regularly creamed off by the same senior NKVD staff who were busily castigating their juniors for their untrustworthy behaviour. Nor were they above taking a fancy to a gold watch or a fine cigarette case. They were simply more discreet about it.

Necessity, they say, is the mother of invention and the prisoners were nothing if not inventive in the pastimes they chose to while away long winter evenings. One night in Dr Godlewski's block a young radio engineer brought in coffin lids from the broken tombs. On these, in an atmosphere of mock solemnity, he and his friends would hold evening séances, hiding the lids under his bunk during the day.[24] In Kozelsk one officer claimed to have a direct line to the spirit of Marshal Piłsudski himself (the great man died in 1935). When summoned by the medium to tell the gathered group of enthusiasts when and how the war was going to end, the marshal was said to have replied: 'You are prisoners and yet you are all behaving like a bunch of brats. I refuse to speak to you.'[25]

The author of this account, Kozelsk survivor Stanisław Lubodziecki, judged his fellow officers harshly: he thought too many were obsessed by the idea of escape, indulging in endless speculation, gossip, arguments and infighting, hence the reproach from the 'spirit' of Poland's greatest twentieth-century leader (and author of Polish independence), Józef Piłsudski. One of the communist survivors, Kazimierz Rosen-Zawadzki, analysed the phenomenon from a political standpoint, describing it as a descent into 'backward' mysticism caused by the circumstances in which the men found themselves. 'They would go to the walls and murmur: "Here they shot…" There were all kinds of cabals, with some very strange views.'[26]

There was an element of truth in these observations. The anxiety felt by prisoners about their families and their ignorance about what was going on in Poland left them vulnerable to anything that answered their profound longing for hope in any form, whether it was a séance, a thread of gossip, or a version of world events. (Józef Czapski recalled one rumour from his early days at Starobelsk according to which the French had launched several armed divisions into the heart of Germany and occupied Munich. People claimed Soviet radio was not broadcasting this news because they did not want to irritate their allies.) As a result, rumours and gossip were rife. At their heart were two closely connected themes: the prospect of release from captivity and hope for an Allied victory in the war.

Rumours about leaving sprang up from the very first moment of arrival in the camps and are noted in NKVD reports, diaries and memoirs alike. They continued during the autumn, died down somewhat over the winter before rising again in the spring, this time with some foundation. But the source of many prisoners' greatest hopes and desires was faith in the actions of their Western allies. This led to one specific rumour which took hold in both Ostashkov and Starobelsk.

One day, some prisoners from Ostashkov were working on the road when a stranger passed alongside them. He stopped some distance from their escort and approached the small working party, asking them who they were and which camp they were from. As they informed him they were Polish prisoners from nearby Ostashkov the guard approached and the stranger swiftly moved off. The prisoners who had spoken to this man claimed he neither looked like a Russian nor spoke like one. They were convinced he was either American or British. The story spread swiftly around the camp. As the prisoners speculated on the identity of the mysterious 'Englishman' and his purpose in questioning them, a rumour grew up that the International Red Cross or Poland's Western allies were trying to obtain information about them. When the camp authorities got wind of the story and tried to find out who had spoken with the stranger, the men stopped discussing the matter in public, but during one interrogation an

NKVD officer was said to have remarked to a prisoner, 'You have highly placed protectors – they are interested in you.'[27]

A strikingly similar rumour emerged in Starobelsk. Here, the story went that the United States, through its ambassador in Moscow, was to take over the interests of the Polish embassy and extend its protection over Polish prisoners of war in the Soviet Union. The rumour first took hold in the autumn of 1939 when a middle-aged major named Skarżyński announced to his fellow prisoners the imminent arrival of the US ambassador to Moscow, Laurence Steinhardt, who – Skarżyński claimed – was due to visit the camp the following day for an inspection, accompanied by delegates from the International Red Cross. Skarżyński had lived for many years in the US and had a personal reason for desiring the intervention of the US ambassador: he had somehow found himself imprisoned together with his fourteen-year-old son, who had been born in the US and was an American citizen. The major was constantly petitioning the Soviet authorities to obtain the release of his beloved boy and eagerly embraced any hint of hope for his delivery. The impending ambassadorial visit initially caused enormous excitement, leading Bronisław Młynarski's close friend, Feliks Daszyński, to ask a high-ranking NKVD official visiting from Moscow if the prisoners might be permitted to draw up a mass petition to the American ambassador requesting their immediate release in order to fight the Germans again. Daszyński was perhaps fortunate that his only punishment for such a foolhardy question was to be the first prisoner in his block taken for inter-rogation. The Special Section subsequently summoned him on numerous occasions for nocturnal 'conversations' and he spent several nights in the camp cooler. The son of one of Poland's most prominent socialist politi-cians, Ignacy Daszyński,[28] Feliks Daszyński became increasingly obsessed with ever more outlandish plans for leaving the camp, culminating in what he deemed a foolproof master plan that involved invoking his rights as an Afghan prince. This honorary title had been bestowed on his father and other guests at a reception in Warsaw's Royal Castle held for the Afghan King Amanullah during his 1928 tour of Europe. When Daszyński sent a petition to the Soviet authorities applying for diplomatic protection via the Afghan embassy he was taken from his bunk in the middle of the night and never seen again.[29] According to Bronisław Młynarski, Major Skarżyński's son was sent home along with a group of privates in early November, but his departure did not calm his father's passion for escape. Rather the opposite: Skarżyński's relentless petitioning of the Soviet authorities for his own release evidently irritated the NKVD so much that he too was taken from the camp and never seen again.

It is highly likely the rumours concerning Western 'protectors' were put out by the NKVD as a way of measuring the mood in the camps and catching men who were inclined to rebel. While pessimists among the prisoners foresaw Siberia as their ultimate and inevitable destiny, optimists were convinced Britain and France would inflict a swift defeat on Hitler, after which Stalin would retreat from his temporary alliance with the Nazis and Poland would be resurgent. The NKVD treated this belief with as much contempt as they treated Poland itself, referring to the Allies as 'rotten democracies', the 'imperialist old effigy' (Great Britain) or the 'old disintegrating whore' (France) and addressing the prisoners as 'You former officers of the former Polish Army'. The war was dubbed 'the Second Imperialist War', later amended to 'the Great Patriotic War' after the Nazi invasion of 1941 necessitated a quick political about-face and a change in allies.

5

—

LETTERS

NOVEMBER MERGED INTO DECEMBER; THE GROUND FROZE, SNOW fell. With winter now beginning in earnest, camp life took on a certain monotonous rhythm. The clandestine talks continued, although the men ventured outside less frequently; prisoners sat in freezing barracks scribbling notes, writing poems, sculpting wooden figures, playing chess, gossiping, following the news bulletins with the same avid thirst. The political talks went on (and on), interrogations which had once been a novelty were now part of an unwelcome nocturnal routine. The only external event to arouse intense interest among the prisoners was the outbreak of the 'Winter War' between the Soviet Union and Finland at the end of November 1939. In Ostashkov, situated in the far north of the country, the proximity of the war was literal: to the east was an airport from which bombers set off towards Finland. One night the prisoners heard an explosion from the direction of the airport 'so powerful it made us jump to our feet'.[1] Visible in the distance was a fire, searchlights scanned the sky. In the morning they learned a plane had exploded on landing. As Finnish resistance to the Soviet attack proved unexpectedly resilient, the optimists stirred: was there a nugget of hope to be extracted from this new development? The pessimists responded as they always did: of course there was no hope. What chance did little Finland stand against the might of the Soviet Union? Nothing would change.

It was at this moment, however, that something did occur that was to transform the prisoners' lives.

Despite numerous pleas and complaints by senior officers, the right to correspond with their families had been denied to the prisoners in all three camps for nearly two months. At the end of November or early December, the camp authorities finally gave permission for them to write one card per month. Each man therefore faced the task of deciding not only to whom he would dedicate this first, most precious letter, but also what he might say to summarise all that had passed since September 1939 without attracting the censor's pen.

I'm in Russia, in a camp, healthy and whole. I don't need anything. I worry about all of you a lot. Write back to me immediately and tell me how you got through those heavy days fighting for Warsaw and how you're getting along now. I would really like it if you could send a short telegram letting me know you're alive and doing well, (e.g.) 'We're alive and well', especially since if we move from here I don't know if I will receive your reply. We live in hope of a swift return home. My dearest Tala, write something about all of you, about how our little Ewa is growing. Remember to make Mother feel welcome amongst you all. Get Sternicki to tell you how to secure the windows and doors against the cold. I don't know if you've heard any news of me from my friends, including Bartosiak. Tala, could you go and visit the wife of one of my comrades in misfortune here? Her name is Anna Witkowska. She lives in Mokotów on 16 Konduktorska St, apartment 3 (off Puławska) near Belgijska St. Reassure her that her husband is alright and ask her if she could write him a letter at the same address which I will put at the end of this letter to you.[2]

This letter, from 33-year-old reserve Second Lieutenant Józef Zięcina, a prisoner in Kozelsk, was never sent. He drafted it in his diary sometime towards the end of February before crossing it out. He describes it as an 'extra' one, perhaps indicating that, having already written one card that month, he knew he would be unable to send another. Or perhaps this is the letter he wanted to send but had not felt able to. The rest of his diary, discovered on his body in the Katyń Forest in 1943, consists mainly of single-line descriptions of meals, arrivals and departures, and a list of the titles of films he watched at the camp cinema, which he evidently attended almost daily.

It was mid-December when the first replies began to arrive, first in a trickle, then a steady stream. The effect was profound. The isolation in which the men had existed for so long was suddenly filled with all kinds of news. The letters brought both relief and despair: for some it was the end of a long period of anxiety; for others the news was grim, or there was none. Initially, communication was only possible for those whose families lived in the Soviet zone of occupation. It was not until much later that men with families living in the German zone received word from them. The botanist Edward Ralski had to wait until March 1940 before discovering that the Nazis had thrown his wife and child out of their lodgings in Poznań, along with all his scientific materials and his work on the grasses of Poland, destroying them on the spot.

The cards and letters also brought with them tantalising hints of other developments in the war, detailed in strange allusions and clumsily disguised codes in an attempt to fox the censors. From these clues the prisoners were able to gather news about the Polish government that had reconvened in Paris and to discover that a Polish army had been formed on French soil. Of course, the letters also provided useful intelligence for the NKVD, who would sometimes show a letter to a prisoner during an interrogation, promising to hand it to him for the price of a denunciation or the acknowledgement of some imagined transgression. Sometimes they held them back for future leverage. Obsessed as they were with the connection between foreign travel and espionage, at one point the NKVD put about a rumour suggesting men with family in other countries had a chance of release. 'People went mad. One had someone in Canada, another in Australia, a third in the Bahamas, others in Tahiti.'[3] Of course, the letters were never sent. They lay in the prisoners' personal record files, waiting for judgement.

Many relatives sent parcels containing food or clothing – sausage, paté, even butter, scarves, gloves, socks. Few made it to the prisoners intact. The correspondence address given to prisoners at Kozelsk was 'the Maxim Gorky Rest Home', a name which led to some amusing misunderstandings: one officer received a letter from his wife reproaching him bitterly for loafing around in a rest home while she and her family were starving.[4]

In Starobelsk, the period leading up to Christmas and the New Year saw another significant change. The new barracks, kitchen and baths were finally completed and the men could move into their new accommodation. Gone were the lice-filled bunks; in their place were spacious wooden barracks, cold but clean, furnished with luxuries such as shelves for kit, brick stoves and even, in some, a tiny table. True to camp tradition, the passages between the rows of bunks were swiftly named. When Józef Czapski was finally able to move out of 'the Morgue' shortly after Christmas, he was delighted to learn that his new address was on the corner of Norwid and Lwów Alley. The new kitchen enabled the camp's devoted team of cooks to make further improvements to the food, and the 'gondoliers' – the volunteers who stirred the huge cauldrons of porridge or soup with long wooden sticks – now had a proper range where they would stand on piles of bricks 'rowing' the morning's breakfast or the day's lunch.

This improvement in living conditions was in every way a testament to the efforts of Major Zaleski and his team of planners, architects and engineers. But Zaleski's triumph was also to be his downfall: as soon as the new buildings were opened the camp authorities decided it was time to dispense with his services and those of his deputy, Major Miller. Bronisław Młynarski had worked closely with both men during the autumn. Just before Christmas, he and his friend Józef Laudański (known as Laud) were with Major Zaleski in the cramped room that served as the office of the Polish Command. One of the Polish doctors, Dr Wolfram, was rubbing ointment on Zaleski's badly swollen legs when the camp messenger, Kopyekin, entered the room. Something was up: over the past few days Zaleski had been in an unusually serious mood, distracted and tight-lipped, not making his usual jokes. Just a few minutes before Kopyekin's arrival he had asked Laud and Młynarski to pack a suitcase for him with a few items of clothing, 'just in case'.

We greeted [Kopyekin] with a polite *zdraztvuytye* which he surprisingly acknowledged with the same greeting. Major Zaleski immediately put on a show of joviality. Addressing Kopyekin in his excellent Russian he said: '*Nu*, what is the news from across the road, *tovarisch* Kopyekin? (Meaning the site of the headquarters of the NKVD) The same freezing cold as the monastery or is it perhaps even worse? How is the Commander, did he have a good night's rest? You are apparently getting ready for tomorrow's great feast – the birthday of the "people's leader"![5] *Nu*, take a seat *tovarisch* Kopyekin, and warm yourself up. Have a smoke,' he said amiably offering him some *makhorka*.

Looking somewhat embarrassed Kopyekin sat on the edge of the Major's bunk…. After a long pause and then stammering as if unsure of himself, he interrupted the silence in his queer voice, reminding one of the quack of a duck: '*Nu*, Zalevsky, that will do. Stop being funny, there's plenty of work ahead. *Nu*, get dressed and off we go to the Commander!'

The Major sighed loudly, pulled down his tunic, tightened his belt and reached out for his cap. He looked round the room attentively as if he had left behind something and then looked straight into the eyes of each of us. Laud tried to help him on with his greatcoat, which he would not wear usually, so he reluctantly flung it over his shoulders.

'Hail my friends…and many thanks,' he said, quickly following Kopyekin outdoors.[6]

They never saw Zaleski again. His disappearance was followed, shortly afterwards, by that of Major Miller and the messenger Kopyekin. Miller had recently used his considerable charm to extract from Kopyekin the explosive news that outside the camp, on Kirov Street, was a house in which 100 colonels and lieutenant colonels of the Polish army were living and that eight Polish generals were being held in a cottage in town. Miller had obtained their names and attempted to get in contact with them.

It is not difficult to work out why Zaleski and Miller were removed: they had served a useful purpose in rebuilding and improving Starobelsk but in the process had come to know a lot about the personalities of the camp's leaders as well as the workings of its administrative machinery. Both men had fought hard for the interests of their fellow prisoners, often coming into conflict with Berezhkov and Kirshin as a consequence. The NKVD tolerated them so long as they were useful but once the camp was functioning properly they became expendable. The messenger Kopyekin was simply the latest in a series of camp workers and civilians who paid the price for engaging in any form of human contact with the prisoners.

There is little information about what happened to Major Zaleski and Major Miller between January and April 1940. They were most likely interrogated either in the NKVD prison in Kharkov or in Moscow before being returned briefly to Starobelsk in April 1940 and taken on a transport towards an unknown destination.

At around the same time, the NKVD removed all the priests from Kozelsk and Starobelsk. The Kozelsk priests were transferred to Ostashkov on 23 December, remaining there until the camp was emptied in April 1940. The Starobelsk priests were initially interrogated in Butyrka prison and the Lubyanka in Moscow before being taken to Kozelsk camp in April.[7] All were murdered in April 1940 except two: from Kozelsk, Father Kamil Kantak and, from Starobelsk, Father Franciszek Tyczkowski. Kantak was a professor at a seminary in Pinsk (now in Belarus) who happened to be in the company of some army officers when a Soviet sentry arrested them. It is possible he was spared because he was a citizen of Gdańsk.[8] We do not know why Tyczkowski survived.

It is a measure of the NKVD's success in subduing these once-proud men that the removal of Zaleski, Miller, the priests and several others was greeted not by protests but in passive silence. The prisoners had learned what happened to those who dared rebel.

Christmas was marked in a solemn but quiet manner, noted by the majority of those who recorded it as a melancholy period during which their thoughts, inevitably, turned to home. The group of colonels living on Kirov Street in Starobelsk town were able to obtain decent supplies for their Christmas meal – oil, fish, herring, potatoes, beetroot – which they prepared together. Everything went well until they sat down at the table and started to exchange Christmas wishes, at which point, 'everyone fell apart'.[9] On New Year's Eve one of the colonels tried to hang himself, leaving a card declaring he could not bear it any more. He was discovered alive by one of the kitchen workers and taken to hospital but never seen again.[10]

In Starobelsk camp itself the prisoners received no extra rations for Christmas but their cook, Antoni, dedicated himself to the task of creating seasonal delicacies to be shared among the men. The chef, known sometimes as Saint Antoni for the excellence of his cooking, was renowned in the camp for his ability to conjure delicious little pasties from *sielotek* (salted herring), which Commissar Kirshin was wont to sample greedily during one of his frequent kitchen inspections.[11] Other prisoners deployed considerable ingenuity in creating traditional Christmas symbols from whatever material they had at their disposal: in Ostashkov they made communion wafers from flour and cut branches from nearby trees to serve as miniature

Christmas trees. In Kozelsk it was said that the only female prisoner in the camp, the pilot Janina Lewandowska, had somehow been able to receive communion wafers which she shared amongst her fellow prisoners. In Starobelsk a young craftsman from Warsaw, the painter, illustrator, set designer and wood engraver Edward Manteuffel, decorated communion wafers with intricate designs.

It is perhaps a reflection of Józef Czapski's character that he alone describes this first Christmas in captivity as a moment of profound spiritual meaning. At the time Czapski was still living in 'the Morgue'. After a dispiriting scene during which one of his roommates threw a bucket of soup over another prisoner, splashing Czapski's coat, he decided to visit his friend, a young lawyer named Tomasz Chęciński. Czapski was welcomed into the barracks by a lively crowd of young lieutenants whose Christmas Eve celebration was in full swing: in the narrow space between bunks stood a table covered in a white cloth on top of which they had placed a tiny Christmas tree and, for each guest, a small roll and three boiled sweets. After a long silence during which each man thought of home and family they sang Christmas carols and recited poetry by Mickiewicz and Wyspiański. 'Neither the Red soldiers nor the Bolshevik propagandists dared show their faces that night.'[12]

The lack of action on the part of the NKVD was most likely because they considered Christmas less of an excuse to foment rebellion than Polish Independence Day. Nevertheless, in their December report Commander Berezhkov and temporary commissar Kutovoy noted that, on the evening of 24 December, a group of ten prisoners, with Major Adam Sołtan at their head and including Captains Ślizeń and Kuczyński-Iskander Bej, were interrupted in mid-discussion by a *politruk*, upon whose entrance they abruptly broke off their conversation. When invited to continue their debate the officers claimed they had gathered together, as members of the same regiment, to celebrate Christmas and were discussing the ongoing battles between German and British naval vessels, prompted by the most recent radio bulletin. Another prisoner (presumably an informer) later revealed to Kutovoy that this was merely a pretext and in reality the conversation concerned the rebuilding of Poland after the war with the aid of France and Britain. No immediate punishment followed, although Kuczyński was removed from the camp before the end of the year, possibly because – like others who sought escape via a family connection – he had petitioned the authorities to contact the Turkish embassy on his behalf.[13]

Throughout January and February the only events to interrupt the monotonous rhythm of camp life were bulletins from the Soviet–Finnish war and the continued arrival of letters from home. Now that construction work was complete there was even less to do in Starobelsk and the men focused their attention on reading, writing, language learning and secret talks. But as spring approached a subtle undercurrent began to be felt. Change was afoot.

One of the first signs came, surprisingly, from a dog. 'Deprived of friendship a dog will look for it as any of us would do. And more than that. His unsurpassed instinct has taught him the notion of divine justice: he senses misery, sorrow and also disaster.'[14]

Packs of stray dogs would regularly hang around Starobelsk in the hope of finding food within. The more determined managed to sneak past the guards, hiding behind the wheels of a truck or squeezing through the closing gate. As a consequence, at any one time dozens of dogs roamed around the camp. The prisoners attached themselves to these mangy hounds with an eagerness that speaks eloquently of their desperate need for companionship. The dogs, starved of affection as well as food, reciprocated with equal ardour.

Alongside the hundreds of doctors imprisoned in the camps were several vets, including, in Starobelsk, one of Warsaw's leading veterinary surgeons, 53-year-old Major Maksymilian Łabędź. Łabędź lavished particular attention on the strays, making combs from bits of tin and using them to remove dirt and fleas. He even carried out surgery, bandaging heads or bellies, immobilising a paw with a cleverly-made splint. He was not alone: Dr Levittoux made a splint for a dog whose leg had been broken by a particularly brutal kick from one of the guards, an act that mystified the Soviets, who thought it idiotic to waste such effort on an animal during a war. Dr Levittoux attempted to explain that a dog also had a right to care, even in wartime.[15]

Particular dogs 'adopted' individual prisoners, making themselves at home under their master's bunk and in return being fed on scraps and bestowed with names reflecting the prisoners' preoccupations and range of references. The vet Łabędź's favourite was a cheerful little black and white

Maksymilian Łabędź (1886–1940).

mongrel nicknamed Linek (short for Stalinek, 'little Stalin', named for his moustache); a shaggy sheepdog was dubbed Foch (after Ferdinand Foch, commander-in-chief of the French armies during World War I and the possessor of a magnificent moustache); Sikorka, deemed to be a distant relation to an English setter, was named after General Sikorski, while a dog named Winston apparently bore no resemblance to his namesake and was certainly not a bulldog.

Zygmunt Kwarciński's adopted dog, the shaggy Foch, had an unusual routine. He spent five days a week in the camp but disappeared at the weekends, leading Kwarciński to conclude that Foch must have a master in town who came home from work at the end of each week. In an attempt to establish communications with the outside world the group of friends hid messages under the fur on the dog's neck: 'What do people think of us?... Do you really love the Germans? Do you also suffer from cold and hunger as we do?' They received no reply until the second half of March 1940, just after the end of the Soviet–Finnish war. Foch reappeared in the camp after an absence of several days looking filthy and hungry, and bearing signs of injuries. Around his neck was a tiny bag made of cigarette paper with an inscription in small, distinct Russian characters: 'Dear Friends. According to rumours you will soon be leaving Starobelsk. People are also saying that you might go home. Whether this is true we don't know. We hate the Germans as much as you do. May God protect you.'[16]

Whether this message was genuine we will never know. It is eminently possible that Foch's message was penned not by a sympathetic local but by the NKVD, adding an authentic-sounding flourish to a cheery narrative that the unsuspecting prisoners were only too ready to believe.

6
—
PARROT HOUR

RUMOURS THAT THE PRISONERS WERE TO LEAVE THE CAMPS had persisted ever since their arrival, dying down somewhat over the winter. In the spring of 1940 they returned with a new sense of imminence underscored by signs of increasing activity in the offices of the camp authorities. The prisoners watched with growing curiosity as the gates opened and closed to admit or release mysterious visitors travelling in black official cars. They were not aware that the new arrivals were senior NKVD officers sent from Moscow to oversee the forthcoming 'operation', nor that the cars shuttling back and forth carried a staff member who had been specially designated to journey to the capital in order to receive, in strictest secrecy, the lists of prisoners destined for execution.[1]

Around this time a Kozelsk prisoner, lawyer Tadeusz Wirszyłło, was asked during an interrogation if he knew any professors from Wilno University who might be present in Kozelsk. Not realising his old friend Stanisław Swianiewicz had given false information about his identity at registration, Wirszyłło duly named three colleagues: the lawyer Wacław Komarnicki; neurologist and psychiatrist Dr Włodzimierz Godłowski (who also happened to be director of the Institute of Brain Research in Wilno which, following the death of Marshal Piłsudski in 1935, had been assigned the task of examining the great man's brain); and the well-known economist Stanisław Swianiewicz. According to Wirszyłło, the investigating officer appeared stunned by the news of Swianiewicz's presence in the camp. Shortly afterwards – much to his surprise because usually only staff officers were called – Swianiewicz was called to a meeting with Kozelsk's top interrogator, Major Zarubin.

Zarubin received me very politely. He did not mention anything about his knowledge that I had given false data. He said, though, that he realised we belonged to two different philosophies of thought and our outlook on the world was completely different, but he would enjoy tremendously a discussion with a man of opposite views. Our conversation lasted for more than two hours. It was difficult to find out what interested him the most. He asked me about my journeys to Germany before the war and about my contacts and acquaintances in the Polish Ministry of Foreign Affairs. Otherwise he jumped from one topic to the next; he was investigating my intellectual acumen from various angles in a very intelligent manner. As for me, I avoided talking about my federalist sympathies and my allegiance to the concepts represented by Józef Piłsudski in 1919. I suspect that this conversation played a great part in my future destiny.[2]

Swianiewicz never saw Zarubin again after this conversation. It was to be some time before he understood its importance.

As the rumours of their imminent departure began to spread a mood of excited anticipation gripped even the most cynical of the prisoners. In one of the barracks in Starobelsk officers found an itinerary showing a journey leading towards Romania; on another occasion, a guard woke the men in Czapski's block to ask if any of them spoke Romanian or Greek. Meanwhile, the prisoner who acted as camp postman confessed to Dr Godlewski that he had been instructed to hand out the entire postbag at once rather than distributing letters in small batches as he would normally do. Each of these signs, planted by the NKVD with meticulous attention to detail, was scrutinised by the prisoners with the eagerness of soothsayers scanning the entrails of a sacrificial animal. They led to only one possible conclusion: they were about to be sent away, westwards, towards home or a neutral country.

More details emerged of the planned departures: in Kozelsk, young dentist and facial surgeon Dr Salomon Słowes heard rumours that prisoners were to be transferred to 'classification centres' for repatriation. These reports originated from conversations between the Polish generals and the camp commander; senior officers confirmed them, as did the janitors in the shower room. Of three such centres, the city of Brest-Litovsk was mentioned most frequently. There, on the border between German-occupied

Poland and Soviet-ruled Western Belorussia, a joint German, Russian and Lithuanian committee was to approve the destinations selected by the men in questionnaires which they had filled out in February.³ This information was so widely disseminated that the wife of Kozelsk's most senior Polish doctor, Professor Bolesław Szarecki, travelled from Warsaw to Brest-Litovsk in the hope of meeting her husband. Likewise, Józef Czapski learned from postcards sent to Starobelsk that several women from the Red Cross, including Dr Kołodziejski's wife and Czapski's own two sisters, were taking it in turns to wait at the train stations on the line demarcating the German and Soviet zones of occupation with hundreds of packages for the prisoners because they had been told they would be passing through on their way to German camps.

As we have seen, all prisoners filled out a detailed personal questionnaire shortly after their arrival in the camps. It appears that sometime in February or March 1940 the NKVD handed out a second questionnaire that included a supplementary question asking prisoners to state where they wished to go on leaving.⁴ There were three options: a neutral country such as Turkey, Romania, Bulgaria, Hungary, Norway or Sweden; German-occupied Poland; or the Soviet Union.⁵ Zygmunt Berling recalled that many officers were extremely agitated as they tried to decide which option to select. Clearly, the choices were fraught with difficulty: a return to Nazi-occupied Poland would mean incarceration in a POW camp and the end of any prospect of playing an active part in the war; on the other hand, it would also mean being nearer families and might conceivably lead to better treatment. Germany was a signatory to the Geneva Convention and generally treated POWs according to accepted international norms. Jewish officers, on the other hand (just under two percent of the population in Kozelsk and Starobelsk) had every reason to dread a return to Nazi-occupied Poland. Prisoners whose homes were in the Soviet-occupied zone, meanwhile, feared their return would render them vulnerable to arrest or trial as anti-Soviet 'undesirables'. And while the idea of travelling to a neutral country was deeply appealing to those who wished to continue the fight against Germany, it barely stood up to a moment's scrutiny as a realistic proposition: why would the Soviets release prisoners to fight against their ally? Nevertheless, General Minkiewicz encouraged the officers in Kozelsk to choose this option. Writing in 1948, Lieutenant

Colonel Tadeusz Felsztyn notes bitterly that the camp authorities must have had a good laugh at this.[6]

This second questionnaire receives scant attention in the recollections of the majority of survivors, perhaps because most published accounts were written by men like Józef Czapski, Bronisław Młynarski or Stanisław Swianiewicz, who had in all likelihood chosen similar answers to their murdered comrades; for this reason they would be unlikely to read any significance into their own response. By contrast, the questionnaire crops up several times in a series of recordings made in the 1960s by the so-called 'Berling group' of pro-Soviet officers, Cadet Officer Franciszek Kukuliński, Second Lieutenant Roman Imach, Captain Kazimierz Rosen-Zawadzki and Lieutenant Colonel Leon Bukojemski.[7] Rosen-Zawadzki states that in the captains' block at Starobelsk at least ninety percent of the prisoners expressed a desire to be sent to German-occupied territory, while Bukojemski claims that during one of his interviews with the head of the Special Section in Starobelsk, Mikhail Yefimov, Yefimov urged him to persuade prisoners to say they wanted to remain in the Soviet Union. When Bukojemski next saw Yefimov the NKVD officer showed him the forms: 'Smotri... (Look...) – out of 4,968 prisoners only 64 say they want to stay in the Soviet Union.' He then gave Bukojemski a new set of forms and instructed him to go out and try again. Bukojemski did as he was ordered, but the result was the same.

Recalling events after a 25-year interval, Bukojemski quotes Yefimov using a completely erroneous figure for the total number of prisoners held in Starobelsk (4,968 instead of 3,893), yet the number of officers apparently declaring themselves willing to remain on Soviet territory (64) matches precisely the number in the 'special group' that left Starobelsk on 25 April 1940 and that included Berling, Bukojemski and other pro-Soviet officers. In the absence of any evidence from the Soviet side it is impossible to conclude whether there was a direct link between the answers given by prisoners and their ultimate fate. The likelihood is that the supplementary question was simply one in a long series of tests designed to probe prisoners' loyalties and explore their commitment to various beliefs or ideals. We have no way of knowing whether all prisoners expressing a desire to remain in the Soviet Union found themselves on the list of survivors, but it is reasonable to suppose those who did were more likely to live.

Rumours about their departure reached Ostashkov later than the other camps. As interrogations ceased and work slowed down or stopped altogether, the prisoners were left to wander about aimlessly, prey to a vague sense of foreboding.

> More and more frequently you would see prisoners in the open spaces of the camp, next to the church and under the walls, turning their miserable faces towards the sun. Although the lake was still frozen and piles of snow which had been taken from the camp lay beyond the bars, one could feel the approach of spring. It did not bring us joy, however.[8]

So ignorant were the men of what was to come that when camp commander Major Borisovets received the first list of forty-nine names from Moscow on 1 April 1940, the news electrified the camp. As names were called and the men prepared to leave, levels of excitement rose sharply. Now came the rumours: they were going to Brest-Litovsk, and then they were going home. 'We wanted to believe it, we were only wondering why, amongst the departing prisoners who came from areas under German occupation, there were also some who came from Soviet-occupied areas.' In a bid to maintain the atmosphere of anticipation Major Borisovets instructed the musical group to accompany the departing men. 'The orchestra played and this did indeed make a good impression on us all. Both officers and men quit the camp joyfully, and they left their comrades with the cry: "See you in Poland!"'[9]

In Kozelsk, Major Kazimierz Szczekowski recorded in his diary the build-up of tension towards the much-anticipated day of departure. His observations reveal several salient details: that the NKVD had been ordered to close the prisoners' personal records prior to departure; that the moment of change coincided with the end of the Soviet–Finnish war (later to form the basis of one theory concerning the timing of the massacre[10]); and that, despite the best efforts of the NKVD to cream off supplies destined for the prisoners, some food parcels did actually make it into the camps.

> 16 March – The authorities are in a hurry to complete our records. Something is in the air, but what it is nobody knows, however hard they guess. On 14 March the war with Finland ended suddenly.

19 March – There are rumours going around that we might be sent to neutral countries – that's something new.

24 March – Easter. I was invited to breakfast by Goszczyński, who has received a parcel from home.

25 -26 March – There was excellent bacon, paté and dry sausage. I ate like a pig, it's a long time since I've eaten anything so good, the bacon especially was delicious.

1 April – The bomb has finally exploded. Today the first transport of 100 men left – of varying ranks, age and background, where to we don't know.

6 April – More departures. I'm ready – linen washed, boots polished.

7 April – Today a large group left with three generals.[11]

The three generals to whom Szczekowski refers were Henryk Minkiewicz, Mieczysław Smorawiński and Bronisław Bohaterewicz. The evening before their departure the camp commander gave them a farewell party, with excellent food and decent cigarettes. The three generals left, along with a large group of colonels and majors, 'in a radiant mood through rows of cheering officers who ranged themselves to bid them farewell. It happened on a beautiful, sunny, spring day.'[12] The fourth general held in Kozelsk, Jerzy Wołkowicki, was on the transport list for that day but his name was not called. It appeared instead on another list sent out from Moscow on 29 March 1940, ordering certain prisoners to be held back on the request of the 5th Department of the NKVD, the intelligence service.[13] These men were spared execution.

The NKVD had laid the groundwork of misinformation so carefully that not only did the prisoners leave in excellent spirits and with the firm conviction that they were being set free, but the men left behind envied them.

There was little time for analysis, and very few people had any presentiment about what was to happen, but those who had been chosen were very excited. There were lots of envious goodbyes from those who stayed behind, a whole commotion. You could hear: 'Write as soon as you can, and say hello to my family…you've got the address, haven't you?' and so on.[14]

Not for a single moment did the NKVD relinquish control of the happy narrative they had established in the prisoners' minds: when, in Kozelsk, the lawyer Wacław Komarnicki asked NKVD Captain Alexandrovich where they were sending the prisoners, Alexandrovich replied: 'Westward – closer to your families.' Alexandrovich was also said to have shown another survivor, Dr Włodzimierz Missiuro, a border post on the map where the prisoners would be handed over to the Germans and Missiuro's camera returned to him. In Starobelsk, Commander Berezhkov and Commissar Kirshin assured senior officers they would be evacuated towards central points, then sent to Poland to their place of birth, whether it was under German or Soviet occupation.

> Standing on the big staircase of the central church, the commander waved goodbye to the groups who were leaving with a big smile full of promises. 'You are leaving,' he said, 'for a place where I would like to go myself.'[15]

From the very first transports the prisoners found it impossible to understand the principle on which the groups were chosen: it was not by age, rank, profession, social status, political opinion or regional origin. The choice seemed so random the prisoners named the time at which the lists were read out 'parrot hour', in reference to street organ-grinders in pre-war Poland, who were often accompanied by a parrot which picked lottery tickets at random from a hat. Whatever the logic, or lack of it, every prisoner waited feverishly for the moment when he would hear his own name read out. Although a member of staff travelled to and from Moscow to receive the transport lists directly, officials double-checked them by telephone, noting any last-minute changes. Some of the more daring prisoners would sneak close to the camp offices to eavesdrop on these conversations, rushing back to tell their comrades who was on the list that day. Once details were confirmed a guard was sent to the blocks to call out the names of those who were leaving, instructing them to gather their belongings and wait in a particular place in preparation for departure. The chosen men received a parcel of herrings for the journey, wrapped in clean white paper, an unusually luxurious touch in a country where paper was always in short supply. They were then subjected to a thorough search during which all sharp implements were taken from them, as well as some of their documents.[16]

After the search they were marched out of the camp and the gates closed behind them for ever.

Second Lieutenant Wacław Kruk made only two diary entries during his time in Kozelsk, one on 8 April, when he recorded the departure of the three generals the previous day, the other on 9 April 1940, when his own name was called:

> Before we left the Skit we had an unofficial concert with the choir. My sculptures won me many fans. I had to make two relief carvings for Major Gołąbów (a highlander and a Virgin Mary), a cross for Cavalry Captain Deszert, a tobacco box…but it was my chess pieces that won the most admiration. People were worried because the gossip said they were taking all wooden pieces off prisoners during the search. Luckily it turned out to be just gossip. They took my knife, though.[17]

Throughout April and early May transports left every couple of days in groups ranging from sixty to three hundred. For those prisoners who were left behind all semblance of routine disappeared.

> We walked around in a state of excitement, went off on our own to daydream, then once again sought others for explanations. The desire to escape from those huge prison gates blotted out everything else. Everyone was jealous of those who had left and the greatest fear was that this one transport would be it. 'What do you think?' people would ask. 'Are they going to take any more?' Rarely did anyone ask: 'Where are they taking them?'[18]

Every day, Józef Czapski watched with envy as someone from Barrack 21, Lwów Alley (where he had been living since Christmas), was called. 'There were forty of us and we had become very close during the winter, but the goodbyes were nevertheless filled with joy. Everyone was living in hope of a better future, full of surprises.'[19] In Kozelsk, the skit had been closed and its inhabitants moved to the main camp. Zdzisław Peszkowski decided that wherever they were taken next he would try to escape, so to pass the intervening time he started learning Russian. As more men departed, the questions for those who were left behind grew more pressing:

> We said goodbye to each group as they left. We who remained gave them addresses, and more or less coded requests, and reports. Often with the sentence: 'If you get to Poland first, if by any chance you see any of my family, tell them we were together, and this is my fate.' It was a terrible feeling to say goodbye to someone whose departure was absolutely under a question mark: where, why, how? And that dramatic question: Why not me? When will it be my turn?[20]

Spring had arrived in all its brief northern glory. Bright sunlight warmed the broken tombstones, melting the last patches of ice and snow. As the end of April approached Dr Godlewski waited impatiently for his name to be called. Although he mistrusted the departures the constant waiting had left him in a state of nervous irritation. On 25 April the usual departure list was read out as well as another, shorter, list of sixty-four names, including his own. Godlewski could scarcely contain his excitement, only stopping briefly to wonder about the significance of the second list and why men in this group were permitted to take a blanket and a knife for cutting bread. Swiftly he packed his few remaining items of linen, his army coat and various camp lectures which he had noted down on cigarette papers, then he bid goodbye to the last few friends remaining in his barracks. There was one man he could not find, a mining engineer named Augustyn Jelonek whom Godlewski held in very high regard.

> I could not leave without saying goodbye to Jelonek. Where could he be? Suddenly I remembered a warning he had given me about my departure: 'You're leaving, but look who you are leaving with!' and he had turned away. It was true that leaving with me were many communists and men who had behaved very badly. When I was already at the gate and about to leave, I saw him and waved at him warmly; he did not reply and I did not see a friendly smile on his face. Apart from Jelonek's suspicious reaction, the other prisoners, lining the path as we marched by with our escort of armed guards, bid us goodbye with envy and sadness. I remember their reaction very clearly.[21]

Alongside Dr Godlewski in this 'special group' were Lieutenant Colonel Berling, Lieutenant Colonel Dudziński, Lieutenant Colonel Bukojemski and several others who had demonstrated a willingness to cooperate with the Soviet authorities – and some who had not. Of the sixty-four names on the list, sixty-three men left the camp (one prisoner remained behind in hospital). They were not aware of it at the time but their destination was different to that of previous transports. They were to be taken to the transit camp of Pavlishchev Bor (also known as Yukhnov), and they would survive.

Chief Inspector Jan Bober left Ostashkov on a transport of around three hundred men on 28 April. Stanisław Swianiewicz's name was called in Kozelsk the following day.

> The farewell with Professor Komarnicki stands out in my mind. After we had kissed each other goodbye, and I was already walking away, he called out to me. When I turned around, he got up, approached me and with the thumb of his right hand made the sign of the cross on my forehead. It was a symbol of delivering me into God's hands. The expression on his face and his gesture moved me deeply.[22]

As April turned to May silence and boredom reigned. In Kozelsk, of the staff officers only Admiral Czernicki and the paediatrician Dr Kopeć remained, along with the lawyer Wacław Komarnicki, growing daily more depressed. Starobelsk, too, was almost empty. Józef Czapski wandered alone through the empty barracks. 'I spent hours in the sunshine in the place where only yesterday thousands of boots had trod. How I envied my "lucky" comrades who had left the ring of barbed wire and gone out into the wide world.'[23] On 12 May 1940, Józef Czapski and Bronisław Młynarski finally left Starobelsk in a group of fifteen men. They were the last to quit the camp.

PART II

Griazovets 1940–41

Pencil sketch of Griazovets camp watchtower by
Second Lieutenant Władysław Chmura.

7

PAVLISHCHEV BOR

OUTSIDE THE GATES OF STAROBELSK A LINE OF TRUCKS WAITED, flanked by armed guards and snarling dogs. The excitement dissipated, to be replaced by a sense of uncertainty as the convoy set off. At the railway station the prisoners were confronted not by cattle trains but prison wagons, known colloquially as *stolypinkas*.[1]

> All the windows, even those giving onto the corridors, were painted over and reinforced with a metal grille. All the compartments were closed in such a way that we could not open them ourselves. If someone wanted to answer a call of nature one of the *boytzy* who was standing guard would open the door. I remember I immediately climbed up onto the overhead shelf. We were all happy and thanked God that at least for the moment we were alive.[2]

Hope returned as the train moved off: this was movement at last, after so long confined within the camp; it signified change – whether for better or worse nobody knew, but something had finally happened. There was a light in the ceiling. The officers noticed faint outlines of words scratched in various places – under the seat, on the top of the lampshade – 'They have brought us to Kharkov, they're getting out and bringing cars…' The names were familiar: they belonged to other prisoners from Starobelsk.

After a journey of several days the train reached a station named Babynino. Here the men were transferred onto trucks for a twenty-mile drive through sleeping villages and a beautiful pine forest, to arrive, on a glorious spring morning, at a cluster of buildings resembling a farm. A second glance revealed the wire fences and watchtowers. 'The mirage of France or Poland evaporated immediately.'[3]

The transit camp of Pavlishchev Bor, also known as Yukhnov after the nearby town, was situated 150 miles south-west of Moscow on land formerly belonging to Polish aristocrats. After the revolution it was turned into a rest home for NKVD functionaries; in September 1939 it became a transit prison camp for Polish prisoners and by May 1940 several thousand Polish prisoners of war had already passed through it. The setting was pleasant, with an abundance of trees and flowering shrubs; the buildings had previously been used as exercise grounds for the owner's horses and were in reasonably good shape. The biggest surprise came when, on arrival, prisoners were ordered into a wooden cabin which turned out to contain a spacious bath house. They were handed clean underwear and blocks of soap. 'Hastily we stripped, tearing away the shreds of our worn, sweaty underwear which we threw into a pile. Naked, the men burst into the adjacent shower stalls with a commotion and cries of joy.'[4] The warm shower was an unexpected luxury. It also revealed the damage wrought by seven months in captivity.

> The young bodies were skinny and pale, and the faces, tanned and exhausted, looked like masks on tall skeletons. The older men were spent, and the folds of dry skin hung loosely on their necks and abdomens. They moved slowly, precariously maintaining their balance on the wet boards as the water cascaded onto their hands. The men exploited the rare opportunity and eagerly scrubbed away, singing and whistling lustily, oblivious to their surroundings.[5]

Out of all the transports leaving Kozelsk, Starobelsk and Ostashkov throughout April and May there were two sets from each – one at the end of April, one in mid-May – whose destination was different to the rest. At eighty miles the distance from Kozelsk to Pavlishchev Bor was relatively short; the journey from Starobelsk took several days and from Ostashkov it took five. First to reach the camp was a group of ninety-six officers from Kozelsk that included the men who would form the core of command in Pavlishchev Bor and, later, Griazovets: General Wołkowicki, Colonels Bolesławicz, Mara-Meyer and Prokop, Professor Szarecki, Lieutenant Colonel Felsztyn and Captain Ginsbert, as well as a young pianist, Zbigniew Grzybowski, and Dr Salomon Słowes. Next to arrive was the 'special' group from Starobelsk in which Dr Godlewski travelled in the company of Zygmunt Berling and other pro-Soviet officers. Chief Inspector Bober, meanwhile, had left Ostashkov on 28 April on a train with three hundred prisoners on board. Somewhere along the way the wagon in which he was travelling was uncoupled and he disembarked at Babynino to discover that only thirty men from the original transport had arrived with him.[6] Józef Czapski and Bronisław Młynarski were among the last to reach the camp.

The unaccustomed luxury of a warm shower and clean clothes was followed by more novel comforts: the rooms in which the prisoners slept accommodated no more than eight to ten men and contained proper beds; there was a dining room with plentiful food and a decent lending library. Better still, there was space and air.

Enjoyable as it was to stretch out on the grass in the sun there was one question nobody could yet answer: the camp was small, only 400 men out of a total of 14,800 prisoners from the three camps had appeared. Where was everybody else?

NKVD records list a total of 395 prisoners brought to Pavlishchev Bor: 205 from Kozelsk, 78 from Starobelsk, 112 from Ostashkov.[7] This is the number accepted by most Russian and Polish historians, but it is not definitive. Records kept by the prisoners themselves produce slightly different numbers, listing 430 or 431 men in total: 427 taken to Pavlishchev Bor, plus a further 4 who arrived at Griazovets separately (including the two priests, Kamil Kantak and Franciszek Tyczkowski, sent directly from the Lubyanka in Moscow on the orders of the 1st Special Department of the NKVD). The discrepancy could possibly be explained by different methods of counting: there were twenty-seven men suffering from TB who, according to Jan Bober, were kept separate from the main camp: if one discounts these plus the further four who arrived at Griazovets later, the numbers are much closer.[8]

Nearly two-thirds of the prisoners were officers, the majority of these junior ranks (137 lieutenants and second lieutenants, 73 officer cadets and ensigns). There was a single general (Wołkowicki), plus 24 colonels and lieutenant colonels, 8 majors and 18 captains (including 3 naval captains). The remaining third of the camp population was made up of police and army sergeants, corporals and privates, along with 38 men listed as 'refugees' from Soviet and German-held territory, three fugitives from Lithuania, a handful of agents, officials and civilians, and seven former convicted prisoners

(including, according to Dr Salomon Słowes, a Ukrainian murderer[9]). None
of these men were aware of the fate of their fellow prisoners. They could
only look around and observe that Professor Szarecki was here but not Dr
Levittoux, Major Lis but not Major Sołtan, General Wołkowicki but not
Mickiewicz, Haller, Smorawiński or any of the other eleven generals held
captive in Kozelsk and Starobelsk. The botanist Edward Ralski, the forester
Zygmunt Kwarciński, the avant-garde poet Lech Piwowar, the dog-loving
vet Maksymilian Łabędź, rosy-cheeked Józef Laudański, graphic designer
Edward Manteuffel, mathematician Józef Marcinkiewicz, engineer Zygmunt
Mitera, Major Zaleski, Major Miller – so many friends and comrades were
absent. Why?

A report from head of the UPV Pyotr Soprunenko dated (after) 25 May
1940 lists six categories of prisoner whose names had been removed from
the execution lists.

Top Secret

Information on the Prisoners of War detained at Yukhnov NKVD Camp

[Note: the Russians refer to Pavlishchev Bor as Yukhnov]

Total sent to Yukhnov camp: . . . . 395 people
Including:

a)   On the instruction of the GUGB 5th department. . . . . 47 people
b)   At the request of the German embassy. . . . . 47 people
c)   At the request of the Lithuanian mission . . . . 19 people
d)   Germans. . . . . 24 people

                                                        ———
                                                        137 people

e)   On instruction from USSR Deputy People's Commissar
       of Internal Affairs Comrade Merkulov. . . . . 91 people
f)   Others . . . . 167 people

                                                        ———
                                                        258
                                                        ———

[Total] . . . . 395 people

Head of the USSR NKVD UPV
GB [State Security] Captain
P. Soprunenko[10]

The names of the forty-seven prisoners in the first category appear on lists sent out to all three camps on 29 March 1940, shortly before the transports began. These men were saved 'on the instruction of the GUGB 5th department' – the intelligence section of the NKVD. Information about them was passed on to the 1st Special Department of the NKVD, where it was checked. Their records were not sent 'for consideration' by the central troika of Merkulov, Kobulov and Bashtakov. Thus they were not 'judged' like their fellow prisoners. They escaped execution.[11] The names on these lists include many pro-Soviet officers: Berling, Gorczyński, Bukojemski, Morawski, Dudziński, Tyszyński, Rosen-Zawadzki and others. But they also include many passionate Polish patriots: Wołkowicki, Grobicki, Künstler, Felsztyn, Domoń, Lis, Ginsbert, Bober, Mintowt-Czyż. Some of these men had a background in intelligence; others were known for their military or specialist skills. The work of the Special Sections investigating them over the preceding months had evidently thrown up information of sufficient interest to the higher-ups in Moscow that they were prepared to overlook the men's hostile political stance in the hope that their particular expertise or knowledge could somehow serve the interests of the Soviet state.

The second and third categories included prisoners whose fate was of interest to the German or Lithuanian authorities, either because relatives had appealed to them on the basis of German or Lithuanian descent, or because of professional prominence, or because persons of note had intervened on their behalf.[12] Prince Jan Lubomirski was a young second lieutenant, a member of one of Poland's most prominent aristocratic families. He was released in July 1940 thanks to the efforts of highly placed diplomatic connections.[13] The artist Józef Czapski (also born into an aristocratic family although he chose not to advertise the fact; his full name was Count Józef Hutten-Czapski) was singled out for attention through the intervention of the Belgian Ambassador to Rome, Ferdinand du Chastel de la Howarderie. In January 1940, du Chastel wrote to the chargé d'affaires at the German embassy in Rome, Baron Johann von Plessen, to ask if von Plessen could intervene to obtain Czapski's freedom. 'The Pole I mentioned to you on the phone is "Count Józef Czapski" … He is apparently a very brave and honourable man, and his fate in a prisoner of war camp is particularly unpleasant!'[14] Apart from Prince Lubomirski, none of the prisoners requested in this manner were actually handed over to the Germans, but they were at least kept alive.

As the transports continued throughout April and May 1940 and the lists of those destined for execution were checked and cross-checked, every so often a note was sent to one of the camp commanders asking for individuals to be removed from the list on the grounds that they had not been 'convicted' or 'judged'. Among these, in a note dated 9 April 1940 from GB Captain Gertsovsky to head of the UPV Pyotr Soprunenko mentioning six prisoners, is Bronisław Młynarski.[15] Although we have no documentary evidence explaining why Młynarski was saved (he possessed little military expertise and certainly did not work for the intelligence services), it is possible his survival was linked to his family: either his late father's prominence among Russian musicians or his connection to the famous pianist Artur Rubinstein, married to Młynarski's sister Aniela. Such exceptions continued to be made right up until the final moment. As we will see later, the economist Stanisław Swianiewicz, whose real identity had been discovered by the NKVD only in March 1940, was separated from his comrades when their train stopped at Gnezdovo, near Smolensk. He was taken to an NKVD prison, they to the Katyń Forest.[16]

The fourth category, 'Germans', were Polish citizens of German origin, or *volksdeutsche*. They were saved as a direct consequence of the Nazi–Soviet alliance. The fifth group, chosen 'On instruction from USSR Deputy People's Commissar of Internal Affairs Comrade Merkulov', were most probably informers or prisoners deemed likely to be useful in that capacity.[17] Presumably the seven convicted prisoners ticked this particular box. That leaves the final group of 'others', 167 men who fell outside the categories qualifying prisoners as 'irremediable enemies of Soviet power' and leading to their death. These were rank-and-file soldiers, NCOs, cadets, members of semi-military youth organisations and certain civilians.[18] In the absence of the personal records kept on prisoners by the NKVD (destroyed by the KGB in 1959), we will never truly understand the basis on which these few men were selected for survival or, conversely, why their companions – so similar in so many respects – were sent to their deaths.

A few days after their arrival in Pavlishchev Bor the former prisoners of Kozelsk were surprised to discover that many familiar faces from the Kozelsk Special Section had followed them, including NKVD officers

Elman, Alexandrovich and Vasilevsky, along with most of the *politruks*. When questioned about the whereabouts of their friends, Elman replied, 'You will be sent home as have all your comrades – your turn has come now.'[19] Pavlishchev Bor was a transit camp. There was no reason to suppose Elman was lying. For a few glorious weeks the prisoners took advantage of the sunshine and their relatively comfortable conditions to relax. Captain Ginsbert entertained them with humorous reports concocted on the basis of the official war bulletins; Czapski gave lectures on art and literature; the young cadets played basketball and football. There was a vegetable patch in which prisoners planted beetroot, carrots, onions, cucumbers and sunflowers, although they did not have time to harvest them. To complete the atmosphere of bucolic tranquillity, there were several horses in the camp, as well as cows tended by a milkmaid.

The prisoners were so little scrutinised during this brief period that Chief Inspector Bober, Major Lis and Major Domoń (who had reappeared following his removal from Starobelsk after 11 November) began wondering whether they could plot an escape. The bathhouse lay just beyond the camp fence, next to the river. Prisoners were taken there under escort by two soldiers. Nobody hurried them, they had all the water they wanted, they could scrub themselves and wash their linen in peace. The conspirators came up with various plans: hiding in the thickets after their bath, or swimming across to the other side of the river. They even got as far as instructing Bober, as the best Russian speaker among them, to engage the garrulous milkmaid in conversation. 'And if they had not suddenly taken us to the camp in Griazovets, who knows whether we might not have risked an escape under those favourable conditions.'[20]

The NKVD offered no explanation for the departure nor any hint as to their destination. They simply ordered the prisoners to pack up their belongings in preparation for another journey which, they said, would take up to a week. The group left Pavlishchev Bor on 14 June 1940, travelling by truck to Babynino railway station where, once again, prison wagons awaited them. Shortly before their departure the loudspeakers delivered some shocking news: the Nazis had occupied Belgium and the Netherlands. The fate of France hung in the balance.

As the train set off the optimists began to hope: this time, surely, they were homeward bound, just as Major Elman had promised. Perhaps they would be able to rejoin the war before it was too late. When the train passed Moscow and, instead of veering west, headed further north, the pessimists said: We told you so; we predicted Siberia all along. In the early hours of 18 June 1940 the train pulled in at the station of Griazovets, fifteen miles from the district city of Vologda, about halfway between Moscow and the Arctic port of Arkhangelsk. It was not quite Siberia, but the short journey from the station revealed a depressingly familiar sight: the high walls of a former convent, mounted with barbed wire and watchtowers.

8
—
GRIAZOVETS

We began this new period of captivity with a new great uncertainty: what are we going to do here? How long are we going to stay?[1]

THE CHURCH THAT WAS ONCE THE CENTREPIECE OF THE CONVENT at Griazovets had been dynamited during the revolution, leaving only ruins standing on a low hill next to a small river, the Muromka, which ran through the middle of the camp. Around the ruins stood clusters of birch and pine trees and several smaller wooden buildings. A bathhouse perched on the river bank, with three wooden buildings on one side and, beyond it, a medical centre with a little hospital on the first floor. There was the usual 'club room' used as a cinema, a camp shop and a kitchen, and a well-stocked library. On a warm June day the surroundings were not unpleasant, and with only four hundred men in the camp there was plenty of space.

When NKVD Major Volkov arrived at the end of June to take charge of the camp he found the prisoners lounging around, sunbathing and swimming. He swiftly set about replacing the lax regime with some not unduly onerous rules: as in the previous camps, the prisoners were expected to run the kitchen, laundry, barber shop and carpentry workshop themselves; volunteers could earn extra rations by joining work groups digging potatoes, moving rubble or chopping wood in the nearby forest. Junior officers cleaned their own quarters, a local woman cleaned for the staff officers. Professor Szarecki ran the clinic alongside a female Soviet doctor and a nurse. Dr Godlewski was in charge of camp hygiene. Dr Słowes worked as Professor Szarecki's assistant, taking on the role of camp dentist. With little equipment at his disposal, Słowes improvised as best he could when patients came to see him in pain, as Józef Czapski did one day after breaking a front tooth biting into a piece of stale bread. Słowes fashioned a replacement crown from a piece of wire and animal bone, earning effusive thanks from the grateful artist. Professor Szarecki's reputation spread quickly: Major Volkov himself came for treatment, followed by a number of senior district officials from beyond the barbed wire fence. Such 'outpatients' expressed their appreciation by giving the doctors handfuls of sweets, or little bottles of Russian vodka.[2]

Behind the scenes, meanwhile, the Special Section was preparing for a fresh round of interrogations. Moscow had recalled all the original personal record files when the three previous camps were closed; new ones now had to be opened on the men in Griazovets.[3] The camp commissar and his team of *politruks* were preparing a fresh programme of cultural 'work', with the customary schedule of lectures, film screenings and discussions.

Everything pointed to a long, possibly indefinite stay.

Summer in the far north of Russia is a brief season. Shortly after the prisoners' arrival came devastating news, delivered with gleeful triumph over the loudspeakers: France had fallen, the British had been forced into a humiliating withdrawal at Dunkirk. The belief in a swift Allied victory which had sustained the men through the winter of 1939–40 was shattered. The hopelessness of their own situation could no longer be concealed by optimism or blind faith. Within the confines of the larger camps the prisoners had remained relatively united. Now, as each man turned to face his own future, their unity began to fracture. More than that: the make-up of the prisoners selected for survival was almost guaranteed to lead to conflict. Factions began to form, each defined by their response to the progress of the war.

The first group can be characterised broadly as Polish patriots ('nationalist-chauvinists', in NKVD terms). At their head stood the charismatic figure of General Jerzy Wołkowicki, the senior Polish officer in the camp. Aged fifty-seven, 'tall, straight as a reed, with a reddish nose which was evidence of his fondness for the divine gifts of Bacchus',[4] Wołkowicki was a fervent patriot with strict notions regarding the appropriate behaviour of the prisoners, whom he regarded as his personal responsibility. General Wołkowicki occupied a particular place in Russian history. Like many of the older Polish officers he had spent his early career in the service of the Tsarist Russian military. As a young naval lieutenant during the 1905 Battle

General Jerzy Wołkowicki (centre) lays a wreath at the
Tomb of the Unknown Insurgent, Katowice, 1939

of Tsushima he had shown outstanding courage in resisting surrender to the Japanese and for his bravery was awarded the St George's Cross. More than that: a Soviet writer, Aleksei Ivanovich-Novikov Priboi, was so inspired by his feats that he immortalised Wołkowicki in fictional form as the hero of a popular historical novel, *Tsushima*. It is quite possibly because of this that, despite his open contempt for communism and frequent involvement in 'counter-revolutionary' activities in both Kozelsk and Griazovets, Wołkowicki was never punished by the NKVD. He was a living legend. Even the NKVD were in awe of him.

General Wołkowicki gathered around him a group of intensely loyal officers, at the head of which stood Major Ludwik Domoń, whose protracted stay in an NKVD prison had left his enthusiasm for fomenting rebellion undimmed. Noted by Chief Inspector Bober as being 'in charge of' conspiratorial activities, described by a less sympathetic prisoner as 'a twister and…an unsuccessful small-time politician,'[5] Domoń had a talent for intrigue, possibly honed working for Polish intelligence before the war.[6] Other key members in Wołkowicki's circle included the staff officers who shared his quarters (Colonel Grobicki, Lieutenant Colonels Czyź, Felsztyn and Kierkowski and Major Józef Lis) as well as Captain Ginsbert and Chief Inspector Bober, who shared Wołkowicki's rabid dislike of communists and Nazis. Around these officers hovered a large group of junior officers and cadets notable mainly for their physical energy and over-zealous patriotism. Some of the more extreme of these espoused ultra right-wing, nationalistic and anti-Semitic views.

The majority of the prisoners in Griazovets remained loyal to the Polish government in exile throughout their captivity and could thus be said to belong to the group of 'patriots'. However, not all were enthusiastic supporters of Wołkowicki's particular brand of nationalism nor in favour of his rigid notions of what constituted acceptable behaviour. Nobody could deny Wołkowicki's passionate patriotism but he was an overbearing man who inspired as much irritation as he did loyalty. A group of university academics and specialists were quartered together in Block 7, nicknamed 'the Professors' Room'. Like Czapski and Młynarski, these (mainly reserve) officers were generally more cosmopolitan, less political and distinctly more socially liberal than many of the professional officers. They frequently clashed with General Wołkowicki as he attempted to exert control over his fellow prisoners, although they cooperated with him on other matters, notably the establishment of an educational programme for prisoners under the leadership of Lieutenant Colonel Tadeusz Felsztyn.[7]

The second distinct group in the camp, led by Major Julian Jerzy Fischer von Drauenegg, comprised thirty prisoners belonging to Poland's German minority. After their arrival in Griazovets they began identifying themselves as *volksdeutsche*, openly espousing pro-Nazi views. Their habit of speaking to one another in German and their apparently arrogant behaviour inevitably led to conflicts with members of Wołkowicki's group: 'I warned Major Fischer their behaviour might lead to incidents,' declares Wołkowicki. 'Finally at lunch Lieutenant Mintowt-Czyż slapped a German officer in the face and after that they were quiet.'[8] This incident, which saw the bold young air force observer Lieutenant Jan Mintowt-Czyż chastise Second Lieutenant Dr Michał Lewin for insulting the Polish nation, ensured Mintowt-Czyż's enduring popularity amongst the crowd of patriotic young cadets. 'A thunderbolt couldn't have knocked him off balance faster than that powerful blow. And another thing: our fine Jasio had hands like loaves of bread.'[9]

Shortly after their arrival in Griazovets Major Fischer von Drauenegg and his followers wrote to the German ambassador in Moscow requesting permission to leave the camp and join the German army. As a result of their petition ten of the group left Griazovets in July–August 1940 and were taken to Germany. General Wołkowicki's unbending hatred of these men was such that when Józef Czapski and another officer, Witold Kaczkowski, had the temerity to say farewell to their former comrades they were hauled before the general and given a severe dressing down, despite the fact that one of the departing officers came from Kaczkowski's home town of Łódź and was carrying a letter for his mother.[10] Whether all the men in the *volksdeutsche* group were convinced Nazis is debatable. In Czapski's (distinctly more compassionate) view, many of them had made the choice out of despair, concluding that reclaiming German roots offered their only chance of returning home. It is a credible thesis.

The third group in Griazovets consisted of forty to fifty pro-Soviet prisoners. At its core were three devoted Marxists: Captain Kazimierz Rosen-Zawadzki, Lieutenant Roman Imach and Second Lieutenant Stanisław Szczypiorski. In the three larger camps the NKVD had permitted no political gatherings and favoured no one group over another. In Griazovets this policy changed. The pro-Soviet group were given permission to form a 'Marxist Circle', aimed at introducing their fellow prisoners to the ideology of Marxist-Leninism 'through the discussion of international themes'. They were afforded privileges, including use of the club room for lectures, talks and musical rehearsals. This they furnished with a homemade bust of Lenin (later destroyed at night by a 'patriot' in one of many arguments between the two factions). The room – and by extension the group itself – became known as 'the Red Corner'.

General Wołkowicki liked to keep close track of his fellow prisoners' loyalty, aided by fellow patriot and general busybody Chief Inspector Bober. Their methods were simple, using volunteers to spy through the windows to see who was attending the Red Corner lectures, then writing down their names.[11] Wołkowicki's notes on Griazovets, made at an unspecified later date, show him dividing prisoners according to their nationality and perceived loyalty to Poland: he lists 31 Germans in the camp, 20 'disloyal' Belorussians and 33 Jews, whom he sub-divides between those he designates as loyal (20) or disloyal (13). The 'disloyal' Jews mainly came from

Handwritten notes by General Wołkowicki listing (l–r) the number of prisoners from the three camps compared with those in Griazovets, their ranks and nationalities, prisoners taken from the camp or who died, those taken into the Polish army and those rejected.

eastern Poland, now incorporated into the Soviet Union; the 'loyal' group were principally from central or western Poland.[12] It was even rumoured Chief Inspector Bober kept a list of names with death sentences attached to them, aimed mainly at members of the Red Corner.[13] As time passed the Red Corner received ever greater privileges from the camp authorities and habitually snitched on their rivals, which in turn led to greater resentment among the patriots.

The hostility between the factions led to frequent disputes that sometimes spilled over into physical violence, presenting a major challenge to camp commander Major Volkov, who grew increasingly frustrated at his inability to control Wołkowicki and his supporters. An inspection of the camp by the regional NKVD head, Pyotr Kondakov, raised sufficient concern that on 29 September 1940 he sent a special report to Beria on the 'Counter-revolutionary Activities of a Group of Prisoners of War in the Griazovets NKVD camp':

Recently the UNKVD has received several reports from the camp which make it clear that a group of POWs made up of former higher and senior commanders of the Polish army including General Wołkowicki, Colonel Grabowski, Majors Domoń and Lis, military priest Tyczkowski, Naval Captain Ginsbert, and Chief Inspector Bober, are conducting active counter-revolutionary [c-r] activity among the POWs aimed at individuals loyally inclined towards the Soviet Union.

...

During the period when lectures on the history of the VKP (b)[14] are being conducted at the behest of a significant portion of the POWs, they are conducting parallel lectures and discussions of a nationalist chauvinist character and organising the singing of c-r nationalist songs.

They are poisoning [the minds of] individual officer cadets and second lieutenants against the POWs who are participating in mass political work. They threaten the latter that they will settle with them in the 'future Poland' or upon their return to German territory. It has been established that similar threats against several POWs have been made by Chief Inspector Bober, who keeps a so-called blacklist of POWs who are loyally inclined towards the Soviet Union.

Out of fear of reprisal, several POWs have stopped attending lectures on the history of the VKP(b) that are being conducted in the camp.[15]

Most prisoners tried to steer clear of the arguments, preferring instead to seek opportunities to share and acquire knowledge as they had in the previous camps. Informal lectures took place sporadically over the summer months, with knowledgeable prisoners giving talks on their favourite subjects to interested friends. A programme of language classes in English, German, French and Russian proved popular with the younger men and met with no official interference so long as the groups remained small. Keen linguist Zdzisław Peszkowski recalled that the very first book he borrowed from the camp library as his guide to learning English was *Life Begins at Forty*, a bestselling American self-help book by Walter B. Pitkin (published in 1932). How it arrived in the hands of the NKVD is a mystery; most likely it had been confiscated from a previous prisoner. Father Tyczkowski, who taught the students from the book, was in his forties at the time and, according to Peszkowski, 'most interested to read on'.[16] By contrast, talks on sensitive subjects such as military history or politics took place in closed circles.

As well as lecturing on art, Józef Czapski gave a series of talks on the work of Marcel Proust which he delivered entirely from memory, captivating his audience with his eloquence.[17] 'He had no paints. He could only speak. And he spoke. One could become completely engrossed in what he said.'[18] Yet even Czapski, the most apolitical of men, was the subject of a report to Moscow in which Major Elman accuses the artist of demonstrating 'fierce nationalism' and supporting the rebirth of Poland. Worse, in Starobelsk Czapski had apparently turned down the opportunity of placing his skills at the service of the camp authorities on the grounds that the Soviet Union had 'stabbed Poland in the back' while she was engaged in fighting Germany.[19]

One of the most prolific lecturers was Professor Stefan Sienicki, an eminent architect and professor at the Warsaw University of Technology whose talks on the history of furniture made a profound impression on Dr Słowes: 'With great skill and astonishing powers of recall, he would use bits of chalk and an improvised blackboard to reproduce grand halls, citadel towers, turrets of medieval castles, and the domes of famous European churches.'[20] Father Kamil Kantak lectured on the history of art; Second Lieutenant Ehrlich spoke on medieval literature and the work of Homer; the pianist Grzybowski lectured on the history of music and composition; Professor Komarnicki lectured on law.

It was not until later in the year that a formal programme of educational courses took shape. Known by the prisoners as 'the University at Griazovets', it owed its existence primarily to a senior NKVD officer, Nikolai Pronin, dispatched from Moscow in late November to address Major Volkov's continuing difficulties in controlling General Wołkowicki and his band of unruly officer cadets.[21]

And meanwhile the autumn of 1940 arrived and there was no sign that our situation was going to change at all. We stewed in our own juice, arguing sometimes violently although sometimes not without a certain comic element for an outside observer. The state of people's nerves grew worse and arguments often broke out about silly things, about closing or opening the window, or whose turn it was to use a bowl or a can, about sweeping the room etc. And when it came to political discussions the temperature rose to dangerous levels and one had to find ways of calming the violence to avoid the scandal of a fight breaking out.[22]

In autumn 1940 a change took place in NKVD policy. Stalin's pact with Hitler had always been a marriage of convenience, but the swiftness and ease with which the Nazis swept across Europe in the summer of 1940 unsettled the Soviet leader, prompting him to reassess the alliance. He had been prepared to do business with the Nazis out of pragmatic self-interest. Hitler, on the other hand, harboured a deep-seated hatred of Bolshevism which could not be suppressed indefinitely. As the two ill-suited allies clashed over interests in central and eastern Europe, Soviet thinking began to crystal-lise around the idea that war between Russia and Germany was inevitable and the situation might arise sooner rather than later. The scenario most commonly envisaged saw Hitler following his victory over Western Europe by invading Britain; the ensuing conflict would (conveniently) exhaust Hitler's resources, leaving the path open for the Red Army to march across an unresisting, battle-flattened Europe to impose Soviet rule and complete the Revolution. Since, in order to achieve this goal, the Red Army would have to cross Poland, Lavrenty Beria began to contemplate ways to minimise inevitable Polish resistance to this fresh invasion. Despite the fact that only seven months previously he had presided over the murder of nearly 22,000 Polish prisoners of war, a large number of Polish POWs remained in NKVD captivity. Ever the pragmatist, Beria decided to put these men to good use by forming a Polish division within the Red Army. There were two advantages to this proposal: given the weakened state of Soviet forces (Stalin had, after all, dispatched most of his top military leaders in the purges of 1937–38), skilled men were badly needed. More crucially, the involvement of Polish soldiers in the liberation of their own country would lend a friendly face to the arrival of their new occupiers.

Stalin approved the plan and tasked Beria and Merkulov with finding a suitable leader for the proposed division, ideally a general of sufficient renown amongst the Poles whose presence would convince others to follow him. Eleven out of the twelve generals held in Kozelsk and Starobelsk were dead, and no NKVD officer in his right mind would consider General Wołkowicki open to the idea of Soviet cooperation. But a handful of Polish generals remained in captivity, notably General Marian Januszajtis-Żegota, General Mieczysław Boruta-Śpiechowicz and General Wacław Przeździecki. The first two were already in the Lubyanka; General Przeździecki was brought to Moscow from Kozelsk camp, where he had been held since June

1940. The results were not promising: Boruta-Śpiechowicz and Przeździecki would agree to the proposal only on orders from the Polish government in London. Januszajtis declared that, although he did not consider himself dependent on an order from Sikorski's government, he wanted to create a special political platform to discuss the future fate of Poland and desired a 'softening of the climate' for Poles living in Western Ukraine and Belorussia.[23] Thwarted but not defeated, Beria did not give up on the idea of eventually persuading Januszajtis or Boruta-Śpiechowicz to cooperate. Przeździecki was presumably too anti-Soviet to be seriously considered. He was sent back to Butyrka prison and then to Putyvl camp, where he remained until June 1941.[24]

A fourth general was being held in the Lubyanka at that time, one of Poland's most distinguished, General Władysław Anders. Commander of the Nowogródek Cavalry Brigade, Anders had been captured and severely wounded as he tried to escape to Hungary in September 1939.[25] In hospital in Lwów Anders received several visits from NKVD officers hoping to recruit him to the Red Army. On one occasion a visiting Soviet general even asked him what he thought about forming a Polish government under Soviet protection. Anders' replies were unequivocal on each occasion: no, no and again no. The NKVD did not give up. If persuasion would not convince him, perhaps coercion would be more effective. Anders was on the point of leaving Lwów for Poland with a convoy of injured soldiers when the NKVD arrested him. This time they were less polite: they interrogated him, accusing him of crimes against the Soviet Union for which, they insisted, the only way out was to become an officer in the Red Army. When Anders again refused he was taken to Brygitki Prison in Lwów where he was kept in isolation for eight weeks, his wounds left untreated and in such freezing conditions he suffered from frostbite. In March 1940 he was transferred briefly to the Lubyanka. Here he was questioned by NKVD Colonel Kondratik, 'a lean and lanky sadist' who threatened to send him to a regular Soviet prison where he would be beaten and tortured if he did not cooperate.[26] When Anders continued to resist they took him to Butyrka prison in Moscow and kept him in solitary confinement for several months until he was finally brought back to the Lubyanka in September 1940, where he remained for almost a further year without being called to interrogation. Given

his subsequent role as leader of the Polish army in the USSR, it is somewhat ironic that Anders appears to have been excluded from the list of
potential generals in October 1940.[27]

With no general yet in the bag, Beria and Merkulov set their sights on
the next rung of the military ladder and began a search to identify suitable
staff officers for the putative new division.

Since the summer, interrogations had continued in Griazovets just as
they had in the larger camps. The investigating team was led by Major
Volkov's deputy, Major Elman, assisted by Captains Alexandrovich and
Vasilevsky, and two lieutenants. Although the same questions were repeated
endlessly and the prisoners' answers painstakingly noted down, the substance of the interviews had gradually begun to shift in emphasis. The
focus of the questions was now less on the prisoners' past than on 'what we
think of the Soviet Union, what we like about it, how we see our future'.[28]
Those most frequently called to interview were officers thought to be
open to cooperation with the Soviet authorities, but senior officers of all
convictions were canvassed repeatedly on their willingness to collaborate.
Lieutenant Colonel Tadeusz Felsztyn recalled several conversations with
NKVD Captain Gubanov:

> His arguments were as follows: England had already lost the war. The con-
> flict might drag on for a few years, but nothing will save her from losing in
> the end. And even if she won, Poland would only be an exploited English
> colony. But there was no point thinking about this because England was
> going to lose for certain. Sikorski's government won't help Poland because
> it is trapped in England. So the only help for Poland is Russia. We Russians
> cannot, with our Slavic hearts, look on quietly as the Germans destroy the
> Polish nation. Russia wants to offer the Poles a brotherly helping hand.
> When the moment comes, and come it will, we will arm the Poles so they
> can stand against the Germans and we will come to their aid with arms. But
> when the time comes there need to be people in Poland who know how to
> spur the nation into action. You are a patriot; you love your country. So you
> could play a brilliant role in Poland's rebirth. Just trust us.[29]

Many officers received similar propositions, 'and after several conversations,
depending on how resistant they thought the rascal would be, the cat came

out of the bag: the request to sign a declaration of willingness to cooperate with the USSR and strict obedience to the orders of the NKVD.'[30]

Most refused. But a small number of senior officers were prepared to contemplate a different course of action. It was these men, along with a few whose military skills were deemed of particular interest to the NKVD, who were singled out by Beria and Merkulov to be taken to Moscow for a period of assessment.

9

'GUESTS'

SHORTLY AFTER BREAKFAST ON 8 OCTOBER 1940, THE CAMP
messenger appeared unexpectedly in the doorway of the room where
Lieutenant Colonel Berling, Colonel Künstler, Lieutenant Colonel
Bukojemski and another officer were seated playing bridge using cards
made from matchboxes. Since card games were forbidden in the camp the
men hurriedly hid what they were doing and watched in mute astonishment
as the messenger, somewhat flustered and apparently in possession of an
important communication from the camp authorities, scrabbled in his
leather bag.[1] Finally, he drew out a paper and proceeded to read out seven
names: Gorczyński, Künstler, Bukojemski, Berling, Tyszyński, Morawski,
Lis. Two colonels, four lieutenant colonels, one major; seven of the most
senior officers in the camp. They were told to prepare themselves for an
immediate departure with the now-familiar phrase: 'Get ready and bring
your things.'

Six of the officers were answered for. The seventh, Lieutenant Colonel
Tyszyński, was nowhere to be found. The messenger ordered the officers
to look for him, explaining that this was an important matter that could
not wait. The men went off in search of their missing comrade, eventually
locating him sitting by the stream with Lieutenant Colonel Dudziński,
fishing. Later, Tyszyński confessed to Berling that he had recently joined
Dudziński in his favourite pastime as a way of calming his nerves and had
borrowed a rod from one of the guards.[2]

The seven men were taken to the camp offices and told they were to
leave for Moscow immediately. No further explanation was offered. The
remaining prisoners gathered to see them off, their departure another in
a lengthening line of mysteries. These were all high-ranking officers, but
not the most senior in the camp; of the seven, five (Berling, Gorczyński,

Tyszyński, Morawski and Bukojemski) were known to be sympathetic to the activities of the Red Corner, with Berling considered by most – despite his protestations to the contrary – to be its unofficial leader. But the others had exhibited no desire to collaborate with their captors. On the contrary, both Major Lis and Colonel Künstler were well known for their patriotic stance. The only distinguishing feature shared by all these officers was their undoubted military talent and the cross-section of skills they possessed between them: Berling was from the infantry, Gorczyński and Tyszyński from the engineers, Künstler, Bukojemski, Morawski and Lis from the artillery.

As farewells were said and friends gathered around to offer gifts for the journey – sugar, a piece of sausage, some crumbs of *makhorka* to smoke – General Wołkowicki and Major Domoń called Major Lis aside. They urged him to keep his eyes open and observe events. Above all, don't sign anything.[3] With this warning ringing in his ears, Lis marched out of the camp with his six companions. It was to be nine months before the crowd of onlookers waving them goodbye received news of their fate.

The seven officers were taken first to Butyrka prison, an imposing eighteenth-century building mainly used as a transit prison before or after an investigation. In the brutal hierarchy of Moscow prisons the regime at Butyrka was considered relatively relaxed. Each man was called for a short interview with one of the NKVD's top officials, Lieutenant Colonel Yegorov, who took their details, asked them if they wanted to fight the Germans, and sent them directly back to their cell. When the group transferred to the Lubyanka prison two days later Colonel Künstler remained behind, having apparently responded angrily to one of Yegorov's questions.

The Lubyanka occupies a dominant position in a large square in central Moscow. The prison sat next door to the headquarters of the NKVD (later the KGB, today the FSB), allowing the top brass to interview at their leisure prisoners in whom they had a particular interest. Yegorov conducted the opening conversations with the Polish officers, often alongside the deputy head of the NKVD's 2nd Department (counter-intelligence) and head of the NKVD's Polish office, GB Major Leonid Raikhman. Beria's refined and urbane deputy Vsevolod Merkulov spoke to the more senior officers. The questions always followed the same pattern, summarised thus by Berling:

1. Participation in the 1920 Polish–Russian war.
2. Present attitude towards the USSR and its genesis.
3. Attitude towards the Germans and our participation in an eventual war between the USSR and Germany, and how that participation could be realised from the Soviet side.
4. Attitude towards the Soviet occupation of our former eastern territories.
5. They were endlessly prying into our personal background, our political views, our travels, relatives abroad, social work, membership of civilian societies etc.

In short, everything we had already been asked dozens of times in the last year since our imprisonment.[4]

Since the main goal was to sound these men out about their readiness to fight the Germans alongside the Red Army, Merkulov was particularly interested in their answers to two key questions: what was their attitude to the Polish government in London, and how did they envisage Polish–Soviet cooperation in practice?

Although the Soviet Union had never made a formal declaration of war against Poland, as far as the Polish government in London was concerned their invasion of eastern Poland in alliance with Nazi Germany placed them firmly in the category of 'enemy power'. Any Polish officer prepared to collaborate with the Soviets was thus fully aware that such an act could be judged treasonous. For the NKVD, the attitude of Polish officers towards the Sikorski government (or 'so-called government' as they named it) was of paramount importance. The standard response of a Polish officer loyal to the oath of service he had taken on joining the army was that he would happily fight the Germans in a Polish army under Soviet command if the order to do so came from the Polish government in London. This was the answer given by Colonel Künstler which sent him directly back to his cell; it was also the unequivocal response of General Przeździecki when he was brought to Moscow and of General Anders on numerous occasions. When Merkulov asked Berling about his attitude towards this knotty problem, Berling replied that, speaking personally, if the price of Soviet aid was a break with the London government then in his view so be it.[5]

*

One evening towards the end of October 1940 Lavrenty Beria invited Berling, Gorczyński, Bukojemski and Tyszyński to a lavish supper in his offices at the Lubyanka. The conversation chiefly concerned the organisation of the planned Polish division and a future war with Germany. At a certain moment, Beria pointed to a map of Southern Russia and said: 'We shall retreat to the Volga and we shall strike at the Germans from the direction of the North Caucasus.' When Berling asked Beria whether their comrades from Starobelsk and Kozelsk would be available to provide the skilled officers necessary for this future army, Beria responded with a sentence which later came to take on a profound and sinister meaning. 'No, you cannot have these men,' he is said to have replied. 'They are not available. *My zdjielali bolshuyu oshibku* – We made a big mistake.'[6]

At the time the Polish officers thought the comment strange but hardly sinister; it was to take on a darker significance during the search for the missing officers in 1941–42. Major Józef Lis, who was not present at the supper, stated in a deposition to the Polish government in exile in 1948 that Colonel Gorczyński told him of the comment the same evening or the following morning when they were in the bathroom together. During the 1952 Madden Committee hearings in London, Lis offered his testimony anonymously, using the pseudonym 'Mr A' for fear of reprisals towards his family in Poland. He offered a fuller account of the occasion, stating that Colonel Gorczyński told him of the conversation that night.

> Mr. Machrowicz: That same night?
>
> Mr. A: Yes. He suggested to me that we go to the washroom, because he wants to tell me something very important.
>
> Mr. Machrowicz: Did he then tell you?
>
> Mr. A: We knocked on the door and were released from our cells to go to the washroom. We sat down on the stools in the washroom, and he proceeded to tell me of his conversations earlier that evening with Beria.
>
> Mr. Machrowicz: In other words, that was the same evening as the conversations took place?
>
> Mr. A: They returned after midnight; so this was early in the morning.
>
> Mr. Machrowicz: A few hours after the conversations?

Mr. A: Yes.

Mr. Machrowicz: Will you tell us exactly what he related to you as to the
conversations with Beria?

Mr. A: He said that there was a discussion proposing the formation of
a Panzer division. Beria said that he wants to form or organise a
Panzer first. To this Berling asked or inquired: 'And where will we
get officers? I would want to have my officers from Starobelsk and
from Kozelsk.' Ostashkov did not enter into the conversation because
Ostashkov had primarily border police and guards. To this Beria
replied – in Russian, of course – that 'We have committed a great
blunder'; and he repeated that twice: 'We have made a great mistake;
we have made a great mistake.'[7]

After informing Major Lis and, subsequently, Józef Czapski what Beria had
said in terms similar to the version given above, Colonel Gorczyński made
a further statement to Army Headquarters in the Middle East in May 1943,
shortly after the discovery of the bodies in the Katyń Forest. This version
contains a slight variation: to Berling's request for the officers of Starobelsk
and Kozelsk, Gorczyński quotes Beria as replying, 'Make a list of them, but
there are not many left, because we made a great mistake in turning the
majority of them over to the Germans.'[8]

In another version of the conversation, Captain Narcyz Łopianowski
(whom we will meet shortly) stated that Berling told him of the conversation personally and Captain Rosen-Zawadzki confirmed it. According
to Łopianowski, Berling was speaking to Yegorov at the time. When the
question of the missing officers came up, Beria said to Yegorov, 'Well then,
I think we should hand over to Berling these officers if he wishes to have
them.' To which Yegorov replied, 'Unfortunately I think it will be rather
difficult, if at all feasible, to trace these officers.' Beria then said, 'It was a
great mistake' and Yegorov added, 'We shall try to find them – perhaps
it can still be done.' When Łopianowski asked Rosen-Zawadzki what he
thought had happened to these officers, Rosen-Zawadzki replied that 'they
had probably been sent to such places from which the Bolsheviks were
unable to retrieve them'.[9]

The subtle changes in these statements reflect not only the unreliability
of memory but also the motivation of each narrator in placing a particular

emphasis on his role (or absence of it) in the narrative. Major Lis and Captain Łopianowski were both loyal to the Polish government in London; after the war they lived in exile in the West and had no motivation to hide their true opinions. Berling, on the other hand, writing many years after the events in question, omits any mention of the missing officers in his own account of the lavish supper with Beria. Instead, he places the crucial conversation in a completely different timeframe, according to which he and Colonel Gorczyński visited Beria and Merkulov in January 1941 with a list of 500 officers from Starobelsk and Kozelsk whom they wanted for the Polish army division. When Beria asked if the list comprised only officers imprisoned in Starobelsk and Kozelsk, Berling answered in the affirmative, to which Beria replied: 'Nothing will come of this. These people are not in the Soviet Union.' 'We made a big mistake with them,' added Merkulov.

Berling adds by way of self-justification: 'We were convinced we were too late with our list and our comrades had recently left the Soviet Union. It remained only for us to nod our heads in understanding and to express regret that this is what had happened.'[10] Even though Berling briefly acknowledges Soviet guilt for Katyń at a later point in his memoirs, he was clearly keen to absolve himself of any accusation that, having so conclusively thrown in his lot with the Soviets in 1940, he had any inkling at the time that the NKVD had committed a terrible crime. Likewise, in the context of the discovery of thousands of bodies in the Katyń Forest in 1943, and at a moment when he was trying to re-establish his loyalty to Poland, Colonel Gorczyński evidently felt the need to modify his statement to emphasise Soviet lies rather than suggest he felt any suspicion during a period when he was actively collaborating with the NKVD.

The precise timing and wording of Beria's statement regarding the missing officers thus remains fluid and the words have become distilled into the single phrase which appears in every account. *My zdjielali bolshuyu oshibku.* We made a big mistake.

Berling's own version of the lavish supper in October 1940 is explosive enough even without the inclusion of Beria's comment. He describes a tense meeting during which Beria and Merkulov asked the Polish officers present if they were willing to agree to three things: to fight for the liberation of Poland alongside the Red Army; to support a future alliance and close cooperation with the USSR; and to confirm that they agreed to the idea of organising a Polish army division on Soviet territory. Nobody raised any objections. Beria then proposed that the officers present be charged, in the name of the Soviet government, with organising the said Polish division, to be formed in Central Siberia. Details could be agreed at a later date. None of this was written down, claims Berling, but had the character of a 'gentlemen's agreement' (he writes the words in English). As they began to discuss the practical arrangements for the coming weeks and months, Merkulov stunned the Polish officers by apologising profusely for having kept them in prison until now: 'For many reasons,' he said, 'our conversations had to take place in Moscow, where the hotels are so full up we could find no other solution.' The awkward silence which followed was filled only when Berling obligingly declared that he and his fellow officers had been perfectly happy to endure the minor discomfort of a stay in the Lubyanka. Merkulov then announced that the group would shortly be leaving Moscow for the suburb of Malakhovka, where a house would be placed at their disposal for the preparatory work involved in their new roles. At the end of the meeting Beria offered the men coffee, cigarettes and cognac.[11]

Shortly after the supper the group of six officers was transferred, as promised, to an NKVD villa in the suburb of Malakhovka. It later acquired a nickname: the 'Villa of Bliss'.

At around the same time, another group of Polish officers was brought to the Lubyanka from Butyrka prison, arriving just one day after Berling and his companions. For a while the two groups were to follow parallel paths but it was only in December 1940 that they became aware of one another's existence. This second group consisted of twenty-one officers originally captured in Lithuania. At its head was 57-year-old Brigadier General Wacław Przeździecki. As we have seen earlier, General Przeździecki was the object of NKVD interest as a potential leader for their proposed Polish division in the Red Army.

Przeździecki had cut his military teeth in the Tsarist Russian army before distinguishing himself in the Polish army after independence and participating in the 1919–21 Polish–Soviet war. Captured by the Soviets in 1918, he had been briefly imprisoned in Minsk. Since 1936 he had been living in retirement, returning to service in September 1939 to lead a reserve cavalry regiment during the battle of Grodno. After heavy fighting he was captured trying to cross the Lithuanian border at the head of a large group of men. These included Captain Narcyz Łopianowski, a cavalry officer who had marked himself out as an outstanding military talent after leading his heavily-outnumbered unit to destroy seventeen Soviet tanks during a battle at Kodziowce, one of the great military achievements of the brief Polish campaign. The captured men were first interned in camps in Rokiškis and Kalvarija in Lithuania. Following the Soviet occupation of the Baltic states in June 1940 they were transferred to Kozelsk, which had remained empty following the departure of the previous Polish prisoners in April 1940.[12]

After two days in Butyrka prison General Przeździecki and ten of his men were moved to the Lubyanka, leaving the other ten officers behind, presumably because they had failed to give sufficiently encouraging responses to the questions put to them, or were deemed of little interest to the NKVD. From the outset General Przeździecki was deeply suspicious of the NKVD's

General Wacław Przezdziecki.

motives, uneasy at the sight of a black limousine waiting outside rather than a 'black raven' (*chorney voron*) prison van. 'I know them so well, they do nothing for free! They want something from us!' As the driver took them on a guided tour of the city Przeździecki's concern grew. Only when they pulled up outside the Lubyanka did he relax: thank goodness it was a prison! Had it been a hotel 'they' would undoubtedly have demanded something in exchange for the luxury.[13]

Cell no. 63 was eleven by eight feet, almost square, boasting two windows with iron bars. In the cell were eleven beds in three rows with mattresses, pillows, sheets and blankets, and a cupboard in which to put their clothes. The guard brought them white rolls, cheese, butter, cigarettes and tea, luxuries that did nothing to calm Przeździecki's suspicions ('They want to buy us, to buy me!'). The small peephole in the door – known colloquially as a '*judas*' – was almost always open; the prisoners were under close supervision. The interviews began. As usual, the NKVD called their 'guests' at night, the general first.

Passing down wide corridors covered in plush red carpet, General Przeździecki was taken through an office into a large room with a table and club armchairs, the usual portraits of Stalin and Lenin adorning the walls. Seated in the armchairs were four men dressed in civilian clothes. The guard told Przeździecki to wait. He sat, listening to voices in the next room, a burst of laughter. Then, after twenty minutes, he was ushered inside. Two NKVD dignitaries greeted him without revealing their names. One of them he recognised as Merkulov. The other, plump and wearing a pince-nez, 'resembled a banker'. The interview began.

Asked how he felt about Germany, Przeździecki replied, 'Personally, I hate the Germans and my only desire is to be able to fight them again and either win or die on the field of battle.'

His interlocutors then asked him his opinion of the USSR. Conscious of the need to answer firmly but not too outspokenly, Przeździecki remarked that he had known Tsarist Russia well but was not familiar with the USSR and the Soviets were like a 'sphinx' to him. He could not resist adding that, although Russia and Poland were both Slavic nations, Russia had attacked Poland in collaboration with the Germans, therefore his attitude towards them inevitably mirrored his attitude towards Germany.

Then came the crucial question: with whom would he be willing to fight the Germans? Przeździecki replied that he would fight alongside the devil himself if he could only beat the Germans, adding – more rationally – that he would ally himself with whomsoever his government ordered him to do so. The unknown NKVD dignitary laughed. 'Your government! Where is it? Do you know? Perhaps you think your Sikorski is in England? Oh no! England is already finished. Your Sikorski is doubtless swimming with Johnny English to Canada right now!' The insulting tone continued: 'Your government! Your Poland.' Przeździecki, growing angry, declared he would not answer any more questions if they continued insulting the prime minister of his government in his presence. The plump little man stopped laughing. There was a long silence, lasting several minutes. The conversation resumed, the nameless inquisitor commenting on the excellence of the general's Russian. 'So, you think the Germans are going to go to war with us?' he asked. Przeździecki replied that it was inevitable, since it was written in Hitler's *Mein Kampf*. In which case, replied the man, they should start preparing for such a war, and proposed that Przeździecki begin organising a Polish division.

> Astonished by this proposal, I asked how I was to understand this – a Polish division! He replied that it would be a good idea to create a Polish army under the Soviet standard and I should start organising the first division and, once it was ready, a second, then a third and so on… I was so astounded for a while I didn't speak.

When asked under what conditions he would undertake such a task, Przeździecki replied, 'Only on the order of my Prime Minister, on the order of our government, would the entire nation be ready to fight.'

To the same questions, posed again and again, Przeździecki wearily reiterated his previous statement. Finally, the man who led the questioning said: 'General, you've not slept for several nights, you're tired, go and get some sleep. I will speak with you again.'

Przeździecki returned to his cell. A few days after this interview he saw in a newspaper a picture of the man who had questioned him: it was Lavrenty Beria himself. The interview was never repeated.[14] It is easy to see from Przeździecki's account why his name was dropped from the NKVD's list of potential leaders: there was no hint of compromise.

Lavrenty Beria.

Although they did not realise it, the ten officers who had accompanied Prześdziecki were also being assessed as potential collaborators, with brilliant cavalry officer Captain Łopianowski the object of intense NKVD interest. Shortly after Prześdziecki's return to their cell, Łopianowski too was called to interview.

> I found myself in a very large room with walls covered with grey tapestries and luxurious office furniture. To the right, very close to the entrance, I noticed an ash cupboard of abnormal height. The cupboard was rather eye-catching against the background of the grey tapestries. Upon the words, 'Go ahead' which a female clerk present in the room uttered, the NKVD colonel opened the cupboard with a little key and disappeared behind the door. The two guards ordered me to stand with my face to the wall. After some time a voice invited me to enter the cupboard. I went in and found myself before a door with a dark red curtain. I pulled it aside and found myself in another room.[15]

The pattern of the ensuing conversation was to become intensely familiar to Łopianowski and the other Polish 'guests' during their stay: a guard led the officers into an ante-room and told them to wait, after which they were taken into the next office via the enormous cupboard, which presumably concealed some kind of security mechanism. The same four senior NKVD officers conducted all the interviews: Beria, Merkulov, Raikhman and Yegorov. One NKVD officer asked the questions, a second observed, usually in silence. At each interview they posed the same questions, asking the officers about their military experiences, their views on the Soviet system and their willingness to cooperate in the organisation of a Polish army on Soviet territory. Łopianowski's answer was identical to that of General Przeździecki, Colonel Künstler and other loyal officers: he would follow orders from his commander-in-chief or any man duly authorised by the government in London.

> 'You're all obsessed with your Government in London,' snapped Yegorov. 'You think England will help you. You are mad if you believe what the English say. England is like a prostitute who sells herself to the highest bidder. She will sell you in the same way if it suits her.'[16]

Captain Narcyz Łopianowski.

Łopianowski was not the only officer to recall the NKVD's particular hatred of the British ('perfidious Albion'). Anders, Przeździecki and others remarked on the Soviets' intense dislike of a country that represented a world system they wished fervently to overturn.

Interrogations continued into December. As some of his officers began to show signs of stress General Przeździecki attempted to encourage them: 'It's a good sign if they want to talk to us,' he said. 'It means they need us for something.' He was right, of course. But with the single electric light bulb illuminating their cell day and night and the '*judas*' opening and closing every few minutes, some men lost their nerve. At night they heard screams. Once they heard a woman crying out and one of the officers became convinced it was the voice of his wife. Although the interrogations were conducted in a civil manner, the leading men of the NKVD were not above using emotional manipulation to elicit a response. Yegorov once told Łopianowski that his wife and two children were in the Soviet zone of occupation, living in very difficult conditions. 'We could help them, if you wanted,' he said. 'You only have to ask…'

Just before Christmas, General Przeździecki and five other officers were removed from the cell and taken back to Butyrka prison. Another six potential recruits had been rejected, leaving Captain Łopianowski the senior officer in a group of five junior officers, all lieutenants. Łopianowski felt a heavy burden of responsibility for his little flock. On Christmas Eve 1940 he was encouraging them to spend the evening in quiet reflection when two strangers unexpectedly entered their cell.

One was dressed in the uniform of a Polish colonel; the other wore civilian clothes. They claimed to be fellow Polish prisoners but they looked suspiciously well fed and the guards were friendly towards them. The colonel gave his name as Gorczyński. The civilian introduced himself as Lieutenant Colonel Berling. After a few minutes of small talk Berling asked the men if they were hungry and offered to order them a hot meal. Seeing that his proposal met with distrust rather than enthusiasm Berling, visibly embarrassed, asked Gorczyński to tell the guards to bring supper for two, explaining that they were very hungry and expressing the hope that the others would not object if he and Gorczyński ate in front of them. As they waited for the food to arrive Berling began talking about politics, inviting the men to enjoy a free exchange of opinions as he offered his own analysis of Poland's political and military mistakes during the September campaign. Most of the group said little, unwilling to engage in conversation with strangers, but 33-year-old air force observer Lieutenant Edmund Tacik could not resist: he disagreed violently with Berling's opinions, growing steadily more impassioned as he defended Poland and its government. The arrival of Berling and Gorczyński's dinner put a stop to the political discussion and the five prisoners had no choice but to sit and watch as the two strangers calmly ate their meal. The smell was tantalising. Perhaps this was Berling's intent: to show the men the privileges they could earn if only they would come around to his way of thinking. After they had finished eating Berling knocked on the cell door and the guard let the two men out. They took their leave cheerfully, expressing the certainty that they would all soon meet again.[17]

The following day, 25 December 1940, Lieutenant Tacik was taken from the cell and returned to Butyrka prison, where he joined Colonel Künstler, General Przeździecki and others who had been found 'unsuitable' for cooperation with the Soviet authorities. The remaining group of four were invited to take their seats in a car waiting for them outside the prison. They were driven thirty miles to the quiet Moscow suburb of Malakhovka, accompanied by NKVD Colonel Viktor Kondratik (the 'lean and lanky' interrogator who had threatened General Anders with torture). The cars turned into an empty, snow-covered street lined with villas set discreetly back from the road in the typical manner of a Russian summer resort. As they drew up at a large gate, Kondratik got out and rang a bell. A soldier appeared to open the gates and the cars crossed the thick snow, pulling up in front of a large, single-storey villa. Waiting at the door was a group of six senior Polish officers, including Colonel Gorczyński and Lieutenant Colonel Berling, who greeted the new arrivals as if they were old friends.

In Berlin, on 18 December 1940 Hitler signed a secret directive that would set in motion preparations for 'Operation Barbarossa', his long-planned invasion of the Soviet Union designed to crush Bolshevism once and for all. The fractures in the Soviet–Nazi alliance were growing harder to conceal.

10

—

'VILLA OF BLISS'

'So how are you feeling here with us, at the villa?' asked Captain Rosen-Zawadzki, sitting down next to me. 'Please, eat as much as you like, if there's anything missing, they will bring it. We have bread, butter, eggs, as much as we like, please, help yourself.' He looked at me searchingly, as if he expected to see an expression of delight on my face.

'Well,' I replied after a moment's silence. 'For me this is just the same as any other prison, only with better conditions.'[1]

To Captain Łopianowski and his group of newly-arrived Polish officers the effect of arriving at the villa in Malakhovka was powerful. They had spent the past year eating barely sufficient rations out of a tin, sleeping on hard wooden bunks infested with lice. Now here was food in abundance – eggs, coffee, milk, sugar, jams, sausage, bread. Here were bathrooms with running hot water, beds with feather pillows, tables laid with white linen and fine silver cutlery. An aristocratic-looking cook presided over the kitchen. Two maids served at table. There was a decent library and even a record player on which residents could play French and English records. Were they guests, as Merkulov suggested, or prisoners? An NKVD sentry stood guard at the entrance; their liaison officer, Colonel Kondratik, lived in a small office next door. The men could go out to exercise, even to ski in the nearby woods so long as they did not venture beyond the villa's grounds. But after 9 p.m. a guard dog roamed outside.

Berling's group of officers had spent the first few weeks of their stay absorbed in discussions on military and political topics. At some point during this period Colonel Morawski was sent back to Butyrka prison following a row. It seems Morawski was rather too keen on promoting his personal vision of Poland's socialist future and had dared to offer advice to Stalin and Beria in a stream of increasingly incoherent memos addressed personally to the Soviet leaders. The others in the group deemed him too unstable to continue. Berling suggests he suffered from a mental illness.[2] With the original seven now reduced to five, Berling asked Colonel Kondratik if they could bring some officers from Griazovets to increase their numbers. The names he suggested were those of the key members of the Red Corner: Colonel Dudziński, Captain Rosen-Zawadzki, Flight Lieutenant Wicherkiewicz, Lieutenant Imach, Second Lieutenant Szczypiorski, Cadet Officer Kukuliński. In late October 1940 these men were taken from Griazovets and brought, via Moscow, to Malakhovka. For Major Lis, the arrival in the villa of six of the most fervently pro-communist prisoners in Griazovets marked a change in atmosphere: the lectures and discussions were now dominated by these officers, covering incendiary topics such as the future Soviet–Polish border and whether Poland should join the USSR. In a further effort to boost numbers, shortly before Christmas Colonel Kondratik proposed to Berling that he might like to meet some other Polish officers whom the NKVD were currently hosting in the Lubyanka prison. It was as a consequence of this suggestion that Berling and Gorczyński made their appearance on Christmas Eve in the cell where Captain Łopianowski and his companions were being held.

With the arrival of Łopianowski and his four junior companions the group reached its final capacity of fifteen men. The next few weeks followed an intense rhythm of lectures centred on the study of Soviet military regulations, the history of the Communist Party and readings of Marx and Engels. Much of the work involved translating Soviet military regulations and instructions into Polish: Łopianowski and Tyszyński, as the best Russian speakers, performed the bulk of this work while Gorczyński translated handbooks for sappers. Each resident was required to prepare and deliver a lecture on a subject of his choice, with ample material placed at their disposal in the well-stocked library. Lieutenant Imach gave readings on dialectics and materialism; Colonel Dudziński spoke on the Stalinist constitution. Yegorov visited the villa frequently, spending long hours closeted with Berling.

If the military studies were relatively uncontentious, the main purpose of the political programme developed in the villa was radical and – from the perspective of an officer loyal to the Polish army – treasonous. Not only did it envisage a change in Poland's political structure, to be enforced with the help of the Red Army, but at one point the group was seriously contemplating the wholesale incorporation of Poland into the USSR as its seventeenth Republic.[3] The notion was short-lived, discouraged by the NKVD, who wanted their new military cadre to have an identifiably Polish face. Similarly, when members of the Red Corner started speaking Russian in Griazovets instead of Polish they were firmly reminded that supporting Soviet ideals need not result in jettisoning every aspect of Polish culture. It demonstrates a remarkably self-aware understanding on the part of the NKVD of a country which they were planning to dominate but knew they could never fully control. The 1919–21 Polish–Soviet war had seen the Bolshevik army pushed into a humiliating retreat by Piłsudski's forces in the so-called 'Miracle of the Vistula' (a battle little known in the West but widely credited with preventing the spread of communism to Europe). This had taught Stalin a bitter and enduring lesson: Poland would never be converted to communism.[4] Where Ukraine, Belorussia and the Baltic states could be subsumed into the USSR, Stalin's policy towards Poland was always aimed at Soviet domination at one remove.

Of the fifteen residents in the villa only a handful were committed communists. Like the *volksdeutsche* in Griazovets, the rest of the group had made the choice to cooperate out of self-interest, weakness, or despair. When Captain Łopianowski made a report to the Polish military authorities in 1942 he provided a blistering character analysis of his fellow residents. Gorczyński: 'A man of indisputable honesty with a weak will and aiming at saving himself for the sake of his own family. Could work usefully under normal conditions.' Bukojemski: 'Of vehement and incontrollable temper, would sacrifice everything for women and vodka.' Tyszyński: 'A talented, intelligent man capable of thorough work. Heedful of his own comfort to exaggeration. Scared out of his wits at the prospect of changing his prosperous existence for the wretchedness of prison life. A Pole only by name.'[5] Berling himself he describes as 'talented, enterprising, absolutely without any scruples. Would sacrifice anything to satisfy his own whims.' Zygmunt Berling was a complex figure, universally acknowledged to be an extremely talented military leader but also ruthlessly ambitious. Many Polish officers were highly critical, as he was, of Poland's pre-war military and political regime. It did not lead them to throw in their lot with the Soviets.

From the very first day of his arrival the ultra-patriotic Captain Łopianowski was appalled by the company in which he now found himself. To his further dismay the younger officers who had accompanied him from the Lubyanka appeared all too ready to throw in their lot with Berling and his gang. Unable to trust Major Lis, whose ambivalent attitude he would only later fully understand, Łopianowski grew increasingly isolated, tortured by the idea that his own loyalty could be questioned simply by being here. 'Despite the almost luxurious conditions I began to feel the effects of stress on my nerves, with the endless attacks on Poland knocking me off balance.'[6]

Matters eventually came to a head in February 1941, when Berling put forward a proposal: wouldn't it be a wonderful way of demonstrating their respect for Soviet power if they asked the NKVD to send them portraits of Beria, Merkulov and Kaganovich to hang on the walls of the villa? When Captain Łopianowski objected in violent terms to this request Berling announced they would hold a vote to decide the matter democratically. Each of the men went to Berling's room and, in the presence of Lieutenant Colonel Bukojemski, placed a folded card on a plate. On the card they were to write a plus symbol for 'Yes' and a minus for 'No'. Łopianowski took his card and, in front of Berling, drew a minus sign across it with such vehemence his pencil pierced the card. He tossed it on the plate and left the room, convinced the ballot would reveal a majority against Berling's proposition. He was disappointed: only he and Major Lis voted against the proposal; Cadet Officer Kukuliński left the card blank. The portraits were duly requested and hung on the walls.

While Łopianowski's growing agitation was evident to everyone in the villa, Major Lis succeeded in maintaining an air of studied neutrality for some considerable time before he, too, eventually lost his composure. Lis had two closely related reasons for concealing his true opinions: firstly, General Wołkowicki had tasked him with observing events as they unfolded. It was thus in his interest to play along for as long as possible to find out what was going on. The second reason, and the probable explanation for his success in convincing the other members of the group that he was on their side, lay in his professional background. During one interview in the Lubyanka Major Raikhman asked Lis if he had at any time worked for the Polish intelligence services. Lis denied it, claiming he had only ever served as an officer of the Artillery Corps. The truth was different: from 1925 to 1930 and from 1934 to 1935 he had worked for the Second Section in three areas close to the German border: Poznań, Katowice and Bydgoszcz.[7] Whether Raikhman was convinced by Lis's denial we have no way of knowing. Although Lieutenant Colonel Bukojemski later correctly identified him as a 'counter-intelligence officer' ('Why he was in our group I have no idea!'[8]), at the time Lis's carefully neutral stance appears to have been so successfully maintained that even Łopianowski did not trust him entirely:

> Shrewd, agile and nervous, curious and eager to know everything – [he] appeared to me rather an enigmatic figure. I was rather suspicious of his behaviour because when alone in our room, he used to hold patriotic speeches but the moment all the other officers were present he became another man.[9]

The moment at which Lis's carefully constructed façade finally crumbled came shortly after Łopianowski's argument with Berling over the portraits. The group were studying a recently produced Soviet map of Europe when Lis noticed the eastern half of Poland had already been included within the boundaries of the USSR. When he remarked bitterly that this should give them sufficient indication of Russia's attitude towards their country, adding that even little Abyssinia retained her own borders despite being occupied by Italy, Berling reacted violently. He shouted at Lis, calling him 'a swine and a fascist', threatening to beat him up. A stormy interview followed in Berling's room.[10]

The final straw came in March 1941, when the NKVD sent the group the first edition of a new monthly magazine, New Horizons (Nowe Widnokręgi), edited by the writer Wanda Wasilewska. Wasilewska was the most prominent member of a clique of pro-Soviet Poles being cultivated by Stalin as future political leaders of a Soviet-backed Poland. Eager to curry favour with the fortunate cabal, Berling suggested a contribution to the magazine. Lieutenant Colonel Dudziński duly composed a suitably ingratiating declaration stating that the pre-war Polish government was reactionary and Poland a land of capitalists exploiting the working classes, and only the Soviet Union could lead them on the right path. The text ended with an expression of enthusiastic support for the new magazine and the hope that Poland might soon be permitted to join the 'happy band of nations' of the USSR. Berling suggested all residents of the villa sign the statement and send it to the magazine.

At this point Colonel Gorczyński wobbled, declaring he could not possibly sign the declaration since it would be published in Poland and could lead to reprisals against his family. Berling proposed another vote to decide the matter. Łopianowski, remembering the bitter experience of the portraits, immediately objected. The ensuing argument grew so heated Łopianowski nearly challenged Berling to a duel. Unable to satisfy his sense of honour, he instead begged Berling to request his immediate withdrawal from the villa before taking to his bed with a fever, where he was visited by Berling and Rosen-Zawadzki in a final attempt to convince him to sign.

> They tried to prove to me it was my duty to comply; they spread before me mirages of a glorious future in which I appeared as commander of a regiment stationed in Warsaw; that I would spend my leave in the sunny Caucasus and indulge to my heart's content in my hobby of hunting. Determined to end once and for all similar conversations I begged Colonel Berling to grant me the greatest of favours, namely to persuade the Soviet authorities to shoot me on the steps of the villa in the hope this would bring them all back to their senses.[11]

Everyone signed the document, with the exception of Łopianowski, Gorczyński and Lis.[12]

On 26 March 1941, a car drove up to the villa and returned Łopianowski and Lis to the Lubyanka. Once again they were led down the familiar corridors, through the giant cupboard and into Yegorov's office, where they were roundly berated by the NKVD colonel for their ingratitude. In Butyrka prison they were reunited with Colonel Künstler, Colonel Morawski and Lieutenant Tacik. Łopianowski related the entire story to Künstler, who listened sympathetically to his anguished tale, helping the overwrought Łopianowski to recover both physically and mentally after the weeks of strain. On 1 April, they were joined by General Przeździecki and the five officers who had left the Lubyanka with him just before Christmas. Both Lis and Łopianowski immediately made a full report to Przeździecki. All eleven men were then removed to a camp in Putyvl in Ukraine, where they lived in relatively comfortable conditions until they were transferred to Griazovets in June 1941.

The group of officers gathered together in Malakhovka had been chosen by the NKVD with an eye to a future Poland which would be under Soviet control. Just as Wanda Wasilewska and her circle were being cultivated as a Soviet-friendly political force, so Berling and the other residents of the villa had been chosen to facilitate the military task of taking over German-occupied Poland. The plan was for the putative Polish division to establish itself as the liberator of its own country, thus embedding Soviet control with a friendly Polish face as a 'people's army'. Hitler scuppered the original version of this plan by invading the Soviet Union in June 1941, pushing the Soviets into an alliance with Britain and, by extension, the Polish government in London. The plan was eventually realised in a somewhat different form later in the war with the creation, in May 1943, of the Polish 1st Tadeusz Kościuszko infantry division in the Red Army. The Kościuszko, led by Berling and made up of Poles who had been unable to join General Anders' army before it left the Soviet Union, was to form the core of the Polish People's Army in post-war, communist-run Poland.[13]

Thirteen officers remained in the villa after the departure of Łopianowski and Lis. That from among the many thousands of Polish officers who were taken prisoner by the Soviets at the beginning of the war such a tiny number were willing to collaborate points to the almost complete failure of the NKVD's attempts to coerce or convince the vast majority of the men they had captured. All that political 'work' – all those lectures, discussions, films and talks, all the interviews and interrogations, the special treatment, the persuasion and threats – had been largely in vain.

Despite the violent disagreements that punctuated his stay in Malakhovka, many members of the Red Corner respected Captain Łopianowski as a man of principle who held different views from theirs. (To some extent this sentiment was reciprocated: damning as he was of Berling and the other senior officers, Łopianowski acknowledged Rosen-Zawadzki as 'a man of indisputable talent consciously heading to his chosen goal' and was generally forgiving towards the younger members of the group, particularly Kukuliński, who had served under Berling as an army cadet and was much in awe of him.) Major Lis was another matter. His formidable reputation as an artillery officer goes some way to explaining why the NKVD were willing to overlook his reputation as one of General Wołkowicki's band of 'nationalist-chauvinist' troublemakers. The residents of the villa were not so forgiving. Lieutenant Colonel Bukojemski bumped into Łopianowski in Buzuluk in 1941.

> 'I hold no grudge against you,' he declared. 'You came to us as our enemy from the start. And you remained as such till the end. But as for Major Lis, he sneaked into our confidence as Berling's comrade and then followed you. When I shall leave the USSR I will shoot him.'[14]

Bukojemski never fulfilled his threat. He remained behind in the Soviet Union when the Polish army evacuated in 1942, deserting his post.

II

—

FACTIONS

AFTER THE DEPARTURE OF BERLING AND HIS GROUP FROM Griazovets little had occurred to disrupt the monotonous routine of camp life. In late October, at around the same time as the six Red Corner officers led by Captain Rosen-Zawadzki left the camp, the popular young air force lieutenant, Jan Mintowt-Czyż, was taken separately to Moscow. He returned just before Christmas with a grim tale of interrogations in Butyrka prison, where he was held 'on suspicion of being involved in an anti-Soviet organisation in Griazovets camp'.[1] The NKVD's interest in the young lieutenant most likely stemmed from more than his anti-Soviet activities in Griazovets. Mintowt-Czyż's training as an air force observer had already attracted the attention of the Special Section in Kozelsk, where he had been approached with a proposal to cooperate with the Soviet authorities abroad. And, like Major Lis, Mintowt-Czyż worked for the intelligence services in Poland before the war, a fact of which the NKVD must either have been aware or suspicious.[2] They took a particularly harsh line with the young lieutenant:

> They beat me on my feet, they stood me up against a wall and shot at me, deliberately missing me, they crushed my testicles, hung me up with my hands and feet tied from behind – I still bleed from my legs – they starved me and kept me in a dark cell. For six weeks every day, not just once but several times a day I was taken to my cell unconscious.[3]

At the beginning of December 1940 the interrogations ceased. The NKVD fed him up and allowed the scars of the beatings to heal before sending him back to Griazovets on 24 December 1940.

The brutal questioning endured by Mintowt-Czyż may well have reflected not just a desire to extract intelligence but a resolve to make an example of a well-liked member of the group of 'patriots' in Griazovets. In a report to Soprunenko dated February 1941, Major Volkov and Commissar Sazonov claim that Mintowt-Czyż's return from Butyrka had a salutary effect on the behaviour of the unruly young cadets when he revealed to them that the NKVD possessed precise information about who visited him in his room in Griazovets and what he discussed with his friends. As a result, many of the more active nationalist POWs toned down their behaviour, at least in public, for fear of being sent to Moscow and made to answer for their 'crimes'.[4]

Most remarkable about Mintowt-Czyż's experience in Moscow was its rarity. Although the prisoners complained frequently about their treatment at the hands of the NKVD, after their release they discovered that in Soviet terms it had been remarkably mild. Beatings and torture were a common feature of NKVD interrogation methods when dealing with people they regarded as criminals, but in the case of the Polish prisoners of war there was a clear policy to eschew violence. The policy is in part a reflection of an acknowledgement at the top of the NKVD that – despite their disregard for internationally-ratified conventions – prisoners of war enjoyed a legal status different to that of criminals. It must also have been glaringly obvious to Beria and Merkulov (Beria's refined, cultured deputy was in charge of dealing with the Polish POWs) that violence would achieve little with this particular group of men. Indeed, several NKVD communications refer to the absolute necessity of treating the Polish prisoners with tact and intelligence. Commissar Sazonov notes in one report that he has been informed by his superiors that 'the word prison should not exist in our vocabulary' and stresses the need to approach the prisoners in Griazovets 'delicately and politely'.[5] This necessity evidently placed a severe strain on NKVD officers dealing with persistent offenders like General Wołkowicki and his circle. At one point Sazonov begs Commissar Nekhoroshev: 'Write, and if you have any material on Wołkowicki and Grobicki, send it to me, speak with them. You have all the personal records.'[6] In October 1940, Merkulov himself intervened to inform the head of the NKVD in the Vologda region, Pyotr Kondakov, that the removal of General Wołkowicki, Colonel Grobicki, Major Domoń, Father Tyczkowski and Chief Inspector Bober from the camp 'is not justified', adding that he has instructed Volkov to improve discipline. (He also notes that Major Lis has been safely dispatched to Moscow.)

Despite Major Volkov's best efforts and Commissar Sazonov's detailed programme of cultural activities (the usual diet of lectures, musical clubs, performances, rehearsals, film screenings and chess tournaments), the arguments between the pro- and anti-Soviet groups reached such a point in late November 1940 that Moscow deemed it necessary to send a specialist officer to Griazovets in an effort to 'normalise' relations and persuade the prisoners to behave loyally towards the camp authorities.[7] Senior Politruk Nikolai Pronin duly arrived on 30 November, beginning his visit with a talk in the cinema (attendance compulsory) that immediately provided him with a taste of what Volkov and Sazonov had been dealing with: when Pronin offered the prisoners the chance to acquire Soviet passports the entire room began to murmur in protest. Major Domoń made an angry remark to which Pronin retorted, 'If you don't like the idea you can leave the room,' at which Domoń promptly stood up and left, followed by everyone except the pro-communists.[8]

Pronin observed that, although the 'nationalists' consisted of 150–170 men, there was 'absolutely no unity of point of view' in the group, leaving them open to being split, or isolated. He decided to isolate Wołkowicki and crush his supporters, reducing them to a 'pitiful, wretched heap' in order to prevent the nationalists 'terrorising' the pro-communists with threats to hang them on their return to Poland.[9]

Despite his aggressive language, Pronin's approach to solving the problem of the camp's factionalism was both practical and intelligent: he embarked on a listening exercise, calling in several prisoners from each of the various groups and asking their advice on the best way to resolve the conflict. As well as pro-Soviet prisoners, Pronin consulted Second Lieutenant Ehrlich, Major Domoń, General Wołkowicki and Colonel Grobicki, as well as the 'professors' and the young leaders of the ultra-nationalist group. The solution he chose was based on suggestions put forward by several of the senior officers: in their view, education was the key to calming the highly-charged atmosphere. A large proportion of the camp population consisted of very young men, some of whom had not even completed their schooling when war broke out. Pronin duly sanctioned a set of courses, to include training in technical, accounting and agricultural skills for the younger prisoners, as well as specialist lectures in science, maths, medicine and the humanities aimed at a wider audience. The courses were to be devised and taught by the many teachers and experts in the camp, with all material subject to approval by the camp authorities. No overt political content was permitted in any of them.[10] Thus the 'University of Griazovets' was born. Pronin asked Lieutenant Colonel Felsztyn to take charge of running the courses. After consulting with General Wołkowicki Felsztyn agreed to take on the role.

Pronin's thinking reflected a two-pronged approach: on the one hand, an educational and training programme would keep the younger prisoners out of mischief by occupying them over the winter months; on the other, members of the pro-Soviet group could use the educational context of the courses to convince their fellow prisoners of the merits of communist ide-ology. Although men like General Wołkowicki would never change their point of view, Pronin believed that the privates and lower-ranking prisoners could be taught, and convinced.[11]

If Pronin's policy was a success – in the first respect at least – it was largely because it coincided with the wishes of the prisoners themselves, who had long sought permission to provide purposeful activity for the younger men. By the new year the camp had settled into a relatively peaceful routine. The programme of classes in foreign languages, science, accountancy and car mechanics proved extremely popular, attended by the majority of prisoners. Despite tensions between the rival factions over access to scarce teaching resources (paper, chalk and books were in peren-nial short supply and the Red Corner generally got first dibs on anything arriving into the camp) relations between the pro- and anti-Soviet groups had finally calmed down.

Two further changes occurred towards the end of 1940: the prisoners began receiving regular pay (twenty roubles for officers, ten for the rest) which allowed them to make small purchases from the camp shop; more significantly, after a gap of nearly nine months they were finally allowed to write to their families.[12] The first letters and packages arrived before Christmas, bringing greatly longed-for news from home. Many of the let-ters contained questions about the men who had left Kozelsk, Starobelsk and Ostashkov the previous spring, from whom nothing had been heard since March 1940. Prisoners often asked NKVD staff about this, but always received vague or evasive replies. 'The most honest was Major Elman, who said simply he was not permitted to say anything.'[13] Although the silence was

Dr Salomon Słowes reading a medical book
received from home, 23 May 1941.

mysterious there was no suspicion, at this stage, that anything untoward had occurred. Most prisoners assumed that their comrades had, like them, been taken to other camps in the Soviet Union and were not permitted to write. When General Wołkowicki questioned Captain Vasilevsky about the matter, the NKVD officer responded: 'They most probably do not want to write to their families' and suggested Wołkowicki prepare a list of names which Vasilevsky would forward to the NKVD administration in Moscow.[14] Needless to say, although Wołkowicki put forward a list of over a hundred names, no answer was forthcoming.

The arrival of letters from families living in the Soviet zone of occupation brought a new bombshell: in April 1940, just at the time when Kozelsk, Starobelsk and Ostashkov were being emptied, the wives and children of prisoners from these camps were deported to Kazakhstan. News of the deportations predictably strengthened anti-Soviet feelings among the 'patriots', but many members of the Red Corner were bitterly resentful of the fact that their families had been taken too. Their anger grew when they learned that the wives of some of the most actively anti-Soviet officers, including General Wołkowicki and Major Domoń, had not been deported, while their wives had.[15]

The Vologda region lies in the far northwest of Russia. The first snows fell at the end of September. By mid-October winter proper had begun. By December it was so cold it was almost impossible to go outside. Most of the prisoners spent their second Christmas in captivity quietly, in small groups. In General Wołkowicki's quarters mass was said in the strictest secrecy by Father Kantak ('pale as a wafer'), assisted by Father Tyczkowski.[16] Witold Kaczkowski recalled a small Christmas tree brought from the forest by the men who went up there to cut wood for heating. The Christmas tree was allowed because for the past three years they had been officially permitted for children under Stalin's slogan 'life has become better and more cheerful'. Official ones were topped with red stars.[17]

The only public celebration of Christmas was a recital given by the 29-year-old piano virtuoso Zbigniew Grzybowski. The concert enjoyed the support of music-loving Major Elman and was sanctioned by Major Volkov so long as there were no demonstrations of patriotic or religious feelings. Grzybowski deemed an ancient piano residing in the club room to be so out of tune that he prevailed upon Major Elman to bring a piano tuner from Vologda to fix it. This charming old man appeared most sympathetic, telling the Polish prisoners how much he loved Chopin, even agreeing to take some letters for Grzybowski and post them in Vologda. Either the old man gave them directly to the camp commander or they were taken off him as he left, for Grzybowski was later called before Major Elman and given a sharp reprimand. Fortunately, the concert went ahead, but as a punishment Grzybowski was denied permission to write to his family for one month.[18]

The concert took place in the camp cinema on Christmas Day in the presence of the entire camp, including the Red Corner, the camp command and the women from the clinic. So carried away was Grzybowski by the emotion of his performance of Chopin's 'Fantasia in F Minor' that he could not resist inserting into the final phrases a few notes of the Polish carol *Bóg się Rodzi* (The Lord is Born). One of the music-loving 'spies' in the audience evidently noticed the digression and Grzybowski was summoned to the camp command. Luckily for him, he escaped further punishment.

New Year passed in icy boredom. Easter came and went with snow still on the ground. Stunning sunsets offered a hint of spring to come. The Germans invaded Greece and Yugoslavia, leading once more to the familiar cycle of debates: some prisoners claimed the Nazis were unstoppable, others maintained they could not be victorious for ever. Then, in June 1941, precisely one year since their arrival in Griazovets, the war took an unexpected turn.

12

—

WAR!

So much had been said before about this war breaking out. I didn't believe two bandits would attack each other, and I kept saying '*C'est trop beau pour être vrai!*' (It's too beautiful to be true!).[1]

DESPITE THE EXTENSIVE PREPARATIONS MADE BY THE NKVD for eventual war with Germany, the conflict came sooner than they had envisaged and in a different form. Stalin had persisted in distrusting intelligence warning of Hitler's intention to attack the USSR (believing it came from British spies) and could not be convinced that Hitler would be foolish enough to open up a new front while Britain remained undefeated. Stalin wanted war when he was ready for it (and when Soviet troops were up to strength) and persisted in hoping for a diplomatic solution right up until the last minute.[2] In his public announcement of the Nazi invasion of 22 June 1941 Molotov refers gravely to 'an act of treachery unprecedented in the history of civilised peoples', declaring that Soviet military might would defeat 'arrogant Hitler, who has turned on our country'. In Griazovets there was initially some confusion as to who was at war with whom. Once it was clear what had happened the camp erupted in excitement. 'God be praised. Let them slaughter each other.'[3]

Over the next few weeks the situation in Griazovets worsened considerably as the Soviet Union was placed on a war footing and the German army advanced with the same terrifying rapidity with which it had conquered most of Europe. Rations were reduced by half, presumably a result of the war effort rather than as a punishment (although the lawyer Wacław Komarnicki suggested it was a deliberate policy to induce prisoners to join the Red Army[4]). This reduction took already meagre rations to a level which camp doctors considered barely sufficient for people who were lying in bed all day, let alone active men trying to lead normal lives.[5] A few officers were removed from the camp: Lieutenant Mintowt-Czyż was again taken to Moscow on 29 June 1941, this time receiving a proposal from NKVD General Zhukov to cooperate with the Soviet Union in diversionary tactics on Polish territory.[6] Mintowt-Czyż gave the usual reply – that he would be happy to carry out any mission on the authority of the Polish government in London – and was duly returned to Griazovets unharmed. He brought with him exciting news: top NKVD officials had informed him that the fate of Polish POWs and internees was to be resolved in the coming days as a matter of urgency. They were going to England![7] This was thrilling news indeed. Joining the Polish army in Britain had long been an obsession for many of the men. On 14 July 1941, General Wołkowicki sent two letters to Moscow: one to Stalin, the other to the British ambassador, making this very request.[8] But as the prisoners listened avidly to the news bulletins, marking the battle zones on a large improvised map of European Russia, they began to fear that the German army was advancing so fast they risked passing straight from Soviet captivity into German hands.[9]

Testament to the swiftness of the advance was the arrival on 22 June of General Przeździecki at the head of a group of twenty-one prisoners from Putyvl camp, which had been evacuated to make space for prisoners arriving from the Baltic countries. Since the members of this group consisted of men who had refused the chance to cooperate with the Soviet authorities, thus showing themselves to be 'active enemies of Soviet authority',[10] Griazovets commander Major Khodas (who had replaced Major Volkov in May) was ordered to place them in separate accommodation, surrounded by a barbed wire fence, to prevent them from communicating with the other prisoners.

General Przeździecki's arrival was followed by the appearance on 2 July of a large group of 1,400 Polish officers previously interned in Lithuania, Estonia and Latvia and then, latterly, Kozelsk. Accompanying them was a group of 181 French POWs, mainly supporters of General de Gaulle who had escaped from German camps in Poland and crossed into the Soviet zone, where they had been arrested. (A further fourteen British POWs had been sent directly to Moscow and handed over to the British embassy.[11])

The influx of so many new prisoners brought chaos to the previously well-organised camp, posing a logistical challenge of almost insurmountable proportions for Major Khodas as he struggled to house, feed and control them all. He put them in the club room, the dining room, the baths, the workshops, the barbers. That still left over six hundred men sleeping in the open air. With a detectable note of grievance, Khodas points out in a report to Moscow that it was on (Head of the UPV – Prisoner of War Administration) Pyotr Soprunenko's own orders that all bed linen was taken from the internees on leaving Kozelsk. They had no underwear or shirts, their boots were in terrible condition, some were sick with TB and needed to be isolated. And then there were the French.[12]

Khodas had received orders from Moscow to keep the French prisoners away from the Poles, necessitating the creation of another enclosure in addition to the one keeping General Przeździecki in 'quarantine'. He housed them temporarily in the club room, enclosing it with a barbed wire fence and issuing strict orders not to communicate with the Polish prisoners. The Frenchmen ignored him. Not only that: 'On 3 July they initiated a concert on the club roof, inciting a large number of Poles to join in. Then the Poles tried to respond with a mass singing of Polish songs, but I cut it all short.'[13] The Polish version of this event is naturally somewhat different: several prisoners recount cheerful scenes as the French performed an enthusiastic rendition of the 'Marseillaise' and other patriotic songs, to which the Poles responded in a similar vein. Khodas found their behaviour scandalous: 'Disobeying the guards, going up to the fence, and when called or ordered by the soldiers they reply with cries, laughter and swearwords.'[14]

The bad behaviour was infectious. Encouraged by the French, the Polish prisoners began acting with increased boldness. There were even rumours of a proposed mass escape attempt. Major Khodas took the unprecedented step of instructing one of the guards to use his weapon as a warning if necessary.

And yet, despite all of this, the interrogations not only continued but accelerated, mainly aimed at the new prisoners, among whom the NKVD sought to identify pro-Nazis and fascists.

For the group of thirteen men still living in the villa in Malakhovka the news of the German attack brought profoundly mixed feelings as the implications of the new political situation began to sink in. On the one hand there was delight at the prospect of their 'work' at last being made public and hope that they would play an active role in any future collaboration between the Soviet authorities and the Polish government in London. On the other there was apprehension: their behaviour was well known to their fellow prisoners in Griazovets, where it was viewed by most as treachery. They waited impatiently for news. Finally, their liaison officer, Colonel Kondratik, arrived to inform them that they would be moving to Moscow. Here they were given an apartment, photographed, issued with Soviet passports and told to wait. They passed the time visiting the city and observing the preparations for war. For a while they even helped with civilian anti-aircraft defence. Initially, the group received visits from high-ranking NKVD officials, at one point receiving an offer to be dropped behind enemy lines in Poland. With the signing of Polish–Soviet political and military alliances in July these offers evaporated, along with their future as leaders of a 'Red' Polish army. It was General Anders, not Berling, who was to lead the Polish forces, a man Berling cordially hated. The group wrote formally to the NKVD asking to join the Red Army, but they were told to join the new Polish army instead. The cool wind blowing from Moscow on these inconvenient acolytes would only grow frostier as time passed.

*

> Comrades torn from their sleep half conscious, having heard the news, fragments of which barely penetrated their consciousness, went mad with joy. Regardless of whether they were friends or not, they threw their arms around one another, many wept, many, not knowing how to express their joy and the feelings that were filling them, began ardently to pray.[15]

On 30 July 1941 a pact was signed in London between the Soviet ambassador, Ivan Maisky, and the Polish prime minister, General Władysław Sikorski. The Sikorski–Maisky agreement, as it became known, restored diplomatic relations between Poland and the USSR, ruptured in September 1939. The agreement carefully brushed over highly contentious issues such as where Poland's eastern border would be drawn after the war. It also included a special protocol granting amnesty to all Polish citizens held on Soviet territory, either as prisoners of war or deportees. Hundreds of thousands of men, women and children deported from eastern Poland in 1940 were to be set free from the labour camps and collective farms to which they had been banished. Immediately, the Polish, British and Soviet governments embarked on discussions about the formation of a Polish army in the Soviet

Union, using deportees and prisoners as its core. After nearly two years in captivity, the men of Griazovets were going to rejoin the war as active participants and free men. 'You have to imagine the crazy enthusiasm that overcame us all…'[16]

> That beautiful, sunny, July morning became for us the most miraculous of all our experiences so far. Everyone felt such a joyful day should be marked in some way, so they pulled from their bundles, their rucksacks or their suitcases the best pieces of their Polish uniform, which despite so many searches and the sometimes great needs had somehow managed to be saved. They cleaned their belts, mended and waxed buttons and buckles, and stitched up the ragged and ruined uniforms and caps.[17]

Not all the prisoners were delighted. Some would have preferred to leave the Soviet Union and join the Polish army in Britain. And they resented the use of the term 'amnesty'. Their question, 'What crime did we commit?' was never to be answered. In London, too, the signing of the agreement led to angry scenes among Polish exiles. Three government ministers resigned due to the lack of explicit Soviet recognition of Poland's pre-war frontiers. But for General Sikorski the pact offered a unique opportunity to transform the fate of vast numbers of Polish citizens. Good relations with Moscow were imperative if he was to achieve his goal of raising an army from the hundreds of thousands of unfortunate souls trapped in the USSR. In particular, he knew that many highly skilled officers had been captured by the Soviets. Their presence would add immeasurably to the prestige of Poland's armed forces abroad.

On 1 August 1941, General Przeździecki and his group were finally allowed to join their comrades in the main camp. Immediately, the two generals began to argue about who should be in charge. General Przeździecki thought the role should fall to him since he was at the head of a much bigger group of men (having until his departure for Moscow been the senior officer among the 1,400 prisoners who had recently arrived). General Wołkowicki argued that as the older of the two it was he who should be in command. The age difference between them was a mere six months. It is a testament to the force of personality of both men that Major Khodas wrote to Soprunenko asking for help in dealing with them.[18]

With the two generals vying for control of the camp and the prisoners no longer willing to submit to Soviet authority, Major Khodas found it impossible to get anything done. Camp staff had no idea what was expected of them any more or who was really in charge. Meanwhile, General Przeździecki and his staff officers were working 'deep underground' reading correspondence, drawing up lists of units, handing out promotions and degrading 'unworthy' officers, placing men on blacklists for not following orders and even putting an officer cadet under house arrest for three days. Major Domoń was up to his usual tricks – 'that blasted legionnaire' – gathering support for a campaign to refuse to join Polish units on Soviet territory.[19]

Despite the chaos, the Special Section did not give up trying to persuade the Poles to join the Red Army. Only now, instead of interrogations they were invited for 'little talks'. Men were sent away, this time of their own free will. The first to go was the lawyer Wacław Komarnicki, on whose behalf General Sikorski had personally intervened with the Soviet ambassador, Ivan Maisky, requesting that he be sent directly to London to help the government. Komarnicki travelled to Moscow in August 1941, later joining two Polish colleagues on a marathon sea voyage from Arkhangelsk to Great Britain, where he was to become minister of justice in General Sikorski's government.[20]

When word reached Griazovets that the Polish and Soviet governments had signed a joint military agreement on 14 August envisaging the formation of a Polish army on Soviet soil, excitement in the camp reached fever pitch. On 22 August the two generals were summoned to Moscow, causing a great commotion as emergency repairs were carried out on their frayed and tired uniforms. They left, seen off by the entire camp. A few days later came news of the imminent arrival of the man who was to lead the new army, General Władysław Anders. More frantic sewing and polishing followed as the prisoners attempted to smarten up uniforms in which they had been living for nearly two years.

General Anders had not been Sikorski's first choice to lead the new army. That honour was to go to General Stanisław Haller, but since nobody knew where Haller was the role was conferred upon Anders instead. (Haller, of course, had been a prisoner in Starobelsk. Nobody had seen him since he left the camp in April 1940.) Anders was steeped in Russian culture and traditions; he had been educated in Russian-controlled Poland and served

in the Tsarist army during World War I. He possessed a profound understanding of the Russian mentality while holding passionately anti-Soviet
views. In July 1941 he was brought from his prison cell in the Lubyanka,
where he had been sitting since September the previous year, for his first
meeting with Beria and Merkulov. They delivered the good news that he
had been chosen to lead the new Polish army, a choice with which they
declared themselves 'very satisfied', particularly since Anders was known
to be the most popular leader among Poles in Russia, ninety-six percent of
his compatriots having declared themselves in his favour. How they arrived
at this figure Anders never knew. It was probably made up.[21]

On 4 August 1941 Anders was finally released from Soviet captivity,
departing from the Lubyanka in Beria's limousine dressed in his prison
clothes and without socks. The prison governor even made a point of
carrying Anders' suitcase for him, only it later transpired that the suitcase
wasn't his: when Anders looked inside it, instead of his belongings he found
someone else's swimming trunks. Since Anders was half-starved and could

General Władysław Anders.

barely walk the NKVD were keen to facilitate his speedy recovery and erase all traces of their former neglect. They assigned him a spacious apartment in central Moscow, complete with a cook, a maid and an ample supply of luxuries – caviar, charcuterie, champagne, vodka. When the cook asked him what he would like to eat Anders chose a simple dish of scrambled eggs and ham. He knew from experience that his stomach could not cope with anything richer. The NKVD officer placed at Anders' disposal was none other than Colonel Kondratik, liaison officer to Berling's group at the Villa of Bliss and the 'sadist' who had threatened Anders with torture in the Lubyanka in March 1940.

Colonel Kondratik informed Anders that Lieutenant Colonels Berling and Dudziński were already at liberty in Moscow. Would he like to meet them? Eager to hear their news, Anders agreed. He listened attentively as the two officers told him about the three camps of Kozelsk, Starobelsk and Ostashkov. As to their own experiences,

> They were both rather vague… They had been separated from their brother officers, kept at first in prison and then in a special villa near Moscow.… I was very careful in my talks with Berling and Dudziński. It seemed to me that they were too insistent on the need for close cooperation with Soviet Russia, while they expressed exaggerated criticisms of conditions in Poland before the war. Coming from Berling, a former officer of the 1st Brigade of Piłsudski's legions, this seemed particularly strange.[22]

Anders devoted a considerable amount of time during his recuperation in Moscow to studying the works of Lenin and Stalin in order to gain an understanding of Stalin's mindset. Berling had spent many weeks in Starobelsk doing exactly the same. Each man reached different conclusions.

It was not until 8 August 1941 that Anders (finally able to walk without crutches) met General Zygmunt Bohusz-Szyszko, sent from London as chief of the Polish Military Mission. Bohusz-Szyszko, who had escaped Poland via Hungary in 1939, spent long hours filling Anders in on world events since 1939 before taking him to meet Brigadier General Mason MacFarlane, head of the British Military Mission in Moscow, with whom Anders was to work closely and become friends ('For the first time I saw an officer wearing shorts').

On 16 August the first official meeting took place between General Anders and representatives of the Soviet military authorities, with General Panfilov presiding and NKVD General Zhukov in attendance.[23] Anders asked the Soviet delegation how many soldiers he had at his disposal for the Polish army and was told 1,000 officers and 20,000 soldiers might be considered as being available. These numbers made a deep impression on Anders, who immediately asked about the three special prisoner of war camps which Berling and Dudziński had described to him and where he knew the majority of Polish officers had been held. The Soviet delegates replied that they were unable to answer his question but promised to try to obtain exact information. Some days later General Wołkowicki arrived in Moscow and was able to offer further information about the three camps, while General Przeździecki gave Anders a brief account of events at the Villa of Bliss. Both men warned him about Berling and his group. Finally, towards the end of August, Anders managed to obtain permission to visit Griazovets.

> Tall, thin, limping, leaning on a cane, his eyes burning as if with fever, his
> face looked as if it was covered with parchment rather than skin.[24]

Anders arrived in Griazovets on the afternoon of 25 August in the company of General Bohusz-Szyszko (resplendent in shiny leather boots and pristine uniform) and NKVD General Zhukov. Everyone, except the *volksdeutsche* and the members of the Red Corner, lined up in ranking order to await the arrival of the great man. He made a powerful impression. 'I will never forget his huge eyes gazing at us. We realised that until a few days ago he had still been in prison.'[25]

Anders saluted each man in turn, gazing into their eyes intently in silence. 'With great emotion I recognised the emaciated faces of many old friends and brother officers. I felt the pleasure my coming gave them, and my statement that they would soon be free again, able to strive for Poland.'[26]

Anders welcomed the men on behalf of General Sikorski in London and declared he would now be forming a Polish army in the Soviet Union of which the prisoners of Griazovets would form the nucleus. After the speech, the men sang *Boże coś Polskę*, at which the Soviet sentries stood to attention, saluting. An irony, considering that only a few weeks before 'anyone found guilty of singing a Polish song would have been thrown into the cooler'.[27] The official meeting over, there were greetings, embraces, recollections. For the first time since their capture the two priests, Fathers Kantak and Tyczkowski, openly celebrated mass in the camp.

Delighted as he was to encounter so many familiar faces, General Anders noticed that none of the officers who had served with him in September 1939 were present – men like his chief of staff, Major Adam Sołtan, who had spent so many evenings with Józef Czapski reading from the works of Sienkiewicz, or Captain Stanisław Kuczyński-Iskander Bej, who had insisted on looking after Anders when he was injured instead of taking his chance to flee abroad. During the visit Anders gained a fuller picture of the winding up of the three POW camps in the spring of 1940, but no one could offer any information as to their comrades' possible whereabouts now. Major Lis and Captain Łopianowski also gave him a detailed report on their stay at the 'Villa of Bliss'. After listening to their account Anders informed the two men that he acknowledged receipt of their important information but at the present moment the political situation meant he must enrol any available men into the new army. He ordered them not to speak of the matter to anyone, an order which both men loyally, if reluctantly, carried out until they left the Soviet Union, at which point they made official statements to the Polish military authorities.

That same day, the men of Griazovets were informed they were no longer prisoners but Polish citizens and members of the Polish Armed Forces. Polish guards replaced the Soviet ones; Chief Inspector Bober was named the garrison's inspecting officer.[28] For a few brief days General Wołkowicki's desire to run the camp according to Polish military rules was finally fulfilled, with morning roll call and prayers as well as a programme of military classes and lectures organised by Lieutenant Colonel Felsztyn.[29] The programme was short-lived. Just a few days later they left Griazovets for good.

The Soviet sentries waved them off in a friendly fashion. The only men who remained behind were those too ill to travel (numbering thirteen), two who were under arrest, a group of twenty-five who had chosen to take Soviet citizenship (consisting mainly of Poles of Jewish, Lithuanian, Belorussian and Russian origin; they were stripped of their Polish citizenship), and fourteen *volksdeutsche* who were wanted neither by the Poles nor the Soviets. Their future looked so bleak their leader hanged himself.[30]

Józef Czapski, Bronisław Młynarski, Zdzisław Peszkowski, Dr Godlewski, Dr Słowes, Chief Inspector Bober, and all those companions in misfortune who had endured so much together, finally left the camp on 2 September 1941, almost exactly two years after the beginning of a war in which they had thus far been active participants for a few short weeks.

> I said goodbye to the patch of earth where I had spent a year of my life, to the wooden hutments, to the massive walls of the monastery which had housed some of us, to the ruin of its seventeenth-century Orthodox Church which the Bolsheviks had blown up with dynamite, the pond in which we had washed our shirts. I also took leave of the birches, the silver-leaved poplars, and of the acacias, in whose shade, among the broken tombstones with Cyrillic inscriptions, we had held so many friendly discussions and listened to so many lectures.[31]

None of the former prisoners yet had the slightest inkling that they were the sole survivors of a massacre that had taken the lives of 14,500 of their comrades from Kozelsk, Starobelsk and Ostashkov. They were looking forward to being reunited with their friends.

In classic Soviet fashion there was a long delay before the train arrived. The men were forced to stand in the pouring rain, cold and wet, their enthusiasm dampened by the overwhelmingly familiar sense of disappointment. They eventually set off around dawn. A brief stop at Yaroslavl for breakfast in a canteen, then Ivanovo, Murom, Arzamas, Ruzayevka. Here the groups split: some went to Tatishchevo, the others (the majority) east to Totskoye. As they travelled farther south the men gazed out at the changing landscape of forests, fields and steppes. The stations they passed were crowded with people, troops, armoured convoys.

'You could feel it was wartime.'[32]

PART III

Czapski's Quest 1941–42

Signing of the Sikorski–Maisky pact, 30 July 1941. L-r: General Władysław Sikorski, Anthony Eden, Winston Churchill, Ivan Maisky.

13

THE NEW POLISH ARMY

For the first time since their capture the men sat on seats in a regular passenger train, unhindered by guards, with an allowance of roubles in their pockets to purchase food. The further south they travelled the more enticing the fare: bilberries, cucumbers, tomatoes, milk, sold by smiling peasants on the railway platforms. Deprived of all fresh fruit and milk since their capture they gorged themselves, with predictable consequences. And for men who had not drunk alcohol for two years a single glass of vodka had the most appalling results. In the corridors Red Army soldiers on their way to the front mingled cheerfully with the Poles.

> 'Not still got a grudge against us for what happened in 1939?' one of them asked.
> 'You'd hardly expect us to have such short memories would you?'
> 'Why not? We're very sorry for what we did.'[1]

The distance from Vologda in the north of Russia to Totskoye in the south is nearly 1,000 miles. The journey took almost a week. Forests gave way to barren steppes, in turn replaced by fields filled with crops of hemp, millet and sunflowers, sprawling villages, thatched houses and huge Orthodox churches. At every station the former prisoners were met by a strange and troubling sight:

> Ragged, bearded figures, dressed in tattered *foufaikis* – or quilted coats – their eyes alight with happiness. One and all, they were half drunk with joy. They had come from Archangel, from the Kola peninsula, from Vorkuta, and elsewhere. They were moving towards the southwest, with the intention of joining the Polish army.[2]

The former prisoners knew that many families living in Soviet-occupied eastern Poland had been deported sometime in the previous year. Until now they had been ignorant of the extent of the deportations. They crowded onto the station platforms: men, women, children, an army of skeletons dressed in rags. On the train, Czapski and his companions listened in horror to their stories.

The Soviet occupation of eastern Poland in September 1939 had been followed in October by sham elections (turnout guaranteed at 99.2%), after which, in November, the newly-elected (pro-Soviet) national assemblies 'requested' the incorporation of the region into the Soviet Union as Western Ukraine and Western Belorussia. The NKVD wasted no time in establishing an iron grip on all areas of life in these conquered territories. Following a well-established pattern of repression, the first step involved mass round-ups and arrests of anyone who could feasibly be considered to present any kind of challenge to Soviet authority. Army officers who had evaded capture, landowners, businessmen, police, members of the judiciary, government officials, members of teaching unions and scouting organisations, military settlers, members of various political parties of right and left. Within weeks the prisons were overflowing. Charges ranged from high treason and espionage to propaganda activities, historical counter-revolution and sabotage. The sentences handed down were harsh, five to eight years in a labour camp, sometimes death.[3] The next step was the conscription, in September and December 1940, of all men aged between eighteen and forty-nine to serve in the Red Army. By this means the Soviets effectively neutralised the threat posed by some 200,000 active young men of Polish, Ukrainian, Jewish and Belorussian origin.

Then came the mass deportations of 'anti-Soviet elements', which took place in four main waves, each with a different profile: in February 1940 they took military settlers and forestry workers and their families; they mainly ended up in the far north of Russia and Siberia. In April 1940 it was the turn of the families of men who had been arrested by the NKVD, including the wives and children of the prisoners of Kozelsk, Starobelsk and Ostashkov. This group was sent to northern Kazakhstan and employed on rural collective and state farms. The third wave, in June 1940, consisted of refugees from central and western Poland who had fled the Germans; these included a high proportion of Jews. The final wave of deportations

took place just before the Nazi invasion in June 1941 and was made up of
citizens from the recently annexed Baltic states. 'Moscow thus carried out
its plan of "beheading" the community, which is always the first step to
the sovietisation of a nation, making it an inert and amorphous mass of
humanity.'[4] Given the harshness of the conditions in which the deported
families were forced to live, and that amongst the deportees were not only
young children but also older family members, the death toll from sickness, fatigue and accidents was high. Firm numbers are hard to ascertain,
but it is estimated that at least thirty percent of the deportees were dead
within a year.[5]

The total number of Polish citizens deported by the Soviets between
1940 and 1941 has never been definitively calculated: different sources come
to differing conclusions depending on how the numbers are arranged.
Estimates made by the Polish wartime government and other, later, sources
set the figure somewhere between 1,250,000 and 1,600,000. NKVD records
offer a far lower figure, just under 400,000.[6] This significant discrepancy is
most probably a result of the fact that the higher figures take into account
Polish citizens conscripted into the Red Army, those placed in Soviet prisons
and those who signed up to work voluntarily in the USSR.[7] Soviet figures,
on the other hand, most likely exclude Ukrainians, Belorussians and Jews
from eastern Poland (now counted as Soviet citizens) and probably do not
take into account the high mortality rate among the deportees.[8]

These former deportees, often entire families or what remained of them,
had now been released as a consequence of the amnesty. They had learned,
in a variety of ways – from the NKVD, from newspapers or the radio – that
a Polish army was being formed on Soviet soil. They were heading towards
it, hundreds of thousands of sickly, starving people, in the hope of finding
a way out of Russia. They were not the only ones: the war brought amnesty
not only for Polish deportees but other prisoners sentenced for minor
misdemeanours, now freed to join the Red Army and adding to the chaos.[9]

When the former prisoners of Griazovets finally arrived at Totskoye
they discovered an army camp consisting of little more than 'some tents,
a few undersized wooden huts without stoves, and that was all'.[10] Here, in
the middle of a barren steppe, with virtually no equipment and thousands
of half-starving civilians converging daily on them, they began the process
of putting together the new Polish army.

*

The military agreement signed in Moscow on 14 August 1941 between General Bohusz-Szyszko and General Vasilevsky, following the reopening of diplomatic relations between Poland and the USSR, stated that the new army would be part of Poland's armed forces and would owe allegiance to the Polish rather than the Soviet government. All Polish citizens currently in the Soviet Union were eligible to serve in it, and 1 October was fixed as the date by which the army should be ready to go into battle (a date General Anders regarded as 'sheer fantasy, but I knew it was a waste of time to make any objection'[11]). Anders had obtained permission to form two divisions and one reserve regiment. A decision on the eventual number of divisions was deferred due to the impossibility of estimating the number of potential recruits. This was later to become a bone of contention between the two sides because the Poles wanted to continue recruiting to the army as long as there were men and women willing to serve, while the Soviet authorities wanted later recruits to be steered towards the Red Army and refused to supply them. It was to be a land force only: Polish air force and navy personnel (like Lieutenant Mintowt-Czyż and Captain Ginsbert) were immediately transported to Britain to join existing Polish services there. Polish army headquarters were in Buzuluk. The 5th Polish Infantry Division, commanded by General Boruta-Śpiechowicz, was based in Tatishchevo and the 6th, commanded by General Karaszewicz-Tokarzewski, at Totskoye near Kuybyshev (now Samara), where most Soviet government agencies and all diplomatic missions were evacuated from Moscow in October 1941.

General Anders had no idea how many men he had at his disposal, what state they were in, how he would equip them or who would command them. When he arrived in Totskoye on 14 September to inspect his new troops it was painfully evident just what a task lay ahead:

> I shall not forget the sight as long as I live, nor the mingled pity and pride with which I reviewed them. Most of them had no boots or shirts, and all were in rags, often the tattered relics of old Polish uniforms. There was not a man who was not an emaciated skeleton and most of them were covered with ulcers, resulting from semi-starvation, but to the great astonishment of the Russians, including General Zhukov, who accompanied me, they were all well shaved and showed a fine soldierly bearing. I asked myself

whether I could ever make an army of them, and whether they could ever stand the strain of a campaign.[12]

The majority of the former prisoners of Griazovets were sent to Totskoye to join the 6th Division under General Karaszewicz-Tokarzewski. General Wołkowicki was made the division's deputy leader, Major Domoń its chief of staff.[13] The officers who had spent so many months in the 'Villa of Bliss', meanwhile, were mainly placed under the command of the left-leaning General Boruta-Śpiechowicz in the 5th Infantry Division, where many of their comrades viewed them with open distrust. Nevertheless, Berling was made chief of staff.[14]

General Anders was well aware of the activities of Berling's group. Major Lis and Captain Łopianowski had briefed him fully on his visit to Griazovets. His decision to allow these men to serve in the new Polish army reflected the realities of the Polish situation: thousands of Polish citizens were being held in Soviet camps and prisons; Anders believed it would be much easier to negotiate with the Soviet authorities if he had men in his ranks who were perceived as friendly towards their hosts. He also acknowledged their undoubted military skill. Above all, his decision reflected the acute shortage of skilled senior officers. The vast bulk of the Polish army's officer cadre was missing. Thousands of officers from Kozelsk and Starobelsk camps had disappeared without trace. It was like looking at a school photograph and discovering the entire sixth form had vanished.

When Generals Anders and Bohusz-Szyszko met Generals Zhukov and Panfilov in August 1941 one of their first requests was for a list of all Polish officers currently being held in the Soviet Union. Neither the Polish government in exile nor the British Mission in the Soviet Union knew precisely how many Polish officers had been captured by the Soviets in 1939. The only numbers they had to go on came from an article, published on the first anniversary of the Soviet invasion of Poland, which Anders had read in prison in the Soviet newspaper *Pravda*. According to this, nearly 200,000 Polish soldiers had been taken by the Red Army, including twelve generals and over 8,000 officers.[15] The former prisoners of Griazovets confirmed that these numbers matched the officer populations of Kozelsk and Starobelsk camps. Zhukov and Panfilov assured Anders that they would provide him with a list of names, but when they did so it consisted of only

1,000 Polish officers and there were only three generals on it: Wołkowicki, Przeździecki (captured in Lithuania) and Jarnuszkiewicz (arrested by the NKVD in 1939 and initially taken to Starobelsk before being transferred to the Lubyanka, where he remained until after the amnesty).[16] Where were Generals Minkiewicz, Bohaterewicz, Smorawiński, Billewicz, Haller, Kowalewski, Orlik-Łukoski, Plisowski, Sikorski, Skierski and Skuratowicz?

Six times Anders and Bohusz-Szyszko met Zhukov and Panfilov between August and September 1941. On each occasion they brought up the subject of the missing officers, even making specific enquiries about Anders' former chief of staff, Major Adam Sołtan, and Bohusz-Szyszko's close friend, Colonel Janiszewski. The Russians always behaved in a thoroughly pleasant manner until the missing officers were mentioned, at which point 'they appeared to become very much disturbed and rattled, and they always managed to evade the particular subject'.[17] When Bohusz-Szyszko asked General Zhukov about Janiszewski for the third time, Zhukov replied bluntly: 'Please do not ask me about these men, because in this particular case I cannot help you.' He nevertheless insisted that the officers were in the Soviet Union and would soon be found.

The official task of pursuing the case of the missing prisoners now fell largely to the newly-appointed Polish ambassador to the Soviet Union, Professor Stanisław Kot. Kot was an odd choice for this supremely political post. An academic, philosopher and historian with no diplomatic experience, Kot spoke no Russian and had little understanding of the Soviet mentality. But he was a close friend of General Sikorski, who persuaded him to take the job. Kot threw himself into the task with admirable dedication, but he struggled to negotiate effectively with a government that operated by a set of opaque rules he simply could not grasp. In the end he succeeded neither in the eyes of the Poles nor the Russians. Many Poles believed General Anders could get something done in a matter of days which Kot would struggle to achieve in weeks or months, while Stalin eventually took to bypassing the ambassador, whom he referred to contemptuously as *vash Kot* ('that Kot of yours'), choosing to deal directly with Anders instead.[18]

Kot arrived in Moscow on 1 September 1941. His main and urgent priority was to lead official diplomatic efforts to locate Polish citizens and ensure they were being released from camps according to the terms of the amnesty. In order to facilitate this process he set up a Polish Welfare

Professor Stanisław Kot.

Committee and created two new departments, the Department of Social Care and the Department of Intervention. These gathered evidence on deportees and organised interventions on behalf of people who needed special protection and assistance from the Polish state. Delegates were sent out to assist newly-released deportees, government representatives waited at key railway stations to direct new arrivals south towards the Polish army. Kot had a personal mission: to find and save men and women whose cultural background, status, or skills he considered vital to the Polish nation. These were academics, politicians, journalists, students, priests, many of whom Kot knew personally. It was a massive undertaking: some deportees did not learn of the amnesty until months after its announcement. For others, the journey south from exile was made drifting down rivers on home-made rafts, on overcrowded trains, or walking barefoot for hundreds of miles. With no money and few items to barter, many were reduced to begging for food. Thousands died on the journey.

In his efforts to find and extract these people Kot was assiduous in pressing the Soviet deputy commissar for foreign affairs, Andrey Vyshinsky (former state prosecutor during the Great Terror), for action on every individual case. At the same time he was tasked with addressing the far larger matter of the 8,500 missing Polish officers so desperately needed for the new army. This was an urgent priority for the military authorities. They knew the men must be somewhere in the Soviet Union because the Polish government in exile had already been in contact with the underground in Poland to ask whether any prisoners from the three camps had been sent home in 1940, as they had been promised. The answer was no. The underground also confirmed that all correspondence to families in Poland had ceased in April–May 1940.

Kot raised the question of the missing officers repeatedly in a series of meetings with Vyshinsky over the autumn of 1941. On each occasion, Vyshinsky responded evasively:

> We will deliver to you all the persons we have, but we cannot hand over those who are not with us. The English, for instance, have given us the names of their nationals who are supposed to be in USSR, but who have actually never been here.[19]

When Kot spoke with Minister for Foreign Affairs Vyacheslav Molotov on 22 October, he pointed out that there were several parts of Soviet territory where the amnesty had not been observed and certain categories of prisoner – officers, judges, public prosecutors and members of the police – who had not been released. Molotov replied that in principle all Polish citizens had been set free but admitted that

> owing to the course of events great transport and administrative difficulties have arisen, for instance the problem of evacuating the Soviet population from areas occupied by the Germans. But please accept my assurance that we shall give the Polish government full help in this matter within the bounds of our possibilities.[20]

Despite the appearance of good faith and repeated assurances by Vyshinsky and Molotov that they were willing to help the Polish authorities, Kot grew increasingly irked by their refusal to admit to keeping any detailed records on the missing officers ('We just haven't any information') and the series of bland and increasingly incredible excuses they used to fob him off. When

Kot pressed Vyshinsky about the lack of information on so many Polish citizens and asked if he could obtain permission to send delegates to visit the camps where these men were detained, Vyshinsky responded as if offended: 'You are putting the case as if we wanted to conceal certain Polish citizens. But where are they?' he exclaimed, adding: 'There have been many changes since 1939. People have shifted from place to place, many of them have been released, many are working, many have returned home...' Kot countered that the officers concerned were prominent men, including several generals. 'After all, these people aren't children, it's impossible to hide them. If any of them have died, please inform us. I cannot believe they don't exist any longer.' Vyshinsky's response was to ask Kot, for the umpteenth time, to provide him with names.

> Vyshinsky: These people aren't trees, they must be somewhere, possibly some of them themselves did not state that they were generals, possibly they figure under other professional categories. After all, I am not in a position to travel all over the Soviet Union looking for them.
>
> Kot: The data I possess I have received from eye-witnesses, from written statements and protocols. At one time or another they have seen a certain number of our officers taken off in some unknown direction. If I had obtained exact data from you I should have used it. People are not like steam, which can fly away, or like those melting flakes of snow (he points to the window).[21]

The minutes recorded by the Polish embassy note: 'The conversation lasted from 13:00 to 14:30 hours. Vyshinsky's tone was not too friendly. The ambassador was very calm and conciliatory.' The only thing on which the two men seemed able to agree was that the missing men were neither children, trees, steam nor flakes of snow. They had to be somewhere.

Frustrated by the lack of progress, the Polish authorities approached the British with a request to mediate. Kot also sent a confidential note to Molotov seeking to persuade the Soviet government to release all Polish POWs before the arrival of General Sikorski in Moscow in early December. It was possibly as a result of these interventions that a week later Molotov sent a note declaring that all Polish citizens detained as POWs had now been released and the Soviet authorities had given all necessary assistance to these persons. Vyshinsky later repeated this claim, informing Kot that it was now only a matter of confirming the men's whereabouts. 'So far as I am concerned,' he concluded, 'this problem simply doesn't exist.'[22]

Ambassador Kot was not able to obtain an audience with Stalin himself until 14 November. When he raised the question of the missing men Stalin claimed to be unaware that some Poles had yet to be released and with an air of great sincerity promised to look into it. At one point during the conversation, as if to underline his personal interest in the matter, Stalin picked up his telephone and made a show of calling the NKVD to ask if all the Polish prisoners had been released ('NKVD? Stalin here...') The 'answer', of course, was yes. This flippant performance, aimed presumably at convincing the ambassador of his good faith, would be comical were the subject in question not so chilling.

While the embassy was pursuing its official enquiries, General Anders made a direct approach to the NKVD, writing to them asking for information about the missing officers, whose number he assessed at 8,772, adding that the list was not yet complete.[23] Receiving no reply, Anders decided to take matters into his own hands. He set up a special section of the General Staff and entrusted Józef Czapski – 'a man of fine character who had been known to me for a very long time' – with the organisation of an 'assistance bureau' to register the men and women who were turning up in Totskoye daily in their thousands. The function of the bureau, housed in a small wooden shed, was to collect information brought in by new arrivals, answer their queries about the army, and explain what was expected of them. It was also to question them with a view to establishing whether any of them had news of the missing men, and to compile a list of names. In this task Czapski was aided by Captain Jan Kaczkowski and a small team of staff, most of whom had been previously imprisoned in one of the three camps.[24]

The chief concern of the men who joined the lengthy queue outside Czapski's little shed was to save their comrades who had been left behind; their second anxiety was to obtain news of their families and let them know their own whereabouts. Czapski and his staff drew up lists of names, recorded statements of men who had come from labour camps, entered the addresses of their relations. It was a laborious and seemingly never-ending task but it placed Czapski at the centre of all information coming into the army. He forwarded the information to the General Staff in Buzuluk and the Polish embassy in Kuybyshev, where his lists were used to support appeals to the Soviet authorities to hand over prisoners who had not yet been released. Czapski also worked on drawing up an alphabetical list of the missing prisoners, asking former inmates of Griazovets to try to recall as many of their comrades as possible. It was by no means a straightforward task: the high-ranking officers were generally well known but it proved much more difficult to name the thousands of junior officers:

> People remembered those with whom they shared the same bunks, and also those with whom they had a closer contact. In relation to those whom they knew less well they remembered generally their last names and ranks, but had forgotten their first names.[25]

Nevertheless, Czapski managed to put together a list of around 4,000 names. This was the list handed to Stalin by General Sikorski and General Anders when they visited the Kremlin on 3 December.

Czapski and his staff lived in daily expectation that at any moment someone would show up with news of their missing comrades. Not only did none of them put in an appearance, but of the hundreds of people arriving from every point of the compass, nobody could offer the slightest crumb of information. Czapski's hopes were momentarily raised by accounts mentioning prisoners from Kozelsk and Starobelsk; these were swiftly shattered when he discovered that these prisoners (like General Przeździecki and those who arrived in Griazovets in July 1941) had been placed in the camps only after June 1940. To avoid confusion, he began calling the camps Kozelsk 2 and Starobelsk 2.

The totality of the silence surrounding the missing men gave rise to a number of theories, the most plausible of which was that they had been sent to one of the Soviet Union's most remote regions and had not yet been able to make their way south. This theory was supported by rumours claiming Polish officers had been seen in the Arctic region of Franz Josef Land, an archipelago which lies beyond the far tip of Arkhangelsk, to the north-east of Svalbard. Another rumour suggested several hundred Polish prisoners were working in the mines and on the construction of airfields in the Gulag region of Kolyma in the far east of the Soviet Union, home to one of the largest camp networks in the USSR. The remoteness of these regions could feasibly account for the men's silence. Kolyma, in particular, was known as a place from which nobody ever returned. In the hope of shedding some light on the matter Czapski decided to take the information he had managed to amass to General Staff headquarters in Buzuluk.

General Anders was away in Moscow when Czapski arrived so he reported instead to Colonel Leopold Okulicki. Stocky, with thick, grizzled hair, Okulicki – whose nickname was 'Bear Cub' – was the physical opposite of Czapski, who at 6'5" was always the tallest man in any room (often the thinnest, too). Okulicki had spent the last two years in a series of Soviet prisons from which he had emerged after the amnesty with all his teeth broken. But he made a positive impression on Czapski, listening attentively to what the artist had to say as he explained that he had compiled not just a list of names but of the places where their vanished comrades might be found. Okulicki immediately transmitted the information to the Soviet authorities and ordered Czapski to draw up a detailed report stating everything he knew about the men.

It was the first time Czapski had written anything about his experiences in Starobelsk. Unnerved by the atmosphere of elegant plenty

Colonel Okulicki, with General Anders, 1941–42.

prevailing at army HQ, Czapski found 'a sympathetic female typist' to whom he began dictating his report. Much to his embarrassment, he discovered that once he began talking about his comrades he was unable to stop. When evening came, he was still dictating. Then there was a power cut, the lights failed and Czapski was forced to wait for power to be restored.

> An hour and a half of conversation! – what a change for one like me, who had come from the life of a camp, from the sort of existence we had known at Totskoye! Chats, flirtatious interchanges with the young ladies at HQ, chocolates from London or Moscow! – all very natural, of course, until one remembers that I was busily engaged in writing the story of my Starobelsk friends. Their faces were vividly present to my mind. I thought of Sołtan, who was determined to get back to Poland, even if he had to 'crawl there on his knees'; of Chęciński, who was obsessed by the idea of a Central European Federation; who, had he been with me at that moment, would never have let the subject alone! To me, in such a state of mind, the atmosphere at HQ seemed something monstrous.[26]

While he was in Buzuluk Czapski met an officer who had recently arrived from the Gulf of Nakhodka. The officer spoke to Czapski at length about the network of Gulag camps and mines that lay strung out along the course of the Kolyma River, which flows into the Arctic Ocean. The climate and conditions there were so brutal few people ever returned. The only way to rejoin the mainland was by boat across the sea of Okhotsk. Even then, thousands of miles of tundra and barren mountains separated the coast and any habitable place. And yet this man had made it out alive, giving Czapski cause to hope. After a further encounter with another Polish deportee who confirmed the rumour that transports, loaded with Poles, had been seen steaming out of Bukhta-Nakhodka around April 1940, Czapski became convinced he was on the right track. Colonel Okulicki assured him General Anders and Ambassador Kot would put in a request with the relevant Soviet authorities to seek the missing men in Kolyma and order their release. Czapski returned to Totskoye in an optimistic mood.

Some weeks later he was recalled to Buzuluk to answer questions about his report. He was to remain based here over the winter months of 1941 to

1942 as he travelled to various parts of the country on his mission to make sense of the mystifying silence surrounding his comrades.

In the camp in Totskoye, meanwhile, Zdzisław Peszkowski and the other army recruits shivered in summer uniforms, sleeping in tents with a stove in the middle, everyone dressed in whatever they could lay their hands on against the cold. Despite their hopes for the future they were still anxious about their families and concerned about the state of the army. Supplies of weapons, uniforms, food and medicines only gradually started arriving in November, but they remained inadequate. Food rations were little different in quantity or quality to what they had received as prisoners in Griazovets: enough to stave off starvation but not to lead active lives. Men already weakened by two years of privation succumbed to sickness; vitamin deficiencies led to temporary blindness; malaria, typhus and dysentery were rife.

At this stage the Polish military authorities, like Czapski, lent most credence to the proposition that their missing officers had been banished to one of the farthest corners of the USSR and had either been prevented from leaving or had perished from the brutal conditions under which they were forced to exist. They even bypassed official Soviet channels and sent some of their own people to follow up on the rumours, but without success and at considerable individual cost: 'From among those that we had sent unofficially and secretly into these northern sections of Russia to get some information on the Polish officers, very few returned, and those who did manage to return could not give us any additional information.'[27]

When General Sikorski arrived in Moscow in early December for the long-planned meeting with Stalin he attempted to elicit a definitive answer to the question of the missing officers by ensuring that the matter was on the official agenda for their conversation. A 'Note on the question of captive soldiers of the Polish Army from the camps at Starobelsk, Kozelsk and Ostashkov, deported to forced labour camps in the Far North and not released by 1.XII.41' was prepared, and the list of the missing men compiled by Józef Czapski submitted alongside it.[28] The meeting took place at the Kremlin on 3 December 1941, with General Sikorski, General Anders, Stalin and Molotov present. When Sikorski broached the question of the officers he told Stalin he knew for sure the men were not in Poland. Since thus far not a single one of them had reappeared, he concluded they must therefore be in the Soviet Union.

> Stalin: That's impossible. They've fled.
>
> Anders: But where could they flee to?
>
> Stalin: Well, to Manchuria, for instance.
>
> Anders: It isn't possible that they have all fled, especially as from the moment of their transfer from prisoner of war camps to labour camps and prisons their correspondence with their families ceased completely.... The majority of the officers named in this list are known to me personally. Among them are my staff officers and commanders. These people are perishing and dying in these terrible conditions.
>
> Stalin: They must have been released, only they haven't arrived yet.[29]

The Poles took Stalin's mocking words at face value, interpreting them to mean that their theory was correct: the men were detained in labour camps in the far north or east, unable as yet to make their way south.

Towards the end of December Czapski suggested to General Anders that he might take advantage of the relatively warm Soviet–Polish relations and present his report to General Nasedkin, head of the Directorate of Labour Camps (GULAG) which had recently been transferred from Moscow to Chkalov (now Orenburg). Here, surely, reasoned Czapski, he might find some more detailed information. Given the complete failure of diplomatic efforts to locate the missing officers, Anders readily agreed, furnishing Czapski with two letters, one to the head of GULAG, the other to the NKVD chief in Chkalov, demanding the immediate release of any prisoners and deported persons who were still being illegally held 'in conformity with the instructions issued by Comrade Stalin'.

On New Year's Day 1942, Czapski set out on his quest.

14

CZAPSKI'S QUEST

THIS NEXT CHAPTER IN EVENTS BELONGS TO JÓZEF CZAPSKI.[1]

The city of Chkalov (present-day Orenburg) lies some 150 miles south-east of Buzuluk, nearly 1,000 miles from Moscow. Through it runs the Ural River, marking the boundary between Europe and Asia. Next to it is Kazakhstan. When Czapski arrived in the city at night he was given a room at the Polish mission, located in the station hotel. On his way there he was struck by the sight of a camel harnessed to a sledge, its coat covered in frost, and by the Asiatic appearance of the city's inhabitants. How far he was from home. Czapski had learned of the presence of GULAG in the city from a Russian who let the information slip by chance, but he had no address and no idea how to find it. He decided to start at the top and duly presented himself to the military commander of the city who informed him, in a very friendly manner, that there was no GULAG in Chkalov. Unwilling to give up so easily, Czapski entered every official-looking building he could find, asking the same question in each of them. Quite unexpectedly, in one of these buildings an orderly gave him the address 'without the slightest fuss and in the most ordinary way imaginable'.

There was no sign outside to indicate what lay within. However, on the third floor, behind a padded door, Czapski discovered a large suite of rooms in which the head of GULAG, General Nasedkin, had installed his office. Having proffered his letter of introduction, Czapski waited in the over-heated ante room, where a well-dressed secretary was making up an order of the various 'extras' to which NKVD officials were entitled: tins of foreign food, bottles of spirits, chocolate. Before long, Czapski was ushered into the main office.

General Nasedkin ('a large, fleshy individual, wearing a uniform of superfine cloth') received the Polish officer smilingly. On the table before him lay General Anders' letter, adorned with the Polish white eagle, beautifully embossed on paper supplied from London. The letter's formal invocation of 'Comrade Stalin', combined with the fact that the visit had clearly taken Nasedkin by surprise, made it easy for Czapski to explain his business. As he spoke, his attention was drawn to something behind Nasedkin:

> On the wall behind the general hung a large map of the whole of Russia, which, whenever it was possible to do so, I furtively devoured with my eyes. All the prison camps were shown, the most important centres being marked with a large star, the others with stars of a smaller size. I had time enough in which to note that the large constellations were scattered over the Kola peninsula, the Komi Republic and Kolyma.

As Czapski outlined the mystery of the Polish prisoners of war who had disappeared from the three NKVD-run camps, he swiftly formed the impression that Nasedkin knew nothing about the matter. The general explained to Czapski that in April–May 1940 he had not yet been appointed head of GULAG. He was therefore unable to state whether these men had come within the GULAG system, reminding Czapski moreover that he was in charge not of prisoner of war camps, but labour camps, which contained only men who had stood trial and been sentenced for certain specific crimes. It was a subtle but vital category distinction, obscure to an outsider but possessing a certain Soviet logic. 'Even if there were Polish officers in my camps, they were working not as officers, but as condemned criminals.'

Nasedkin promised to look into the matter and asked Czapski to return the following day, when he hoped to be able to give him more positive information. The same evening, Czapski paid a visit to the commander of the local NKVD in Chkalov, Colonel Bzyrov, presenting the second letter of introduction from General Anders. After a short wait in another well-heated ante-room, Czapski, to his astonishment, was shown into Bzyrov's office through the same kind of oversized cupboard the Polish officers had encountered at the Lubyanka. Standing beneath the ubiquitous portrait of Stalin in his spacious and well-furnished office, the young colonel greeted Czapski warmly. Immediately he advised his visitor that the only men likely to be able to answer his questions were those at the very top of the NKVD: Beria, Merkulov, Fedotov, Raikhman or Zhukov. When Czapski explained the theory about Kolyma, Bzyrov appeared not the slightest bit surprised.

> Walking over to a large map of Soviet Russia, he climbed on a stool and pointed out to me the main routes followed by the convoys of prisoners sent to work in the north. He drew my attention to the port of Dodinka, standing at the mouth of the Yenisey. That was the point of departure of all the more important working parties destined for the islands of the Arctic Ocean. Sitting there in the NKVD Commandant's comfortable room, I seemed to be listening to a perfectly innocent and natural exposition of one aspect of a planned economy. Bzyrov even went so far as to give me, in the frankest possible manner, his own views on the matter. He seemed to think it highly probable that our prisoners of war would be found somewhere in the far north.

When Czapski returned to see General Nasedkin the following day there was no trace of the Russian's former friendliness and Czapski quickly surmised that Nasedkin had been reprimanded for entertaining him the previous evening. Without preamble, and clearly eager to see the back of his inconvenient visitor, Nasedkin asked for the list of missing men, which he proposed sending to NKVD headquarters in Kuybyshev. Since the list had already been communicated to Stalin by Polish general staff, Czapski refused the offer. He could see Nasedkin wanted him gone, but he was determined to try to obtain at least something from his visit, so he mentioned the theory concerning Franz Josef Land and Nova Zemlya. Nasedkin's reply was in stark contrast to his friendliness of the previous day:

> Fixing his small grey eyes on the carpet in front of his desk, he replied that what I was saying was not wholly impossible, that the northern labour camps under his control might, in fact, have sent a few small working parties to the places I had mentioned. 'But should that turn out to be so,' said the general with a sullen look, 'the numbers involved could not possibly amount to several thousands as you maintain.'

The interview was over.

Czapski travelled all the way to Kuybyshev to discover that the NKVD bigwigs whom Colonel Bzyrov had encouraged him to consult had returned to Moscow. Reasoning that his only chance of obtaining an answer to his questions was to go directly to the top, he obtained a military pass and, armed once more with letters of introduction signed by General Anders (with an added handwritten appeal to the NKVD generals, in the name of humanity and goodwill, to clear up the mystery surrounding the disappearance of his officers), he prepared to leave for Moscow to seek an audience with Major Raikhman and General Zhukov.

While he waited for his papers Czapski stayed briefly at the Polish embassy, where he was much struck by the strange atmosphere prevailing in a building where half the staff had been sent over from England and the other half were fresh from Soviet labour camps and prisons. The differences were profound, not only in appearance but political and social attitudes. Ambassador Kot's efforts to seek out and rescue persons of note from Soviet captivity had brought dozens of artists, scientists and journalists to the embassy, where Kot did his best to find them work. His staff thus consisted of a gallery of eminent representatives of literature, university professors and journalists from Poland's pre-war elite. Kot's small office was 'in a constant state of siege', his days filled with conferences and interviews, his nights plagued by insomnia.

> When he could not sleep he played endless games of patience and read all the French books the local shops could provide. Any novel of the last century, no matter by whom, was grist to his mill, because it brought him relaxation after the strenuous labour of his days, and occasionally induced sleep.

When Czapski informed Kot of his plan to visit Moscow, Kot responded with a warning: 'Go, by all means, if you want to,' he said, 'but it won't serve any purpose.'

Among Kot's many preoccupations at that time was another troubling mystery: two prominent Jewish Polish politicians, Henryk Ehrlich and Wiktor Alter, had recently gone missing. Ehrlich and Alter were best known as leaders of the pre-war Bund, a non-Zionist Jewish socialist party committed to working closely with the Polish state. Alter was a member of the committee of the Second International and the Polish National Council in London. Both were well-known anti-Nazi activists.

At the beginning of the war Ehrlich and Alter had fled east to escape the Nazi invasion, subsequently falling into Soviet hands. They were arrested, imprisoned in Moscow, interrogated, tortured and eventually sentenced to death, later commuted to ten years in a labour camp. After the amnesty Kot brought them to the Polish embassy in Kuybyshev, where they began working, initially with Soviet approval and encouragement, to persuade communists and non-communists to work together against Hitler. They were invited to meetings with Beria and wrote directly to Stalin to ask him to support the international Jewish anti-fascist committee which the NKVD themselves had suggested they set up and lead. The Soviet authorities even provided them with secretarial staff and transport. Soviet enthusiasm for their efforts soon waned. On 4 December 1941, Ehrlich and Alter went to dine in the diplomatic restaurant at Kuybyshev. At 12.30 a.m. an Intourist employee approached Alter and asked him to come to the telephone. A few moments later, Alter called Ehrlich over and the pair were seen leaving the hotel in the company of an unnamed man. They were never seen again.

After several days the local NKVD admitted to the embassy that they had arrested the pair. The subsequent international outcry included requests for their release by prominent figures such as Eleanor Roosevelt. To no avail. Neither had a diplomatic passport. Nothing could be done. When Ambassador Kot asked Vyshinsky to release them, Vyshinsky replied that he could not because they were German spies. Kot pointed out that they were both well-known socialists and Jews, to which Vyshinsky retorted with unshakeable logic that Trotsky was also a socialist and a Jew and yet proved to be a German spy. The affair sent a ripple of anxiety through the embassy. Most of the staff had only recently escaped Soviet captivity. They, too, lacked diplomatic passports. The case of Ehrlich and Alter highlighted the precariousness of their own situation. How quickly they could find themselves right back where they had started.[2]

Since his capture in 1939 Czapski had become familiar with the peculiar vagaries of Soviet rail travel as he crossed the country in a variety of cattle trucks and prison wagons. When he took his bags to the station at

Kuybyshev he was therefore unsurprised to discover that his train, scheduled to leave that night, had not yet arrived. For three days and nights he waited, alongside crowds of emaciated Polish refugees who slept on the station floor. Communication with Moscow was difficult, the railway system overwhelmed by military traffic and evacuees. The heavy January snowfall only added to the delays. Czapski was lucky. He did not have to sleep on the floor like his compatriots. He passed the days at the embassy or in his hotel and the nights dozing on a chair in the Polish radio operator's tiny office in the station. Here, he sought refuge in nineteenth-century French novels borrowed from the ambassador's library while the loudspeakers played Strauss waltzes to the huddled masses sleeping on the floor.

> During one of the nights I spent waiting for my train, a lorry stopped outside the station. Into this a number of corpses were loaded like logs of wood, to be taken away and buried. These were the bodies of passengers who had died of cold on the journey, prisoners released from labour camps.

Rescue arrived unexpectedly in the form of an officer from the British Military Mission, part of which was temporarily housed in Kuybyshev. On discovering Czapski's plight the officer invited him to join a group of British airmen who were due to travel to Moscow on the same train. The Mission had its own railway coach reserved for its sole use. Would Captain Czapski care to join them? The coach turned out to be a first-class sleeper carriage with seats upholstered in turquoise blue velvet, mahogany fittings, a washroom and all the luxuries of pre-revolutionary Russian travel. For the first time since his capture Czapski was able to ride in comfort, gazing out at the vast snow-covered landscape while the train performed the familiar routine of stopping and starting apparently at random. It took three days to get to Moscow, ample time for Czapski to observe his new companions. Czapski spoke no English; only one of the officers spoke French. They passed the time playing chess and attempting to converse. Czapski was deeply moved by this brief intimacy with the British officers. Their civility towards him struck him all the more powerfully because it brought home the extent to which he had become accustomed to the brutality of Soviet life. It was a painful reminder of a world he had taken for granted before the war.

They were all men of good education, and they treated me as an officer of
an Allied army, the army of a country for which they had feelings of respect.
Their instinctive courtesy (most of them were airmen), their readiness
to help and perform small services, impressed me [deeply].... It was the
normal thing for these Englishmen to shave regularly every day, and wear
well pressed uniforms.

It is a sad reflection of Czapski's two years in Soviet captivity that this deeply
cultivated, multi-lingual aristocrat should feel so grateful to these British
officers for choosing to ignore his shabby uniform and his emaciated frame
and treat him as an equal.

Czapski's co-tenant in his sleeping compartment was a Welsh sergeant
who insisted on showing the Polish officer a photograph of his wife and
child taken in the garden of his home. Each morning the sergeant would
spend a good half hour crumbling biscuit into condensed milk in an effort
to obtain something resembling porridge.

Charmed as Czapski was by his contact with the British officers, he
nevertheless observed that their ability to behave naturally in Soviet Russia
was based on a complete ignorance of its realities. Stopping for lunch at
Morshansk, the airmen were ushered into the station restaurant where a
magnificent lunch had been prepared for them, served by pretty girls in
silk blouses. In order to accommodate the British officers the local NKVD
had emptied the station restaurant of local customers. The crowd gathered
on the station platform had been forced back so the airmen might make
their way to the restaurant unimpeded.

> I can still see those well shaven, immaculately-dressed Englishmen walking
> to their meal with an air of unconcern (what could be more natural than
> luncheon in a station buffet?) without seeming to notice the starved huddle
> of men and women in sheepskins and *foufaikis* staring as if at some spectacle
> from another planet.

Nor did it occur to the Englishmen that both the food and the pink-cheeked
girls had most likely been bussed in that morning and would disappear as
soon as the lunch was over. As they sat at table enjoying the meal set before
them, Czapski's thoughts turned inevitably to the crowd shivering in the

room next door. 'I knew too much about the backstage realities of the feast to share the phlegmatic enjoyment of my English companions.'

There were only two hotels in Moscow reserved for foreigners, both beautifully decorated and half empty. On the evening of their arrival the British airmen dropped Czapski at the first of these, the National. The next morning he was informed without explanation that his reservation was at the second, the Metropole. He duly moved and found more pre-revolutionary luxury, his room decorated with dark blue wallpaper, the armchairs upholstered in sapphire velvet. There was even a telephone, although according to the other guests (a small group of British and American journalists who spent their days waiting around for someone from the Soviet propaganda service to take them to visit 'interesting' sights) the telephone lines were all bugged.

When Czapski entered NKVD headquarters at the Lubyanka the following day he was convinced that the letters he was carrying from General Anders and General Sikorski to General Zhukov and Major Raikhman would immediately secure him an interview. After explaining his business to a young NKVD official, he swiftly realised how naive he had been:

> My request to be allowed to see [Zhukov and Raikhman] was met by a half amused smile on the face of the young man and a blank refusal. It was impossible to make an exception in favour of anybody, no matter who they might be and I talked in vain. The only thing I could do was to hand over the letters and wait patiently for a reply.

He made his way to the British Military Mission, where he was received by Brigadier General Mason MacFarlane who, like Kot, warned Czapski he would find it next to impossible to see either Merkulov or Beria, adding that he himself had to wait several weeks when he wanted an interview. Nevertheless, he offered Czapski use of the Mission as a place to work, suggesting he could also leave papers there if he was reluctant to leave sensitive material in the hotel. Czapski took MacFarlane up on his offer, spending his mornings at the Mission working on a report and using British diplomatic channels to forward documents to the Polish government in London.

Czapski's report contained a detailed account of the capture of the Polish officers, their imprisonment in the three camps, the liquidation of the camps, the situation in Griazovets, efforts made by the Polish government to locate the missing officers, and the current state of thinking in Polish circles in early 1942 about the likely fate of the men. He observed, pointedly, that despite Vyshinsky and Molotov's claims to hold no records on the prisoners, the Polish authorities were fully aware that the NKVD had kept detailed records on each individual prisoner: notes from their interrogations, photographs, personal information gleaned from confiscated documents.

> We knew how carefully and exactly this work of the NKVD was conducted, so none of us [former] prisoners of war can believe for a second that the whereabouts of 15,000 POWs of which more than 8,000 are commissioned officers, could be unknown to the higher authorities of the NKVD.[3]

The point was made with little diplomatic tact but with a certainty born of personal experience: the NKVD had checked and rechecked Czapski's identity dozens of times in Starobelsk and Griazovets. He had filled in questionnaires and watched as interrogating officers noted his words during multiple interviews. He knew for certain that if there was one Soviet body that was not only meticulously well-organised but positively obsessed with record-keeping, it was the NKVD.

The British Military Mission was temporarily housed in premises belonging to the Yugoslav legation. During the time he spent working here Czapski fell further under the spell of the British, whose unflappable poise made a profound impression on him. They seemed to possess a sense of almost mystical certainty which was in profound contrast to the perpetual incertitude of being a Pole:

> We were in the dark-panelled dining room at the Yugoslav legation. At a given moment the Mess President…rose to his feet and gave the traditional toast: 'Gentlemen – the King!' These simple words, expressing homage to their king and country, uttered in the middle of ice-bound Moscow, moved me more deeply than I should have thought possible.

Czapski was a man of exceptional character who had a tendency to see his own goodness reflected in others. Poetically rather than politically minded, his admiration for the British blinded him to the pragmatism and essential self-interest of their political decisions. When Brigadier General Mason MacFarlane forwarded a copy of Czapski's report to London he added the following observation:

> There is not the slightest doubt that the NKVD must know what has happened to these Poles as the most detailed nominal rolls and information are kept up at every concentration camp and prison… I am in close touch with Czapski but propose to keep us out entirely of this business, which is a purely Polish-Russian affair.[4]

This follows a line MacFarlane had suggested in earlier communications to the Foreign Office in relation to Poland's search for its missing citizens: 'We've got to keep out of the affair as much as we can, and when we do intervene we must remember that Russia can help us to beat Hitler, and not Poland.'[5] MacFarlane's view was to be echoed later in the official British government's response to the discovery of the bodies at Katyń.

When Czapski finally received his reply it came – as these things always did – at night. He was summoned to the Lubyanka and ordered to report to the waiting room, after which he would be taken to see Major Raikhman.

The central block of the Lubyanka boasted a large, imposing entrance with glass doors and, inside, a deep piled carpet of vivid red. Passing several guards wearing ankle-length overcoats and pointed caps, Czapski was led through various corridors into a lift and, finally, into a small ante-room where – to his great surprise – he came upon Major Khodas, the last commander of Griazovets, also apparently waiting to see Raikhman. Khodas was called inside before him, leaving Czapski to reflect on the nature of this apparent coincidence. Had Khodas been summoned to supply information about him?

When Czapski was finally called into Raikhman's office, he saw before him 'a thin man of middle size, with a distinguished face and well-kept hands' whose manner throughout the conversation was polite but icy. Following NKVD practice a second man was present, a uniformed

NKVD officer who stood with his back to the light and said nothing throughout the conversation. Czapski handed Raikhman his report, then waited in silence as the Russian read it through with absorbed attention, following each word and each line with a pencil. 'Not a muscle quivered. Raikhman's pencil moved steadily on to the very end. He made not a single note, underlined not a single word.' Finally, Raikhman addressed his visitor:

> Without raising his eyes, and in a clipped voice, he remarked that this business – about which he knew nothing – was not really his concern, but that for the sake of General Anders he was prepared to look into it. He would communicate with me in a few days' time when he hoped to be in possession of the required information. The tall man with the broad shoulders standing in the shadow cast by the curtain still maintained his earlier silence. I begged General Raikhman to facilitate my task of getting an interview with Beria or Merkulov.[6] With, perhaps, rather too feverish an air of eagerness, I added certain comments, and quoted certain facts, which instinctively, desperately, I hoped might bring the discussion on to a more human level. To all I said General Raikhman replied with the same icy and laconic politeness. He very much doubted whether I should be able to see either of the two officials. As a matter of fact, he said, Merkulov was not, at the moment, in Moscow. General Zhukov, to whom General Anders' second letter was addressed, also happened to be away – in Turkestan, whither he had gone on business connected with the organisation of the Polish army. It was impossible to say when he would return. In these circumstances the only thing for me to do was to leave the letters with Raikhman.

The interview was over. Czapski may not have understood Major Raikhman's precise role in the NKVD (he was head of the NKVD's Polish office), but he was well aware Raikhman had been in charge of the Polish section of the Lubyanka and was intimately involved in all matters pertaining to Polish POWs. He could not plausibly plead ignorance of the fate of 14,500 missing men.

On his way out Czapski bumped into Major Khodas. As they left the Lubyanka together, crossing Dzerzhinsky Square, Czapski reminded Khodas of Griazovets, where the pair had enjoyed a relatively cordial relationship in the final months. On an impulse he asked Khodas to join him for lunch, hoping to persuade him to talk.

> But Khodas hurried at breakneck speed along the slippery pavement of the Dzerzhinsky Square. I could feel that he was as terrified of me as the Devil is of Holy Water and that he was seeking the first excuse to get away. Quite politely but very firmly he declined to arrange any further meeting. He was not, he said, living in Moscow. It would be utterly impossible for him to see me again. I went back to the Hotel Metropole. What more could I do?

One has to admire Czapski's optimism. Despite everything he had learned about the NKVD since his capture he never gave up hoping that one day he would be able to form a simple human bond with one of their men.

Czapski waited a further twelve long days for his next summons from Raikhman. His papers for Moscow were about to expire when he was woken late one night by the ringing of the telephone:

> General Raikhman in person was on the line. He had tried, he said, to ring me three times without success and expressed surprise that the hotel staff, though informed that I was the person he wanted, had failed to find me. He would very much have liked to see me again but had, unfortunately, to leave Moscow next morning, so that any further meeting was now out of the question. His voice was friendly, charming, even cordial. Finally, he came to the point. He had looked into the matter we had discussed and had been assured that all documents relating to Polish prisoners of war had been forwarded by the NKVD to NKID (the Russian Foreign Office). He advised me, therefore, to go back to Kuybyshev and apply for information either to Comrade Vyshinsky or to Comrade Novikov. 'Or maybe you have done so already?' he asked in a tone that sounded a little too innocent.

Czapski attempted to explain that Ambassador Kot had spoken to Vyshinsky on multiple occasions about this very matter. As he spoke, it dawned on him that Raikhman's only purpose in calling him was to get rid of him without offending General Anders. Raikhman continued the conversation, informing Czapski helpfully that he had received information concerning a large number of prisoners of war who had recently been moved south-wards to the army at Irkutsk. Czapski responded that he was aware of this but these men were from different camps. 'Is that really so?' he said. 'How unfortunate it is that I'm not really up on all this and so cannot give you the information you want.'

The conversation concluded with Raikhman cordially informing Czapski that he had authorised an extension to his permit: Czapski was welcome to remain in Moscow for as long as he desired, although the best course of action – in Raikhman's view – was to go back to Kuybyshev and contact Vyshinsky. Czapski's mission in Moscow was over. Behind Raikhman's polite obfuscations lay a silence which Czapski now realised he would never penetrate. There was nothing more he could do except return to General Anders to confess that in the many weeks he had spent in Kuybyshev and Moscow he had learned precisely nothing.

The NKVD made sure Czapski left Moscow in style. They issued him with several bottles of good wine, white bread, sausages and jam, and booked him a place on a train in the category of seat reserved for the privileged: 'soft with reservation' (the other categories being, in descending order of desirability, 'soft without reservation', 'hard with reservation' and – least coveted – 'hard without reservation').

It was now February 1942. Czapski had been away for almost two months. In his absence the army had moved south to Uzbekistan, its headquarters at Yangiyul, close to Tashkent. The move, which took place between 15 January and 25 February, had been made at General Sikorski's request so that Polish forces could benefit from the milder climate rather than freez-ing in tents. Being closer to the southern border would also make it easier for the British to supply the Poles from Iran or India. The Polish army in the Soviet Union was finally beginning to take shape. Czapski wrapped up his work at the embassy and then set out to rejoin the army and report his findings to General Anders.

Czapski left Buzuluk in deepest winter. When he arrived in Yangiyul, 1,300 miles farther south, it was almost spring. Staff headquarters occupied a large house set in the middle of a fine orchard of apple, cherry, peach and apricot trees that sloped down towards a small river. Nearby was a cluster of small white houses with terraces in which General Anders and some of the senior officers lived. The rest of the staff were either accommodated in tents or billeted with locals. It was a pleasant setting to work in and Czapski did his best to take up where he had left off. He continued recording the names of men who could not be found, but he no longer felt the same energetic determination to pursue his task. His failed mission to Moscow had left him disheartened, increasingly convinced he would never unlock the mystery of his missing comrades. It was just at this moment that a new piece of information came to light.

In the early spring of 1942 two former residents of the Villa of Bliss, Colonel Gorczyński and Lieutenant Colonel Bukojemski, approached Czapski. They had heard of his search for the missing officers and wanted to report the conversation between Beria and Berling which had taken place in Moscow in October 1940, highlighting Beria's mysterious reply to Berling's request for access to the officers of Kozelsk and Starobelsk. As discussed earlier, there are several versions of this conversation, but the central message remains the same: *My zdjielali bolshuyu oshibku* – 'We made a big mistake.' Czapski immediately went to see General Anders and told him what he had heard.

> Anders listened to me without blinking an eyelid. Seated in front of his desk, he looked not at me but the window. He did not want to discourage me from pursuing my investigations, but neither was he willing to hide from me what he believed to be the truth. I saw upon his face a flicker of hesitation. 'You know,' he said after a moment's pause, as though speaking to himself, 'I think of them all as comrades and friends whom we have lost in action.'

The first piece of relevant information to come to Czapski since he began his quest confirmed nothing. Nobody could yet define the precise meaning of the 'big mistake' to which Beria referred. But the mystery surrounding the men's absence had now grown darker. General Anders was the first person to articulate a possibility which until now Czapski had been unwilling to contemplate: that he might never see his friends from Starobelsk again.

Journey from Griazovets camp to the Polish army
and out of the USSR, 1941–2.

15

EVACUATION

SINCE ITS INCEPTION THE SITUATION OF THE POLISH ARMY IN the USSR had been precarious, but from the beginning of January 1942 things grew steadily worse. The move south had not been an unqualified success: the camps were scattered over a vast area, making transport and communication difficult, and the warmth brought with it deadly outbreaks of malaria, typhus and dysentery.[1] The army now stood at almost 80,000 and was still growing. General Anders needed to feed the ever-increasing numbers of soldiers (as well as the civilians who were sharing their rations), but Stalin was refusing to supply them. If something did not change soon they would starve to death. Stalin, meanwhile, was becoming impatient with the Poles and their endless demands. He wanted them to fight, but General Anders claimed that his men were not yet ready for battle. This was true, but Anders also feared the Soviets would divide his men up between larger units, thus undermining the agreed notion of a fully Polish army under Polish command.[2] Matters came to a head during a meeting between General Anders and Stalin on 18 March 1942. Stalin threatened to reduce Polish rations to 26,000 before relenting slightly and raising his offer to 44,000. When Anders asked what would happen to the 30–40,000 Poles who would go unfed under such a plan, Stalin suggested they could be sent to work on collective farms, a path Anders refused to contemplate. Finally, they arrived at a compromise: Stalin agreed to allow 40,000 Polish soldiers to be evacuated to Iran, where the British could supply them. The Russians would supply those remaining in the USSR.[3]

At the same meeting Anders again raised the question of the missing officers. 'I do not know where they are,' responded Stalin. 'Why should we keep them? It may be that they were in camps in territories which have been taken by the Germans and come to be dispersed.'⁴ This reply, subtly different from previous ones and doubtless reflecting the changing face of the war, was later to form the basis of the official Soviet version of events.

The first evacuation took place in March–April 1942. Boats left from Krasnovodsk (now Turkmenbashi) in Turkmenistan, crossing the Caspian Sea to arrive in the port of Pahlavi (now Bandar Anzali). General Zhukov ran the evacuation from the Soviet side, demonstrating once again just how efficient the NKVD could be when it came to moving large numbers of people. On the Polish side the evacuation was overseen by Lieutenant Colonel Zygmunt Berling.

A total of 45,000 Polish military personnel were evacuated between the end of March and early April 1942, along with over 16,000 civilian adults and 9,500 children.⁵ The large number of Polish civilians arriving in Pahlavi caused considerable alarm to the British, who felt they had been 'bamboozled' by the Poles.⁶ They soon discovered that the Polish government had also been left largely in the dark by General Anders, who was determined to get as many people out of the Soviet Union as possible and was willing to ignore orders to achieve his aim. The presence of thousands of malnourished, sickly refugees, mainly women and children, presented a huge challenge to the British and Polish authorities, who had to find somewhere to put them. Eventually the British government came to an agreement with the governments of the East African British territories to allow families to settle temporarily in Kenya, Uganda and Tanganyika, as well as North and South Rhodesia and South Africa. India accepted 11,000 unaccompanied children. The Mexican government also agreed to host several thousand Poles.⁷

After the first evacuation the Soviet authorities increasingly found ways of obstructing further recruitment to the army, notably by insisting that Polish citizens of Jewish, Ukrainian or Belorussian origin from eastern Poland were Soviet citizens and therefore ineligible to join. Despite this, the army soon swelled to over 45,000 men and women, at which point Stalin reminded the Poles that he had agreed to a ceiling of 44,000 and recruitment must therefore cease. By now Anders was desperate to get the rest of the army out of the Soviet Union. He pressed Sikorski repeatedly, stressing the appalling conditions in which the Polish divisions were living.

Sikorski had hoped that a sizeable Polish military presence alongside the Red Army would allow Poland greater influence when the moment came to liberate their country from the Nazis, but the ongoing discussions in London about the future Polish–Soviet border were going badly; relations with Stalin were steadily deteriorating. Eventually, Sikorski asked the British and Americans to intervene with Stalin, as a result of which, in July 1942, Stalin agreed to allow the remaining Polish troops to be transferred to Iran, presenting the move as a magnanimous concession on his part to aid the British in Egypt.[8] In reality, Stalin had had enough of the 'reactionary' Polish army and was glad to see the back of it. The Battle of Stalingrad was just getting under way. After months on the back foot, the Red Army was about to fight its greatest battle.

The second evacuation took place in August–September 1942. Once again, Anders chose to ignore orders to leave civilians behind. Out of 44,000 evacuees, 11,000 were civilians.[9]

Just before he left for Iran in the first evacuation, Officer Cadet (now Lieutenant) Zdzisław Peszkowski bumped into Zygmunt Berling in Krasnovodsk. The two had formed an unlikely friendship in Griazovets and for a while Berling (described by Peszkowski as 'a very cultured man') taught Peszkowski English. Many times during their lengthy conversations Berling had attempted to convince his young friend to cooperate with the NKVD. His words fell on deaf ears, Peszkowski owning up to twin hatreds, 'one of the Bolsheviks, the other of the Germans'. But they remained close despite their political differences. On one occasion Berling begged Peszkowski to remember, when people spoke about his behaviour in the future, that 'I was not a pig. I also love Poland.' Peszkowski did not understand Berling's words but dared not question the older officer about their meaning.[10]

When the two men met again in March 1942 Berling called Peszkowski to his quarters and asked him if he had any local currency to use in Iran. When Peszkowski told him he only had roubles, Berling gave him some cash to share with his comrades once they left the Soviet Union. Peszkowski was deeply touched by this generous gesture and the two men parted warmly. As they did so, Berling asked Peszkowski to remember what he had said to him in Griazovets. Still baffled by Berling's cryptic words, Peszkowski promised he would bear it in mind. It was only later, in August, when news reached him of Berling's decision to desert his post and remain behind in the Soviet Union, that he finally understood what his friend had been trying to tell him.[11]

From September 1942 the Soviets stopped all further recruitment to the Polish army and refused any additional evacuations. Polish citizens unable to get out in time had to survive as best they could. Many of them ended up joining the Kościuszko Infantry Division in the Red Army after its formation in May 1943 in the hope of finding a route back to Poland.

After Czapski's fruitless trip to Moscow the Polish authorities had not entirely ceased their quest for answers on the missing officers. Between March and August 1942 several notes, memoranda and aide-memoires on the subject were exchanged between the two governments. The Soviet stance varied little from their previous line of claiming that the prisoners had either left for home, escaped abroad or died along the way. Once the Polish army left the Soviet Union the matter inevitably ceased to be an active subject of discussion on an official level. The Polish ministry of foreign affairs in London raised the question one last time in diplomatic correspondence on 27 August 1942 in a note simply recording the difficulties encountered by the Polish government in trying to track down the missing men.

It was perhaps fortunate for his own state of mind that around this time Józef Czapski took on a new role which would occupy him for the remainder of the war. In April 1942 General Anders appointed him head of the Army Propaganda Service. His responsibilities were extensive: he was to oversee publication of the army's two printed bulletins, plus the weekly journal *The White Eagle*, as well as looking after cultural relations with the Russians, the supply of news, the cinematographic and photographic sections of the propaganda service, publicity, the design and printing of posters, provision of music and entertainment, training of military orchestras, and the education of the young. The task was enormous but a welcome diversion from the hopeless quest on which Czapski had been engaged for so long. It also meant he could choose his own staff. For the next two years Czapski surrounded himself with the kind of people he liked best: intellectuals and artists, men and women who shared his interests and outlook, not one of

*General Anders (in beret) with Józef Czapski
on his left, Monte Cassino 1944.*

them a professional soldier. With characteristic fair-mindedness, Czapski was even prepared to admit that there was a lot the Poles could learn from the Soviets when it came to propaganda.

Czapski remained in Yangiyul until the summer, busy with his new job. He had not forgotten his comrades. There was one last thread of hope to which he clung: July and August were the only months when boats could cross the Arctic Ocean from the distant islands of Franz Josef Land. But still nobody appeared. In July 1942 the strain of the past three years took its toll; Czapski fell ill with a combination of typhoid and malaria. He was transferred to a hospital at Ak-Altyn where he spent several blissful weeks recuperating, seated outside the little hospital where he could admire the beauty of the Tashkent landscape as he ate fresh fruit and fielded visits from concerned friends. By the end of August he was well enough to make the journey to Iran. Along with a group of orphaned Polish children he travelled by road across the mountains in the last convoy to leave the USSR. When he arrived in al-Mashad on 3 September 1942 the children were taken to a Polish reception centre where they would stay until a convoy could be arranged to take them to refugee camps in India. The reception centre was under the care of an eminent Polish paediatrician, Professor Kopeć, a former prisoner of Kozelsk and Griazovets.

In al-Mashad Czapski succumbed to a further bout of illness that delayed his departure for Iraq. He recovered slowly, dividing his time between long hours of rest in his hotel room and solitary excursions onto the city streets. Here, he discovered an exhilarating new culture that was in complete contrast to the country he had left behind. After three years of Soviet grey he rediscovered his passion for colour: it exploded around him in the clothes people wore, in the sparkling gems for sale in the markets, in the brilliant blue sky. The sheer, raw power of humanity in the bustling streets excited him, just as the terrible poverty appalled him.

It was only now, in this foreign city, that Czapski was able to accept that this important chapter in his life was finally over. He had left the Soviet Union for good. The fear that had weighed on him constantly for the past three years had vanished. To mark this new beginning he bought himself a new notebook (as writers do), choosing one with a turquoise blue cover and a Persian inscription in gold. In the long, humid afternoons in his hotel room he began to write the memoir that would become one of the most important testimonies of Polish wartime experience in the USSR, *The Inhuman Land*:

> I could finally write down everything I could remember, everything that, in spite of my well-nigh indecipherable handwriting, I had never, while in Russia, dared to mention except indirectly, or in code. Here, in the midst of golden minarets, of blue and gilded domes, among the human tides of Persians, Arabs and Hindus, I could drive deeper and deeper, for several hours each day, into my Soviet memories.[12]

For the men who emerged alive from Kozelsk, Starobelsk and Ostashkov the Soviet episode was finally at an end. Over the next few months their lives were to be entirely taken up by the business of training and preparing to return to the war. From Iran the army was transferred to Iraq, where it was absorbed into the British Army under the command of General Sir Henry Maitland Wilson. Headquarters were in Qizil Rabat, with the bulk of the army based near Khanaqin, 125 miles north of Baghdad.

Józef Czapski, Bronisław Młynarski, Dr Zbigniew Godlewski, Zdzisław Peszkowski, Jan Bober, Josef Lis, Dr Salomon Słowes, Tadeusz Felsztyn, General Wołkowicki, Major Domoń and all the other men of Griazovets were absorbed into army life. The mystery of their missing comrades was temporarily put aside.

16

THE WITNESS

They were transferring not only persons but our personal files. The thing
that struck me at that moment, even if I could not explain it, was the fact
that my file was of a different colour from the files of the other prisoners....
I cannot remember the colours, but it seems to me that all the files were
red while mine was white.[1]

BEFORE ADVANCING IN THE CHRONOLOGY OF EVENTS, WE MUST
turn back briefly to examine the role of a single former prisoner of Kozelsk
camp. Like Józef Czapski, he was to play a vital role in the unfolding narrative of the missing men.

In September 1939, reserve Lieutenant Stanisław Swianiewicz was captured, along with a group of around a hundred officers (including General
Wołkowicki, Colonel Künstler and Lieutenant Colonel Tyszyński) in a small
village close to Lwów following his regiment's retreat from Piotrków. They
were imprisoned first in Putyvl in Ukraine then, in October 1939, handed
over to the NKVD and taken to Kozelsk. When he first arrived in Kozelsk
Swianiewicz concealed his true identity. Only in March 1940 did the NKVD
discover, through a chance comment of one of his friends, that they had in
their hands a distinguished professor of economics from the Stefan Batory
University in Wilno.[2]

Swianiewicz had established his reputation in the 1930s with two important pieces of research. The first gained him his doctorate; its subject was
the Soviet economy and it was published as a book, *Lenin as an Economist*,
in 1930. His next book, *The Economic Policies of Nazi Germany*, published
in 1938, was the result of an extensive period of research in Germany in
1936–37. Unexpectedly summoned to an interview with NKVD Major Vasily
Zarubin in March 1940, Swianiewicz could not work out what interested

Stanisław Swianiewicz, Jerusalem 1943.

Zarubin most. His first instinct was that it must be his research into the Soviet economy.

Józef Czapski's memoirs show us a man motivated above all by his dedication to art and his profound faith in humanity. He *sees* and *feels* the world around him, his writings packed with observations about colour and light. When he describes his lost comrades he vividly evokes his joy in their character, his pain at their absence. His quest among the bigwigs of the NKVD reveals his almost naive insistence in believing the best of others. Like Bronisław Młynarski when he tried to engage his NKVD interrogator in Starobelsk on the subject of music, Czapski searched tirelessly for the human being behind the NKVD uniform. Stanisław Swianiewicz is at the other intellectual extreme: possessed of a highly analytical mind, he observes events in meticulous detail, weighing up the evidence before him with lawyerly precision. Where Czapski is perpetually baffled by the behaviour of the individual NKVD officials he encounters, Swianiewicz applies himself to understanding the system itself that holds his fate in its unfeeling hands. That is not to say that Swianiewicz felt his situation with any less intensity than Czapski. He simply applied his skills as an economist and academic, just as Czapski applied his as a painter and writer.

When he left Kozelsk camp on 29 April 1940 on a transport of just over 400 men Swianiewicz was surprised to observe that it was not just the prisoners who were being transferred but also their personal files. He had no idea what this meant, but he knew that these records contained all the information on the officers gathered by the Special Section since their arrival, including notes from interrogations and the prisoners' own responses to the questionnaires. He also noticed that his own file was a different colour to the rest, and that their new escorts behaved far more brutally than the guards inside the camp.

The prisoners were taken to a railway siding where six prison carriages, the infamous *stolypinkas*, awaited them. Fourteen men squeezed into a compartment designed for eight; the doors were locked. After a short delay the train set off, heading west. So far, so good: west meant the border; it meant home, just as the NKVD had promised. When the train arrived at Smolensk early the following morning there was nothing to suggest that anything was amiss. They were still going in the right direction. After another delay the train continued for a few miles, stopped again, waited, moved off again, covered another ten miles, before finally grinding to a halt at a small station named Gnezdovo.

> From outside we could hear the sound of movement of a large number of people, the sound of running motors and the abrupt voices of command. There was no window in our compartment; therefore, it was difficult to find out where we were and what was happening outside. From compartment to compartment they started giving the news that the disembarkation had begun.

Swianiewicz waited in the crowded compartment, listening to the sounds of the neighbouring wagons emptying onto the platform outside. After about half an hour an NKVD colonel appeared in the doorway looking for prisoner Swianiewicz. 'Identify yourself, collect your things and come with me.' Swianiewicz's comrades watched in silence as he fumbled for his belongings and pushed his way towards the door. An NKVD colonel bringing a message in person. What did it mean?

The initial order came from Moscow just two days before Swianiewicz left Kozelsk. On 27 April Captain Gertsovsky of the 1st Special Department of the NKVD wrote to the Deputy Head of NKVD Prisoner of War Affairs, Ivan Khokhlov, passing on a directive from Merkulov himself: Stanisław Swianiewicz and another prisoner, Michał Romm from Ostashkov, were to be held back from the transports.[3] This was followed on 28 April by a telegram with more detailed instructions:

> On the instruction of USSR People's Commissar of Internal Affairs Com. Beria, I request you to issue an instruction on the transit by stages to Moscow, to the interior prison of the USSR NKVD, to the charge of the 2nd Department of the GUGB[4] of prisoner of war Stanisław Swianiewicz, born 1899 (file no. 4287), who is being held in Kozelsk camp. Please inform me of the day of dispatch.[5]

The order arrived too late to hold Swianiewicz back in Kozelsk. Instead, they caught up with him en route.

As he emerged from the prison wagon Swianiewicz was struck by the beautiful spring scene before him: the warm breeze that carried the scent of the nearby forest, the brilliant blue sky, the little patches of snow melting into the earth. He also noticed that the station was deserted: there were no railway employees in sight, no passengers waiting on the platform; the train locomotive had already gone. On the other side something was happening, he could not see what. The colonel took Swianiewicz to one of the empty railway carriages and told him to find himself a place inside before leaving him with a guard, whom he instructed to bring tea. The soldier brought Swianiewicz a kettle of boiling water into which he put some tea. 'I took out sugar, bread and herring, given to us the previous day, and I ate breakfast, which – under the conditions of Soviet prison transport – could be called a bountiful meal.'

After his breakfast, Swianiewicz pretended he wanted to lie down and climbed onto the luggage shelf near the ceiling where there was a small opening in the window. Every time the guard looked away Swianiewicz peered outside. He saw a road leading away from the railway tracks at a right angle. Along the road stood a row of NKVD guards with bayonets. After a while a small bus with whitewashed windows approached. It backed up to the nearest railway carriage, a group of prisoners stepped into it, the bus drove off. After about half an hour it returned to take the next contingent. In charge of the operation was the NKVD colonel who had separated Swianiewicz from his companions. Another large, box-shaped car was parked nearby which Swianiewicz recognised as a 'black raven' – a prison van. After several hours the colonel returned. He ordered Swianiewicz out of the train and into the prison van. Inside were three narrow cells, each with a low bench, and two seats for the guards. The doors slammed, leaving Swianiewicz crouching in absolute darkness. As the car started moving, he made the sign of the cross. 'The thought struck my mind that I was going to be executed.'

After a short journey the van pulled up outside a small building with barred basement windows. In answer to Swianiewicz's question, 'Where am I?' an NKVD captain politely informed him that he was in the internal prison of the NKVD in Smolensk, then led him to the basement, to an empty cell big enough to house thirty prisoners. The guard brought him a mattress, bed sheets, blankets and pillows, and told him he could choose any bed and sleep as much as he wanted. A dinner of bread, sugar and tea followed. He was even allowed to purchase extra sugar and butter from the prison store. The captain asked if he would like some books.

Swianiewicz spent five days in the Smolensk prison enjoying the relative luxury of cleanliness, space, decent food and books in a solitude which puzzled and disturbed him. The prison appeared to be empty: he could hear no footsteps, no voices except that of the guard. The day after his arrival was the May Day holiday, its festive spirit marked by the appearance of the NKVD captain with some books for him to read (on polar expeditions and Soviet investments in the Far North) and a friendly conversation on the subject of the captain's granddaughter, upon whom he clearly doted. When Swianiewicz asked why he had been separated from his comrades the captain replied that he did not know. He was just the commander of the prison. 'As far as he could tell, he considered that I must be some kind of a "great man" because the Soviet government was interested in me, so obviously I had to be treated differently from other Polish officers.' When asked why this 'special interest' had been expressed through his arrest, the captain replied, 'You are not under arrest.'

> He explained that he had received an order to hold me for a certain time until further orders as to my fate would come from Moscow. What he was able to do in this situation, he did. He could not place me in a hotel because he did not have the means of guarding me there, nor did he have the funds for it in his budget. So he decided to place me in the internal prison of the

NKVD where from time to time they used to place Soviet people of high
rank, and in this way he made sure that I was comfortable.

Swianiewicz concluded that the NKVD captain genuinely knew nothing
either about his own status or the destination of his comrades. He was left
to turn over in his mind the scenes he had witnessed from the train: the
guards with bayonets, the whitewashed windows of the bus, the absence
of any onlookers or local people. Like the men of Griazovets, Swianiewicz
concluded that his comrades must have been taken to a different camp
elsewhere while he had been singled out for further investigation. Whether
this was good or bad he did not yet know.

On 5 May 1940 Swianiewicz was transferred from Smolensk to the
Lubyanka prison in Moscow. Here, he was photographed, fingerprinted
and – for the first time since his capture – subjected to a full body
search, including a rectal examination. After a pleasantly warm shower
(the baths of Moscow's two most notorious prisons – Lubyanka and
Butyrka – enjoyed a reputation among prisoners for relative luxury), he
was given clean undergarments and his clothes were returned to him,
still hot from disinfection.

For the first forty-eight hours in the Lubyanka Swianiewicz was kept in
solitary confinement in a basement area known as the *pryomnik* (which
translates roughly as 'acceptor' – a kind of reception or preparation area).
There was barely enough room to stand in the small windowless cell, lit day
and night by a single light bulb. The peephole in the door – the *'judas'* –
would slide open at regular intervals, revealing the guard's eye. Since there
was only room for the prisoner to sit or lie on the bed, Swianiewicz spent
much of his time lying down, his arms over the blanket as he had been
instructed, in a state bordering sleep and waking. From the corridor he
could hear other prisoners moaning. At first he thought these were sound
effects, part of a deliberate policy to terrify inmates into confession, but
eventually concluded that they were genuine.

Swianiewicz passed the time in reflection, surprised by his own sense
of calm, in striking contrast to the panic he had felt on leaving Kozelsk. He
later surmised that this was the primary purpose of the *pryomnik*: to alle-
viate anxiety in prisoners so that they would be in a suitable state of mind
for the questioning that would inevitably follow. The guards were polite,

they allowed prisoners to leave their cells to go to the toilet, the food was passable, they could sleep when they wanted. There were even rumours that the food was drugged.

Swianiewicz knew the Lubyanka was not a regular prison. Situated as it was right next to the main administrative centre of the NKVD, its purpose was to investigate cases in which the NKVD's top officials were especially interested. Prisoners were held here only for as long as those interests were active and relevant; after that, they were transferred to other prisons such as Butyrka. Swianiewicz waited, lying on his bed with little to do except eat the food that appeared at regular intervals, hungrily accepting the second helpings offered each time. As he waited he tried to work out which elements in his past life could be of such particular interest to the NKVD. There was no shortage of angles from which he might be viewed as an enemy of the Soviet state: in 1918 in Russia he had belonged to the Polish Military Organisation (a secret intelligence organisation created by Józef Piłsudski in 1914 during his campaign for Polish independence[6]). In 1919 he was operating against the Soviets in Latvia. At Wilno University he had studied the problems of the Soviet economy and been instrumental in setting up the Centre for Soviet Studies attached to the Institute of Eastern Europe, one of the first institutes of Sovietology in the world. During his research for his thesis he had sometimes been critical of the Soviet Five-Year Plan. But the most likely source of the NKVD's intense interest in him, he concluded, was his participation in a group known as the 'Wilno Federalists', who believed that the rebuilding of Poland after World War I should go hand in hand with that of neighbouring nations such as Ukraine, Belorussia, Lithuania, Latvia and Estonia. Their aim was to form a federation or commonwealth of independent nations, including (but not being ruled by) Poland. This programme had put the Wilno Federalists in direct conflict not just with Russian imperialism but also Polish nationalism.

After two days in the *pryomnik* Swianiewicz was moved to another cell in the main part of the Lubyanka. He was to remain here until December 1940.

A few days after his arrival in the new cell Swianiewicz was taken for a nocturnal interrogation, an experience repeated at irregular intervals over the next eight months. Prisoners in the Lubyanka were led to their investigations in a very particular manner: their hands were placed behind their backs; the escort on the left took the right wrist while the escort on the right took the left, thus producing pressure in the small of the back. After a warning, the group of three would run through the prison corridors, slowing down as they crossed into the offices of the NKVD. This method is mentioned by one of the Villa of Bliss residents, Captain Rosen-Zawadzki, who recalled an incident when he was mistakenly taken for interview in the 'typical' manner instead of walking freely as he and his companions were usually permitted to do.[7]

During his first interview at the Lubyanka Swianiewicz learned he was being charged with espionage. The document handed to him by the Soviet prosecutor also explained that he was no longer a prisoner of war but an offender who had acted against the Soviet state. 'Appropriate passages from the Book of Statutes were given to me to read which prescribed the highest degree of punishment for this crime; that is, execution.' To his protestations that he was not a Soviet citizen the prosecutor replied that 'hostile deeds committed anywhere in the world against the Soviet Union are punishable by the Soviet State'. His Polish citizenship was meaningless, he was told, since the Polish state no longer existed. The differentiation between prisoners of war and criminals has been noted previously. The fact that the Soviets apparently viewed Swianiewicz's Polish citizenship as meaningless is interesting. The Soviets had been designating Polish citizens of Ukrainian, Belorussian and Jewish origin as Soviet citizens since November 1939. In August 1940 Lithuania (including its capital, Swianiewicz's home city of Wilno) was fully incorporated into the Soviet Union. Only after November 1941 were ethnic Polish citizens stranded in the USSR told that their Polish citizenship was no longer recognised.

The accusations against Swianiewicz were broadly as follows: cooperation with Polish Intelligence when he led the study of the Soviet Economy at the Institute of Eastern Europe in Wilno before the war; again during his 1937 trip to Germany and his subsequent book about the economic policy of Hitlerite Germany. Time after time during his eight-month stay Swianiewicz was asked by a variety of investigators to disclose the names of Polish intelligence agents sent to Russia. The demand was put in different forms, sometimes involving physical threat (pushing him against a wall), at other times in a more persuasive tone: 'Tell us everything you know, clear your conscience and you'll see, it will be lighter on your heart.' It was the invitation of a priest to a sinner to unburden his soul through confession.

Swianiewicz made it clear to his inquisitors that he had no reason to hide anything: his activities had always been open, he had lectured at university, published books and written articles, and had often spoken to people with communist sympathies. Why, therefore, he reasoned, would Polish Intelligence entrust its secrets to such a garrulous character? As the investigation progressed he became convinced that of the two charges – spying against Russia and spying against Germany – the second was of more interest to his interrogators. More than anything, it was his book on Nazi economic policy that had created the most intense interest in the upper echelons of the NKVD. This impression was confirmed when the examining magistrate ordered him to submit a written account of the methods used by the Germans to finance their rearmament. From this moment on Swianiewicz was no longer taken for questioning but led late in the evening to an investigator's office where throughout the following night he wrote down what he knew about the 'economic model of German rearmament', essentially recapitulating the contents of his book.

Swianiewicz's investigation began in May 1940 and continued throughout the autumn and winter of 1940, a period coinciding with the NKVD's change of strategy regarding Germany and their search for Polish officers to cooperate within the structures of the Red Army. Whether their interest in him had initially been motivated by his knowledge of the Nazi economy or whether the emphasis of the investigation changed along with Soviet policy we cannot know. However, by Christmas 1940 the NKVD had evidently concluded that his potential as a source of useful intelligence was exhausted because they transferred him from the Lubyanka to Butyrka prison. As they moved him, Swianiewicz overheard someone speaking Polish. It is possible that this was one of the prisoners in General Przeździecki's group: they were taken from the Lubyanka to Butyrka at the same time.

Swianiewicz had learned much about the workings of the Lubyanka during his eight-month stay. The conditions in which he and a revolving cast of four cellmates lived were reasonable. Food rations were adequate and they were supplied with books from a well-stocked prison library (apparently created shortly after the revolution from books confiscated from the homes of executed members of the bourgeoisie). Each prisoner had the right to borrow six books over a ten-day period. The reading matter was varied and of high quality, although no books in foreign languages were allowed, nor any political works, including Marx and Lenin. Inevitably, much of the prisoners' time was spent either reading or discussing what they had read. Most of his cellmates were engineers and industry administrators from every corner of the Soviet Union – Georgians, Tartars, Armenians – many of whom had formerly held important roles in the Soviet state. One cellmate confessed to Swianiewicz that the average time a person held a high-ranking post in a large Soviet conglomerate was four years.

> During that time, generally, something would happen so that they would end up in prison and, eventually, in a Gulag. They had to live in constant nervous tension because of chronic shortages of supplies and all kinds of structural defects, but all these inconveniences and risks were worth taking because of a high standard of living and the satisfaction they obtained from being in a position of power.

Being a prisoner in the Lubyanka, nevertheless, was acknowledged by all his cellmates as preferable to being in other Soviet prisons such as the notorious Lefortovo, where inmates were tortured. Some prisoners even referred to the Lubyanka as a 'sanatorium', because it provided a respite from the beatings they were subjected to elsewhere.

It was through his conversations with fellow prisoners that Swianiewicz learned more about the brutal regime of Beria's predecessor, Nikolai Yezhov, head of the NKVD between 1936 and 1938 and a key figure in Stalin's Great Terror. Stalin dismissed Yezhov from his post in late 1938, ordered his arrest in April 1939 and had him executed on 4 February 1940. Many prisoners told Swianiewicz that the appointment of Beria as Yezhov's replacement had led to a relative relaxation in NKVD methods of oppression. During the purges, the NKVD evoked such terror in the population that they entirely lost their ability to orient themselves about what was happening in the country because arrestees were so terrified they immediately began to confess to the most fantastical crimes. As a result, it became impossible to distinguish truth from fiction: the NKVD could not discover the shortcomings of industry when every arrested manager of a Soviet enterprise pleaded guilty to sabotage and was ready to write a paper to prove his guilt. 'Beria was trying to put some kind of order into this madhouse and decided that, at least in the beginning of the investigations, it was necessary to bring those frightened people to some state of stability, so that one could talk sensibly with them.' This was not to say Beria was any less ruthless than Yezhov. On the contrary. Beria's main achievement was the rationalisation of Stalinist terror by introducing a systematic approach to the work of the NKVD. If Beria improved conditions in the labour camps and prisons it was not through any concern for the wellbeing of prisoners but because he wanted the Gulags to be more productive and the prisons to produce more confessions.

Not one of Swianiewicz's fellow prisoners had heard about the special camps for Polish officers.

Shortly after his arrival in Butyrka prison Swianiewicz was informed that the NKVD authorities had decided to bring his investigation to an end. The investigating officer set out their conclusions:

> In his opinion, there were certain contradictions in my case that were difficult to explain. The material collected from various people who knew me before the war seemed to indicate that my attitude towards the Soviet Union was more positive than could be concluded from my behaviour during the investigations. He told me that he himself had talked about my case with many people, and it transpired that my attitude was not at all counter-revolutionary, that I was a democrat characterised by tolerance, and that I had an understanding of social problems. In the meantime, from the material collected during the investigation, it came out that I was not sincere; that I gave evasive answers; that I did not want to tell everything that I knew about various pre-war affairs in Poland.

Swianiewicz found the NKVD's assessment remarkably accurate, even fair-minded, although the result was largely pre-ordained and bore little relation to any genuine charge of espionage. Before the war he had often been accused of harbouring Soviet sympathies because he was in favour of state intervention and believed the Polish political system should be based on the ideals of collective action. However, from a philosophical and moral point of view he rejected communism as wholeheartedly as he did nationalism.

At the end of February 1941 Swianiewicz formally received his sentence: eight years in a labour camp, to include the time since his arrest. He was transported via Kotlas to a camp in the Republic of Komi situated on a tributary of the Wym River, a region of taiga (subarctic forest) from which escape, in winter, was impossible. On arrival, he and a group of other new prisoners walked fifteen miles in -20°C to reach the camp. The gate bore the uplifting slogan: 'Moral rebirth of fallen people through the educational virtues of work.'

His abiding impression of that day was the sight of the Aurora Borealis against the dark sky.

17

ESCAPE

STANISŁAW SWIANIEWICZ'S STAY IN THE UST-WYMSK CAMPS lasted just over a year, from March 1941 to April 1942.[1] The first period took place between spring and summer and was relatively bearable. In August 1941 he was briefly released before being returned, along with another Polish officer, on the grounds that they were both excluded from the terms of the amnesty, most likely because in the eyes of the Soviet state they were convicted criminals as opposed to deportees. The second half of his stay coincided with winter and was 'gruesome' as he and his fellow prisoners endured famine in temperatures reaching -50°C. During the deepest part of winter, between January and March, prisoners frequently died in their sleep, their deaths only discovered at morning reveille when they failed to get up. Swianiewicz's fellow prisoners consisted mainly of citizens of the recently occupied Baltic countries and eastern Poland, as well as members of Soviet minorities of the USSR. There were a great many Chinese, Kazakhs, Tartars and Finns, as well as a large number of Polish Jews.

By February 1942 Swianiewicz's state of health was desperate: his legs were covered with lesions due to frostbite and he could barely walk. In camp terminology he was what was known as *dokhodiaga* ('coming to an end'). He attributed his survival to the actions of the Romanian camp doctor, who asked for Swianiewicz to be transferred to the camp hospital, officially on grounds of sickness but in reality because he needed a Russian speaker who could communicate with him in German to help with the backlog of death certificates. A female doctor, Dr Orlov, also managed to obtain the right for doctors to extend normal food rations to a percentage of prisoners regardless of the amount of work performed. Swianiewicz benefited from this change. He later discovered that this easing of conditions may well have been due to the intervention of the Polish embassy on his behalf. In early January 1942 some Polish Jews who had been released from the camp informed Professor Kot of Swianiewicz's presence there and his poor state of health, warning Kot that Swianiewicz was close to death. Given the urgency of the situation, Kot decided to bypass the proper diplomatic channels, instead contacting the commander of the Ust-Wymsk camps directly by telegram to demand Swianiewicz's release according to the terms of the amnesty and to ask that the prisoner be put on a plane to Kuybyshev at the embassy's expense. The camp administration would not release him without permission from the higher Soviet authorities, but they evidently realised it would be a good idea to keep him alive to avoid future recriminations. Swianiewicz was also helped by the kindness of one of his fellow prisoners, a sixty-year-old anarchist who worked as the caretaker of the disinfection building. This was a small chamber which fulfilled a triple function: disinfecting clothes, drying the clothes of prisoners who worked in the snow, and as a storage facility for dead bodies to be thawed when the doctor had been ordered to determine the cause of death. The caretaker told Swianiewicz that the warmth at the bottom of the chamber was very helpful against the cold, confessing he sometimes sneaked a prisoner inside to warm up. Seeing Swianiewicz's weakened state, the anarchist offered to let him try this method, so Swianiewicz started coming to the chamber and lying at the bottom alongside the dead bodies. 'After several hours of this cure, when one walked out, the frost did not seem so terrible.'

Swianiewicz's release in April 1942 came nine months after the amnesty was declared and had only been secured thanks to the personal interventions of Ambassador Kot, former Kozelsk prisoner Wacław Komarnicki (now a government minister in London) and Polish foreign minister Kajetan Morawski, all of whom had directly approached the Soviet ambassador in London on his account. For all the criticism of Kot's tenure as ambassador this was one of his success stories and serves as an example of his remarkable tenacity in pushing for the release of Polish citizens from Soviet captivity. It also explains why he was unpopular with the Soviet authorities. Fortunately, in Swianiewicz's case the Polish authorities knew exactly where he was. The NKVD could not pretend they had no record of his fate.

The network of Polish embassy officials who met and aided Swianiewicz on his journey to Kuybyshev amply illustrates Kot's achievement in setting up the Welfare and Intervention Departments to help newly released deportees.

In Kotlas Swianiewicz was greeted by an officer wearing an armband marked 'Poland' who sent him to a nearby barracks for provisions and documents for the journey. It was Swianiewicz's first opportunity to obtain detailed information about what had been happening in the outside world since he was taken to Smolensk in April 1940.

> One of the first questions I asked him was where the other Kozelsk prisoners, my friends and comrades of misery, were. I already imagined that they most likely had formed the main cadre of that army, about which I had learned from the occasional newspapers arriving in the camp. This officer told me that a great mystery surrounded Kozelsk, and that there was only a small group of Kozelsk prisoners in the camp at Griazovets, and no further information about the rest of them at all. Equally, the fate of the majority of officers of Starobelsk and Ostashkov remained unknown. Generally speaking we were short about 10,000 officers who had been taken prisoner by the Russians. He also told me that all the delegates of the army and the embassy had instructions to collect as much information as possible that might lead to some trace of them, for up to now nothing concrete was found.

Swianiewicz wanted to enlist immediately in the Polish army but the officer told him that he had precise instructions to send him to Kirov, where the main delegate of the embassy for Northern Russia wished to speak to him personally. The delegate in question was Otto Pehr, a lawyer and well-known socialist activist who, like Swianiewicz, had only recently been released from Soviet captivity. Pehr received Swianiewicz with delight, informing him that extricating him from the camp had been one of his specific assignments, adding that the government in London had shown great interest in his case.

As Swianiewicz gave Pehr an account of his experiences since his capture in 1939 he began to realise that the interest surrounding him was not so much personal as due to the fact that he was the first – and so far only – officer to reappear from the transports that had left Kozelsk during its liquidation in April–May 1940. The Polish authorities were hoping he might be able to shed some light on the mystery of the missing men. After listening to Swianiewicz's story, however, Pehr concluded that the mystery, instead of becoming clearer, had become even more obscure. The news that the transport on which Swianiewicz travelled from Kozelsk had stopped near Smolensk completely contradicted the theories holding sway until then. If the prisoners had been sent to camps in the remote north or east of the Soviet Union, why did the transports head west instead of north?

Swianiewicz again expressed his desire to report to the closest military unit for active service, reminding Pehr that as an officer it was his duty to do so. Pehr, however, insisted he needed first to get Swianiewicz to the embassy in Kuybyshev, reassuring him that he would be able to join the Polish army from there. The journey, he added, needed to be arranged in a particular manner:

> We have conducted your case in such a way that they had to release you. The text of the Polish–Soviet agreement concerning the release of Polish citizens staying in Soviet prisons is abundantly clear. The NKVD couldn't possibly tell us that they could not find you because for some time we had correct and precise information about what was happening to you and where you were. Now, I am afraid that if we were to issue you with ordinary documents for travel to Kuybyshev or to the army, you simply would not arrive there. So, we have to organize the journey in such a way that we are sure you will. It will require time to extract the necessary documents from the local NKVD.

Swianiewicz did not immediately understand why it was necessary to take such elaborate precautions. The notion that the NKVD might try to ambush him en route seemed far-fetched, but he was nevertheless grateful to Pehr for organising the journey in such a way that it would be difficult to do away with him 'on the sly'.

Pehr's talent for dealing with the NKVD authorities was impressive. To Swianiewicz it revealed a paradox at the heart of Soviet society: he had often observed that a Pole who spoke Russian well was suspected of being a spy, whereas one who spoke it badly aroused sympathy and confidence. Pehr spoke poor Russian with a strong German accent, he wore a well-cut suit and had a certain distinction of manner that came from his time as a reserve officer in the Austrian cavalry during World War I. As a consequence, the local Soviet functionaries in Kirov treated him with special respect. Swianiewicz interpreted this contradictory behaviour as the expression of an inferiority complex towards the West, manifest also in the fact that foreign communists were thrown in prison whereas Europeans with aristocratic connections were set free soon after arrest. (This impression is reinforced by the release from Soviet captivity of two members of Poland's aristocracy, Prince Jan Lubomirski and Prince Edmund Radziwiłł, following intervention from foreign dignitaries. Ambassador Kot also remarked half-jokingly on this phenomenon in a meeting with Molotov on 21 October 1941, 'You have released several princes, counts, two Piłsudskis, but so far I have seen no representatives of the Peasant Party...'[2])

Swianiewicz travelled in the company of Pehr's representative, who was carrying diplomatic mail. The NKVD issued them with formal documents and tickets in the 'soft carriage' with reservations from Kirov to Gorky (now Nizhny Novgorod), where Pehr had reserved places on a boat sailing down the Volga to Kuybyshev. Thanks to Pehr's careful planning, the journey proceeded without incident.

As Czapski had already discovered, the Polish embassy in Kuybyshev was crowded with outstanding representatives of pre-war Poland's literary and academic world whose release Kot had engineered and who now enjoyed posts as embassy staff. Swianiewicz was delighted to find himself in such stimulating company and especially glad to encounter his old friend, the journalist Bernard Singer. Through him he made the acquaintance of another well-known journalist, Ksawery Pruszyński, who had been brought over from London to work as the embassy's press attaché and was to become a close friend.

Swianiewicz reported to the military attaché, General Wolikowski, who asked him to write a statement about his journey from Kozelsk to the internal NKVD prison in Smolensk. Swianiewicz set down everything he could remember about the train's arrival in Gnezdovo and what he had seen there while he waited for the NKVD colonel to take him to Smolensk. Copies were sent simultaneously to Kot and the Department of Intervention. Swianiewicz was then invited for a lengthy conversation with Kot himself. As his earlier conversation with Otto Pehr suggested, Swianiewicz's statement completely changed the focus of the embassy's enquiries, until now centred on the remote regions of Kolyma and Franz

Józef Land. It begged the question: why had the Soviet authorities never once mentioned that the prisoners of Kozelsk were taken in the direction of Smolensk or Gnezdovo?

After less than a year as ambassador, in July 1942 Kot left his position and returned to London. He had asked to be recalled in March on health grounds, but in reality his brief tenure had not been a success. He had irritated the Russians and was considered ineffective by the Poles, especially the military. His two main objectives had been to save tens of thousands of Polish citizens, among them many representatives of the nation's intellectual elite, and to create conditions of trust and cooperation between Poland and the Soviet Union. While one could argue that he had some success in achieving the first objective, he failed conclusively in the second. Whether anyone else could have done better remains open to question. The Soviets were accustomed to exercising complete control over their citizens. The presence of so many foreigners on Soviet territory represented a significant challenge both logistically and psychologically. There were the vast numbers of Polish refugees cluttering up their railways and roads for starters. There was also the irritating fact that the Poles were allowed to move around as they pleased, to set up offices and schools, organise religious services and hand out food and clothing supplied by foreign powers, including the Americans. This was a privilege no Soviet citizen could enjoy. Local Soviet officials were supposed to prevent citizens coming into contact with 'dangerous' outsiders. How were they supposed to deal with the Polish embassy representatives who popped up in every corner of the USSR, setting up welfare offices and waving official papers that demanded their cooperation?

The personal toll on Kot of his short ambassadorial stint was high: as well as insomnia, he suffered from high blood pressure and migraines. The Polish government in London decided to replace him with an experienced professional diplomat in the person of Tadeusz Romer, previously Polish ambassador to Italy, Portugal and Japan.[3]

On 8 July 1942, shortly before his departure, Kot went to see Vyshinsky for a farewell visit. According to diplomatic custom a departing ambassador may make a request which as a rule is not refused. Kot first asked if he could take with him the two prominent Jewish politicians, Henryk Ehrlich and Wiktor Alter, arrested by the NKVD in December 1941. Vyshinsky replied that unfortunately this was impossible but offered no reason why.

(In reality they were dead, executed shortly after their arrest.) Kot then asked if he might take Swianiewicz with him instead. Vyshinsky suggested that this might be possible, but he could not guarantee it, advising that Swianiewicz make an application for the required exit visa to the proper authorities in Kuybyshev.

It was during this meeting that a final discussion between Kot and Vyshinsky took place on the subject of the missing Polish officers. Vyshinsky assured Kot that he had looked into the matter thoroughly and ascertained there were no Poles in camps in the far north or east or anywhere else: 'Maybe they are outside the USSR, maybe some have died.... Everybody has been released. Some were released before our war with Germany, some after.'[4] Surfacing in this final sentence is the beginning of the suggestion, also visible in Stalin's comments on the matter in March 1942, of a link between the fate of the prisoners and the German advance into Russia. Vyshinsky's remark may also reflect an accommodation of Swianiewicz's eye-witness statement, which had rocked Polish faith in the 'remote corner of the USSR' theory that had proved so convenient for the Soviets until now. When Kot asked (again) for a list of the prisoners who had been freed, pointing out that the Soviet government had always kept such records, Vyshinsky replied, 'Unfortunately we have no such lists.'[5] The denial was barely even the pretence of a lie. Everyone knew the NKVD were meticulous record keepers. No self-respecting security force could keep tabs on their citizens without also keeping files on them. Kot himself had heard Vyshinsky boast on many occasions that they had lists of all Polish POWs in the Soviet Union.

Although employed by the Polish embassy and in possession of a Polish passport, Swianiewicz was not protected by diplomatic immunity. In order to leave the Soviet Union he needed an exit visa. He duly applied to the local militia for the relevant stamp on his passport.

> I was told to come back a few days later. When I reported back, they told me to come the next day. When I came the next day, they told me again to come the next day and so it went on and on.

On the morning of the ambassador's departure Swianiewicz reported again to the militia, who informed him that his exit visa was not yet ready and advised him to come in the afternoon. When he replied that his ship was sailing that afternoon, they told him to come back forty-five minutes before the scheduled departure time. Swianiewicz knew they were stalling him. There was nothing he could do but return to the embassy and wait. Kot and his companions, meanwhile, were already leaving for the river port. Swianiewicz arranged with the embassy chauffeur that he would return immediately after dropping off the ambassador, take Swianiewicz to militia headquarters and wait outside to drive him to the port.

The chauffeur duly dropped Kot off and returned to take Swianiewicz to the militia office. Once again Swianiewicz was forced to wait as officials found endless reasons to fiddle with his passport. Finally, just fifteen minutes before the ship's departure, they ran out of excuses and pronounced the visa ready. Swianiewicz urged the chauffeur to put his foot down and drive to the river port at top speed, ignoring the speed limit and traffic lights. 'I was trembling, afraid that the militia would stop us, even if the car did have a diplomatic flag. We reached the river port, and someone told me that the ship was actually moving away.'

Swianiewicz showed his visa to the NKVD officer at the barrier then ran at full pelt towards the port, past a pavilion filled with Soviet dignitaries gathered to bid the Polish ambassador farewell – NKVD men in splendid uniforms and shiny leather boots, members of the diplomatic corps and foreign military attachés in the uniforms of their armies. Ahead, the ship's engines throbbed as it moved slowly away from the quayside. The sailors were pulling up the gangplank.

> There was a space between the gangplank and the deck of the ship of about three-quarters of a meter. I jumped with my suitcase straight onto Ksawery [Pruszyński] who was standing by the edge of the deck entrance; he grabbed my left side, afraid I might lose my balance, and a sailor steadied me from the right.

Once they were down in the passenger cabins, Pruszyński hugged his friend, weeping.

> He told me, 'I went through several hours of dreadful anxiety, for I was sure that they would never let you out of Russia.' Indeed, while the ambassador with his escorts was standing on the upper deck making courteous bows

to the people sending him off, Ksawery was standing together with the sailors who were going to lift the gangplank, waiting, hoping that at the last moment I would appear.... I was overwhelmed with gratitude for his concern and friendship.

Below deck a first-class cabin had been prepared with his name on the door, written out in full: Professor Stanisław Swianiewicz. He now realised how close he had come to sharing the fate of Ehrlich and Alter. The NKVD had promised the Polish ambassador that Swianiewicz could accompany him to Iran, so they could not openly prevent him from leaving. Instead, they had prepared an elegant cabin for 'the Professor' while doing everything possible to keep him from reaching the boat. Had it departed without him he would certainly have been arrested. Without diplomatic immunity he would either have been shot or sent back to die in a labour camp.

At last they were on their way, sailing down the Volga River on a luxurious pre-revolutionary steamer in the brilliant summer sunshine, their destination the port of Pahlavi, then (by land to) Tehran. Kot had brought with him a group of his closest colleagues and friends, and in the evenings the insomniac ambassador would invite Ksawery Pruszyński, Bernard Singer and Swianiewicz to his cabin where they would talk late into the night. Their route took them close to the front line at Stalingrad, where they stopped overnight, listening to the artillery thundering from the west.

At Astrakhan they transferred from a flat-bottomed river boat to a seagoing vessel, passing through Dagestan to arrive in Baku, capital of the Soviet Socialist Republic of Azerbaijan. Here a polite official informed them that regretfully there were no ships to Pahlavi for the next few days. A representative of the local NKVD appeared, most apologetic, eager to smooth away the inconvenience. Places had been made available for the party at a newly-built Intourist hotel, he explained. Caviar and vodka were on the house, the hotel would supply them with any theatre or concert tickets they desired.

The passengers spent a pleasant week enjoying this largesse, swimming in the sea, attending an outdoor concert of Chopin, continuing their nocturnal discussions. Just one puzzling thing occurred: when Ambassador Kot tried to contact the embassy in Kuybyshev and the Polish authorities in Tehran, the long-distance telephone connections did not work. He sent telegrams but received no replies. Finally, news came that a ship would be sailing to Pahlavi the following day. After a further twenty-four hours at sea they docked in Pahlavi and continued their journey by land, stopping overnight in a luxurious palace with a beautiful view of the Caspian Sea, en route to their final destination of Tehran.

The following morning, Swianiewicz was seated outside enjoying a leisurely breakfast with his friends when a messenger arrived from Tehran with urgent mail for the ambassador. The party fell silent, fearing bad news. Their instinct was right. The letter informed Kot that immediately after his departure from Kuybyshev the Soviet authorities had started liquidating the embassy delegations that had been set up across the Soviet Union. They confiscated the tinned food, the medical supplies, the clothes sent from America. Then they started arresting embassy staff, all the cultural, academic and scientific luminaries whom Kot had worked so hard to release. With no diplomatic protection there was nothing to stop the NKVD from imprisoning these men and women again. Kot was heartbroken. His principal achievement as ambassador had been the creation of a network of social care for the hundreds of thousands of Polish deportees released by the amnesty. This network now lay in ruins. By mid-August 150 staff working for the embassy had been arrested and their archives confiscated. There was even talk of a show trial.[6]

The delay in Baku and the mysterious failure in communications to Kuybyshev and Tehran now made grim sense.

> It was more than likely that for some time the Soviet authorities had a liquidation plan for the Polish network of social care, and for taking the supply of food from the embassy outposts…. They chose to perform this blow at the moment when the representation of Polish interest in the Soviet Union was weakened by the absence of its ambassador.

While Polish citizens were trying desperately to get in touch with their ambassador to alert him to what was going on, he was stuck in Baku, along with his press attaché, cut off from the outside world. Officially, they were privileged travellers living in comparative luxury. 'In reality, we had been interned.'

The liquidation of Polish welfare organisations on Soviet territory worsened after the second evacuation in August 1942 and continued for several months after that. In January 1943 the Polish chargé d'affaires at Kuybyshev received a note stating that the Soviet government would no longer recognise as a Polish citizen anyone who was in Soviet-occupied Poland on 1 November 1939, including ethnic Poles. The welfare organisations, it argued, were no longer necessary since all concerned were now Soviet citizens. Some of Kot's staff were eventually released. Hundreds of others disappeared without trace. For Swianiewicz, reflecting many years later, the loss of so many distinguished men and women constituted a 'small Katyń' still waiting for its historian to document their fate.

In Tehran, Kot invited Swianiewicz to the Polish legation for a long conversation during which he suggested Swianiewicz prepare a report on the missing officers. Amongst the many criticisms levelled at Kot during his ambassadorship was one that particularly rankled: some people, particularly in military circles, accused him of making insufficient efforts to find the missing prisoners of Kozelsk, Starobelsk and Ostashkov. Quite apart from a desire to ensure that the government was in possession of detailed records covering every aspect of the case, Kot was also keen to demonstrate that this accusation was completely untrue.

Like Czapski, it was only once he had left the Soviet Union that Swianiewicz began to understand the full significance of his own experience. As he sat on the veranda at the Polish legation, his work punctuated by midday swims, he began to study the files provided to him by Kot. These contained the correspondence between the embassy and Narkomindel (the Soviet ministry of foreign affairs), as well as correspondence from London to the Soviet ambassador and Józef Czapski's report. As he read these documents Swianiewicz slowly began to comprehend his own role in events. Until now, he had been an 'outside observer of this drama in which I was unknowingly an actor'. Now his part became clear, and the meaning of the special precautions taken by Otto Pehr to protect him finally made sense. He was the first and only person from the transports that left Kozelsk in April and May 1940 ever to reappear. He had travelled further in the company of the missing men than any of the other 395 survivors, all of whom had been taken directly from the three camps to Pavlishchev Bor. While they had waved goodbye to their comrades at the camp gates,

Swianiewicz's journey from Kozelsk to Smolensk and Gnezdovo had followed the trail of the missing officers to the very point where it grew cold. He had watched as his comrades were loaded onto trucks and driven off in the direction of a forest. Thereafter, who knew? The mystery remained, sinister and unfathomable.

From the perspective of the NKVD, as long as Swianiewicz was in a labour camp he could do no harm. It was only once he was released that he became a witness, and thus a threat. Perhaps it was fortunate that he had not fully appreciated the danger he was in from the moment of his release to the day of his departure. He might have shared Professor Kot's insomnia.

PART IV

The Forest 1943–44

Katyń, 1943. Lieutenant Slovenzik liked to leave large numbers of bodies on display to maximise the shock for visitors.

18

—

BODIES

On 9 April 1943 the President of the Polish Red Cross in Warsaw, Wacław Lachert, received a phone call from the propaganda department of the German government in Warsaw, summoning him to come at once to a meeting at the Bruhl Palace, headquarters of the Nazi governor, where a special envoy of Dr Goebbels was to give a speech. Suspecting that this was some kind of propaganda initiative on the part of the German authorities, Lachert made an excuse, citing a previous engagement. To his surprise – for it was not the custom of Nazi officials to waste niceties on Poles – the official received his refusal very politely, reassuring Lachert that he was not to worry if he could not attend and promising to telephone again later the same day to inform him of the result of the meeting.

The official kept his word and telephoned Lachert that afternoon to relay to him the contents of the speech made to a number of Polish organisations by the special envoy from Berlin. A mass grave of around 10,000 Polish officers had been discovered by the German army in the Katyń Forest near Smolensk in Russia, he said. They had been murdered by the Russians. The official added that he was of the opinion, and the German government shared this view, that the time had come for a reconciliation between Poles and Germans under the banner of a joint effort to fight for the civilisation of Europe against the barbaric East. Similar meetings, he concluded, had taken place in Kraków and Lublin.

Those who attended the meetings had been obliged to listen to long speeches on the subject of the German mission to defend European civilisation against the 'communist flood'. The massacred officers were a testament, they declared, to 'the bestiality of the Bolshevik regime'. Those present had also been asked to prepare themselves for a journey, for they were invited to travel by plane to the scene of the graves, where they would see for themselves the truth of the German assertions. The first delegation left Warsaw the following morning.

On the same day, Reich Minister of Propaganda Dr Joseph Goebbels wrote in his diary:

> Polish mass graves have been found near Smolensk. The Bolsheviks simply shot down and then shovelled into mass graves some 10,000 Polish prisoners, among them civilian captives, bishops, intellectuals, artists, et cetera. Above these mass graves they built installations of various kinds to cover up any possible traces of their dastardly deeds. The secret of these executions leaked out through local inhabitants and their gruesome aberrations of the human soul were revealed. I saw to it that the Polish mass graves were inspected by neutral journalists from Berlin. I also had Polish intellectuals taken there. They are to see for themselves what is in store for them if their wish for a German defeat at the hands of the Bolsheviks should ever be fulfilled.[1]

The first public announcement of the discovery was made on 11 April 1943 via a German radio station, Trans-Ocean. It reached a limited audience, as did the Soviet-backed Polish-language Radio Kościuszko's broadcast refuting the claims the following day. It was not until Berlin Radio broadcast the news on 13 April that the story made international headlines. It was followed, on 15 April, by Moscow Radio's furious rebuttal of the German version of events:

> In the past two or three days Goebbels's slanderers have been spreading vile fabrications alleging that the Soviet authorities carried out a mass shooting of Polish officers in the spring of 1940, in the Smolensk area. In launching this monstrous invention the German-Fascist scoundrels did not hesitate to spread the most unscrupulous and base lies, in their attempts to cover up crimes which, as has now become evident, were perpetrated by themselves.
>
> The German-Fascist report on the subject leaves no doubt as to the tragic fate of the former Polish prisoners of war who in 1941 were engaged in construction work in areas west of the Smolensk region and then fell into the hands of German fascist hangmen in the summer of 1941, after the withdrawal of the Soviet troops from the Smolensk area.[2]

Thus began one of the most explosive rows of World War II, resulting not only in the breaking-off of diplomatic relations between the Soviets and the Polish government in exile, but in a lie which was to stand for over forty years.

The context for these revelations was the German occupation of the Smolensk region in July 1941 following the Nazi invasion of the USSR. A German signals regiment chose as its headquarters a former NKVD rest home in Koze Gory (Goat Hills) on the eastern fringes of the Katyń Forest. Here, in the summer of 1942, Polish workers labouring for the German organisation Todt were told by locals that somewhere in the forest were graves of Polish officers who had been shot and buried nearby. The Poles did some digging and found human bones and military insignia. They showed their findings to the Germans, who initially paid little attention to the discovery. It was only in January 1943, when the commander of the signals regiment, Lieutenant Friedrich Ahrens, was informed of their find, that he ordered the area to be dug up and the mass graves were discovered. Since the ground was still frozen they had to wait until the spring thaw before investigating further. The graves were opened in late March 1943.[3]

Goebbels immediately saw in this discovery an opportunity to drive a wedge between the Allies and ordered his propaganda department to use all means necessary to demonstrate to the world this evidence of Bolshevik brutality. Every opportunity should be taken to invite witnesses to inspect the graves for themselves.

Present at the meeting that Red Cross president Wacław Lachert had declined to attend was the Polish writer and dramatist, Ferdynand Goetel. A prominent figure on the Warsaw literary scene (formerly president of Polish PEN and president of the Main Board of the Union of Professional Polish Writers), Goetel was an outspoken and sometimes controversial figure. His association with the pre-war Sanacja regime and authorship of a 1938 book favourable to fascist ideology left him vulnerable to accusations of pro-Nazi sentiment, claims vehemently denied by Goetel himself and belied by his close association with the Polish underground throughout the war. Goetel was contacted as early as 7 April by the local Warsaw Nazi propaganda officer, Dr Grundmann. Like Wacław Lachert, Goetel was surprised by the unusual nature of the approach. Grundmann came in person to see him at his home address; on learning that Goetel was out

Ferdynand Goetel.

he left a message asking the writer to come to his office immediately on a matter of great importance. 'This puzzling visit, carried out without any police presence and without threats, persuaded me to go.'⁴

The magnificent Bruhl Palace was formerly the seat of the Polish foreign ministry. Now it served as the headquarters of Warsaw's brutal governor, Ludwig Fischer (it was later completely destroyed by the Germans following the Warsaw Uprising in 1944). On arrival, Goetel found himself in a room with several representatives of what remained of Warsaw's civic life: someone from the municipality of Warsaw, another from the city's welfare office, a priest, two writers, some members of the legal profession and representatives of women's and artisans' organisations. The German authorities were represented by an official from Berlin and by Monzes and Grundmann, respectively the head and a member of the Warsaw district Nazi propaganda office. The delegate from Berlin addressed the meeting with Dr Grundmann. After offering brief details of the German discoveries, along with reflections on the barbarity of the Bolsheviks, Dr Grundmann invited the representatives present to travel to Smolensk and participate, voluntarily, in a visit to the graves to form their own judgements about who was responsible for this terrible crime.

The speeches were greeted with stunned silence. At the invitation to visit the graves, however, Goetel observed a ripple of fear passing through the audience. Everyone suddenly discovered urgent reasons why they were unable to oblige: the priest was willing to go, but didn't dare get on a plane; another couldn't fly due to a stomach condition; someone else had a very important meeting… 'I looked around me with anger and shame in my heart. Everyone was overcome by the fear of being caught up in this matter, the dangerous gravity of which was felt by everyone present, and everyone wanted to get out of its way.'[5]

Goetel's judgement of his Warsaw colleagues was harsh (he was later to be equally harshly judged for participating in the visit to Katyń) but the terrifying implications of the German revelations were impossible for any of those present to grasp immediately. For the last three and a half years Poland had been living under brutal Nazi occupation, the harshest in Europe. In Nazi ideology the Slavic races were only a step up from Jews in terms of their perceived 'worth' as human beings. Their designated future role was to serve their Nazi masters in the expansion of the Reich that would provide the *lebensraum* (living space) for future generations of Aryan settlers. For this reason the Nazis closed all Polish educational establishments above primary level – Poles only needed to be able to write and count. Like the Soviets, the Nazis sought to 'decapitate' Polish culture, persecuting political, religious and intellectual leaders, most notoriously in the Sonderaktion Krakau when, on 6 November 1939, 183 Polish academics were invited to a lecture by the German authorities. Instead of a lecture they were arrested and taken to Dachau and Sachsenhausen concentration camps. Random killings were a daily feature of Warsaw life, with particularly harsh punishment for any action connected with the AK – the *Armia Krajowa* (the Home Army, or Polish underground resistance).

It was thus understandable that the gathered representatives initially responded to the horrific news by treating it as some kind of 'Nazi trick', especially since the meeting took place before any public announcement had been made.[6] In the end a group of five men agreed to go, including two doctors and Goetel himself, who consented on condition that whatever he found at Katyń he would report immediately to the Polish Red Cross. Before he left, he asked permission of the AK, who advised him to go but warned him to be wary of being taken in. A handful of others from Kraków joined them on the trip: three doctors, a labourer and a second well-known writer, Nazi sympathiser Jan Emil Skiwski. There were also three journalists from the so-called *prasa gadzinowa* (the collaborationist or 'gutter' press). One of these, Władysław Krawecki, was to visit Katyń more than once. A few Germans accompanied them, including members of the Gestapo.

The delegation travelled by plane to Smolensk, where they were greeted by three officers from the propaganda section of the Smolensk army led by Lieutenant Slovenzik, an Austrian journalist who oversaw all the day-to-day aspects of 'running' the site. Slovenzik gave the delegates a more detailed version of the Katyń discoveries, showing them photographs of the woods, the corpses and the documents discovered on the bodies. The visit to the graves was to take place the following morning.

The Katyń Forest lies around ten miles outside Smolensk, just off the main road that connects Smolensk and Vitebsk. The area is hilly, with wooded patches on the higher ground and marshland on the lower level. Over the hills run woodland paths leading towards the Dnieper River. Beside the river sits a dacha, previously used by the NKVD as a rest house. The visitors travelled by car to the edge of the woods before proceeding further on foot, passing through pines, spruce, silver birch and alder to arrive at an area near the largest hill. The sight that greeted them there was unforgettable. Next to a long, excavated ditch a mass grave gaped open, filled with bodies all wearing the uniform of Polish officers. Since work had only recently started on the excavation it was unclear how many layers of bodies there were but it was already evident that the graves were deep and the layers many. The bodies were lying face down with their hands either beside them or tied behind their backs.

Next to the grave was a temporary hut where a team of pathologists was working under the leadership of Professor Gerhard Buhtz, head of army group medical services and professor of forensic medicine from Breslau (Wrocław). On the grass nearby lay dozens of bodies, numbered and placed in rows. Draped on the branches of the trees were fragments of uniform. Buhtz, whose 'face and manner suggested a German of the old school from the Germany of the past, when the profession of doctor was accompanied by a dedication to knowledge rather than to any kind of social doctrine,' invited the visitors to choose a body at random and explained that he would perform a post-mortem on it in their presence.[7] He also gave

Ferdynand Goetel a list of about thirty names of the dead whom he had already identified.[8]

> They bring over the body we have pointed out. A robust, broad-shouldered man with the insignia of a cavalry captain. His uniform intact. Beautiful 'Warsaw' boots. His face: a waxen mask.[9]

Professor Buhtz performed an autopsy, separating the head from the body and scalping it, almost causing Goetel to pass out. The post-mortem showed a shot through the skull, the entry point of the bullet at the base of the occiput and its exit point close to the brow. He cut open the pockets of the man's jacket to reveal a postcard from the Grodno region of Poland, addressed to a cavalry captain from his wife and sent to Kozelsk camp.

> 'Another one?' asks the professor.
> 'No, no, that's enough!'[10]

Among the bodies already laid out were those of two generals: Smorawiński and Bohaterewicz, both prisoners of Kozelsk camp. Goetel and his colleagues recognised them by their insignia, their medals and the remains of their facial features.

Throughout the visit Germans holding microphones followed members of the delegation around, repeatedly asking them for their thoughts on what they saw and whether they believed the Bolsheviks had committed the massacre. Whatever personal view they were forming, none of the Poles wished to provide material for Nazi propaganda and refused to express an opinion in public. Aside from these recordings and the constant presence of photographers, the visitors were allowed to explore the site freely and to speak with a small group of locals who claimed to have witnessed the arrival of Polish officers in the area in the spring of 1940. As he walked around the site, Goetel began to discern the shape of the graves: their sunken edges, their uneven surfaces. Standing out against the wild forest were neat rows of small young pine trees planted atop the graves. Before their departure the Polish delegation were granted a few minutes alone to say prayers. Dr Seyfried asked them to observe a minute's silence in order to 'pay homage to those Poles who died so that Poland might live'.

On the return journey to Smolensk the party stopped at a village. Here, in a roadside building, artefacts found on the bodies lay neatly arranged in glass showcases: letters, diaries, religious medals, identification papers, visiting cards. Professor Buhtz had used these to identify the bodies. Goetel observed that Lieutenant Slovenzik did not seem to understand why the postcards and letters found on the corpses bore the name 'Kozelsk'. When Goetel told him what he knew about the three special prison camps, he had the impression Slovenzik was hearing the information for the first time. At this stage, the Germans had announced the discovery of 10,000–12,000 bodies, a figure chosen largely for maximum propaganda effect since the Nazis knew of the Polish search for a similar number of missing officers. It was immediately evident to Goetel that the Germans had no idea how many bodies would be found since they had only just begun to excavate.

On his return to Warsaw Goetel wrote a report for the Polish Red Cross in the form of an open letter describing what he had seen on the trip and recommending the International Committee of the Red Cross be entrusted with investigation of the site. He gave copies of the report to various trusted people and asked for a copy to be sent to Dr Grundmann. In doing this, Goetel hoped both to force the German authorities to put the investigation into the hands of the Polish Red Cross and to overcome the reluctance of the Red Cross to investigate the Katyń affair. The report also reached the AK and was sent on to the government in London. Goetel took a copy in person to the general secretary of the Polish Red Cross, Kazimierz Skarżyński. He described to Skarżyński what he had seen and told him privately what he dared not say openly in public: everything pointed to a Soviet crime, just as the Germans were claiming.

The public announcement on 13 April came shortly after Goetel's return from Katyń. On 14 April an article by the second writer present during the visit, Jan Emil Skiwski, appeared in the Nazi-sponsored newspaper *Nowy Kurier Warszawski*. The headline ran: 'Bolsheviks murdered thousands of Polish officers. A delegation of Poles, headed by Ferdynand Goetel, view this shocking graveyard.' This was followed by a sub-heading: 'This terrible crime was managed by Jews from the Smolensk NKVD' and, in smaller print: 'What I saw there was more terrifying than my worst nightmare, says writer Emil Skiwski.'[11] A photograph of the first delegation features

Skiwski and Goetel standing with others by one of the mass graves. In the febrile atmosphere prevailing in Warsaw after the announcement, Goetel was accused of being a German agent. One rumour even claimed he had received a bottle of vodka in payment for participating in the visit.

Loudspeakers in the streets announced the shocking news, giving out the first names of the dead. Despite the protests of the Polish Red Cross this practice continued across occupied Poland for weeks, the loudspeakers blaring out names taken from documents which in some cases had been incorrectly deciphered by the Germans, leading sometimes to painful mis-understandings. The German press also published lists of names in all its Polish-language publications on occupied Polish territory. In this manner many families learned of the fate of their relatives.

> Days of waiting followed, filled with pain and torment. In June, on my way home from school, I bought 'Kurier'. I looked down the list, and the world turned upside down, everything went dark, I fainted. Under the exhumation number 2658 I found the name of my husband.[12]

Initially, most people in occupied Poland believed Katyń was a German crime and the publicity a particularly sadistic kind of Nazi propaganda game. Few people knew about the missing prisoners and the search for them in the Soviet Union. It was only as more evidence became available that public opinion changed.

To Ferdynand Goetel's intense relief, the initial reluctance of the Polish Red Cross to become embroiled in the 'Nazi trick' soon gave way to a realisation that, however dubious the motivation of the Germans, it was their duty to ensure the bodies of the dead officers were identified and properly reburied. The day after the Berlin radio communiqué stunned an international audience, the first Red Cross delegation, led by General Secretary Kazimierz Skarżyński, left Warsaw for Smolensk. Joining him from Kraków was the director of the Kraków branch of the Polish Red Cross, Dr Adam Schebesta.

When Skarżyński arrived at Katyń he realised at once that they were dealing with 'a mass execution' carried out by expert hands.[13] Every corpse had been shot in the back of the neck at close range, fired at the victims in a standing position. After concluding a brief joint prayer the

Father Stanisław Jasiński at Katyń, April 1943.

priest accompanying the delegation fainted. 'Poor man, he couldn't stand the smell. We had to revive him.'[14] The Polish uniforms, decorations, insignia, regimental badges, coats and boots were in good condition. Skarżyński noted the high proportion of senior officers but, like Goetel, also realised that the Germans had grossly overestimated the number of the dead.

Several times Skarżyński was asked to say something into one of the microphones that were constantly being thrust before him. He kept his opinion to himself, emphasising to Lieutenant Slovenzik that the Polish Red Cross had agreed to come to Katyń for one purpose only: to ascertain the situation of the graves and leave behind a technical commission to assess the scope of the work needed to identify the corpses, rebury them and safeguard personal artefacts with a view to returning them to the victims' families. Slovenzik assured Skarżyński that the Red Cross would have the complete cooperation of the German authorities and full access to all graves for exhumation and identification purposes, as well as access to the collection of documents being kept in a separate office away from the main site. The documents would be retained by the German Field Police (*Geheimfeldpolizei*) until they had finished with them, after which they would be delivered to the Polish Red Cross to be given to families.

Before leaving, Skarżyński permitted himself a brief comment for the German microphones. He stated how moved he was by the terrible sight before him, and acknowledged the work being carried out by the German army on the grave sites. He departed, leaving behind three Red Cross members to form the beginnings of a technical commission.

On his return to Warsaw, the propaganda department immediately started pressurising Skarżyński to make a public statement about what he had seen. When he dared refuse this request – an act which he later confessed terrified him – he was ordered to prepare a written report instead and present it that same day, 17 April, at the propaganda office.

Skarżyński met with the other members of the Polish Red Cross board of directors to discuss the text of the report, which had to present an accurate reflection of what he had surmised from his visit without drawing any conclusions that could serve the Germans. They settled on a brief statement featuring eight points, the most significant of which was that the visit had led Skarżyński to conclude that the murders were probably carried out in March–April 1940. The implications were clear: the Soviet case for Nazi guilt rested on the claim that the murders were carried out in the summer of 1941, over a year later. Meanwhile, Skarżyński made a verbal report to Stefan Korboński of the Polish Underground in which he gave a far more detailed account of his impressions. To Korboński he confessed his true opinion: like Goetel, he was convinced the Soviets were responsible for the massacre.

19

POLITICS

In London a furious political row was under way. The Germans knew they had not killed the Polish officers. Their goal was therefore to marshal all means at their disposal to show the outside world what the 'bestial Bolsheviks' were capable of, thus dividing the Allies at a crucial moment in the progress of the war. The Soviets, on the other hand, needed above all to control the story of Katyń in order to convince the world, specifically Britain and the US, that it was the 'fascist hangmen' who were responsible for the crime.

Unlike the public in Nazi-occupied Poland, the Polish government in exile in London was fully aware of the efforts made by the Polish authorities in the Soviet Union to find the missing prisoners in 1941–42. To them the notion of Soviet guilt was not just likely but almost certain. What, though, of the Allies, Britain and the US? From their perspective it was not at all clear who was responsible for the crime, and the wartime situation made it next to impossible to verify claims on either side. Politically, the situation was explosive: here was their greatest enemy accusing their much-needed but little-trusted ally of a heinous crime. That same ally was equally vociferously pointing the finger of blame right back at their mutual enemy. In the middle stood powerless Poland, loudly and most inconveniently demanding justice.

On 15 April 1943, Winston Churchill and the permanent undersecretary for foreign affairs, Sir Alexander Cadogan, lunched alone with General Sikorski and Edward Raczyński (who was serving both as ambassador and foreign minister in General Sikorski's government). The main topic of discussion was the long-running dispute over the future Soviet–Polish border, but the conversation inevitably touched on the revelations concerning Katyń. Churchill offered to intervene with Moscow on Poland's behalf, but also warned Sikorski against provoking their important ally. When Sikorski and Raczyński told Churchill that they had good reason to believe the murder of the Polish officers was the work of the NKVD, both Cadogan and Raczyński noted Churchill's response:

> Churchill, without committing himself, showed by his manner that he had no doubt of it. He remarked: 'The Bolsheviks can be very cruel.' He added, however, that their ruthlessness was a source of strength, and was to our advantage as far as destroying Germans was concerned.[1]

On the same day, a meeting of the Polish cabinet in London concluded that the only way of ensuring a credible and trustworthy investigation of the graves was to ask the International Committee of the Red Cross in Switzerland to undertake the task. Unfortunately, instead of consulting the British before doing so – or indeed their own foreign minister, Edward Raczyński – they rushed out the announcement prematurely. Goebbels was delighted:

> This declaration changes the whole Katyń affair fundamentally in that the Polish government in exile now demands that the International Red Cross should take part in the investigation. That suits us perfectly. I immediately got in touch with the Führer, who gave me permission to send a telegram to the International Red Cross, requesting it to collaborate to the uppermost in identifying the corpses.... In my opinion, something has thus been started which may have simply unimaginable repercussions.[2]

Goebbels had immediately grasped that two apparently simultaneous appeals to the International Committee of the Red Cross by the Germans and the Poles would inevitably create the appearance of a degree of cooperation between the two parties. Sure enough, two days later an article appeared in the Soviet press with a headline referring to 'Hitler's Polish Collaborators', followed by a flurry of indignant finger-pointing and furious accusations aimed at the Polish government. The Russians rejected the proposed Red Cross investigation, thus dooming it to failure. The International Red Cross could not intervene unless the request came from all parties involved.

Without the consent of the Soviet Union there could be no international investigation.

With the political row growing more acrimonious every day, for a short time the subject of Katyń became a major international news story. It was even discussed by the British war cabinet. But the wartime situation was not favourable to the notion of Soviet guilt: the Allies were focused on fighting Hitler, not Stalin, and it was Nazi brutality that preoccupied them, not Soviet crimes. In such a context, and with the full force of the Soviet-sponsored press (and parts of the British press) ranged against them, attempts by the Polish government to convince the world that the Soviets were the perpetrators of the Katyń Massacre fell on infertile soil.[3]

On 21 April, Stalin informed Roosevelt and Churchill that, as a result of the Polish government's 'unreasonable behaviour', he was going to break off diplomatic relations with Poland. When the two leaders attempted to persuade him not to take such a drastic step, Stalin offered to rethink the decision if two conditions were met: first, if the Polish government in exile withdrew its request to the International Red Cross; and second, if it blamed the Germans for the massacre. Inevitably, General Sikorski refused to contemplate either course of action.

Stalin knew perfectly well that the Poles would not acquiesce to his demands. He did not want them to. His apparent umbrage was simply a cover for a strategic decision that had been a long time in planning: to remove the exiled government from the political equation in order to cultivate an alternative centre of Polish power friendly to Soviet interests.

Ever since the first months of the Soviet occupation of eastern Poland in 1939 Stalin had been providing support and encouragement to a group of Polish communists, led by the writer Wanda Wasilewska. In January 1943, a full three months before the Katyń revelations, Stalin summoned Wasilewska to Moscow and informed her that he expected an imminent breakdown in Polish–Soviet relations. They then discussed what measures could be taken to develop the influence of Wasilewska's group. For some time Wasilewska had been pressing Stalin for permission to create a Polish political body within the Soviet Union that could provide a focus for the many thousands of Poles who remained on Soviet territory following the evacuation of the Polish army. Stalin agreed the time was now ripe for the formation of such a body. Thus, in March 1943, the Union of Polish

Patriots in the USSR (*Związek Patriotów Polskich w ZSSR*, or ZPP) was born, with its own newspaper, *Free Poland* (*Wolna Polska*), edited by Wasilewska.[4]

The BBC broadcast news of the break between the Soviet Union and the Polish government in exile on the evening of Easter Monday, 26 April 1943. Despite British attempts to mend matters, Stalin did not relent. He knew the Allies could not afford to offend him. Poland was in the invidious position of being Britain's most loyal ally but a strategically unimportant one. As an occupied country with a small but determined number of troops and airmen at liberty in the West, her contribution to the war effort was valiant but insignificant compared to the might of the Soviet Union, without whom the Allies could not defeat Hitler.

Shortly after the public declaration of the rupture Stalin made a statement in the press expressing his desire to see a 'strong and free' Poland. This was followed, on 6 May, by a statement from Vyshinsky accusing the Polish embassy and its welfare representatives of espionage. Ever since Professor Kot's departure in July 1942 the Soviets had been steadily dismantling the embassy's various outposts and departments. The breakdown of diplomatic relations meant the withdrawal of the Polish ambassador and his staff, leaving Wanda Wasilewska's Union of Polish Patriots to take over many of the welfare and educational provisions previously provided by the embassy. At the same time, in May 1943 the Polish infantry division originally envisaged by Lavrenty Beria in October 1940 finally came into being. Named the Polish 1st Tadeusz Kościuszko Infantry Division, it was fully integrated into the Red Army and led by the newly-promoted General Zygmunt Berling. Along with Wanda Wasilewska, he had been pivotal in its creation, aided by his former Griazovets comrade and fellow deserter, Lieutenant Colonel Leon Bukojemski. All Polish citizens remaining in the Soviet Union, including those of Ukrainian, Jewish and Belorussian origin, were eligible to serve in the Kościuszko. The division was later to form the core of the Polish People's Army in communist-run Poland, thus fulfilling another element of Beria's original plan.

In the aftermath of the diplomatic rupture some sections of the British press portrayed the Polish government in exile as hysterical and reactionary, and their attitude towards the Soviet Union unnecessarily and unhelpfully hostile. An article in *The Times* on 1 May 1943 illustrates the supremely

Reich Minister of Propaganda, Dr Joseph Goebbels.

misplaced self-confidence evinced by British commentators (and the government) in misreading Stalin's motives:

> To clear up some apprehensions, it can be said outright that the Germans are wrong when they declare that the Soviet Government is going to establish a rival Left-Wing Polish 'Government' in Moscow. There are good grounds for confidence that Moscow has no such intention.

Goebbels' diary, by contrast, reveals his remarkably accurate reading of the state of affairs:

> The Soviets at the moment are extremely insolent and arrogant. They are quite conscious of the security of their position. They have no consideration whatever for the Anglo-Saxon Allies, nor need they have, as they are under no obligation to them for military achievements. The men in power in the Kremlin know exactly how far they can go.

It also showed a triumphant, and profoundly narcissistic, assessment of his own success in driving a wedge between the Allies:

> The most important theme of all international discussion is naturally the break between Moscow and the Polish émigré government... All enemy broadcasts and newspapers agree that this break represents 100% victory for German propaganda and especially for me personally. The commentators marvel at the extraordinary cleverness with which we've been able to convert the Katyń incident into a highly political question... There is talk of a total victory by Goebbels![5]

Although the British government had automatically viewed any claims made by the Nazis with profound distrust, as the Polish government in exile supplied them with more information it became increasingly clear that in the case of Katyń the Germans were telling the truth. But, for the sake of the war effort, neither the British nor the Americans wanted to be seen to take the Polish side by supporting their claims against the Soviets. Following the diplomatic rupture, both governments suppressed further public revelations about Katyń, adopting an official position of what might at best be called 'constructive ambiguity'. They justified it on the grounds that under present circumstances it was impossible to make a definitive judgement as to who was responsible for the Katyń Massacre. In reality, they were swallowing their reservations for the sake of keeping Stalin onside.

One of those who took a close interest in Katyń was the British ambassador to the Polish government in exile, Sir Owen O'Malley. On 23 May 1943 O'Malley produced a report for the foreign secretary, Anthony Eden, offering a detailed analysis of the information he had received from the Poles and concluding that the material provided convincing evidence of Soviet guilt. At the end of his report O'Malley expresses in the most powerful terms the sense of moral distaste felt by him – undoubtedly shared by some others in the cabinet – at the situation in which the British government found itself:

> In handling the publicity side of the Katyń affair we have been constrained by the urgent need for cordial relations with the Soviet government to appear to appraise the evidence with more hesitation and lenience than we should

do in forming a common-sense judgment on events occurring in normal times or in the ordinary course of our private lives; we have been obliged to appear to distort the normal and healthy operation of our intellectual and moral judgments; we have been obliged to give undue prominence to the tactlessness or impulsiveness of the Poles, to restrain the Poles from putting their case clearly before the public…. We have in fact perforce used the good name of England like the murderers used the little conifers to cover up a massacre; and, in view of the immense importance of an appearance of Allied unity and of the heroic resistance of Russia to Germany, few would think that any other course would have been wise or right.[6]

The notes by officials responding to O'Malley's report remain recorded in the Foreign Office archives, handwritten in its margins. They provide an illuminating snapshot of the debate going on inside the British government at the time:

'O'Malley urges that we should follow the example which the Poles themselves are unhappily so prone to offer us and in our diplomacy allow our heads to be governed by our hearts.' [David Allen]

'It is obviously a very awkward matter when we are fighting for a moral cause and when we intend to deal adequately with war criminals, that our Allies should be open to accusations of this kind.' [Frank Roberts]

'I should be inclined to print this as it stands and circulate to King and War cabinet only. It is a powerful piece of work and deserves to be read.' [Sir William Strang]

'I confess that in cowardly fashion, I had rather turned my head away from the scene at Katyń – for fear of what I should find there.' [Sir Alexander Cadogan][7]

As Sir Alexander Cadogan went on to point out, in purely numerical terms the death of 14,500 Poles at the hands of the NKVD was insignificant compared to the millions of Soviet citizens who had died under Stalin's regime. Moreover, the number of Polish citizens who perished during the deportations of 1940–41 was infinitely greater, in the hundreds rather than the tens of thousands. Yet the imagery of the crime, its symbolic importance above all, possessed a particularly powerful emotional resonance that continued to trouble men like Sir Owen O'Malley long after the affair had faded from public consciousness.

Before the Allies could look away entirely there was to be one more twist in the tale: in July 1943 Poland's prime minister and commander-in-chief, General Władysław Sikorski, was killed in a plane crash while taking off from Gibraltar in circumstances that have never been fully clarified. Although the incident had the appearance of a tragic accident, many on the Polish side saw the hand of the NKVD in Sikorski's death.

With their most charismatic leader gone and diplomatic recognition withdrawn on the Soviet side, the government in exile was gravely weakened both in influence and effectiveness. Sikorski was respected by both the Allies and the Soviets; his replacement, Stanisław Mikołajczyk, could never hope to hold a position of such importance. Increasingly riven by factional infighting, sidelined by the British and Americans, the Polish government was at the beginning of a long and painful slide towards irrelevance.

20

IN THE FOREST

For as long as the political arguments about Katyń continued to dominate Western headlines Goebbels remained committed to extracting the maximum advantage from the situation. With the Red Army advancing steadily westwards towards Smolensk, the Germans decided it was vital to obtain as much concrete evidence from the graves as possible before they lost control of the site. In the absence of an International Red Cross investigation, they decided to organise their own. They 'invited' an international committee of well-respected medical specialists from Nazi-occupied countries to conduct post-mortems on the bodies and produce a report on their findings. The committee arrived on 28 April 1943 and spent three days at the site.[1]

At the same time, in an effort to speed up the process of exhumation and identification of the bodies, Professor Buhtz proposed bringing in Polish forensic medical specialists to direct the work of the three-man Polish Red Cross Technical Commission. The specialists were to be chosen by his former assistant, Dr Werner Beck, who since 1940 had been director of the Medical Institute of the Jagiellonian University in Kraków. Dr Beck in turn asked Kraków's Red Cross director, Dr Adam Schebesta, to recommend suitable candidates.

On Tuesday 27 April 1943, 29-year-old Dr Marian Wodziński received an invitation to visit Dr Schebesta in his office.[2] Dr Wodziński's official role at the Medical Institute was that of senior assistant in forensic medicine. His boss, the eminent forensic expert Professor Jan Olbrycht, had been arrested by the Gestapo in 1942 and taken to Auschwitz, leaving Wodziński the only specialist in the department. In addition to his role at the Institute he worked for the Polish Red Cross in Kraków and was a sergeant in the AK. He knew Schebesta well.

Dr Marian Wodziński.

Dr Schebesta explained that he had a proposal of some importance to put to his young colleague. Would he agree to participate in the exhumation of the graves discovered in the Katyń Forest? Wodziński was stunned. Conscious of the gravity of the request, he asked for time to reflect but Schebesta insisted he needed an immediate reply. He assured Wodziński that he had recommended two other Polish forensic experts, one from Lwów and another from Warsaw, so he would not have to work alone. But Wodziński was the only one who could set out directly from Kraków, so Schebesta was keen for him to leave immediately. Somewhat reassured, Dr Wodziński decided to accept the mission.

He set out late that same evening, travelling to Warsaw by train accompanied by three laboratory assistants and as much technical equipment as they could carry: lancets, saws, metal callipers, overalls, rubber boots and gloves, phials for specimens, as well as a Leica camera for his personal use and some film. He received no instructions from the Red Cross as to what line of action he should take once he arrived, only that he should cooperate with the Technical Commission who were already on site. Two members of the Polish Red Cross administration joined him in Warsaw and on 28 April they flew together from Warsaw to Smolensk. On arrival in Katyń,

Dr Wodziński was dismayed to discover he was the only medical expert in the party. It fell to him alone to negotiate with the Germans and organise the exhumation and identification of thousands of bodies. The other two forensic experts never materialised.

German military police guarded the entrance to the Katyń site. By the barrier were two large notices: 'Entrance to Katyń woods is absolutely forbidden except to those working there' and 'It is absolutely forbidden to take photographs of the scene of the crime.' The entire perimeter of the woods was fenced off with barbed wire.

The exhumation had advanced since Ferdynand Goetel's visit earlier in the month. Seven grave pits were now open, each two to three metres deep and filled with up to twelve layers of bodies. In the process of uncovering the graves the little pine trees that Goetel had observed had been removed. The first sight of such a great mass of bodies wearing Polish uniforms, noted Dr Wodziński, 'caused everyone a great nervous shock'.

Dr Wodziński's arrival on 29 April coincided with the visit of the international medical commission. Since Lieutenant Slovenzik had ordered all other work to cease for the duration of the visit, Wodziński could only stand by and watch.

The 'European Commission of Medical Experts' consisted of thirteen forensic specialists from countries occupied by or friendly to the Germans: Belgium, Bulgaria, Denmark, Finland, Croatia, Italy, Holland, the Bohemian Protectorate, Romania, Slovakia, Hungary, and a medical inspector from France. The only member from a neutral country was the Swiss representative, Professor François Naville. Eager to form an idea of how his own work would proceed, Dr Wodziński observed carefully how the Germans treated their visitors. He found little to criticise: Professor Buhtz and Lieutenant Slovenzik behaved with courtesy, allowing the doctors freedom to work as they wished and inviting them to choose bodies at random on which to conduct autopsies. The doctors themselves behaved with professional thoroughness. They examined the graves, the bodies and the surrounding area, dictating their reports to German army typists. Everywhere they went, a photographer followed. None of the committee addressed the Polish doctor except the Slovakian, Professor Šubik, who confessed in a whisper that he hated the Germans. Nonetheless, he added, he was convinced this was a Soviet crime.

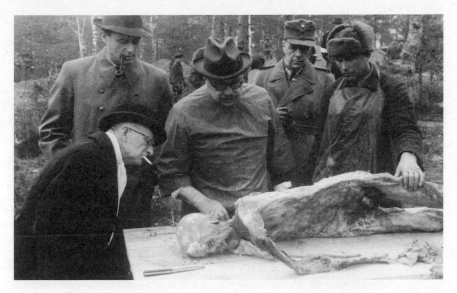

The International Medical Commission at Katyń, April 1943.

Three locals were brought to the scene: an old peasant, Parfemon Kiselev, whose family farm lay close to the forest, and two younger men, Ivan Krivovertsov and Semyon Andreev. Professor Orsós of Hungary was the only one able to converse with them without an interpreter. He questioned the witnesses at length in Russian. Wodziński listened.

Kiselev claimed to have seen 'black raven' prison vans bringing foreign soldiers into the Katyń woods in the spring of 1940. Later, he heard cries and gunshots. Andreev said he had learned from local railway workers that trains arriving in Smolensk were broken up into small groups of railway cars. These were sent on to Gnezdovo, where they halted on a dead-end track near the station. Krivovertsov described seeing trains arriving at Gnezdovo station from the direction of Smolensk. He had initially assumed that the prisoners were Finnish (since the Soviet Union was at war with Finland until mid-March 1940) but soon recognised the uniforms as Polish. Krivovertsov also confirmed that there had never been any camps for Polish POWs in the vicinity, nor were any road works carried out by POWs in the area, as claimed by the Russians.[3] None of those present was aware that these statements tallied precisely with what Stanisław Swianiewicz had witnessed before he was taken off to the NKVD prison in Smolensk. The Polish government would piece this information together at a later date.

Ivan Krivovertsov talks to the International Medical
Commission , Katyn, April 1943.

The official report of the international medical commission was published some days later. On the basis of nine post-mortem examinations performed on site, as well as observations made during the visit and the result of conversations with local villagers, the medical experts concluded unanimously that the officers had been shot in the spring of 1940. Inevitably, however, as far as the Allies were concerned a report written by medical experts drawn from Nazi-occupied countries could never be fully trusted. Accurate and professional it may have been, but without the guaranteed neutrality of an International Red Cross investigation it was just more Nazi propaganda.

With the international committee gone Dr Wodziński could now begin work. Before him lay a monumental task. So far only 310 bodies had been exhumed, identified and reburied in a communal grave. The Germans had created two individual graves for the bodies of General Bohaterewicz and General Smorawiński (the latter dug up for a second time in the presence of his brother-in-law so that he could identify it). Dr Wodziński had somehow to organise the removal of thousands of bodies from the mass grave pits; search, number and examine them in order to establish the cause of death; and identify and then rebury them in new graves.

The work was traumatic and difficult, made all the more complex by the team's peculiar status as 'free' experts operating on enemy territory. Throughout the five weeks spent by Dr Wodziński at Katyń the Germans never restricted his actions, but he and his colleagues continually felt they were being watched. Lieutenant Slovenzik visited the graves every morning and afternoon, devoting himself entirely to the exploitation of the site for propaganda purposes. Every time a group of visitors appeared work had to cease, and there were constant requests for interviews or photographs. Inevitably this led to tensions. Slovenzik liked to leave large numbers of bodies on display to maximise the shock for his visitors. This prevented Dr Wodziński from emptying each grave methodically, as he wished. It also delayed reburial of the bodies. Wodziński argued frequently with Slovenzik about this but the lieutenant, inevitably, prevailed. Even so, some of Dr Wodziński's colleagues felt he was too accommodating.

Diffident, reserved, meticulously professional, Dr Wodziński was a young man catapulted into a position of responsibility that he had no desire to occupy. It fell to him to make decisions on behalf of the Polish Red Cross, it was he who had to negotiate with the Germans. Several times he asked Lieutenant Slovenzik and Professor Buhtz for more experts to work with him, reminding them that he had been promised two colleagues. He even tried to persuade them to free his boss, Professor Olbrycht, from Auschwitz to help with the work, but the ministry of propaganda in Berlin refused his request. He remained alone.

Initially, Wodziński personally examined all the bodies as they were dug up. He also liked to be present when the bodies were searched, noting the last date of entry in diaries, on letters received or not yet sent, or on newspapers found in pockets. There was not a single document dated later than March or April 1940, no camp address other than Kozelsk. More than once he found himself examining the body of someone he had known before the war: a colleague, a friend.

Grave no. 1 was by far the largest, containing around 2,500 bodies. The lower layers were arranged methodically, but on the top layers the bodies had been thrown in chaotically, as if in haste. The bodies in the upper layers were light and fragile, their facial features partially mummified; those lower down were better preserved, with distinct facial features covered with a layer of adipocere (a white, wax-like substance) which had a putrid smell, a sign of fatty degeneration. The bodies at the bottom, lying in peaty soil, were the best preserved but had been flattened by the pressure of the other layers above them. All the bodies in this grave wore winter clothes, warm underwear, sweaters and coats, with wooden soles attached to their boots. A few had their hands tied behind their backs.

The other graves were in a similar state: the dead wore winter clothing and lay face down, some with their hands tied, others not. Their bodies were relatively well preserved. One striking aspect of the arrangement of the bodies (which only became apparent once the Polish authorities had examined the lists of names and cross-checked them with statements from survivors) was the fact that the order in which they were found in the graves was more or less the same as that in which the men had left Kozelsk, following the pattern of the transports. The Soviet version of events claimed the prisoners spent nearly a year and a half working in the Smolensk area after April 1940. It stretched credibility wafer-thin to suggest that the Nazis had killed the officers in the summer of 1941 in the exact same order in which they had been sent out of the NKVD camps some fifteen months earlier.[4]

The work of removing the bodies from the graves was carried out by Russian civilians. It was an unpleasant task: the smell was overpowering, the state of decomposition and compression of the bodies made it very difficult not to damage them. Many were so firmly stuck together that the workers had to use iron hooks to lift them out, sometimes even shovels and picks. Dr Wodziński encouraged the civilians to use their hands as far as possible but, understandably, they were extremely reluctant to do this. Despite repeated warnings from the technical team to take care, they often damaged bodies and uniforms in the process of removing them.

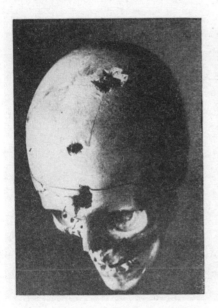 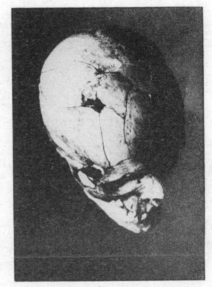

The most important part of Dr Wodziński's work was his examination of the bodies themselves. After shaving off the hair on the back of the head he generally found an entry wound just below the occipital protuberance. Beneath the skin was a bullet-shaped channel, running forwards and upwards into the cranial cavity through the base of the occipital bone. After clearing the entry cavity of soft tissue he measured its diameter: it was just short of 8mm. The entry aperture was characterised by smooth outer edges that expanded, crater-like, towards the interior of the cranium. The exit wound was almost always on the forehead, at the edge of the scalp. The shot went right through the centre of the medulla, causing instantaneous death. In a tiny number of cases he found 7.65mm calibre revolver bullets stuck under the skin of the forehead or in the exit wound. As Red Cross General Secretary Kazimierz Skarżyński had observed when he visited the site, this was clearly the work of expert killers, men who were trained to dispatch victims swiftly and with the minimum loss of blood. A shot to the back of the neck was a well-known method employed by the Cheka after the Russian revolution and frequently used by the NKVD during the Great Terror. The Russians later sought out examples of Nazi atrocities committed in the Soviet Union in an effort to prove that these methods were not unique to Soviet executioners.

The question of the ammunition was controversial: the bullets were made by a German manufacturer, Geco, a fact which the Germans were anxious to avoid. Lieutenant Slovenzik was always keen to point out that the Germans supplied large quantities of Geco ammunition to the Baltic states and the Soviet Union before the war. Dr Wodziński had no way of knowing if this was true, but the Polish government in London made their own enquiries to Polish army HQ in the Middle East, who confirmed that, although the official Polish military pistol was a 9mm Wis, these guns had only been supplied from 1939 and were not much in use at the start of the war. Many Polish officers owned their own pistols, bought privately or dating from the previous war. A large number of these were 7.65 calibre weapons. Ammunition for these pistols was held in Polish Ordnance Stores and would either have been purchased abroad or come from older stocks that would certainly have included ammunition supplied by Geco. The Russians could therefore have easily obtained Geco bullets after they occupied eastern Poland in 1939. Moreover, NKVD officers were known to carry the 7.65mm Tokarev pistol and often confiscated 7.65mm calibre pistols from their Polish captives for personal use. Although there was no conclusive proof regarding the precise provenance of the Geco bullets, their German manufacture did not exclude the possibility that they had been used by the Russians.[5]

Dr Wodziński and his colleagues tried to establish where the shootings had taken place, but it was not wholly clear. They found a large number of bullet cartridges under the pine needles near the graves as well as scattered amongst the bodies. They also found bullets stuck in pine trees growing close to the edge of the longer arm of grave no. 1, leading them to conclude that some of the executions had been carried out on the spot: it seemed that the men had been shot by the side of the pit and fallen directly into their own grave. It has never been precisely established where the rest of the men were killed.[6]

As summer and the military front approached, Dr Wodziński was forced to speed up the pace of work. He had so far examined around eight hundred bodies but now decided to limit himself to a thorough examination only of those bodies on which no documents had been found and which were listed as N.N. [*Nicht Namen* – No Name]. Members of the Technical Commission undertook the searches, under the supervision of NCOs from the German Field Police, cutting open coat pockets to extract objects of value, which they placed in numbered envelopes. A metal disc with a number on it was attached to the uniform or the bones, and the corresponding number written on the envelope containing the artefacts. They slit open boots, often finding penknives and other valuables hidden there. Banknotes were left on the spot. They threw newspapers away after dating them. If they found no documents on a body and no other evidence of rank they took one epaulette and placed it in the envelope. Russian prisoners brought in from Smolensk dug new communal graves. The Technical Commission marked crosses in the earth running the length of each grave and planted red and white flowers on top. They kept detailed information about the position of the bodies in the hope that one day they might be repatriated to Poland.

Dr Wodziński's work was constantly being interrupted by visitors, mainly large groups of German soldiers led by special propaganda officers issuing dire warnings that the same terrible fate would await the soldiers if they were ever taken prisoner by the Bolsheviks. On 12 May there was a change in the usual routine:

> When I arrived for work the next day at about 8 a.m. I noticed that the Germans were in their best uniforms and that at the entrance to the Katyń Forest there was a larger contingent than usual of German *Ordnungpolizei*. The Germans did not let us set to work, saying that it would only be possible once the delegation had gone.

The delegation in question consisted of eight prisoners of war who had been 'invited' to visit Katyń. There was a Scottish doctor, Captain Stanley Gilder; a South African, Lieutenant Colonel Stevenson; two American

officers, Colonel John H. Van Vliet and Captain Donald Stewart; plus
three British privates and one British civilian. Captain Gilder was medical
officer to British patients at the prisoner of war hospital of Rottenmünster
in southern Germany. The others were from a camp in northern Germany,
Oflag IX, A/Z Rotenburg.

The men were flown from Germany to Smolensk, where they spent the
evening in the officers' mess being wined and dined by 'German officers
[who] were as charming as only Germans can be, when they have orders
to be charming'. A pianist and accordionist serenaded them with popular
American and British songs. An English-speaking mess waiter, born in
Brixton, was deployed to converse with the lower-ranking men, who treated
him with predictable suspicion. Lieutenant Slovenzik gave his usual illus-
trated talk about Katyń before taking them the following morning to see
the site for themselves.[7]

As always, Dr Wodziński was forced to stop work while Lieutenant
Slovenzik led the party on a tour of the graves. The visitors were then shown
an exhibition of objects found on the bodies and invited to inspect some
of the corpses before the local witnesses were brought forward. Captain

The delegation of 'Anglo-Saxon' POWs at Katyń, May 1943.

Gilder was the only one in the party to speak Russian and German. He questioned Parfemon Kiselev. He also attempted to speak to Dr Wodziński privately, asking him what he thought about the massacre. At first Wodziński could not answer as there were German soldiers nearby. When Gilder tried again, noting that the Polish doctor was 'very discreet', Wodziński found an opportunity to reply:

> During the walk the English medical captain and I moved a little apart from the rest of the party and he asked me once more what was my opinion of the Katyń crime. I told him that so far I had been unable to find any evidence that could be used against the Germans, and that all the known circumstances and all the evidence pointed to the Soviets having committed the crime.

After the delegation left, some of Wodziński's colleagues told him that they had noticed concealed microphones installed among the trees.

The principal goal of all this effort on the part of the German propaganda department was always to persuade credible witnesses to speak out publicly about what they had seen at Katyń and express their belief in Soviet guilt. In this respect the presence of visitors from Allied countries was something of a triumph. Their statements could potentially influence opinion in Britain or the US. Lieutenant Slovenzik bent over backwards to try to capture the impressions of his 'Anglo-Saxon' visitors, yet despite promises of improved conditions for any prisoner of war willing to make a public statement, they refused to oblige. No self-respecting POW would say anything that could possibly serve the Nazi cause. Only at the end of the war did the senior officers in the party make reports to their respective military authorities.[8]

One of the two US officers present at the visit, Captain (later Colonel) Stewart, subsequently stated that, despite their reluctance to speak to the Germans, everyone came away convinced of Soviet guilt. It was not the documents that persuaded them (those could easily be falsified) nor the autopsy performed in their presence. What really convinced Stewart and his companions that the Polish officers had been killed in the early spring of 1940 was the state of their clothes:

> Colonel Stewart: Most of the stuff we saw there – most individual items – could be discounted. But the things that struck us, other than the fact

that a large number of Polish officers had been killed, was the fact
that many of those bodies, those in the larger grave, were in overcoats
and in good condition; Polish overcoats. We saw several hundred
bodies of the Polish officers in uniforms of very good quality that
had not been worn. I was a prisoner myself, and my clothes got worn.
Each one of us noted that individually, and the conclusion that we
drew from our examination of those uniforms was that those officers
could not have been prisoners very long at the time of their deaths.

Mr. Madden. Did that same thing apply to the boots, the shoes, too?

Colonel Stewart. The boots; yes, sir. The boots were not worn at all; very
little wear on them. They could not have been worn, those boots, very
long without showing more wear than they did. They were less worn
than the heels on my shoes right now, and those things made a very
strong impression on us. When we left the grave site, the Germans –

Mr. Madden. That circumstance or fact regarding the newness of the
uniforms and the boots and shoes was not called to your attention
by the Germans?

Colonel Stewart. No, sir; we noticed it individually. You see, we did not
talk as long as there were any Germans near us, and we tried to keep
any expression from being shown on our faces.[9]

This observation was made repeatedly by visitors to the site. Indeed, it was
such a potent argument in favour of Soviet guilt that when the Russians
commissioned their own report in January 1944 the date for the massacre,
initially given as 'summer 1941', was subsequently amended to 'sometime
between September and December 1941' to account for the prisoners' heavy
clothing.

Stewart and his companions also observed that, despite their brutality
in so many other respects, the Germans generally observed international
conventions when it came to the treatment of prisoners of war and did not
use officers for hard labour. This undermined the central Soviet claim that
the Polish officers had been put to work by the Germans building roads.

Accompanying the group of Allied POWs was a Polish journalist,
Władysław Kawecki, the editor of a Nazi-sponsored newspaper published
in Kraków, *Goniec Krakowski*. Kawecki had been part of the first delegation to visit Katyń in early April. He spent most of his second visit either

talking with Lieutenant Slovenzik or irritating the Red Cross team by trying to eavesdrop on their private conversations. Kawecki must have been a persuasive man, because he somehow convinced Dr Wodziński to agree to an interview, promising the doctor he would not mention his name in any subsequent article. As soon as he returned to Poland Kawecki broke his promise and quoted Dr Wodziński directly. He later claimed the Germans pressurised him to do it. Like Ferdynand Goetel, Dr Wodziński was later to suffer severe consequences for this 'public' statement.

As the graves were emptied it became clear that the number of bodies (around 4,000) bore no resemblance to 10,000–12,000 announced by the Germans. What it did tally with was the number of prisoners missing from Kozelsk camp. All documents discovered on the bodies referred to Kozelsk alone. To the Polish team it was obvious that the prisoners of Starobelsk and Ostashkov would not be found at Katyń, but Lieutenant Slovenzik was not yet willing to accept defeat: a number had been given out, and this was the number of bodies he needed to find. Failure to do so would constitute a political embarrassment and – more importantly – would displease his superiors. He ordered his men to start searching the surrounding area and towards the end of May was rewarded with the discovery of two new graves, each containing fewer than twenty corpses in a state of extreme decomposition. These turned out to be Soviet citizens, some in military uniform, others civilians, and including several women. Their skulls bore the marks of gunshots similar to those that had killed the Polish officers: the entry point at the base of the skull, the exit point through the forehead. Dr Wodziński estimated that they had been in the ground between five to ten years. More victims of the NKVD.

It was late May 1943. The Eastern Front was approaching, the weather growing warmer, threatening disease. Dr Wodziński and his colleagues were anxious to leave. Their work was nearly done. But when Wodziński asked Lieutenant Slovenzik when they might return home Slovenzik insisted that they complete the search for additional graves first. Unless… If the good doctor would only agree to use the figure of 12,000 bodies in his final report he could leave immediately. Wodziński refused, so they worked on.

There was only one grave left to be emptied: the smallest, no. 5, which was waterlogged. Until now only five bodies had been retrieved from it when they rose spontaneously to the surface. Slovenzik had promised to supply a pump but it never materialised. As the weather grew warmer and the water level dropped the smell became unbearable. Slovenzik refused to ask the Russians to work in such unpleasant conditions so the Red Cross team had to pull the bodies out themselves, forty-six of them, all in a state of advanced putrefaction due to the damp. It was a horrible task, but the grave revealed a new aspect to the crime: all the victims had their hands tied behind their backs, their greatcoats pulled over their heads. Around each man's neck was a cord that ran down to his wrists, pulling his hands up to his shoulder blades. In this way, if the victim struggled he would choke himself. In one case Wodziński found sawdust in the victim's mouth; in others, felt gags. The victims had been shot in the back of the head through their greatcoats. Dr Wodziński concluded that these victims were younger men who – on realising what was about to happen – tried to put up a fight and had to be restrained.

As the Polish team were working on these bodies Slovenzik approached in a state of great excitement. He had found an eighth grave. Inside it were ten bodies in Polish uniforms, wearing only shirts and jackets. The newspapers in the grave dated from early May 1940. All documents, like the others, referred to Kozelsk. Dr Wodziński surmised that these were the bodies of the last group of men to leave the camp. When he informed Slovenzik that the grave's dimensions suggested it could contain no more than two hundred bodies in total the Austrian's reaction was a mixture of nerves and fury. At some point he would have to find the courage to inform his superiors of the inconvenient discrepancy between the desired and actual number of bodies found at Katyń. And yet still he would not give up. He insisted that he would continue searching until all the bodies were found.

The sun shone, the stench worsened, the risk of disease grew. With the front approaching ever closer, the threat of Soviet capture became daily more real. Dr Wodziński again appealed to Slovenzik to allow the Red Cross team to leave. Finally, Slovenzik relented. They could leave on two conditions: they must return in the autumn to complete the work, and Dr Wodziński must report to the local Nazi propaganda office as soon as he arrived in Kraków.

Dr Wodziński and three members of the Red Cross Technical Commission left Katyń on 3 June 1943, travelling by train from Smolensk to reach Warsaw several days later. The rest of the Commission remained behind to finish work on grave no. 5 before they, too, left. When Wodziński finally arrived in Kraków he was mentally and physically exhausted. In no mood to be used as fodder for Nazi propaganda, he ignored Slovenzik's orders to report to the propaganda office and headed instead to the mountain resort of Zakopane, where he spent several weeks recuperating before returning to his job at the Institute of Forensic Medicine. When he saw Lieutenant Slovenzik again in the autumn of 1943 Katyń was again under Soviet control and Slovenzik had travelled to Kraków to announce that work on the site could not continue. Wodziński never saw the Austrian again.

Dr Wodziński had every reason to believe that his central role in the drama of Katyń was over. He had endured five weeks on enemy territory as the sole medical expert investigating the murder of thousands of his compatriots, some known to him personally. He had done his best to avoid the endless propaganda initiatives run by the Germans and given only a single interview to a Polish journalist on condition of anonymity. He submitted his detailed report to the Polish Red Cross, but his fervent hope remained that an International Red Cross commission would one day travel to Katyń to corroborate his findings. He knew their voice would carry far more weight than that of a lone Polish 'expert'.

When the Red Cross Technical Commission left Katyń there was one outstanding matter to be resolved with the German authorities: what to do with the thousands of documents that they had not been able to decipher on site. The Germans agreed to send them to Poland, to the Chemical Section of the Polish State Institute of Forensic Medicine in Kraków. Here, work on them would continue under the direction of Dr Beck.

There were ten large boxes of documents, plus an additional smaller box containing items found in the graves that the Germans intended to use in an exhibition on Katyń that never took place. For the next few months a small team of Polish experts, led by the head of the Chemical Section at the Institute, Dr Jan Zygmunt Robel, undertook the painstakingly slow task of analysing the documents.[10] Their aim was to gather as much information as possible about the circumstances of the victims' deaths and to create a reliable and comprehensive list of the victims' names. This was of particular importance since many of the documents had been incorrectly deciphered by the Germans, resulting in the wrong names being placed on the list of the dead.[11]

The Germans largely left Dr Robel to himself, periodically applying pressure to get the work finished as quickly as possible so that they could make use of the material to support their propaganda efforts. But Robel was not to be hurried. The Red Cross wanted to keep as much material as possible in Polish hands and had accordingly instructed Robel to take his time identifying the dead in order to delay handing over the completed work to the Germans. In reality, both the technical work and the process of establishing a reliable list of victims were so complex that there was no need to slow them artificially. The documents had to be placed in a chemical bath to remove the adipocere before any attempt could be made to decipher them under infra-red lights. Once the documents could be read there were hundreds of details to cross-check, relatives to contact, records to consult. Each victim was assigned a folder into which documents and objects were placed, along with a physical description and a declaration of the degree of certainty of the identification, according to whether it was 'absolutely certain' or 'most probable' that they belonged to the individual named.[12] It cost the Germans little to allow Robel and his team to devote their time to this painstaking process. The importance of Katyń to the Poles was self-evident: the death of several thousand members of Poland's elite was profoundly significant even in the context of wartime's brutality. From a German perspective evidence of Soviet guilt provided ammunition for their propaganda war; it also supplied essential proof that the Nazis themselves were not guilty of a heinous crime which they too stood accused of committing.

Among the items found in the graves and preserved in the smallest box were twenty-two diaries, the content of which provided vital information about the last days, sometimes hours, of the men's lives. Not a single diary contained an entry dated later than April 1940. Some continued right up to the day the writer left Kozelsk. Major Adam Solski's diary breaks off only when he is brought to the Katyń Forest itself:

> 8.04 3.30 a. m. departure from Kozelsk station, moving west; 9.45 am at Jelnia station.
> 9.04 Just before 5 a.m., reveille in the prison trucks and preparations for leaving. We are to go somewhere by car. What next?

9.04 5 a.m. Since dawn, the day began strangely. Departure in a prison
coach in cell-like compartments (terrible). They've taken us somewhere into a wood, something like a summer resort. Here a thorough
search. I was relieved of my watch, which showed 6.30 (8.30) a.m.
They asked me about my wedding ring, which…Roubles, belt and
pocket knife taken away....[13]

*

While Dr Robel worked on undisturbed, in the background a new and
dangerous clock was ticking: on 5 January 1944 the Red Army entered
Polish territory. By summer they were nearing Kraków, the heart of the Nazi
occupation of Poland and administrative centre of the General Government
(the part of Nazi-occupied Poland not incorporated into the Reich).

Dr Robel and his team had examined fewer than three hundred of
the envelopes. The Polish Red Cross feared that the NKVD would come
looking for the documents, thus eliminating the most compelling evidence
of Soviet guilt as well as valuable personal mementoes of the dead men.
Together with the Kraków AK they hatched a dramatic plan to substitute
fake boxes for the originals, which would be hidden in a nearby lake until
they could be safely retrieved at a later date. Dr Schebesta and Dr Robel
(both members of the AK) prepared the fake boxes. They even managed
to smuggle them into the Chemical Institute. Unfortunately, the plan was
compromised by one of the institute's workers, whether accidentally or
deliberately is not clear. Somebody talked; the Germans were alerted to
the plot. Ironically, it was to Dr Robel himself that Dr Beck confided the
information that German police had received a tip-off about the proposed
'kidnapping' of the boxes. Beck immediately ordered their removal, taking
them under heavy guard to the Institute of Forensic Medicine. After this,
Dr Robel and his team were given access to the documents only with the
explicit permission of Dr Beck.

With the Red Army within a few miles of Kraków, Dr Beck received
orders from Berlin to destroy the boxes rather than let them fall into Soviet
hands. Beck was acutely conscious of the importance of the documents not
only to the Poles but to the Germans in providing vital proof that they were
not responsible for the crime. He decided to ignore his orders and attempt
to rescue them. His first plan, conceived in cooperation with Dr Robel, was

to distribute the documents among a network of trusted Poles in Kraków. They swiftly abandoned this idea when they realised that the penetrating smell would immediately give the game away. Instead, he drove the boxes to the Anatomical Institute at the University of Breslau (Wrocław), storing them there while he and Robel continued working on them, making the 170-mile journey from Kraków to Wrocław several times over the following few months.

When the Red Army occupied Kraków in January 1945 Beck and his administration retreated briefly to Wrocław until the swift advance of Soviet troops forced them to move again. Beck took the boxes by truck to Radebeul, just outside Dresden, where his parents lived. He left the boxes at the forwarding department of the railway station while he set off for Prague to ask the International Red Cross to safeguard the documents. Before leaving, Beck gave instructions to a railway agent that if Dresden fell into Soviet hands before his return the boxes were to be burned. It was May 1945, Europe was in chaos. Beck was unable to reach Prague, so he headed instead for Pilsen, occupied by the Americans. While he was waiting for a pass from the US military Dresden fell to the Russians. In accordance with Beck's instructions the boxes were destroyed.[14]

Testifying at the Madden hearings in America in 1952, Dr Beck informed the committee that a source in Dresden, whose name he did not wish to reveal for fear of compromising them (but who was actually Beck's father, Oskar Beck), told him that the NKVD knew where he had left the boxes and had searched Beck's parents' house in Radebeul several times.[15] Not only this: the NKVD had followed him right up to the border of the Soviet-occupied zone and searched the homes of all the people who sheltered him during this time, losing him only when he crossed into the US zone. His 62-year-old mother, he added, spent six months in prison because the Russians wanted his address. The railway agent who burned the documents was deported by the NKVD and never heard of again.[16]

Dr Beck emerges from this narrative as an ambiguous figure: during the 1945 investigations into Katyń conducted by the communist authorities in Poland, staff at the Institute of Forensic Medicine described him as an alcoholic and a sadist. Dr Robel also claimed Beck was an alcoholic who behaved brutally towards some of the Polish personnel.[17] Yet Red Cross secretary general Kazimierz Skarżyński refers to him as a 'decent German'[18] and Beck and Robel clearly cooperated closely for many months. It is hard to disentangle these contradictory accounts from the context in which they were made: in 1945 the communist authorities interrogated everyone who had been associated with the German investigation of Katyń. Polish staff may have deemed it necessary to make Beck out to be a monster in order to avoid any suggestion of collaboration with the Nazis. The only verifiable information we have is the fact that Dr Beck did his best to safeguard important evidence about Katyń. Whether he did this out of self-interest or from altruistic motives we will never know.

Although the boxes were gone, Dr Robel and his colleagues made significant efforts to preserve and hide other material relating to Katyń. Some of it has reappeared; some remains lost. Robel's staff secretly typed up copies of the diaries and in 1944 successfully smuggled them to London via an AK courier. Other copies hidden in private apartments in Kraków have never been found. Several other packages containing documents and objects relating to Katyń, entrusted by Robel to various friends, have been discovered over the years, some as recently as 1990 and 1991.

The fate of the Katyń boxes continues to tantalise historians. The enormity of the loss they represent has tempted some to speculate that they remain hidden somewhere, yet to be discovered. And where there is speculation, conspiracy theories are never far away. The eminent Katyń scholar, Janusz Zawodny, recalled a meeting with the former prime minister of the Polish government in exile, Stanisław Mikołajczyk, at Princeton University in 1957. Discussing the boxes, Mikołajczyk declared: 'One of those nine boxes was not burnt in Germany. The Americans have it. I know that from a very reliable source.'[19]

Perhaps a box of Katyń documents does indeed lie forgotten somewhere, buried deep in a CIA facility in a remote region of the United States. Why the Americans would want the documents is another question.

21

—

BURDENKO

Unfortunately we have had to give up Katyń. The Bolsheviks undoubtedly will soon 'find' that we shot the 12,000 Polish officers. That episode is one that is going to cause us quite a little trouble in the future. The Soviets are undoubtedly going to make it their business to discover as many mass graves as possible and then blame them on us.[1]

WHEN THE GERMANS FIRST DISCOVERED THE BODIES OF THE murdered Polish officers at Katyń, Goebbels eagerly seized the opportunity to drive a wedge between the Allies. By September 1943 even he had to admit that the propaganda war was lost. But the words of the Reich's master propagandist once again demonstrate his remarkably accurate reading of events.

Following publication of the Germans' 'white book' report on Katyń,[2] in September 1943, which contained the findings of the International Medical Commission and accused the Soviets of the massacre, the Soviet authorities decided to produce their own medical report. To facilitate this task, members of the Special State Commission for Investigating the Crimes of the German Fascist Aggressors (established in late 1942) joined with the Soviet intelligence services to form a special commission. In overall charge of the project was Vsevolod Merkulov, who had overseen the three special prisoner of war camps and been closely involved in their liquidation. Just as the Nazi-sponsored medical commission was made up of forensic experts from German-occupied territory, so the Soviet commission consisted of five experts from areas under Soviet control, along with several high-ranking military and other dignitaries. The chair of the commission was the chief surgeon of the Red Army, lieutenant general of the Medical Corps and one-time personal doctor to Stalin, brain specialist Nikolai Burdenko.

In late September 1943, shortly after the Red Army liberated the Smolensk area, a group of NKVD operational workers arrived in Katyń led by another familiar figure, GB Major Leonid Raikhman. The task of this special group was to 'rearrange' the Katyń site so that it produced the evidence required to suggest German guilt. The workers duly dug up the graves created by the Polish Red Cross, destroyed any evidence that could implicate the Soviets (specifically documents bearing dates earlier than April 1940) and planted forged documents with dates later than May 1940 in the clothes of selected victims.[3]

At the same time, they prepared local 'witnesses' while arresting and brutally interrogating anyone who had cooperated with the Germans. Since, according to a 1943 Soviet decree, the crime of 'cooperating with the enemy' was punishable by death, many villagers agreed to say whatever they were told. Of the three principal witnesses mentioned previously, Parfemon Kiselev ended up signing a declaration that he had been coerced by the Nazis into making a false statement; Semyon Andreev was arrested and given a long prison sentence;[4] although Ivan Krivovertsov managed to escape to the West and made further statements to the Polish authorities about what he had witnessed, his death in Britain in an apparent suicide in 1947 has long been regarded as suspicious.[5]

The 'Special State Commission for Ascertaining and Investigating the Circumstances of the Shooting of the Polish Prisoners of War by the German Fascist Invaders in the Katyń Forest', commonly referred to as the Burdenko Commission after its chair, was officially established on 13 January 1944. Its main purpose was to refute the conclusions drawn by the German-sponsored International Medical Commission and provide evidence to contradict German claims. Work officially began on 14 January 1944 with the ceremonial 'opening' of the pre-prepared graves by a group of 200 Russian sappers, accompanied by a film crew. Burdenko and his medical colleagues then conducted post-mortems on a total of 925 bodies while the non-medical members of the commission spoke to witnesses and inspected the documents 'discovered' at the site.

Like the Germans, the Russians were keen for international observers to inspect their findings and publicise them. Accordingly, on 22 January 1944 they brought a group of journalists to Katyń, consisting of Moscow correspondents for Associated Press, the *New York Times*, Reuters and the

Toronto Star. Among them was the Russian-born British war correspondent Alexander Werth, who worked for (among others) the *Sunday Times*, the *Guardian* and the BBC. They were all experienced hacks, well versed in Soviet propaganda techniques and determined not to be taken in. Noting the presence on the commission of the well-known writer Alexei Tolstoy and Nikolai, the Metropolitan of Kiev and Galicia[6], Alexander Werth was immediately cynical: 'What qualifications these "personalities" had for judging the "freshness" or "antiquity" of unearthed corpses was not quite clear.'[7] Also accompanying the group was the daughter of the US ambassador to Moscow, Kathleen Harriman, who was in Moscow as the American correspondent for the International News Service, and the third secretary of the embassy, John Melby. Only one Polish journalist was invited, Jerzy Borejsza, representing *Wolna Polska* (Free Poland), the official organ of the Soviet-backed Union of Polish Patriots (ZPP).

The journalists were invited to inspect the graves and witness an autopsy on three bodies, the evident aim of which was to demonstrate that they had been in the graves not for four years but two: 'Professor Burdenko, wearing a green frontier guard cap, was busy dissecting corpses and, waving a bit

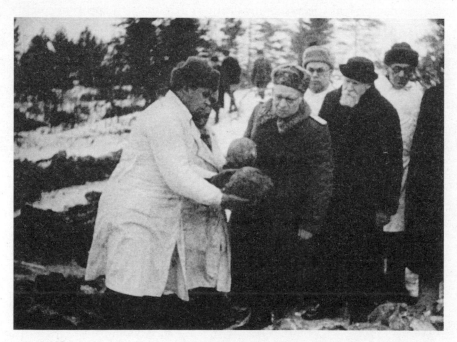

Nikolai Burdenko and the Soviet Medical Commission at Katyń, January 1944.

of greenish stinking liver at the tip of his scalpel, would say "Look how lovely and fresh it looks."[8] The journalists were not permitted to question the forensic specialists; at a press conference afterwards they could put questions to the commission members but not the witnesses. Like the British and US prisoners of war who visited before them, the journalists immediately noticed that the bodies were dressed in heavy coats and winter boots. When questioned about this, the writer Alexei Tolstoy responded by declaring that this was because the prisoners were wearing the same clothing in which they had been captured by the Red Army in September 1939. This was true. However, had they been killed in 1941, as the Soviets claimed, 'That would mean that for a year and a half they had been wearing furs, summer and winter.'[9]

The entire visit lasted only a couple of hours before the journalists were whisked back to Moscow, where the general consensus was that they were unconvinced by what they had seen. Alexander Werth pronounced the evidence 'very thin', declaring 'the whole procedure had a distinctly pre-fabricated appearance'.[10] He pointed out that the Germans had displayed hundreds of objects and documents, whereas the Soviet material consisted of a tiny number of artefacts dating from 1941. 'The Russians, in presenting their case to the outside world, had certainly taken no notice at all of what would, in Western terms, be regarded as evidence.'[11] What troubled Werth most was the Soviet tale of three prison camps supposedly 'near Smolensk', of which there was no sign. Nevertheless, as he diligently questioned both versions of events, Werth was convinced that the style of the murder was more typical of the Gestapo than the NKVD:

> The record of the NKVD…rather suggested that people in their care did frequently die in large numbers – but through neglect, overwork, bad food and exposure to cold, rather than in any kind of mass murders. Secondly, why kill them in 1940 when Russia was at peace and there could be no urgency for exterminating even these 'class enemies'?[12]

This was a very good question, but Werth's first observation about the 'style' of the murders reflects widespread Western ignorance of Stalin's Great Terror of 1937–38, during which the NKVD carried out mass executions of entire categories of people considered enemies of the Soviet state. The

German discovery in May 1943 of mass graves in the Ukrainian city of Vinnytsia, where over 9,000 (mainly) Ukrainian citizens were massacred by the NKVD in 1937–38, garnered far less international publicity than Katyń. But for anyone paying attention the parallels were striking: the victims had been shot in the back of the head, their hands bound, their bodies buried under a recreational park.[13]

There was one member of the delegation who was prepared to believe the Soviet version of events. After the visit, the US secretary of state received a telegram confirming 'the general evidence and testimony are inconclusive, but Kathleen and embassy staff member believe probability massacre perpetrated by Germans'.[14] During her testimony at the Madden hearings in 1952, Kathleen Harriman (now Mortimer) spoke of her visit:

> We heard one girl testify (Anna Mihailovna Alexeyeva) that towards the end of August 1941 she and the other girls noted that often opened and closed cars and trucks could be heard turning off the highway at the Goat Hill entrance. When this happened invariably the Germans in the dacha would go out into the woods. About ten minutes later single shots, fired at regular intervals, would be heard. When the shots ceased the officers, accompanied by German non-commissioned officers and enlisted men driving empty trucks, would return to the dacha. Always on these days the bath house water was heated. The men went directly to the baths and returned to be served a 'particularly tasty meal' plus double the usual hard liquor ration. The girl said on these days the soldiers seemed noisier than usual and talked more. Once Alexeyeva was asked to wash off fresh blood from one of the non-commissioned officers' sleeves.[15]

Another female witness described how

> she heard noises near the dacha and looked out and saw two Poles hovering around under guard. She was ordered back into the kitchen, but her 'feminine curiosity' got the best of her. She went back to the window and saw the Poles were being led away into the woods. Soon after two single shots were heard.[16]

The level of detail woven into these statements echoes the fiction created around the prisoners' departure from the camps in the spring of 1940. By creating a narrative rich in apparently trivial details, the NKVD aimed to convince their audience that no fictional version of events could possibly be so comprehensive. The use of female witnesses, with their apparently artless references to 'feminine curiosity' and 'tasty meals' was evidently designed to induce the visitors to trust their honesty. It had little effect on the hard-boiled male journalists; the less experienced Harriman was perhaps more susceptible. In this case, however, the NKVD were sloppy: the witness Anna Mihailovna places the shootings in August 1941, the date initially given out by Moscow Radio, whereas the report's conclusion claims the killings took place between September and December 1941.

Kathleen Harriman was later criticised for not questioning the Soviet version of events, the implication being that she was gullible and naive. But Alexander Werth conceded that the Western correspondents who visited Katyń were placed in an impossible position: 'They could do little more than say what they had been shown; and even any implied criticism of the Russian handling of the whole case, however mild, was deleted by the Soviet censorship.' Another of the journalists in the group, W.L. White, wrote in 1945 that their reports were censored in such a way that all qualifying words such as 'in my opinion' or 'probably' were cut out so that 'the stories as received in America were as firmly damning of the Germans as *Pravda*'s editorials.'[17] The journalists were also motivated by a powerful imperative not to play into German hands: 'Might it not also have been *this* consideration,' asks Werth, 'which prompted Miss Harriman to state in January 1944 that she was "satisfied" that the Russian version was correct?'[18] The position of Kathleen Harriman's father, Averill Harriman, may also have influenced her views: Harriman was US ambassador to Moscow. It would have been politically awkward had his daughter pointed the finger of blame at America's Soviet allies.

The Burdenko report was published in Russian on 25 January 1944. The English version appeared a few days later. Unsurprisingly, the report concluded that the Germans were responsible for the Katyń Massacre, declaring the methods used to kill the victims to be typical of the Nazis. The commission's findings were widely publicised, supported by a small selection of documents 'discovered' on the bodies bearing dates later than April 1940. Whereas the Germans had painstakingly compiled a comprehensive list of names and amassed over 3,000 objects, the Burdenko Commission offered up as evidence a sum total of nine items. They made no effort to identify any of the victims beyond the few they had selected as possessing documents bearing the appropriate dates.

The version of the Katyń story proposed by the Burdenko Commission went as follows: the occupants of the camps of Kozelsk, Starobelsk and Ostashkov were moved in April and May 1940 to three special ON (*Osobovego Naznechenya*) POW camps near Smolensk named 'No. 1 – ON, No. 2 – ON, and No. 3 – ON'. Following the occupation of the Smolensk area by the German army in the summer of 1941, the Polish prisoners fell into German hands. Some time between September and December 1941 the Germans executed these men, using German-manufactured Geco 7.65mm ammunition. The Soviet chief of one of the ON camps declared that orders for the evacuation of the camp in July 1941 did not reach him. In the face of the rapid German advance, he attempted on his own initiative to secure railway cars for the Poles but the railway official in Smolensk (who gave evidence to corroborate this claim) was unable to supply them, so he fled, leaving the prisoners to their fate. The number of victims was given as 11,000 (matching the German claim), and the date of the killings adjusted from 'summer 1941' to 'between September and December 1941' in response to the much-noted fact that the men were wearing winter uniforms. The Commission even went so far as to name three German officers of the 537th Construction Battalion who were supposedly responsible for carrying out the massacre: Lieutenants Ahrens, Rekst and Hodt. The men existed, although their names and military designations were incorrect.

The intended audience for both Nazi and Soviet propaganda was primarily the Allied powers, Britain and the US. For this audience the detailed forensic information – arguments about layers of calcium in a skull, the number of rings on a pine tree or the state of decomposition of bodies – as well as circumstantial evidence such as the type of bullets used or the documents found on the bodies – could feasibly be argued to be inconclusive on either side. Since the site was occupied in turn by both the supposed perpetrators of the crime, any investigations conducted *in situ* could be open to accusations of falsification for political purposes. Similarly, any witness statements were open to accusations that the witnesses had been intimidated or bribed into saying whatever would please their interrogators.

However, for anyone with even a passing knowledge of the Polish experience in the Soviet Union between 1939 and 1942, the report presented numerous inconsistencies, many of which were patently absurd: the wildly inaccurate number of victims given; the claim that there were three camps for Polish prisoners near Smolensk, which was demonstrably untrue. It was also widely known that the Soviets never let their prisoners fall into enemy hands, preferring either to deport them eastwards or liquidate them. Most damning of all was the fact that, in the many meetings between Polish and Soviet authorities during 1941–42, when the Poles repeatedly asked about the fate of their missing officers, not once had anyone on the Soviet side ever suggested that these men had been captured by the Germans. Only at the tail end of months of Polish enquiries did Stalin suggest to General Anders (in their meeting on 18 March 1942) that the prisoners might have been 'in camps in territories which have been taken by the Germans and come to be dispersed'. Vyshinsky later echoed this shift in emphasis in his final meeting with Ambassador Kot in July 1942. 'Everybody has been released. Some were released before our war with Germany, some after.'[19]

Following publication of the Burdenko Commission's report, the British ambassador to the Polish government in exile, Sir Owen O'Malley, wrote a second dispatch to Foreign Secretary Sir Anthony Eden (his first, quoted earlier, dealt with German claims) in which he expressed his views on the claims made by the Soviets.

O'Malley points out the similarities and differences between the propaganda methods employed by the Nazis and the Soviets. The Germans relied primarily on the findings of an international commission of medical experts and invited Polish delegations and the Polish Red Cross to the site, whereas the Soviet commission consisted uniquely of Soviet forensic experts and state officials (or, as American journalist W.L. White put it, 'If the German Commission was a 90 percent Axis party, the Russian Commission was a 100 percent Soviet picnic.'[20]). Both invited foreign journalists to the scene, making sure the visits were as luxurious as possible in the context of war: 'The most up-to-date sleeping cars were provided by the Russians and aeroplanes by the Germans for their guests: and in both cases, after a busy day among the corpses, these were served with smoked salmon, caviar, champagne and other delicacies.'[21]

For O'Malley, one of the strongest reasons for believing in Soviet guilt was because this was the conclusion the Poles themselves had come to. He pointed out that the Poles who visited Katyń (among whom were members of the Polish underground) hated the Nazis and Soviets in equal measure and had no incentive to conclude in favour of one side over another. He also observed that none of the British and American correspondents who visited Katyń, with the exception of Kathleen Harriman, were convinced by Soviet claims. O'Malley gives both sides fair consideration, admitting that 'if the evidence of the Soviet Government's witnesses and experts could be trusted, it would be just possible to believe in the truth of the Russian story'. But there was a particular element in the Soviet version of events which for O'Malley simply did not stand up:

> The Russian story assumes that about 10,000 Polish officers and men, employed in forced labour, lived in the district of Smolensk from April 1940 till July 1941 and passed into German captivity when the Germans captured it in July 1941 without a single one of them having escaped and fallen again into Russian hands or reported to a Polish consul in Russia or to the Polish Underground movement in Poland. This is quite incredible; not only to those who know anything about prisoner of war camps in Russia, or who pictures to himself the disorganisation and confusion which must have attended the Russian exit and German entry into Smolensk, but the assumption which I have described as essential to the Russian case is actually destroyed by the words of the Russian investigating committee itself. The commission asserts that many Polish prisoners did in fact escape after the district of Smolensk had been overrun by the Germans, and describes the frequent 'round-ups' of escaped prisoners which the Germans organised. The Russian story gives no explanation why in these circumstances not a single one of the Poles who were allegedly transferred from Kozelsk, Starobelsk and Ostashkov to the labour camps Nos. 1 O.N., 2 O.N. and 3 O.N. has ever been seen or heard of alive again.[22]

To conclude, O'Malley notes that not a single letter, postcard or telegram had ever been received by families of the missing officers after April 1940; not one of the enquiries addressed by the Polish Red Cross and the Polish government to the Soviet government had ever been answered. If the prisoners had been transferred to these camps then why, he asks, did the Soviet government not say so long ago?

O'Malley's dispatches are a lesson in eloquently restrained outrage. 'Let us think of these things always and speak of them never,' he concludes.

> To speak of them never is the advice which I have been giving to the Polish government, but it has been unnecessary. They have received the Russian report in silence. Affliction and residence in this country seem to be teaching them how much better it is in political life to leave unsaid those things about which one feels most passionately.[23]

After Eden and Churchill had read it, O'Malley's dispatch was not circulated widely in the British government, where the prevailing sentiment was that the less said about Katyń the better. However, Churchill asked Eden in a personal minute of 30 January 1944 to enquire secretly of O'Malley what his opinion was concerning the trees: 'How does the argument about the length of time the birch trees had grown over the grave fit in with this new tale? Did anybody look at the birch trees? All this is merely to ascertain the facts, because we should none of us ever speak a word about it.'[24]

O'Malley's reply was addressed to the permanent undersecretary for foreign affairs, Sir Alexander Cadogan:

> The little conifers also deserve more attention than they have received. In the first place they are presumptive evidence of Russian guilt; for, considering the conditions under which the German army advanced through Smolensk in July 1941 in full expectation of early and complete victory, it is most unlikely, if the Polish officers had been murdered by Germans and not Russians, that the Germans would have bothered to cover up their victims' graves with young trees. In the second place, one of these young trees under examination by a competent botanist would reveal beyond any possibility of doubt whether it had last been transplanted in May 1940 or some time subsequent to July 1941. Perhaps this test of Russian veracity will presently be made.[25]

O'Malley continued making enquiries of various experts concerning the reliability of both the German and Soviet reports, but to little effect. In February

1944 the Soviet Section of the Foreign Office Research Department, under the direction of Russian expert Professor Benedict Humphrey Sumner, was given the official task of analysing the Burdenko Commission's report. Unlike O'Malley, Sumner based his conclusions only on examination of the Soviet report, not taking into consideration the material provided by the Poles and accepting large portions of the Soviet report at face value. Comparing the two versions of events, Sumner concluded 'the report of the Special Commission may be said to make out a good, though not a conclusive, case for the perpetration of the massacres by the Germans'.[26] The same question that exercised O'Malley so much – namely the fact that the Soviets had given no response to any of the multiple enquiries about the whereabouts of the missing men – is addressed by Sumner in the following manner:

> The only possible explanation seems to be that there had been terrible confusion and that the GPU or other officials had blundered badly or disobeyed orders and had taken refuge in evasion and extreme procrastination in order to save their faces and perhaps their skins.

Given the significance of the 'big mistake' to which Beria alluded in conversation with Berling in 1940, there is a certain irony in a British official seeking to explain away facts that did not fit by concluding that Soviet silence on the missing officers was the result of their desire to cover up a mistake. The reading was partially correct; unfortunately, Sumner deployed it in the service of the wrong conclusion. Likewise, his answer to the absence of correspondence after the spring of 1940 was to pounce upon a single piece of 'evidence' appearing in the Soviet newspaper *Pravda*, in which a member of a delegation of Poles visiting the Katyń site on 30 January 1944 informed the Pravda correspondent that 'he had been in one of the Katyń camps until June 1940, had then been transferred elsewhere, and in February 1941 had received a letter from a Polish officer friend (name and regiment given) from that Katyń camp dated January 1941'. Sumner omits to mention, or is unaware of the fact, that those present at the ceremony were members of the 1st Tadeusz Kościuszko Division, the Soviet-sponsored Polish infantry division within the Red Army, led by General Zygmunt Berling. Whether the obliging delegate had actually been a prisoner in one of the three camps is dubious.

The official stance of the British Foreign Office on Katyń eventually settled on the view formulated by Sir William Malkin, legal adviser to the Foreign Office, who considered the Soviet case to be 'stronger than was first thought and calls, at any rate, for suspension of judgement'.[27] Sir Alexander Cadogan responded less ambiguously to Sumner's view of the Soviet Commission's case as a strong one, describing it as 'absolute nonsense' before adding that all evidence on both sides was faked. 'But, as I say, it may be as well, as we have given an estimate from one angle, to correct it from the other.'[28] Foreign Secretary Anthony Eden initialled Cadogan's comment with two words: 'I agree', and thus the British government effectively washed its hands of the whole awkward affair. Their stance was to remain essentially unchanged for the next forty-five years, at which point it became irrelevant.

Meanwhile, as mentioned above, on 30 January 1944 a ceremony was held in the Katyń Forest beside the freshly re-covered graves. Six hundred representatives of the 1st Kościuszko Division, accompanied by an orchestra, joined in a mass to commemorate the dead. General Berling gave a speech, after which the men marched ceremoniously past the graves, on which a plaque had been placed with the inscription, 'In memory of the fallen, 1941' alongside an image of the Polish eagle. By the entrance to the Katyń Forest stood a large sign, written in Russian and Polish: 'Here, in the Katyń Forest, in the autumn of 1941 the Nazi monsters shot 11,000 Polish prisoners of war, soldiers and officers. Soldier of the Red Army – avenge them!'

In his memoirs (written many years later and only published in full in 1990, after the collapse of communism and several years after his death), Zygmunt Berling acknowledges Soviet responsibility for Katyń, proposing that it was the refusal of Polish officers to cooperate with the NKVD that 'most likely influenced the subsequent decision of the Soviet authorities which resulted in the terrible tragedy of Katyń'.[29] Whether he ever believed the Soviet version of events we will never know. During and after the war he most likely found himself unable to reconcile the idea of Soviet guilt with his own acceptance of a Soviet-backed Polish state. Like the governments of Britain and the US, he chose simply to look away.

In the 11 February edition of *Wolna Polska*, the leader of the Union of Polish Patriots, Wanda Wasilewska, issued a stirring call to arms:

For the third time the graves of Katyń have been opened. They cry out and call to the entire world… The blood of Katyń calls us to unforgiving and merciless revenge. Listen to that voice, soldiers of our Corps…When you go west, as you stab the enemy in the chest, through gritted teeth whisper these words to yourself: for Warsaw, for Westerplatte, for Kutno – and do not forget to add: for Katyń![30]

The war was reaching its final act. In August 1944 Warsaw rose in a doomed attempt to wrest control of the capital from the Nazis before the arrival of the Red Army sealed Poland's fate. For two months they fought, alone and unaided, soldiers and civilians, men, women, boys, girls, in one last, desperate act of fatal heroism. Mistimed, miscalculated, undertaken against all rational advice, the Warsaw Rising is seared into Poland's collective memory as one of its noblest and most catastrophic defeats. District by district the German tanks and planes moved inexorably to crush the insurgents. In September, General Berling's Polish divisions arrived in the Warsaw district of Praga, on the south side of the River Vistula, taking heavy casualties as they attempted to bridge the river before being ordered to withdraw. No other help from the Soviets was forthcoming; Stalin denied British and US planes landing rights that would have enabled them to drop aid to the beleaguered city; he denounced the AK as criminals. On 2 October General Bór-Komorowski signed the act of capitulation. The AK were taken as prisoners of war, the rest of the city evacuated before Hitler vindictively ordered it razed to the ground. All that was left for the triumphant Red Army when they entered Warsaw in January 1945 was a city of ashes and ghosts.

We do not know if the members of the Burdenko Commission acted in good faith, but Nikolai Burdenko himself may have known or suspected the truth. Burdenko was a close family friend of Boris Olshansky, formerly an associate professor of mathematics at the University of Voronezh who served as an officer in the Red Army during the war but escaped to the West in 1948 while stationed in Germany. Burdenko had helped Olshansky academically and financially after his father's death in 1929 and the pair had subsequently remained in touch. In a statement to the Madden Committee in 1952 Olshansky claimed that during a work-related visit to Moscow in April 1946 he went to visit his father's old friend. Burdenko, now in his late sixties, was seriously ill and had withdrawn from public life. During their conversation the subject of Katyń came up, causing Burdenko to react nervously. He told Olshansky that he believed there were and would continue to be many 'Katyńs' in Russia. Anyone digging in Russian soil would find such things. He then confessed he had been under personal orders from Stalin to investigate the graves at Katyń. When he inspected the bodies it was clear to him they were four years old and the men had been killed in 1940. Using the same terms as Beria in the oft-reported conversation with Berling, Burdenko concluded that, in his view, 'our NKVD friends made a mistake'.[31]

The Soviet prosecution presented an extract of the Burdenko Commission report as evidence at the 1946 Nuremberg trials. After the war the report was cited in all Soviet media, encyclopaedias, history books and notes to foreign governments, right up until the official admission of Soviet guilt on 13 April 1990.

PART V

Cold War 1945–

*Yalta, February 1945. Winston Churchill and Stalin share
a joke with the help of Stalin's interpreter, Pavlov.*

22

—

PURSUIT

As the Red Army approached Kraków in early January 1945, many of the people who had been involved in the German-led investigation of Katyń began to feel nervous about what would follow once the Russians established control over the city. Dr Marian Wodziński took the precaution of leaving Kraków to stay with friends in Jędrzejów, a town about fifty miles away where he had family, including a cousin, Stefania Wanda Cioch. His plan was to remain there until he had a better idea of the situation. The Red Army 'liberated' ruined Warsaw on 17 January 1945; two days later they entered Kraków. Wodziński waited, unsure whether it was safe for him to return.

Since Stefania Cioch was able to travel freely she agreed to take a letter from her cousin to Dr Robel at the Institute of Forensic Medicine, letting him know where Wodziński was and asking for news. Robel informed her that as soon as the Soviets entered Kraków the NKVD went directly to the Institute, asking the caretakers if they knew where Dr Wodziński was and wanting information on the whereabouts of the boxes containing the Katyń documents. The caretakers replied that they knew nothing about Wodziński, and that the boxes had been taken away by the Germans. Dr Robel tried to reassure Cioch: he did not believe that Dr Wodziński was in any real danger because if the NKVD arrested him it would surely point too obviously to Soviet guilt. Wodziński nevertheless decided it was safer to remain in Jędrzejów, where there was no sign of the NKVD as yet. He moved in with his cousin's family and waited for further news. In March 1945 he learned that Dr Robel had been arrested by the NKVD, along with three colleagues.

Dr Robel was detained not in a prison but a house, isolated from his colleagues and family. His interrogation was conducted in a supremely 'gentlemanly' manner by an NKVD general who insisted (as senior NKVD officers desiring cooperation were wont to do) that Robel was not a prisoner: the general simply wanted some information from him. Robel later confessed to Stefania Cioch that after a prolonged period of this 'soft' but persistent questioning he was convinced that anyone would say whatever the interviewer wanted and that he now finally understood how so many Soviet citizens had signed confessions accusing themselves during the trials of the 1930s.[1]

The NKVD general asked Dr Robel repeatedly about Dr Wodziński. What was he like? Who were his friends? Where was he staying? And where had he hidden the Katyń boxes? The same questions were put to Robel's colleagues, again and again. Robel tried to downplay Wodziński's role at Katyń, claiming he was just a Red Cross doctor doing his job and that he suffered from a serious heart problem. To which the NKVD general supposedly replied, 'That sick man could still ruin our international policies in ten years' time with some stupid article or book about this.'[2] After eight weeks Dr Robel and his colleagues were released thanks to the joint intervention of the rector and deacon of Kraków's Jagiellonian University. Robel's experience of arrest convinced him of two things: the NKVD was the most effective security force in the world, and Dr Wodziński was in grave danger. Not only did the NKVD apparently believe he knew where the boxes were hidden, but during one conversation the NKVD general told Robel he wanted Wodziński to make a public statement naming the Germans as the perpetrators of the Katyń Massacre. When Dr Robel next saw Stefania Cioch he urged her to tell her cousin to move out of her family's apartment and change his name immediately.

Dr Wodziński followed Robel's advice. He changed his name to Cioch and moved from Jędrzejów to the city of Katowice, where he hid with the help of AK colleagues. Meanwhile, Stefania kept in touch with Dr Robel and her cousin's former boss, Professor Olbrycht (who had returned to his post at the Institute of Forensic Medicine after his release from Auschwitz). From Olbrycht she learned that the search for Dr Wodziński was now in the hands of the UB (*Urząd Bezpieczeństwa*), the newly-created Polish equivalent of the NKVD, and that a succession of 'friends' and 'colleagues' had been turning up at Wodziński's parents' flat in Kraków looking for him on various slim pretexts.

Since the Red Army's entry into Polish territory, the familiar pattern of persecution had been in full swing, courtesy of the NKVD[3] and their Polish acolytes. As the Red Army swept west, the Soviet security forces tidied up in their wake, removing any obstacles (in the form of human beings deemed unfriendly to Soviet rule) in preparation for the new order. In July 1944 the Soviets had parachuted in a group of pro-Soviet Polish communists to form a rival administration to the government in exile in London. The Polish Committee of National Liberation (*Polski Komitet Wyzwolenia Narodowego* – PKWN), or the 'Lublin Committee' after the city where it was based, was the offspring of a union between Wanda Wasilewska's Union of Polish Patriots (ZPP) and the Polish Workers' Party (*Polska Partia Robotnicza* – PPR). In January 1945 Stalin informed Churchill that the Soviet Union had decided to recognise the Lublin Committee unilaterally as the Provisional Government of the Polish Republic on the basis that the London government was no longer functioning (the same argument employed by the Soviets when they invaded eastern Poland in 1939). At the Yalta Conference in February 1945 Churchill and Roosevelt declared themselves willing to recognise the Provisional Government on condition that members of other political parties from inside and outside Poland were included within it, with 'free and unfettered elections' to take place at a later date. The resulting Provisional Government of National Unity was something of a misnomer: a handful of non-communists were handed minor cabinet posts to appease the Allies; in reality the government was under Soviet control. In July 1945 Britain and the USA formally withdrew recognition of the Polish government in exile in London and accepted the legitimacy of the Provisional Government of National Unity.

The provisional Polish government wasted no time in asserting its desire to please Moscow. In June 1945 it launched an official investigation into Katyń, headed by the chief prosecutor of the Supreme Court and Supreme National Tribunal for the Pursuit of War Crimes in Poland, Dr Jerzy Sawicki. The aim of the investigation was to seek out Polish citizens who had cooperated with the occupying German forces 'to the detriment of the Polish state'.[4] The idea was to prepare for a public trial which, like the Burdenko Commission report, would serve to shore up the Soviet version of the Katyń narrative by providing solid 'evidence' of German culpability while simultaneously suppressing the counter-narrative of Soviet guilt.

The investigation zealously pursued anyone who had spoken in public about Katyń and was deemed to exert an influence on Polish public opinion. Three men in particular were singled out: the writer Ferdynand Goetel, who had made a public statement about his visit to Katyń and was closely involved in convincing the Polish Red Cross to investigate the crime; Jan Emil Skiwski, who accompanied Goetel in the first Polish delegation to Katyń and wrote about Soviet guilt in the Nazi-sponsored press; and Dr Marian Wodziński, who had not only compiled a detailed forensic report on his five weeks at Katyń but had made the mistake of speaking to the journalist Władysław Kawecki in May 1943, unwisely trusting Kawecki's promise not to mention Wodziński's name in his subsequent article. Kawecki had ignored Wodziński's request and 'quoted' the doctor as saying the murders definitely took place in 1940.[5]

On 21 June 1945 a formal investigation was launched against Ferdynand Goetel and Jan Emil Skiwski and a warrant issued by prosecutor Dr Roman Martini for their arrest. On 7 July he added Dr Marian Wodziński's name to the list. Three days later, on 10 July, the three arrest warrants appeared in the Kraków press accusing the men of collaborating with the Nazis. This pattern was repeated all over Poland as the new regime employed the accusation of Nazi collaboration as a pretext to rid themselves of a host of undesirables: members of the AK and other anti-Soviet resistance groups, opposition politicians, inconveniently independent thinkers and insufficiently cooperative witnesses. A series of show trials in the immediate post-war period resulted in the imprisonment, deportation or public execution of some of Poland's most courageous citizens, men and women who had fought six years of Nazi oppression only to fall foul of their own puppet Stalinist regime.

When Stefania Cioch discovered a public trial was planned at which her cousin would be the principal defendant, she immediately warned Dr Wodziński, who accordingly uprooted himself again, leaving Katowice for Poznań, where he was once more sheltered by former members of the AK.[6] He escaped to Britain in December 1945, remaining there for the rest of his life. Although Dr Wodziński gave a deposition to the Polish military authorities in London in 1947 he did not testify at the 1952 Madden hearings and never spoke publicly about Katyń again. For most of his career he worked as a GP in Liverpool.

Ferdynand Goetel was in hiding in a convent in Kraków when he learned that Polish investigators were seeking him.

> I sent word to the chief investigator of Katyń, Sawicki, and asked: 'What is the matter, what do they want from me?' He answered, 'Oh, we have nothing against Mr. Goetel, who is a famous writer, but if he signs a statement that he was kept by force at Katyń and that his main impression in Katyń was that the massacre was done by Germans, Oh, we have nothing; he can live here and write books and so on.' I refused.[7]

Goetel escaped from Poland in December 1945 using a false passport. He made his way to Italy, where he joined the Polish II Corps, later travelling with them to England. While he was in Italy Goetel came across Ivan Krivovertsov, one of the local witnesses in the German investigations at Katyń. Krivovertsov had correctly concluded that his cooperation with the Germans would not go well for him once the Soviets re-occupied the Smolensk region. He escaped, first to West Germany, where he gave his story to a Polish liaison officer and made a statement to a field court in May 1945. Then, in the autumn of 1946, he travelled with the Polish II Corps to Italy, where he gave a full statement not only to Ferdynand Goetel but to another writer who had participated in one of the delegations to Katyń, Józef Mackiewicz.[8] Krivovertsov's fate thereafter is somewhat cloudy: using the pseudonym Mikhail Loboda he accompanied the Polish army to Britain and was sent to a resettlement camp in Sussex. For a while he worked for the Polish Red Cross but soon proved disruptive, drinking heavily with a friend and telling anyone who would listen that he was the only living witness to the Katyń Massacre and demanding special treatment. He was transferred to Stowell Park camp near Cheltenham, then in October 1947 to Easton-in-Gordano in Somerset, where he was found hanged on 30 October 1947 in an apparent suicide.[9] It is possible, although not verifiable, that the 'suicide' was the work of the NKVD.

Like Dr Wodziński, Ferdynand Goetel remained in exile in London for the rest of his life. He wrote and spoke frequently about Katyń before his death in 1960. Meanwhile Jan Emil Skiwski, who really had collaborated with the Nazis, escaped with the retreating Germans and was no longer in Poland when the warrant for his arrest was published.

The investigation of Ferdynand Goetel and Jan Emil Skiwski served as a pretext for the Polish communist authorities to interview many prominent Polish literary figures. This was not just an exercise in obtaining information on the two writers (about whom the prosecutors seemed to know very little). It was also an attempt to take the temperature of Polish public opinion regarding Katyń. The esteemed intellectuals were supposed to explain how it was that, during a brutal Nazi occupation, the Polish people had allowed themselves to be 'taken in' by German propaganda about Katyń rather than heeding what Moscow had to say. A local Kraków vice-prosecutor, Władysław Wyrobków, decided in 1961 to keep the interviews for posterity. The transcripts convey an impression of Ferdynand Goetel as a man who, despite his questionable political opinions, was popular with his fellow writers and highly respected by them. He used his prominent position to help many artists during the war and they in turn recognised his generosity and commitment. Jan Emil Skiwski, on the other hand, was viewed as a straightforward collaborator. As to public opinion on Katyń, feelings in Poland during and just after the war were profoundly conflicted about this painful subject. Since 1943 the Poles had been subjected to a barrage of propaganda from both sides. Although many were initially receptive to the idea of Nazi guilt, the mounting evidence to the contrary had led most people to conclude that the Soviets were responsible for the crime. Although some of the writers interviewed were willing to concede that the systematic brutality of the crime was more 'in the style of' the Nazis than the Bolsheviks, one can only speculate whether they were saying this because they believed it or in order to avoid arrest. After all, they were hardly going to tell a government vice-prosecutor that they thought the Russians did it.[10]

The idea of a trial of the 'participants in the Katyń provocation', featuring Ferdynand Goetel, Dr Marian Wodziński and Jan Emil Skiwski as the prime exhibits had been given prior approval by the Soviet deputy commissar for foreign affairs, Andrey Vyshinsky. Polish prosecutors also proposed that the trial take evidence from members of the Burdenko Commission as well as Bulgarian, Czech and Finnish doctors who had participated in the German International Medical Commission and been 'exploited' by the Germans into providing false testimony.[11] However, for reasons unknown the Katyń trial never went ahead. In March 1946 the prosecutor Roman Martini, who had been tasked with interrogating witnesses, was murdered. For many years his death was thought to be connected to Katyń: it was rumoured he had been killed by the NKVD after discovering evidence in Gestapo archives in Minsk that convinced him of Soviet guilt and then writing a report citing several NKVD officers by name. A competing rumour connected the murder to an accusation that Martini had seduced a young girl. A third theory suggested that in fact it was the anti-communist underground who killed him as a communist collaborator. The truth has never been established.[12] After his death, the impetus for the trial was lost and the idea quietly shelved. Nevertheless, as late as 1956 Skiwski, Goetel and Wodziński remained on a list of persons 'of interest' to the communist Polish authorities. Friends and relatives still received visits from the militia asking if they had seen them. It was fortunate that Dr Wodziński escaped Poland: according to his cousin, once the idea of a trial was dropped in September 1945 the UB received orders that if they found him they should simply dispose of him on the quiet.[13] It is little surprise that he never returned to Poland during his lifetime and rarely spoke about Katyń, even to his family.[14]

Aside from the three principal figures of Goetel, Dr Wodziński and Skiwski, the list of those who were arrested, bullied, interrogated, intimidated or imprisoned because of their involvement in the Katyń investigations is extensive.

On 1 May 1945 almost the entirety of the board of directors of the Polish Red Cross was replaced. Of those involved in the Katyń investigations, Kazimierz Skarżyński was interrogated several times in June and July 1945 before fleeing Poland in May 1946, later settling in Canada. Other members of the Red Cross were kept under surveillance, experienced difficulties finding work or were pressured into signing false statements. Kraków's Red Cross director, Dr Adam Schebesta, initially continued working in the Silesia region (at around this time he also changed the spelling of his name from Schebesta to Szebesta). Despite an extraordinary record of public service, in 1950 the UB arrested Szebesta and imprisoned him for his participation in the Katyń investigations and his wartime involvement with the AK (perhaps also for his membership of the Polish Socialist Party, of which he was a member between 1945–48). They freed him after two months, possibly thanks to the intervention of the International Red Cross.[15] Two years later, an interview appeared in the state-backed newspaper *Dziennik Zachodny* in which Szebesta appears to accuse the Germans of the Katyń crime. Although there is no detailed evidence to corroborate this, it is possible that he was coerced into signing a declaration to this effect while he was in prison.[16]

After his release from NKVD arrest in May 1945 Dr Jan Zygmunt Robel was allowed to continue his work in peace and was even appointed director of the newly-reopened Polish State Institute of Forensic Medicine in Kraków. Robel attributed his good fortune to the fact that during one of his conversations with the NKVD general he had (in an effort to deflect interest from Dr Wodziński) rather boldly claimed to know far more than Wodziński about who was really responsible for Katyń and declared that he would be prepared to make a public statement, whatever the personal cost to him. In his view the NKVD were reluctant to murder such a prominent scientist for fear it would point strongly to their guilt, so they left him alone.[17] Dr Wodziński's former boss, the forensic expert and former Auschwitz inmate Professor Olbrycht, played a major role in Poland's post-war investigations of Nazi war crimes. He and his wife communicated regularly with Stefania Cioch, providing her with information to pass on to her cousin.

The discovery of the graves at Katyń in 1943 and subsequent German efforts to publicise the crime had greatly expanded the number of people who could potentially question the Soviet version of events. In order to control the narrative, therefore, the NKVD had to spread their net beyond Poland's borders. They had already dealt with the local witnesses. Next in line were the forensic experts who had participated in the German-sponsored International Medical Commission. The NKVD pressured several of the doctors whose countries were now under communist control to retract their statements: the Bulgarian expert, Dr Markov, was accused of collaboration with the enemy and in February 1945 pleaded guilty before a people's court in Sofia, confessing he had signed his statement under duress. He later gave evidence for the Soviet side at the Nuremberg trials. The Czech doctor, Professor Hájek, was also coerced into making a statement blaming the Germans. Others fled: following the arrest of his family by the NKVD in November 1944 the Romanian doctor, Professor Birkle, left for Switzerland on a false passport, later settling in Peru. The Croatian, Dr Miloslavich, emigrated to the USA in 1944. Professor Orsós of Hungary went into exile, as did the Slovakian, Professor Šubik, who was imprisoned after 1945 and fled abroad in 1952.[18]

The long reach of the NKVD even stretched as far as Western Europe. In 1948 the Italian communist party accused Professor Palmieri of collaboration with the Nazis; he was forbidden to lecture at his university. The Finn, Professor Saxen, was interrogated and pressured to change his statement, although he did not retract it. Left-wing deputies in the Geneva National Council attacked Professor Naville of Switzerland (the only representative of a neutral country to participate in the commission), attempting to bring a motion demanding that he either revoke his statement or be dismissed from his post for participating in the 'Katyń provocation'. The Council fully vindicated Naville, who went on to give evidence to the 1952 Madden Committee, confirming that the statement of the medical experts was correct and had been arrived at without pressure from the Germans. Five of the forensic specialists who participated in the International Medical Commission testified at the Madden hearings: Palmieri, Miloslavich, Orsos, Naville and Tramsen. The communist activists in Italy and Switzerland who brought accusations against these doctors presumably acted in good faith: primed to believe the Nazis guilty of all manner of crimes, ignorant of the facts, they believed what they were told by their Soviet contacts and acted accordingly.

In Poland the work begun by the NKVD was continued by the UB. Families of the victims were arrested and interrogated, their apartments searched, their belongings removed. Widows were issued with falsified death certificates, their pension benefits denied. Records referring to the public achievements of victims were erased: sporting heroes disappeared, scientific research was ignored. Children soon learned that, when asked what happened to their father during the war, they were to answer, 'He went away and never came back.' When filling in the section of a form asking 'Occupation of father/husband', the accepted formula was 'He died during the war.'

At least the families of the Kozelsk prisoners knew their fate. The wives of the prisoners of Starobelsk and Ostashkov had no such certainty. Some persisted in hoping that their husbands would one day return. 'To the very end [she] refused to believe her husband had died.... She always held on to the hope he was alive. She would ask everywhere, read every newspaper announcement, even though the disappearance of the Polish officers was hush-hush.'[19] Other women simply never mentioned their husbands again, for the sake of their children maintaining a silence so absolute as to be utterly mystifying to the children concerned. As one recalled: 'He didn't write, he gave no sign of life.' From time to time strangers would turn up at their flat, mainly privates from the army, and tell them he was in the Omsk region, where things were very tough. 'These were most likely informers recruited by the Soviets.'[20] History books and school textbooks referred to Katyń as a Nazi crime. All monuments relating to the Katyń Massacre bore the date 1941, with inscriptions dedicated to the victims of the 'German–Fascist occupiers'.

Shortly after the end of the war, in August 1945, the Allies came to an agreement concerning an International Military Tribunal to try enemy war criminals. The tribunal was to sit in the German city of Nuremberg, in the American zone of occupation. Britain, the US, the Soviet Union and France would run it as a joint enterprise with judges and prosecutors representing all four countries. Each country was allotted a specific sphere of responsibility. Soviet prosecutors were given responsibility for Nazi crimes committed in the Soviet zone of occupation.

The main focus of the Allies' attention at Nuremberg was the prosecution of high-ranking Nazis for war crimes, of which the Holocaust was naturally the most significant. Among the Soviet charges against Nazi leaders, however, was the murder of the Polish officers at Katyń. It read: 'In September 1941, 11,000 Polish officers, who were prisoners of war, were killed in the Katyń Forest, near Smolensk.' The charge had been added against the advice of both British and US prosecutors, aware of its controversial nature and not wishing the tribunal to be seen as a forum for 'victors' justice'. Nevertheless, the Soviets persisted. The indictment was presented to the International Military Tribunal in Berlin on 18 October 1945.

The Soviet deputy prosecutor, Colonel Yuri Povrovsky, opened the case for the prosecution on 13–14 February 1946. Submitting an extract of the Burdenko Commission report as evidence, he claimed that the Katyń Massacre had been committed in 1941 by the 537th Sapper Regiment of the Wehrmacht under the orders of officers Ahrens, Rekst and Hodt.

Since Hermann Göring was the highest-ranking officer to be tried at Nuremberg he was cited in all cases presented before the Tribunal. When his defence lawyer, Dr Otto Stahmer, noticed Katyń among the charges he decided that here was one accusation, at least, on which he could argue for Göring's innocence. Accordingly, Stahmer asked permission to call the German officers listed in the Soviet accusation as witnesses for the defence. Although his request met with opposition from the Soviet prosecutor, permission was granted to call three witnesses for each side. On 1–2 July 1946 the defence called Colonel (formerly Lieutenant) Friedrich Ahrens, commanding officer of the Army Group Centre (AGC) 537th Signals Regiment; Lieutenant Reinhard von Eichborn, who arrived in Smolensk with the AGC Communications Department in late September 1941; and Major General Eugene Oberhäuser, head of AGC communications. The three witnesses appearing for the prosecution were the former deputy mayor of Smolensk, Boris Bazilevsky; Soviet professor of forensic medicine and member of the Burdenko Commission, Victor Prozorovsky; and the Bulgarian forensic medical expert Professor Anton Marko Markov, who – as noted previously – had been arrested and accused of collaboration with the enemy and in February 1945 confessed he had signed his statement for the International Medical Commission under duress.[21]

After representations by both sides the tribunal judged the evidence insufficient to charge the Nazis with the crime. The question of Soviet guilt was never discussed. How could it be? The only charge under consideration was against the Nazis. The final judgment of the International Tribunal in Nuremberg makes no mention of Katyń. It is simply left out.

For the Polish government in exile – the 'London Poles' as they were increasingly referred to – Nuremberg represented the last bitter insult in a series of disappointments that had piled up since the end of the war. The prosecution of the Katyń Massacre had been entrusted to the representatives of one of the two governments suspected of the crime. The Soviets had effectively been placed in charge of judging themselves. Moreover, not a single Polish representative or adviser was invited to participate. Despite several attempts to present information to the International Military Tribunal, no documentary evidence had been accepted from them.

For the British and American governments the Nuremberg fudge provided a convenient excuse to park the 'Katyń question' for the foreseeable future. Neither had wanted to become entangled in what they viewed as a matter between Poland and the Soviet Union. The post-war political situation now made this approach even more desirable. When the promised 'free and unfettered' Polish elections of January 1947 duly produced a Soviet-backed communist government, both the Americans and the British concluded there was little to be gained diplomatically by continuing to stir up this particular hornet's nest. Official government policy thereafter on both sides of the Atlantic could be summed up in four words: let sleeping dogs lie.

It was an unhappy time to be a Pole.

23

THE SURVIVORS

Very few Poles can be happy at this moment, except opportunists or young people who have chosen this unseasonable time to fall in love; the rest of us are all cruelly anxious for our loved ones and for our country. Moreover, the Yalta decisions have brought almost every member of the émigré community face to face with a problem about which we preferred not to think while the end of the war still seemed far off: what shall we be doing tomorrow, or in a few weeks' time, and what are we going to live on?[1]

WHEN GRIAZOVETS CAMP WAS CLOSED IN EARLY SEPTEMBER 1941 the majority of the former prisoners joined the Polish army. The only exceptions were twenty-five men who wished to take Soviet citizenship and fourteen *volksdeutsche* who were neither permitted to join the Polish army nor wanted by the Soviets. A further thirteen men remained behind due to illness; two were under arrest.[2] The rest travelled south to Totskoye or Tatishchevo, were evacuated to Iran, and later moved on to Iraq. The army remained in Iraq until the summer of 1943, when it was transferred to Palestine and Egypt for further training and renamed the Polish II Corps. In 1944 the former prisoners finally achieved their dream of rejoining the war as active participants. They fought mainly in Italy, most notably at Monte Cassino. Once the war ended the question on everybody's lips was: where now? After an odyssey that had taken them halfway around the globe the choices were stark: home to communist-ruled Poland or exile.

The Yalta Conference of February 1945 had left most of eastern Europe under Soviet control. In Poland the eastern borderlands – the *kresy* – were now permanently incorporated into the Soviet Union, divided between the Socialist Republics of Ukraine and Belorussia.[3] The rest of Poland was ruled by the Provisional Government of National Unity which in reality was under Soviet control. The vast majority of Poles who served in the British Army came from the *kresy*. They no longer had homes to return to. Even if they did, the mere fact of having served with the Allied forces could mean arrest, persecution, even execution. Citizens from central and western Poland faced the same dilemma. Rumours swirled around the Italian towns where Polish forces were stationed: grim tales of repression and arrests, the notorious 'Trial of the Sixteen'.[4] The fear felt by many was compounded by a sense of bitterness that it was their great ally, Britain, who had betrayed them by conceding so much to Stalin.

The former British ambassador to the Polish government in exile, Sir Owen O'Malley, was scathing in his appraisal of the manner in which Churchill and Roosevelt dealt with the Soviet leader. In his view, they had failed entirely to get the measure of 'Uncle Joe', comprehending neither his intentions nor his character, both mistakenly (arrogantly) believing they could 'handle' him:

> In my view it was of no more substantial use to argue and negotiate with Stalin and his associates than to argue and negotiate with a lot of gorillas and rattlesnakes. There was in the sombre depth of their hearts and minds no desire for a genuine accommodation, nor any moral principle or sentiment to which we could successfully appeal....
>
> Between 1943 and the autumn of 1945 much more than the sacrifice of Poland was esteemed necessary to keep Stalin in a good temper; and to appease him an indifferent eye was turned upon his destruction and dismemberment of a number of smaller nations. One after the other they were seized: Estonia, Latvia, Lithuania, parts of Finland, a quarter of Poland, all Poland, Czechoslovakia, Ruthenia, Yugoslavia, Hungary, Bulgaria, Romania, Albania, a quarter of Austria and a third of Germany.[5]

The thorny question of what to do with the thousands of Polish citizens who had fought loyally for the Allies but now had nowhere to go was eventually resolved by the British government in the form of the 1947 Polish Resettlement Act. This granted Poles serving in the British armed forces, and their families, the right to settle permanently in the UK. To facilitate their entry into British life they could join the Polish Resettlement Corps, a quasi-military organisation which would give them a salary, accommodation and training for a period of up to two years. Accommodation was in former army and RAF barracks dotted all over the country, consisting mainly of Nissen huts (nicknamed *beczki śmiechu* – 'barrels of laughs'). Some families stayed only briefly, others remained in the camps for several years. In the late 1940s the men's families were brought over from the refugee camps in India, Africa and other regions to which they had been sent after the 1942 evacuation to Iran. Of nearly a quarter of a million Polish citizens who arrived in the UK after the war approximately 120,000 eventually settled there permanently, forming the bedrock of the Polish community in Britain. Many others emigrated to the USA, Canada, Australia and other countries.

The influx of a large number of Polish men (and there were, inevitably, more men than women among those who came out of the British forces) into a depressed post-war labour situation was not without friction. Where once the Polish pilots had been feted for their courage, now people asked: why are the Poles still here? Some saw them as unwelcome competitors for a limited pool of work. Others, particularly on the political left, viewed them as reactionaries whose hostility towards communism stemmed from prejudice and social conservatism. There was no shortage of reactionaries among the Poles who settled in Britain, but those who accused them had little understanding of what they had been through: that, for people who had been deported, imprisoned, starved or tortured by the Soviets, communism was not a byword for fairness, equality or freedom.

The former prisoners of Griazovets faced the same dilemma as their compatriots, their situation compounded by the added danger they faced if they returned to Poland because of their connection to Katyń. Of the three hundred or so survivors who emerged from the British armed forces at the end of the war, the vast majority chose exile in the West rather than return to risk arrest in communist-run Poland. Most came to Britain. Here they lived anonymously and quietly, moving mainly in Polish circles centred on London – where the government in exile continued to meet and most of the major Polish expatriate organisations were based – and Wales, where the presence of a Polish hospital in Penley and a retirement home in Penrhos, Pwllheli, ensured a steady population of former servicemen.

Józef Lis, Stanisław Swianiewicz, Jan Mintowt-Czyż, Julian Ginsbert, Jerzy Wołkowicki, Ludwik Domoń, Jan Bober, Tadeusz Felsztyn – all made their homes in Britain. Some were fortunate enough to be reunited with their wives and children; others had family in Poland who either eventually joined them or whom they never saw again. A few had a sufficient command of English to find professional work (Tadeusz Felsztyn taught mathematics and physics at secondary school, writing and publishing books on science in his spare time). Most had to take whatever work they could find. Younger officers fared better: they could learn English, gain qualifications, work their way up. Doctors were always in demand. But for many of the older officers the transition to life in Britain was never fully made: without a decent command of English they had no chance of finding work consummate with their seniority or status in Polish life. Many high-ranking officers were forced to take menial jobs as labourers or waiters, sometimes working for men who were their subordinates in the army. The other alternative was employment within the Polish community – Józef Lis became director of archives at Foxley Camp in Herefordshire, Adam Moszyński worked for the administration at the Penrhos camp in Wales, where General Wołkowicki lived in retirement (later moving to a Polish care home in Chislehurst, where he died in 1983 at the grand old age of ninety-nine). A few returned to Poland in later years, drawn by longing or necessity. Ludwik Domoń ('that blasted legionnaire') was heavily wounded at Monte Cassino; he remained in the UK until 1958, when he returned to Poland having apparently signed an undertaking not to act against the Polish state.[6] Jan Bober went back to Poland in 1971 for reasons unknown; he referred to it as his 'bad fate' so it was evidently not through choice. He left behind him the draft manuscript of a memoir that he consigned to the Sikorski Institute in London for safekeeping. It was eventually published in 2016.[7]

Józef Czapski and Bronisław Młynarski had both spent a substantial portion of their pre-war lives abroad. For these cultured and cosmopolitan travellers the question of where to live once the war was over was easily settled: Józef Czapski returned to his beloved Paris, where he continued writing, painting and participating in expatriate Polish cultural life until his death in 1993 at the age of ninety-six. He shared an apartment with his sister Maria, who had survived the war in Warsaw. Bronisław Młynarski emigrated to the US where his sisters lived (one of whom, it may be remembered, was married to the celebrated pianist Artur Rubinstein). He settled in California, marrying a former silent movie star, Doris Kenyon, and earning a living as an antiquarian bookseller. Dr Salomon Słowes settled in Israel, where he continued his profession as a surgeon specialising in maxillofacial injuries.

Zdzisław Peszkowski was only twenty-two when he was captured by the Red Army in 1939. Scouting had always played a vital role in his life, and in 1944 he was sent by the Polish army to work as a scout leader in a refugee camp for Polish children in Valivade, India. Once the war was over he left for Britain, studying theology in the UK and then the US. In 1954 he was ordained as a Catholic priest, later becoming head chaplain of the Polish Scouts abroad. A devoted advocate of peace and forgiveness, Father Peszkowski became closely involved in the remembrance of Katyń and in 1989 returned to Poland, where he served as chaplain to the Katyń Families Association, a post he held until his death in 2007.

Józef Czapski at his home in Maisons-Laffitte, 1988.

The economist and lone 'witness' to the Katyń Massacre, Stanisław Swianiewicz, ended up in London after the war before settling permanently in Canada. His wife and four children remained in Poland and when he testified at the Madden hearings he did so anonymously for fear of reprisals against them (as did Józef Lis, whose family were also in Poland). In 1949 his eldest son Witold escaped from the Polish navy in a manner almost as dramatic as his father's flight from Soviet Russia, jumping ship in Sweden and hiding in a forest until the ship left harbour. He claimed asylum in Sweden, later joining his father in London.[8] It was not until 1957 that Swianiewicz's wife Olimpia was finally granted permission to leave Poland and the couple were reunited after an interval of almost twenty years. For Swianiewicz, the sense of paranoia created by his experiences in the Soviet Union never fully went away, perhaps justly so: in 1975 he was invited to Copenhagen to an inquiry organised by Dr Andrei Sakharov on human rights violations perpetrated by the USSR. Two weeks before the hearings he was seriously beaten up on the street in London. The British police saw it as a random attack. Swianiewicz saw in it the hand of the NKVD's successor, the KGB.

Around thirty of the survivors returned to Poland immediately after the war, including Dr Zbigniew Godlewski.[9] At some point between 1942 and 1943 Godlewski had fallen sick with typhus and was cared for by a young Polish nurse, Zofia Pamfiłowska. The pair fell in love but had to wait until after the war to be reunited. They married in Edinburgh, where Zofia was completing her medical studies, and the two doctors left for Poland in 1946. Although he avoided the worst excesses of the persecution of the post-war era, it seems the path of Dr Godlewski's career was not straightforward, but he finally found a post in a hospital in Warsaw where he worked until his retirement. He lived quietly, a devoted family man who never lost his love of learning or his dedication to his students.[10] We know little of Dr Godlewski's political beliefs. In Griazovets he was a popular figure generally identified with the 'patriots'. At one point he was placed under camp arrest by Major Volkov for protesting about the use of river water for cooking (he was head of camp hygiene). His fellow prisoners staged a three-day hunger strike in protest at this unduly harsh treatment, and even the Red Corner thought Volkov overreacted. One of the pro-Soviet group, Stanisław Szczypiorski, mentions bumping into Dr Godlewski in London in 1946 and remarked that the pair became friendly.[11] Godlewski wrote a brief account of his time in Starobelsk based on his wartime notes but makes no reference to his experiences after the war.[12]

And what of the communist group, the members of the Red Corner sent to Moscow and the Villa of Bliss? The fate of its core members – Kazimierz Rosen-Zawadzki, Roman Imach, Stanisław Szczypiorski and Franciszek Kukuliński – is worth outlining.

Although the group were all accepted into the Polish army in 1941 they continued cooperating with the NKVD, maintaining active contact with a liaison officer to whom they provided information and from whom they received instructions. They were not spies, if only because everyone knew about their behaviour in Griazovets and treated them accordingly. Where they could, they cultivated communist cells among their compatriots, but the pickings were slim and they were under constant surveillance by Polish military intelligence. Hostility towards the group was initially mitigated by the widely-held belief that they would all soon be fighting side by side with the Russians against Hitler. The evacuation to Iran in 1942 changed everything. None of the four wished to leave the Soviet Union, but if they remained behind while the rest of their unit left they risked being arrested, possibly shot, for desertion. Unless the NKVD gave them a direct assurance regarding their future, none was willing to take such a drastic step.

In a telegram to General Zhukov dated 17 April 1942 the head of the Comintern, Georgy Dimitrov, expressed his concern about the fate of their Polish informers once abroad. In his view, sending these officers outside the USSR was pointless since their communist activity was already known and their influence on the strongly anti-Soviet Polish units would be reduced almost to zero. Moreover, it would put the men themselves in danger. He recommended that where possible these men should be transferred to Polish divisions remaining in the USSR. Alternatively, they should be 'demobilised' and provided with the appropriate documents to return to their former homes.[13] The subsequent actions of the NKVD suggest that Dimitrov's concerns fell on deaf ears.

When they heard about the evacuation of the Polish army in March 1942 Rosen-Zawadzki, Imach, Szczypiorski and Kukuliński immediately asked for guidance from their NKVD liaison officer. He recommended that they speak to Lieutenant Colonel Berling, who was in Krasnovodsk organising the Polish side of the operation. Berling's advice was to stay

in the Soviet Union. He feared that once they were outside Soviet territory the men risked being arrested by the Polish military authorities.
The only solution on offer from the NKVD, however, was for the men to
pretend they were ill with typhus so that they would be left behind when
the others left. This pretence seemed not only cowardly but to offer little
guarantee of success. When Berling asked for further guidance from the
NKVD he was told the officers should leave the Soviet Union. When he
raised the question of their safety he was assured that the NKVD 'had
people everywhere' and would keep an eye on the group. Captain Rosen-
Zawadzki received a similar reply from his liaison officer: 'You can work
for the Soviet Union anywhere. Go. You will work, we will keep in touch.'
Despite their reservations, all four did as they were instructed. Only Berling,
Lieutenant Colonel Bukojemski and Flight Lieutenant Wicherkiewicz
remained behind, deserting their posts.[14]

Once the four men were outside the Soviet Union little changed at
first, but gradually they found themselves sidelined by the Polish military
authorities. They were removed from active service and placed in reserve
posts such as supply depots where they had little chance of influencing
others. Isolated from one another, with no word from their NKVD handlers
and under constant surveillance by Polish military intelligence, it seemed
their days of political activity were over. In 1943, Rosen-Zawadzki bumped
into Szczypiorski and Imach by chance in Palestine. The three began to
meet up regularly, together with a few other like-minded men, including
Kukuliński. They made contact with the Jewish–Arab communist party,
then the Jewish communist party, who encouraged them to become active.
They duly organised regular party meetings and even made a few attempts
to counter 'anti-Soviet propaganda', but with little success. Despite multiple
attempts to make contact with the NKVD they received no instructions,
no guidance, no support. Their usefulness at an end, they had been left
out in the cold.[15]

The group's renewed political activity did not go unnoticed. In October
1943 Rosen-Zawadzki, Imach, Szczypiorski, Kukuliński and two others were
arrested by the Polish military authorities in Palestine. They were interrogated and tried in 1944, accused of espionage. Imach and Szczypiorski
received a sentence of fifteen years and were expelled from the Polish
army. Rosen-Zawadzki was charged with 'betrayal of the state' and received

a sentence of life imprisonment. Kukuliński, as the most junior of the group, was given a much shorter sentence. Still the NKVD did not come to their aid.

The unity of the group had been fracturing for some time. After the trial they turned on one another. Imach accused Rosen-Zawadzki of being a 'megalomaniac'. Szczypiorski detested him. All were shocked during the trial by how much the prosecutors knew about their activities: testament to the efficiency of the Second Section? Or perhaps a sign of an 'imperialist mole' in their midst? A more likely possibility was that Captain Janusz Siewierski, one of Captain Łopianowski's group in the Villa of Bliss, had been spying on them.

As the war in Europe drew to a close, in May 1945 the prisoners were moved from Palestine to Qassasin in Egypt, where they were kept in a tented enclosure in the desert until their release and eventual repatriation to Poland, organised by the British.

On their return to communist-run Poland the men were not hailed as heroes as they might have hoped. In the brave new world of Stalinist paranoia the mere fact of having served in Anders' Army was sufficient to cast doubt on their communist bona fides. Rosen-Zawadzki was accused (by Szczypiorski) of being a capitalist provocateur and imprisoned between 1952–55. Kukuliński joined the Polish People's Army but in 1948 was deemed insufficiently enthusiastic about collective farming and was packed off to teach in an officers' school in Wrocław, where he was accused of 'nationalist tendencies'. He was investigated and his life made difficult, then he was told to resign from the army which, seeing no alternative, he did. He ended up working in his previous trade in a car factory. Eventually he was given the right to return to the army and was rehabilitated in 1956 by the very same people who had accused him.

After deserting from the Polish army in August 1942 during the evacuation to Iran, Lieutenant Colonel Zygmunt Berling remained in the Soviet Union, where he played a pivotal role in organising the 1st Tadeusz Kościuszko Infantry Division, which he then led. For a while things went well: he was promoted to general and in 1944 was made commander of the Polish army in the USSR. It was not long before problems began to surface. Always a controversial figure, a loner of no fixed political abode, Berling soon found himself in conflict with members of Poland's new cadre

of communist leaders, including Wanda Wasilewska. Disagreements centred largely on Berling's dislike of the role of political commissars within
the army and his attempts to bypass their influence. Questions were then
raised about his effectiveness as a military leader, particularly following his
attempt to intervene to help the Warsaw Uprising. At the end of September
1944 he was dismissed from his post on the personal order of Stalin himself, effectively putting an end to his career. He was sent to study at the
Military War Academy in Moscow before finally receiving permission to
return to Poland in 1947, where he taught at the Military Academy for the
General Staff until he retired from the army in 1953. He held a variety of
minor government posts until his retirement and died in 1980 at the age
of eighty-four.

Poland lay in ruins, twenty percent of its population dead, millions dis-
placed. Between them the Nazis and the Soviets had succeeded in killing,
imprisoning or sending into exile vast swathes of the country's professional
class. The war had also fundamentally changed the ethnic composition of
the country. Prior to 1939 Poland was a multi-ethnic society with substantial
Ukrainian, Jewish, Belorussian and German minorities. The Soviet takeover
of Poland's eastern territories had removed the Ukrainians and Belorussians.
The formerly German western territories awarded to Poland in compensation for the loss of the kresy were divested of their German population in a
giant post-war population swap as the Poles from the east were moved west
and the Germans pushed back over the new German–Polish border. Where
once the country had been the centre of European Jewry it was now a giant
cemetery. Three million Polish Jews had been murdered in the Holocaust,
ninety percent of Poland's pre-war Jewish population. For the first time in
its history Poland was a country of ethnic Poles, predominantly of Catholic
faith. The change was a profound one, its effect still resonant today. The
Nazi occupation of Poland had lasted six years. Soviet rule was to endure
for nearly half a century.

24

COLD WAR

IN THE WEST, POST-WAR UNCERTAINTY SOON GAVE WAY TO A new, cold war. The rhetoric which had encouraged the American and British public to regard 'Uncle Joe' Stalin as the saviour who helped defeat Hitler changed to one of hostility and distrust. With the advent of the McCarthy era in the US, press interest in the Katyń Massacre, suppressed for the sake of the war effort, grew again. In 1949 an American journalist, Julius Epstein, published articles about Katyń in the *New York Herald Tribune* calling for an official US investigation into the matter. Momentum grew when Epstein persuaded the former US ambassador to Poland, Arthur Bliss Lane, to establish the American Committee for the Investigation of the Katyń Massacre. In 1951, the US House of Representatives convened a select committee to 'Conduct an Investigation and Study of the Facts, Evidence, and Circumstances of the Katyń Forest Massacre', known as the Madden Committee after its chairman, Democratic congressman Ray Madden. The committee gathered together all available documents relating to the Katyń Massacre and conducted extensive hearings in April–May 1952 in the United States, London and Frankfurt. The hearings were notable for assembling a wide-ranging cast of Polish, German and American witnesses, including many of the survivors of the three camps. Unsurprisingly, no representative from communist Poland or the Soviet side took part. Some of the Polish witnesses gave their testimony anonymously, fearful of possible repercussions for their families back home. The stories were familiar, even if the names were disguised: Józef Lis used the pseudonym Mr A as he described his experiences in the Villa of Bliss; Stanisław Swianiewicz testified in the guise of Mr B.[1]

The purpose of the Madden Committee investigation was not to ask who was responsible for the Katyń Massacre. They were looking for evidence of

Soviet guilt and they found it, in abundance. At the conclusion of the hearings the Committee determined unanimously that the NKVD were responsible for the murders and recommended a trial before the International World Court of Justice. A supplementary question as to whether the US government had actively sought to suppress public discussion of the Katyń affair during the war and the manner in which the matter had been dealt with at Nuremberg was less clear-cut: of the many high-ranking US officials called to appear before the committee none would admit that the State Department had ever deliberately sought to suppress evidence incriminating the Soviet Union, and they all emphasised the importance that had been placed on remaining on good terms with Stalin for the sake of winning the war against Hitler. No satisfactory explanation was offered for the disappearance of a report submitted by Colonel Van Vliet in 1945 concerning his visit to Katyń in 1943, nor for the suppression of other American reports on Katyń.[2]

The Madden Committee's final report was submitted to the United Nations in February 1953, but they never achieved their goal of an international trial of the Katyń case. Despite the anti-communist rhetoric that dominated the era, newly-elected Republican president Dwight Eisenhower was no more eager to rock the diplomatic boat on account of Katyń than his predecessors. Likewise, calls for an international trial by the Polish government in exile in London, which had no official role in post-war Britain and was widely perceived as irrelevant and out of touch, fell largely on deaf ears.

In the UK, after a lull in Katyń-related activity during the 1960s a flurry of publications in the 1970s led to renewed interest in the subject. Debates in parliament followed the publication of author and campaigner Louis Fitzgibbon's book, *Katyń: A Crime Without Parallel* (1971), which appeared in the same year as the UK edition of Janusz Zawodny's book *Death in the Forest* (published in the US in 1962, in the UK in 1971) and a BBC documentary about Katyń. Foreign Office archives for the wartime period were declassified in 1972, leading to the publication by the recently-established Katyń Memorial Fund (founded by Fitzgibbon) of a pamphlet containing Sir Owen O'Malley's two searing dispatches to the foreign secretary, Anthony Eden. These were also reprinted in Louis Fitzgibbon's second book, *The Katyń Cover-Up* (London, 1972). Nevertheless, despite efforts by several MPs to urge a re-examination of the case by the United

Nations, the attitude of British governments of every political persuasion throughout the Cold War remained as determinedly ambiguous as ever. The lack of conclusive evidence was always cited as the principal reason for not condemning the Soviet Union. In reality, the need to maintain civil relations with the communist governments of Poland and the USSR continued to be the dominant diplomatic priority for both British and US governments right up until 1989.

Amongst the large Polish diaspora Katyń was neither forgotten nor forgiven. Monuments and plaques bearing the all-important date of 1940 sprang up in places as diverse as Paris, Chicago, Buenos Aires, Melbourne, Rome, Johannesburg and Glasgow, largely the result of initiatives by local Polish societies. But politics continued to play an influential role when it came to more prominent displays of remembrance. In the mid-1970s attempts by the Katyń Memorial Fund to erect a monument to the victims of the massacre in London met with objections from the Soviet embassy, who were under instructions from the Politburo to pressure the British government to put an end to this campaign. A protocol on the subject employs terms of such outraged self-righteousness that one might almost conclude that, thirty years after the event, the Soviets had come to believe their own propaganda:

> What is particularly scandalous…is the character of the inscriptions approved for the aforementioned 'memorial.' In a coarse manner they distort the historical facts about the real culprits of the Katyń tragedy. In effect they reproduce the base inventions put about by the Nazis during World War II in order to hide the bloody crime of the Gestapo murderers, which is known to the whole world.[3]

These words certainly give pause for thought: how far up the Soviet hierarchy did one have to be to be aware of Soviet guilt? The men at the top certainly knew about it: the information passed from one generation of leaders to the next. As for those who occupied the lower echelons of the Communist Party or the KGB, who knows?

Soviet pressure was successful in achieving the rejection of the first location for the memorial, offered by the Royal Borough of Kensington and Chelsea in London, St Luke's Cemetery in Chelsea, but they could not prevent the monument from going ahead entirely. Kensington and Chelsea proposed another site on land owned by them in Gunnersbury Cemetery near Acton in west London. The monument was finally unveiled here in 1976, much to the ire of the Soviets. In keeping with the continued policy of studied fence-sitting with regard to Katyń, no official representative of James Callaghan's Labour government attended the ceremony. Meanwhile, the Politburo urged diplomatic representatives of the Polish People's Republic to 'Firmly resist provocative attempts to use the so-called Katyń Question to harm Polish–Soviet friendship', and exhorted the KGB to 'make it clear to persons in government circles of appropriate Western countries that the renewed use of various anti-Soviet forgeries is seen by the Soviet government as especially intentional provocation aimed at worsening the international situation'.[4] At around this time the Soviet authorities in the Smolensk region received orders to 'undertake supplementary measures to ensure the proper maintenance of the monument to the Polish officers and the surrounding area'. In short, they were to see to it that nobody tampered with the false information given on the official memorial at Katyń.

In post-war Poland the subject of Katyń remained taboo – unless, of course, you were prepared to support the Soviet version of events. Throughout the 1940s and 50s articles regularly appeared in the state-run press accusing the Germans of the crime; there was even a book published in 1953, not long after the Madden Committee hearings. Entitled *The Truth about Katyń* (*Prawda o Katyniu*, Warsaw 1953) by Bolesław Wójcicki, it simply regurgitates the Soviet version of the narrative before moving on to a prolonged attack on the capitalist West. The death of Stalin in 1953 brought a significant change in the direction of Soviet politics. In a 1956 speech at the Twentieth Party Congress the Soviet Union's new leader, Nikita Khrushchev, set about denouncing many of Stalin's acts as crimes. Katyń was not among them, doubtless because in official Soviet history it was listed not as a Soviet but a Nazi crime. But it had not been forgotten. Far from it. In March 1959, the head of the KGB, Aleksandr Shelepin, sent a memo to Khrushchev:

> To Comrade Khrushchev, N.S.
>   Since 1940, records and other materials regarding prisoners and interned officers, policemen, gendarmes, [military] settlers, landlords and so on,

and persons from former bourgeois Poland who were shot in that same year, have been kept in the Committee of State Security of the Council of Ministers, USSR. On the basis of the decision by the special Troika of the NKVD USSR, a total of 21,857 persons were shot; of these, 4,421 [were shot] in the Katyń Forest (Smolensk Oblast), 3,820 in the camp of Starobelsk, close to Kharkov, 6,311 in the camp of Ostashkov (Kalinin Oblast), and 7,305 persons were shot in other camps and prisons of Western Ukraine and Western Belorussia.

The whole operation of liquidating the above-mentioned persons was carried out on the basis of the decision of the CC CPSU of 5 March 1940. All of them were sentenced to the highest order of punishment according to the files started for them as POWs and internees in 1939.

From the time when the above-mentioned operation was carried out, that is, from 1940, no information has been released to anybody relating to the case, and all of the 21,857 files have been stored in a sealed location.

All these files are of no operational or historical value to Soviet organs. It is also highly doubtful whether they could be of any real value to our Polish friends. On the contrary, any unforeseen incident may lead to revealing the operation, with all the undesirable consequences for our country, especially since, regarding the persons shot in the Katyń Forest, the official version was confirmed by an investigation carried out on the initiative of the organs of Soviet authorities in 1944, under the name of the 'Special Commission to Establish and Investigate the Shooting of Polish Prisoner-of-War Officers in Katyń Forest by the German-Fascist Aggressors'.

According to the conclusion of that commission, all the Poles liqui-dated there are considered to have been killed by the German occupiers. The materials of the inquiry were extensively covered in the Soviet and foreign press. The commission's conclusions became firmly established in international public opinion.

On the basis of the above statements, it seems expedient to destroy all the records on the persons shot in 1940 in the above-mentioned operation.

In order to answer possible questions along the lines of the CC CPSU or the Soviet government guidelines, the protocols of the meetings of the NKVD USSR Troika that sentenced these persons to be shot, also the doc-uments on carrying out this decision, could be preserved. The volume of these documents is not large and they could be kept in a special file.

Attached is the draft of the [relevant] decision by the CC CPSU.

Chairman of the Committee for State Security of the Council of Ministers of USSR

A. Shelepin

3 March 1959[5]

This memo, like all Soviet documents quoted in this book, was not made public until after the collapse of communism in the 1990s. The Polish 'friends' to whom Shelepin refers are members of the communist Polish government. The records he mentions are the personal files kept on every prisoner which contained all the details amassed by the NKVD from interrogations, questionnaires, correspondence and other sources. It is also likely that the files contained some indication of the reasoning behind the decision to sentence individual prisoners to be shot. The figure of 21,857 given by Shelepin adds a further 7,305 Polish prisoners of war to the 14,552 hitherto considered to be the victims of the Katyń Massacre. Since the men shot in Western Ukraine and Belorussia were killed on the basis of the same order of 5 March 1940, they have since been added to the final total.[6] Only one personal file has ever been found (of a prisoner of Ostashkov). The Russian government has never released any of the protocols of the Troika meetings nor any documents relating to the decision to sentence the prisoners to which Shelepin refers. Whether they too were destroyed is not known. Since Shelepin suggests that they could be kept in a 'special file', it is tempting to think they were preserved but have never been approved for public release. One can only speculate.

Why destroy the personal records in 1959? Shelepin first argues that they are of no 'operational or historical value' to either Soviet or Polish government bodies. This is debatable. His next suggestion offers a more convincing reason: since the official version of the crime of Katyń is so well established, why keep material that could potentially damage the credibility of this narrative and, in the process, harm the reputation of the Soviet Union at a time when Khrushchev was supposedly repudiating Stalinist crimes? If the aim was to place Stalinism firmly in the past then it would be deeply embarrassing if evidence emerged that the freshly-painted new regime had colluded in covering up one of Stalin's most contentious crimes.

In Poland the situation remained essentially unchanged for decades. Right up until the late 1980s it was still dangerous for anyone to speak or write publicly about Katyń. People did not forget, however, and they did not give up trying to commemorate the victims: the Military Cemetery in the Powązki area of Warsaw became the symbolic centre of unofficial commemorations not just of Katyń but other significant events that could not be openly remembered, such as the 1944 Warsaw Uprising. With the advent of the Polish pope, Karol Wojtyła, in 1978, Poles began to hope that one day the truth would come out. In 1979 an underground 'Katyń Institute' began to research the subject; 1980 was unofficially declared 'the Year of Katyń'. With the rise of the Solidarity movement the impetus grew. Underground printing presses published many of the documents that had already appeared in the West. Leaflets proliferated. Still the SB (*Służba Bezpieczeństwa*[7]) arrested people, confiscated documents, searched apartments, broke up meetings. They even blockaded the Powązki cemetery to prevent an attempted commemoration on 13 April 1980.[8] Yet despite the imposition of Martial Law in Poland in 1981 – the response of Polish president General Wojciech Jaruzelski to the growing influence of the Solidarity movement – efforts to commemorate Katyń and research the truth continued throughout the 1980s. Families of the victims began to form groups to press for public recognition of the crime. There was even a final 'victim' of Katyń when a priest, Father Stefan Niedzielak, one of the founders of the Katyń Families Association and the man responsible for hanging a memorial cross for the Katyń victims in the Powązki cemetery in 1981, was murdered by 'persons unknown' on the night of 20 January 1989.[9]

However desperately the Poles wanted it, there could never be a conclusive answer to 'the Katyń question' without Soviet consent.

25

REVELATIONS

DURING THE 1980S PRESIDENT MIKHAIL GORBACHEV'S POLICY of *glasnost* opened the door to public discussion of many previously taboo subjects in the Soviet Union. In the case of Poland this inevitably meant demonstrating a willingness to discuss their difficult shared history. Accordingly, in 1985 Gorbachev and Polish president Wojciech Jaruzelski signed a declaration of 'Cooperation in the Sphere of Culture, Learning and Ideology' followed, in 1987, by the creation of a Joint Commission of Soviet–Polish Party Historians whose task was to examine various problematic historical events – or 'blank spots' – between the two countries, of which the Katyń Massacre was the most prominent. The initial progress made by the commission was slow to non-existent: since the only official material available on the Soviet side was the Burdenko Commission report, the Soviet historians could bring nothing new to the debate. The Polish historians, by contrast, had access to many documents published in the West. Having examined the available evidence, they concluded that the massacre was the responsibility of the NKVD. In March 1989 the Polish government spokesman, Jerzy Urban, took the profoundly significant step of announcing that his government agreed with the commission's findings.[1]

The announcement was a reflection of the Polish government's increasingly precarious domestic situation as it sought to retain some sense of legitimacy in a fast-changing landscape. General Jaruzelski evidently hoped that by finally addressing one of Poland's most painful historical grievances he might shore up his own standing in the eyes of the Polish public, fatally damaged by his imposition of Martial Law in 1981. But it was too late: the political situation was changing too rapidly. Round-table talks in April 1989 between the government and the Solidarity-led opposition led to democratic elections in June and July that produced the first non-communist government for over forty years. As the Poles became more and more willing to place the accusation of NKVD guilt in the public domain, the creaking edifice on which the fiction of Katyń stood began to crumble.

With public pressure in Poland mounting and Soviet historians beginning to openly question the official version of events, Soviet foreign minister Eduard Shevardnadze, along with KGB head Vladimir Kriuchkov and director of the International Department of the Soviet Communist Party Valentin Falin, suggested to the Central Committee of the Soviet Communist Party that perhaps the time had come to offer the Polish people an explanation:

> In this case, time is not our ally. Perhaps it is more advisable to say what really happened and exactly who is guilty, thus effecting closure to the problem. The costs of this kind of action would, in the final reckoning, be less in comparison with the losses [resulting from] present inaction.[2]

The suggestion was a sign of the changing times, in striking contrast to KGB head Aleksandr Shelepin's 1959 proposal to keep Katyń under the carpet.

The policy of *glasnost* included the opening up of certain state archives to a select group of Russian historians. Three of these historians in particular, Valentina Parsadanova, Natalia Lebedeva and Yuri Zoria, were to make a discovery that would transform the landscape in which Soviet discussion of Katyń took place. Although, as we have seen, the KGB destroyed all the personal files kept by the NKVD on the Polish prisoners of war in 1959, the historians found in the archives a substantial number of documents relating to the Polish prisoners that firmly made the connection between the NKVD and the murder of these men. In the Central Archive of the Red Army Lebedeva found the records of the 136th NKVD Convoy battalion that escorted the Kozelsk prisoners to Katyń. Departure dates for the battalion from Kozelsk to Smolensk and Gnezdovo precisely matched the dates of the transports on which the Polish prisoners were taken from Kozelsk. Further records of the Main Administration of the NKVD Convoy troops revealed that their orders came from the UPV (the

Administration for Prisoner of War Affairs). The UPV records were held in the Central Special Archive, to which Valentina Parsadanova and Yuri Zoria had access. Together the three historians managed to piece together different elements of a narrative that eventually proved too conclusive to be ignored.

In February 1990 Valentin Falin sent a note to Gorbachev explaining what the historians had discovered. They were about to publish articles about their findings that would undermine the previous Soviet argument that no new materials had been unearthed in the state archives. 'In view of the approaching fiftieth anniversary of Katyń,' he concludes, 'we should define our position one way or the other.' In Valentin's view the least damaging course of action would be for the Soviet authorities to inform General Jaruzelski, during a planned state visit to Moscow in April 1990, that they had uncovered information contradicting the findings of the 1944 Burdenko Commission report. Although they did not have direct proof in the form of orders or directives, there was enough evidence to suggest that the 'extermination of the Polish officers in the Katyń regions was the work of the NKVD and personally of Beria and Merkulov'.[3]

The Politburo initially rejected Falin's recommendations, but events intervened to force a different course of action. The first of these was an ultimatum issued by General Jaruzelski to the Soviet government declaring that he would not go ahead with the presidential visit unless they admitted the truth about Katyń. In the intervening period the Polish political context had changed rapidly: at the end of January 1990 the Polish communist party disbanded itself. Then, in March, the Polish parliament (*sejm*) passed a resolution on the occasion of the fiftieth anniversary of the Katyń Massacre declaring the NKVD responsible for the crime and demanding Soviet admission of the truth, together with information relating to the reasons for the massacre, the circumstances in which it took place and the burial sites of the prisoners of Starobelsk and Ostashkov. Meanwhile, in Russia, Natalia Lebedeva gave an interview about her new findings that was published in the *Moscow News* without government permission, causing a furore among government officials and nearly costing Lebedeva, as well as the journalist and the editor of the paper, their jobs. Valentin again approached the Politburo with a recommendation to make a public admission of the truth, again suggesting they use General Jaruzelski's state visit as the occasion on which to do so. This time, the Politburo agreed.

On 13 April 1990, the same date on which Berlin Radio first announced the discovery of the mass graves in the Katyń Forest in 1943, President Gorbachev handed over to General Jaruzelski documents containing the NKVD dispatch lists for the prisoners of the three camps. That day, the Soviet news agency TASS issued the following communiqué:

> The archival materials that have been discovered, taken together, permit the conclusion that Beria and Merkulov and their subordinates bear direct responsibility for the evil deeds in Katyń Forest. The Soviet side, expressing deep regret in connection with the Katyń tragedy, declares that it represents one of the heinous crimes of Stalinism.[4]

It was a big step towards an admission of guilt, although the statement mentions only the Katyń Forest, not the other burial sites, and lays the blame squarely on Beria and Merkulov as leaders of the NKVD, and on Stalinism rather than Stalin himself. There was no suggestion that subsequent iterations of the Soviet regime had colluded in covering up the crime. It was as if – hey presto! – they had suddenly unearthed documents that pointed to NKVD guilt and were as surprised by the discovery as anyone. There was also no hint of an apology to the Germans for having spent the past four and a half decades accusing them of the crime.

The crucial execution order of 5 March 1940, signed by Beria and sent to Stalin for his approval, emerged only with the final collapse of the Soviet Union in December 1991. This explosive document was contained in a special envelope, along with other secret files (including the secret protocol to the 1939 Molotov–Ribbentrop Pact) that had apparently been passed from one Soviet president to the next ever since the war. When Mikhail Gorbachev handed over power to Boris Yeltsin as the new president of Russia, the envelope came too. Yeltsin did not immediately share the document with the Polish government. He sat on it for a while, using it for political advantage in his fight to discredit the former Soviet regime and the now-outlawed Communist Party. On 14 October 1992 it was finally handed, along with other secret documents relating to Katyń (including the 1959 note to Khrushchev from KGB boss Aleksandr Shelepin), to the Polish president, Lech Wałęsa, in Warsaw.

The memorandum provides the long-sought proof that the decision to shoot the Polish prisoners of war was taken at the very highest level of Soviet government. And while none of the protocols of the NKVD Troika responsible for sentencing the prisoners have ever surfaced, it does shed at least partial light on the thinking behind the decision.

5 March 1940

No. 794/B

TOP SECRET

Central Committee of the All Union Communist Party (b)

To Comrade Stalin

In the USSR NKVD prisoner of war camps and prisons of the western regions of Ukraine and Belorussia, there are at present a large number of former officers of the Polish army, former workers in the Polish police and intelligence organs, members of Polish nationalist c-r parties, participants in exposed c-r insurgent organisations, refugees, and others. They are all sworn enemies of Soviet power, filled with hatred for the Soviet system of government. Prisoner of war officers and police in the camps are attempting to continue their c-r work and are conducting anti-Soviet agitation. Each one of them is just waiting to be released in order to be able to enter actively into the battle against Soviet power. The NKVD organs in the western oblasts of Ukraine and Belorussia have exposed several c-r insurgent organisations. In all these c-r organisations, an active guiding role is played by former officers of the former Polish army and former police and gendarmes. Among the detained refugees and those who have violated the state border, a significant number of individuals who are participants in c-r espionage and insurgent organisations have also been uncovered. The prisoner of war camps are holding a total (not counting the soldiers and the NCOs) of 14,736 former officers, officials, landowners, police, gendarmes, prison guards, [military] settlers, and intelligence agents, who are more than 97% Polish by nationality.

Among them are:

generals, colonels, and lieutenant colonels. 295

majors and captains 2,080

lieutenants, second lieutenants and ensigns 6,049

police officers, junior officers, border guards, and gendarmes. . . 1,030

rank and file police, gendarmes, prison guards, and intelligence

    agents 5,138

officials, landowners, priests, and military settlers 144

In the prisons of the western oblasts of Ukraine and Belorussia a total of 18,632 arrested people (including 10,685 Poles) are being held, including:

former officers 1,207

former police, intelligence agents, and gendarmes 5,141

spies and saboteurs 347

former landowners, factory owners, and officials 465

members of various c-r and insurgent organisations and various

    c-r elements. 5,345

refugees 6,127

Based on the fact that they are all hardened, irremediable enemies of Soviet power, the NKVD USSR believes it is essential:

I. To direct the NKVD USSR to:

1)   examine the cases of the 14,700 former Polish officers, officials, landowners, police, intelligence agents, gendarmes, military settlers, and prison guards who are now in the prisoner of war camps

2)   and also examine the cases of those who have been arrested and are in the prisons of the western oblasts of Ukraine and Belorussia, numbering 11,000, members of various c-r espionage and sabotage organisations, former landowners, manufacturers, former Polish officers, officials, and refugees, [and] using the special procedure, apply to them the supreme punishment, [execution by] shooting.

II.   Examine [these] cases without calling in the arrested men and with-
       out presenting [them with] the charges, the decision about the end
       of the investigation, or the document of indictment, according to
       the following procedure: a) [examine the cases] against individuals
       in the prisoner of war camps on the basis of information presented
       by the USSR NKVD UPV.

   b) [examine the cases] against individuals who have been arrested
       on the basis of the information from files presented by the UkSSR
       NKVD and the BSSR NKVD. Assign the examination of cases and
       the carrying out of decisions to a troika [threesome] consisting
       of Comrades Beria*, Merkulov, Kobulov, and Bashtakov (Head
       of 1st Special Department NKVD USSR).

USSR peoples commissar of internal affairs

L. Beria

*Crossed out by hand in blue pencil[5]

A criminal in the Lubyanka or Butyrka prison could expect some kind of
trial, however fixed or predetermined its outcome might be. The Polish
prisoners of war, by contrast, were sentenced to death on the basis of the
personal record files that had been transferred to Moscow when they left
the three camps. The prisoners were not 'called in' or presented with their
charges. Their files were scrutinised by the top brass of the NKVD, in whose
hands alone lay the decision whether they would live or die.

Few of the former prisoners of the three camps survived to witness
the admission of Soviet guilt in 1990, let alone the publication of Beria's
execution order in 1992. Of those featured in this book, only Józef Czapski
(aged 95), Stanisław Swianiewicz (92), Dr Salomon Słowes (83) and Father
Zdzisław Peszkowski (74), were living. As chaplain to the Katyń Families
Association, Peszkowski was to play a major role in the exhumations that
took place between 1991–95. He lobbied successfully for the creation of
cemeteries at the three mass burial sites and blessed the remains of each
body found in the graves. He is perhaps the only survivor to have set foot
in the place where his comrades were murdered.

Of those actually involved in the murder, less than a handful were still
alive: the head of the UPV, Pyotr Soprunenko, who was in charge of clearing

Father Zdzisław Peszkowski at the Monument to the
Fallen and Murdered in the East, Warsaw 2006.

out the three camps, blind and unwilling to talk; the head of the NKVD in the Tver (Kalinin) region, Dmitry Tokarev, who oversaw the shooting of the Ostashkov prisoners in the NKVD prison in Tver; and Mitrofan Syromiatnikov, also blind, an NKVD official from Kharkov who offered some details concerning the place where the prisoners of Starobelsk were killed and the method of execution. These few first-hand testimonies, along with the available documentation and the exhumations that took place between 1991–95, allowed historians to piece together with reasonable certainty how the Katyń Massacre was actually carried out.

Location of NKVD prison camps and sites of execution of
Polish prisoners of war in April 1940.

26

DEATH

Despite the powerful and enduring imagery of the Katyń Forest, it transpired that the majority of the prisoners of Kozelsk, Starobelsk and Ostashkov had been shot not in a remote wood but inside the offices or prisons of the NKVD local to each of the camps; their bodies were then transported to burial sites nearby. The prisoners of Starobelsk were buried in Piatykhatky Park, near Kharkov; those of Ostashkov in Mednoye, near Tver.

Between April and May 1940 the 3,739[1] prisoners of Starobelsk camp were transported by train to Kharkov station, thence in 'black ravens' to the headquarters of the NKVD at number 13, ul. Dzierżinskiego. The messages seen by survivors scratched into the carriage ceilings finally made sense: '14.4.40 – we are travelling from the Starobelsk officers' POW camp. We are at a station not far from Kharkov. We are getting out...'

There is no documentary evidence concerning the manner and method of the execution of these men. The only eyewitness account comes from an NKVD militia lieutenant, Mitrofan Syromiatnikov, who was working in the Kharkov NKVD prison at the time. He was interviewed by Russian and Polish prosecutors in the early 1990s. According to Syromiatnikov, the operation was supervised by NKVD officials from Moscow who arrived at the Kharkov prison shortly before the Polish prisoners were brought from Starobelsk. The commander of the prison, Timofei Kupry, was also closely involved. It was he who did the shooting. The procedure followed a precise pattern.

On arrival, the prisoners were ordered to leave their suitcases, to undress down to their shirts and trousers, and to remove their belts. Each prisoner was led individually, hands tied, down a corridor and across a courtyard to a separate building where he was taken down to a sound-proofed cellar. Here, the guard would open the door and ask, 'May I?' to which the response was 'Come in.' Inside the room a prosecutor was seated next to Kupry. The prosecutor asked the prisoner for his name and date of birth, then said, 'You may go.' At this point there was a noise, a 'clack', after which Kupry would call the guards to take the body away and load it onto a truck. The method of shooting used by Kupry was slightly different to that used in Katyń and Mednoye: the victims were shot at extremely close range in the nape of the neck, about the height of the third vertebra, causing instant death and minimal loss of blood. The prisoners' coats were pulled over their heads to prevent blood spilling onto the truck. The gun used to shoot the victims was a Soviet-manufactured 7.62 mm Nagant pistol. Syromiatnikov recalled seeing several on a table being loaded. Lawyer and writer Stanisław Mikke recalled the interview:

> Syromiatnikov said that, although the cellars in which they were killed were soundproofed, sounds of gunshot could still be heard. When the next Pole was taken downstairs there were two or three others waiting there before him. In his opinion, those people knew what was waiting for them. 'How did they react?' asked the Polish prosecutor. 'They didn't make a fuss,' answered the old man.[2]

The bodies were taken by truck and buried in mass graves in the sixth quadrant of Piatykhatky Park, about seven miles from Kharkov. Like Katyń, this was the site of an NKVD rest home; and like Katyń, the Polish officers were not the only victims buried there. The area had been used as an NKVD burial ground since 1938.

NKVD units dug mass graves on either side of a track that was covered with black cinders to enable the trucks to manoeuvre more easily; they scattered the bodies with lime to speed up decomposition. The area was then sealed off and designated for use by the NKVD (later KGB) only, and a boarding house constructed under the name 'Relaxing Base', with a guardroom nearby. KGB functionaries staying at the house (still operational in 1989) could roam along pleasant forest paths in the 'recuperation' park. One wonders who came up with this uniquely twisted formula, applied in more than one mass burial location. Presumably some NKVD bright spark decided that the optimum means of concealing mass graves was to build holiday accommodation on top aimed at the only guests who could be guaranteed not to talk if they accidentally tripped over a human skull while strolling in the park.

Over the years local children sometimes strayed into the park, finding buttons, insignia, eagles. On 2 June 1969 the KGB in Kharkov were informed that three students from a nearby school had discovered one of the graves, along with a wedding ring, gold tooth crowns and buttons with the Polish eagle, plus two metal plates with the inscriptions 'For the fight against the counter-revolution' from the local GPU training college and 'On the 10th anniversary of the October revolution' from Kiev. They had also identified indentations several metres long and wide in the same part of the park, along with a fragment of bone and the remains of foreign army boots. The Kharkov KGB restored the grave to its original state and filled it in, then informed the local population that the area was unsafe for visitors because during the war the Germans had used it to conceal the bodies of people who had died from communicable diseases such as typhus, cholera and syphilis.[3]

As with Starobelsk, there is no documentation to confirm the exact manner in which the prisoners of Ostashkov were killed, but there was one witness still alive who was prepared to offer some information to the Soviet Katyń investigation in 1991. Ninety-year-old Dmitry Tokarev was the former head of the NKVD for Kalinin Oblast (now Tver). The procedure he describes is almost identical to the process set out by Syromiatnikov. A special detachment of NKVD men arrived from Moscow to supervise the operation. The prisoners were taken by train from Ostashkov to Tver, a journey of roughly 120 miles, thence by truck to the local NKVD prison. One by one the men were led from their cells to a basement where their personal details were checked, after which they were handcuffed and led to a soundproofed room. Here, two men held the prisoner's arms while a third shot him in the base of the skull using a Walther pistol loaded with Geco ammunition. The man doing the shooting was Major Ivan Blokhin, one of the NKVD's most prolific executioners. NKVD guards loaded the bodies onto trucks and drove them to Mednoye, about eighteen miles west of Tver, and dumped them into large pits. After each night's executions the guards would return to their quarters and drink vodka. A total of 6,314 men from Ostashkov were murdered in this manner.[4]

In Mednoye and Kharkov, as in Katyń, one burial pit was discovered in which the bodies lay in disorder, suggesting that in all three cases the NKVD executioners began the operation by shooting the prisoners on the edge of their graves. Evidently they swiftly abandoned this method of execution because it lacked the element of surprise and control. The bullet casings discovered in the graves at Katyń support this conclusion.

There are no NKVD accounts of the fate of the Kozelsk prisoners, but the testimony offered by earlier witnesses allows an approximate picture to emerge. We know from Stanisław Swianiewicz and local witnesses that the trains arrived in Gnezdovo station and a bus or van with whitened windows ferried the prisoners away from the station. According to Major Adam Solski's diary entry for 9 April 1940, the prisoners were taken by prison van 'somewhere into a wood, something like a summer resort'. Here they were searched and any sharp objects, as well as their belts, were confiscated. Local villagers Parfemon Kiselev and Ivan Krivovertsov confirmed this, claiming that the prisoners were taken to or near the NKVD summer resort buildings. Although some prisoners were shot by the burial pits, the majority of the 4,410 men were most probably murdered in one of the resort buildings and brought to the pits later, their bodies stacked neatly in rows.[5]

Of the further victims of Beria's order of 5 March 1940 – the 7,305 Polish prisoners initially held in NKVD prisons in Western Ukraine and Belorussia and later transferred to prisons in Kiev, Minsk, Kharkov and Kherson – very little is known. Researchers have established a total number of 3,435 victims shot in Ukraine, of whom over 2,000 have been identified, but there is little trace of those taken to Minsk from Belorussian prisons.[6] Under the leadership of President Alexander Lukashenko, in power continuously since 1994, the Republic of Belarus remains one of the last outposts of Soviet-style rule in Europe. To date, all requests to release documents or allow investigation of sites of interest have been refused, although in 2020 researchers discovered a partial list of names in the Belarusian State Archive in Minsk.

The NKVD men who carried out Beria's order to execute the Polish prisoners were awarded a financial bonus in October 1940. We know little of their further fortunes, although it is rumoured many were liquidated by the KGB in the 1950s or 1960s and that others committed suicide or took to drink.

The 1990s saw an explosion of activity around the subject of Katyń, notably the exhumation works that were carried out between 1991 and 1996 in Kharkov, Tver and the Katyń Forest (where the graves created by the Polish Red Cross in 1943 were opened once again). Each summer, teams of archaeologists, forensic medical experts, anthropologists, criminologists, conservators, representatives of the Red Cross, technical-engineering experts and students of archaeology worked to exhume and identify as many victims as possible, safeguarding artefacts and reburying the remains in new graves. The 1990s also saw the official formation of the Katyń Families Association to represent relatives of the victims. One of their central campaigns was for the creation of memorials at the burial sites.

The exhumations of the 1990s were markedly different to those of 1943: where Dr Wodziński and his team had been digging up bodies, now the teams were searching for remains. A crime scene had (almost) become an archaeological dig. The work was challenging for many obvious reasons, not least the fact that many of the sites had been 'churned' by bulldozers in the 1970s as the Soviet regime sought to conceal evidence of previous crimes. In Kharkov investigators came across many remains of Soviet citizens shot and buried in the same area as the Polish officers, making identification all the more complex. Yet despite the passing of time, a wealth of objects remained to be discovered: documents, ID tags, letters, Polish money, military insignia, valuables, religious items, eagles from caps, military buttons. There were wooden boxes carved with inscriptions, cigarette holders and

Wooden cigarette box with the initials TB and TJ carved on either side of a pierced heart and a four-leaf clover.

other hand-whittled objects, newspapers dated no later than 1 April 1940. In one of the graves they discovered the remains of burnt belts, obviously taken from the prisoners before execution.

Paediatric surgeon and anaesthesiologist Dr Ewa Gruner-Żarnoch worked as a volunteer at the Kharkov site in 1995–96. Her father, Dr Julian Gruner, was captured by the Soviets on 17 September 1939 along with the entire staff of the military hospital in Stanisławów where he was serving as a doctor. He was taken to Starobelsk, where he worked alongside Dr Levittoux in the camp clinic. A champion athlete in his youth, Dr Gruner, like his daughter, was a specialist paediatrician. Medicine ran in the family.

We went to the site of the exhumation. Traces of earlier excavations were evident in the bones protruding from the ground; here a jaw, there a segment of skull, elsewhere a tibia.... The feeling of the profanation of the place was deepened by the sight of scattered bottles and trash, as well as traces of campfires and recreational footpaths; after all, this had been a rest area for the KGB.

Work conditions were incredibly difficult. It's hard enough to imagine let alone to describe. In the deep excavations, often filled with cadaverous fluid which splashed on us, pieces of bodies would tumble down.... The so-called 'wet' graves [were] 3 metres deep. We are standing in it up to our knees in a greasy substance arising from the decomposition of the soft parts of corpses....

In the largest of the [so-called 'dry' graves] corpses were preserved in their entirety, with hands, legs, toes, nails, faces. They lay in disorder as if thrown from vehicles. Some had their hands tied behind their backs by a rope having two characteristic knots, or by barbed wire. We found complete bodies, but only where the large drills, the so-called 'meat grinders', had not passed over. For in the years 1970–80, here in this cemetery, as it seems in other cemeteries in the Soviet Union, gigantic industrial machines destroyed the traces of Soviet crimes. In some graves in Kharkov sixty to seventy percent of the skulls had been crushed....

During the exhumation work I wanted so much to find my father's remains or some object belonging to him. I knew he could have had on himself a gold ring, an ancestral signet, a watch, a cigarette case with the monogram 'JG'.[7]

Despite over forty years' experience as a doctor, Ewa Gruner-Żarnoch discovered that she had severely underestimated the difficulty, both mental and physical, of working at the burial site. It was, she said, 'like a mental illness'. Whereas for the majority of the participants the exhumation was a difficult but essentially practical challenge – work experience for the students, a job for the professionals – for Gruner-Żarnoch it was 'de facto my father's funeral'. Every day she would wake up hoping to find her father's remains, yet dreading to do so. Eventually, emotionally and physically exhausted, she decided to return to her home in Szczecin, leaving behind with her colleagues some details that might help identify her father's remains:

> Reserve lieutenant and doctor, forty-two years old, teeth in good shape, around 190cm tall, athletic build, he might have been wearing a signet ring, a watch, carrying a monogrammed cigarette case with his initials, JG…which he had engraved himself. A gold wedding ring with the date of his wedding and my mother's initials, MM. Photographs of a thirty-year-old woman, a brunette with long hair, and a girl about five years old with short fair hair, letters or postcards from the Gruner or Deutschman families.[8]

The girl of five with short fair hair was, of course, Ewa Gruner-Żarnoch herself. Some days after her return home she received the news that a signet ring had been found with the monogram 'JG' and a watch.

27

SMOLENSK

DESPITE THE DIFFICULTIES INVOLVED IN EXAMINING, ANALYSING and identifying both mortal remains and archival documents (and the official archives now presented a further complication with the division of former Soviet archives into those of the individual states of Russia, Ukraine and Belarus), the 1990s and early 2000s represented a vital step forward in filling in essential gaps in the history of Katyń. There was growing cooperation between academics, historians and archivists in Russia, Poland and Ukraine. Politically, too, there was some cause for optimism as memorials were established at the three burial sites, opened in 2000 with the official participation of the presidents, prime ministers or foreign ministers of each of the host countries and Poland. The memorials commemorated not just the Polish victims but Soviet ones too, and the discussions around Katyń provided a platform for a wider discussion of Stalinist crimes in Russia and Ukraine. Obstacles remained, notably the lack of information concerning the burial sites of the prisoners who were shot in Western Ukraine and Belorussia. More fundamentally, there was a gulf of understanding between differing points of view about what the crime of Katyń represents, and how recent history should be interpreted. Not everyone in freshly post-Soviet Russia was willing to accept the 'new' version of the Katyń Massacre.

Following the revelations about Katyń in the Russian media, some members of the Soviet military and political hierarchy were unhappy about this questioning of the Soviet past. In their view it endangered 'Soviet patriotic education' – the historical narrative on which the country stood. In 1990 a counter-movement came into being as a riposte to the Polish allegations. Dedicated to highlighting Polish crimes against the Soviet Union, it was known as 'anti-Katyń'. The main focus of attention was a hitherto neglected branch of Polish–Soviet history: the matter of Soviet prisoners of war held by the Poles following the Polish–Soviet war of 1919–21, a conflict little known in the West which culminated in a spectacular victory-against-the-odds for Marshal Józef Piłsudski as Polish troops held back the Red Army on the banks of the Vistula. Credited with preventing the spread of communism to Western Europe, the Polish victory was a humiliating defeat for the Soviet Union and there has been more than one attempt to make the link between Stalin's personal resentment (he took part in the war as a commissar) and his murder of the Polish officers in 1940. According to the 'anti-Katyń' narrative, the Poles deliberately exterminated between 16,000–20,000 Russian POWs held in Polish 'concentration camps' after the end of the 1920 war. The similarity in numbers of victims suggests an equivalence to Katyń itself. It also supplies a convenient motive for Stalin's decision to kill the Polish prisoners of war: Piłsudski committed just as big a crime, only he did it first, making Katyń a tit-for-tat act of revenge.[1] On 7 April 2010, at a press conference after the ceremony commemorating the seventieth anniversary of Katyń, Vladimir Putin offered his 'personal' opinion of Stalin's motives for killing the men: 'I am not a historian,' he said, 'but I cannot rule out the possibility that Stalin – as one of the leaders of the 1920 war – wanted to revenge himself for that unsuccessful campaign.'[2] The reality, supported by evidence from both Polish and Russian scholars, is that after the formal conclusion of the Polish–Soviet war there were 110,000 Soviet prisoners of war on Polish territory. Of these, 66,000 returned to the Soviet Union, 16–17,000 died in the camps, 20–25,000 joined anti-Bolshevik Russian units. The deaths were a result of extremely poor sanitary conditions in overcrowded camps, leading to severe outbreaks of typhus, cholera, dysentery and other infectious diseases. Many also died of cold. This was at a time when Poland had barely recovered independence; the country had been ravaged by the 1914–18 conflict.[3] That Stalin nurtured a particular hatred of Polish officers was likely true; that the humiliation of 1920 rankled is also entirely believable. Whether this provided anything approaching our definition of a 'motive' for Katyń is debatable. Some historians would go further back in Polish–Russian history, referring to ever more distant victories and defeats between the two nations. But where do you stop when looking for a historical motive for such a crime?

Another strain of resistance to the idea of Katyń as a Soviet crime surfaced in the 1990s and persists today among those – notably Russian communists and, increasingly, nationalists – who continue to argue that it was in fact the Nazis who shot the Polish prisoners in 1941. According to this version the documents handed over to the Polish government in 1990 and 1992, including Beria's 5 March 1940 execution order, were falsified by the KGB on Gorbachev's orders, presumably in an effort to disassociate himself from his country's Stalinist past. This is the legacy of decades of falsification: a never-ending hall of mirrors in which historical truths are warped, distorted and – if we are not careful – permanently disfigured.

The official investigation into Katyń on the Russian side which began in 1990 dragged on for several years until the Main Military Prosecutor's Office finally closed it down in 2005 on the grounds that no one could be condemned because everyone involved was dead. What Poland – specifically the Katyń Families Association – had hoped to obtain from Russia was an official apology of the kind offered by the Germans for Nazi crimes committed in Poland. There was also talk of a trial, compensation for the families, and – most controversially – a call for the crime to be recognised as genocide. This 'escalation of demands' according to President Yeltsin (in a letter to President Wałęsa dated 22 May 1995) was seen by the Russians as a step too far. Neither Boris Yeltsin nor his successor, Vladimir Putin, would accept any equivalence between Nazi crimes and Stalinist repression. From the Russian perspective there were many more Soviet victims of Stalinism to be recognised than just the Polish prisoners: the Russian people too were victims and therefore an apology from one group of victims to another was not appropriate. As to the notion of genocide, there were two issues: the first was one of interpretation. Was Beria's resolution to shoot the prisoners based on ethnic or national grounds? Was his aim to eliminate Poles simply for being Polish? The definition of genocide adopted in 1948 by the United Nations General Assembly is 'acts committed with intent to destroy, in whole or in part, a national, ethnical, racial or religious group'. Yet Beria's order states they are to be executed as 'irremediable enemies of Soviet power', thus lending itself to the argument that the massacre was committed for political reasons. The second issue was a legal one: the concept of genocide was only recognised in Russian law in 1997, when the Russian criminal code was brought into line with international law. The new code stated that punishment for newly codified crimes could not be applied retrospectively,

meaning a crime committed in 1940 could not legally be treated as genocide. Moreover, Russian law does not allow the prosecution of criminals
who are no longer living. There could be no possibility of a trial. Although
in 2004 the Polish Institute of National Remembrance [*Instytut Pamięci
Narodowej* – IPN] undertook a Polish investigation, largely under pressure
from the Katyń Families Association, there was little hope of ever being
able to conclude it, given the fact that once the Russians had closed their
own investigation there was no access to the documents they had gathered.[4]

Nevertheless, leading up to the 70th anniversary in 2010 the 'mood music'
at the top of the respective governments was positive: Vladimir Putin, then
prime minister of Russia, came to an agreement with his Polish counterpart,
Donald Tusk, to share archival materials, to encourage greater collaboration
between historians and to broadcast Polish film director Andrzej Wajda's
2007 film *Katyń* on Russian television (a significant step given that public
awareness of Katyń in Russia was minimal). They also agreed to a historically important joint pilgrimage to Katyń to mark the anniversary. The
Poles saw Putin's presence at Katyń as highly significant. For one of the
main organisers of the event, the secretary general of the Council for the
Protection of Struggle and Martyrdom Sites (*Rady Ochrony Pamięci Walk
i Męczeństwa*), Andrzej Przewoźnik, Putin's willingness to come to Katyń
marked 'a new direction in Russian political history'.[5]

Two ceremonies were planned, each designed to be different in character:
the first, on 7 April 2010, was to be an intergovernmental affair with the
Polish prime minister visiting Katyń at the invitation of the Russian head of
state for a joint commemoration of the victims. The second ceremony, on 10
April, was to be the main Polish commemoration of the 70th anniversary
in the form of a pilgrimage led by the Polish president, Lech Kaczyński.
Nearly 100 Polish dignitaries were to attend, alongside hundreds of other
invitees, including 250 members of the Katyń families, scouts from Poland,
Belarus, Ukraine and Lithuania, soldiers, a choir and youth organisations.[6]

On 7 April the government delegations, led by Donald Tusk and Vladimir
Putin, concluded their memorial visit. There were around thirty people in
the Polish group, mainly ministers and members of parliament as well as
special guests including former president Lech Wałęsa, former premier
Tadeusz Mazowiecki and the film director Andrzej Wajda (whose father
was a prisoner at Starobelsk), along with religious leaders of all faiths and

members of the Katyń Families Association. Putin's speech was generally well received, although he stopped short of apologising for the crime, choosing instead to emphasise the shared history of suffering of Russians and Poles. He drew attention to the graves of Russians on the same site who had been killed under the Stalinist repressions, and by the Germans during the war: 'Our nation, which experienced the nightmare of civil war, of enforced collectivisation, of the mass repressions of the 1930s, understands all too well, perhaps better than anyone, what Katyń, Mednoye and Piatykhatky mean to many Polish families…'7 He laid flowers on both Polish and Russian sections of the memorial, and lit candles. These gestures matter, and they were welcomed on the Polish side.

The participants in the second ceremony travelled from Poland in two groups: the dignitaries on the presidential plane, the others by train. The ninety-six guests on board the plane included President Kaczyński and his wife; the governor of the Polish central bank; senior military and other high-ranking officials; leading figures of the Katyń Families Association and other Katyń-related organisations; relatives of General Mieczysław Smorawiński and Major Adam Solski; the lawyer and journalist Stanisław Mikke; and the secretary general of the Council for the Protection of Struggle and Martyrdom Sites, Andrzej Przewoźnik (returning for a second visit). On the morning of 10 April 2010 the Polish air force Tu-154M plane was about to land at Smolensk air base when it crashed, killing everyone on board.

In the immediate aftermath of the crash relations between Russia and Poland seemed to improve: there was a spontaneous outpouring of public sympathy from the Russian people that was entirely unexpected and did much to soften the impact of the disaster, at least in the short term. The awful evocation of previous tragedies – Katyń itself, and the death of General Władysław Sikorski in a plane crash in 1943 – with their strong association in Polish minds with Russian guilt, made it particularly striking that Vladimir Putin and the Russian president, Dmitry Medvedev, went out of their way to demonstrate their sympathy and readiness to help. They promised to facilitate a speedy and transparent investigation of the crash; Andrzej Wajda's film was broadcast widely in Russia, the director decorated with the Order of Friendship for his contribution to Polish–Russian relations; on 11 April Putin himself returned to Smolensk to witness the departure of the coffin of the Polish president, draped in a Polish flag. More significantly still, on 28 April 2010 President Medvedev personally ordered the publication online of the Katyń archive documents that had played such a pivotal role in bringing the truth to light, a gesture greeted by Polish historians as a genuine breakthrough. In another notable step later that year, in November 2010 the Russian State Duma (the lower chamber of the Federal Assembly of the Russian Federation) made an official declaration of Stalin's guilt: 'Published documents, kept in classified archives for many years, not only revealed the scale of this horrific tragedy, but also showed that the Katyń crime was carried out on direct orders of Stalin and other Soviet officials.' It seemed as if the Smolensk crash, despite or perhaps because of the terrible echoes that accompanied it, had opened the door to a new era of understanding between Poland and Russia. It was short-lived. Even at the time many Russian Communist Party MPs voted against the 2010 declaration because, in their view, the notion of Katyń as a Soviet crime remains 'one of the greatest myths of the twentieth century'.[8]

The Russian investigation report, published in January 2011, concluded that the Smolensk crash resulted from a combination of pilot error and bad weather, additionally claiming that the plane's captain was repeatedly warned about the heavy fog but pressed on regardless, apparently under pressure to land from his powerful passengers. Although the Polish authorities criticised many aspects of the Russian investigation, the official Polish report, published in July 2011, did not differ fundamentally in the conclusions drawn about the causes of the crash. Rebutting the Russian claim about the plane's captain, the Polish report stated that Russian air traffic control provided incorrect information to the crew as they approached for landing and drew attention to the fact that the military airport at Smolensk was poorly equipped, lacking modern civil navigation aids, all contributory factors to the disaster. But there was no suggestion of foul play.

At the time of the crash, Donald Tusk's centre-right Civic Platform party (*Platforma Obywatelska* – PO) held a majority in the Polish parliament gained in a 2007 election at the expense of Kaczyński's conservative Law and Justice party (*Prawo i Sprawiedliwość* – PiS), unseating the president's twin brother Jarosław as prime minister and leading to an awkward period of power sharing between Lech Kaczyński (elected president in 2005) and Tusk. After Lech Kaczyński's death his brother took over as leader of the

Law and Justice party. It was not long before the shock of the tragedy gave way to political arguments about the causes of the crash. Jarosław Kaczyński presented the Smolensk air crash as part of a continuum, referring to it not as an accident but a crime – *zbrodnia* – the Polish term used to describe the Katyń Massacre. The insinuation is clear, if not explicitly expressed: the death of his twin brother and ninety-five members of the Polish elite was not the result of poor weather or pilot error but an act of Kremlin-sponsored sabotage.

The 2015 elections in Poland swept the Law and Justice party back to power, with Jarosław Kaczyński widely seen as the 'power behind the throne' despite holding no elected role. The new government considered the 2011 official report to be seriously flawed and were deeply suspicious of its findings. Moscow, having promised full cooperation, had not delivered it: they had not handed the plane wreckage over to the Polish authorities and there were many reported irregularities in the Russian investigation. The new Polish defence minister, Antoni Macierewicz, promised a fresh look at the crash based on evidence that he insisted had been suppressed by the previous government under Donald Tusk, now president of the European Council. Accordingly, the 'Committee for Re-Investigation of the Crash of Tu-154M in Smolensk Russia', known as the Macierewicz Commission, was set up, finally publishing its conclusions in April 2018. The new report declared the previous official Polish version null and void, rebutting the claims that pilot error was the primary cause of the crash. Instead, it concluded that Russian air traffic controllers deliberately misled the Polish crew. Most controversially, it claimed that 'the Tu-154M aircraft was destroyed in the air as a result of several explosions' for which Russia was to blame.

Responses in Poland to these new conclusions roughly mirrored the sharp political divisions within the country: on the one side stood those who believed there was a cover-up by the previous government and who were ready to believe in Russian guilt; on the other side those who accused Law and Justice of using conspiracy theories for political ends. In the middle sat the quiet majority who wished – and continue to wish – that the pain of Katyń could finally be placed safely in the past.

Although the controversy no longer dominates the political agenda as it once did, questions will doubtless persist about the causes of the crash. What can be said with some certainty is that both Smolensk and Katyń continue to evoke feelings far removed from the sentiments of acceptance, reconciliation and shared remembrance that featured so prominently in Vladimir Putin's 2010 speech at the Katyń Memorial.

On both sides the story of Katyń can be moulded to suit a political purpose. Poland has matched its political move to the right since 2015 with rhetoric painting Poland as the eternal victim of malign external forces, a politics of 'inflated victimhood'.[9] In this interpretation of history Katyń is not just a symbol of Soviet terror but plays into a narrative of martyrdom stemming from the years between 1772 and 1918 when Poland was partitioned between the great European powers of Tsarist Russia, Austria and Prussia/Germany. The themes of suppression, rebellion and sacrifice nurtured by romantic poets such as Adam Mickiewicz continue to exert a powerful hold on the Polish imagination, often exploited and encouraged by nationalistic politicians in the name of patriotism. Over the same period, Russia under Vladimir Putin has cultivated a nostalgia for its past that chooses to minimise the brutality of Joseph Stalin in favour of his status as the patriotic leader who led his country to a great victory over Nazism. In this context Katyń acts as an irritant, almost a reproach. By memorialising the victims of a single Stalinist crime, the Poles present Russians with an unwelcome reminder of the numberless Soviet citizens murdered by their own great leader. The Polish victims have names. They are marked out as individuals worthy of remembrance with monuments, candles, plaques, ceremonies. The millions who died in Gulags or were shot in the Great Terror lie in anonymous graves scattered across the former Soviet Union, never commemorated, their families deprived of the opportunity to mourn.

In challenging times nations cling to stories that reassure them about their place in history, whether as victim or victor. National martyrdom remains a potent theme in Poland; external enemies provide a useful point of blame for politicians to conceal internal weaknesses. Russia celebrates patriotism, devotion to Mother Russia above all else. The Red Army soldiers who died in the Great Patriotic War can be commemorated without shame. The role of the NKVD in murdering its own citizens sits uneasily in a narrative which demands that there should be no stain like Stalinism in Russian history. To acknowledge Katyń is to acknowledge Stalinism. Not everyone in Russia is prepared to look that particular ogre in the face.

When governments lead the way in bending facts to suit their political purposes they legitimise a vast cottage industry of conspiracy theorists, historical revisionists and extremists who claim their version of 'the truth' is as valid as anyone else's because you can always disbelieve what the 'authorities' are telling you. In May 2020 activists of the Russian political group National Liberation Front removed two memorial plaques commemorating the victims of the Katyń Massacre and other victims of the NKVD placed on the former NKVD prison in Tver in the early 1990s. They were encouraged to do so by the actions of prosecutors in Tver, who claimed in 2019 that the inscriptions were 'not based on documented facts'.[10]

Conclusion

SURVIVING KATYŃ

Katyń was not only a terrible crime carried out under the majesty of Soviet law; it was also a lie; a lie repeated thousands of times, but one which, for all that, did not cease being a lie.[1]

IN SEEKING TO COME TO TERMS WITH ITS SIGNIFICANCE TO THEIR nation, Poles have always sought an 'answer' to Katyń, a way of explaining it in terms that make it comprehensible. One might argue that Stalin's decision to kill the Polish prisoners of war is simultaneously simple, complex and unknowable.

A 'simple' explanation places Katyń in the context of twentieth-century Soviet history. Here it sits alongside a lengthy list of Stalin's crimes, neither more nor less significant than any other, part of a continuum that begins with the Polish Operation of the Great Terror in 1937–38, continues with the mass deportations of Polish citizens in 1940–41 and ends with the persecution of Poles deemed unfriendly to communist rule after 1945. Examined from this perspective, efforts to seek a more complex motive simply reflect a misunderstanding of Stalinist brutality and Soviet ideology. The primacy placed on the individual in Western culture leads to a search for a personal motivation where in fact there was none. These 22,000 men represented a potential obstruction to the imposition of Soviet rule both in Poland's eastern territories, seen by Stalin as rightfully part of the Soviet Union, and in Poland itself after the war. He therefore ordered their execution with as little concern as he had shown for the millions of others whose deaths he had demanded since he rose to power. They were class enemies, counter-revolutionaries, the elite representatives of a culture that could never be moulded to fit Soviet ideology. In this context, whether he killed the men because he nurtured a particular hatred for Polish officers as a result of the 1919–21 Polish–Soviet war is immaterial.

The isolation in which the Soviet Union existed during the 1920s and 1930s ensured that most people outside the country had little idea of what occurred during the Great Terror of 1937–38. If they knew anything, they were aware mainly of the theatrical bloodbath that engulfed Stalin's enemies and former friends: the show trials, the purge of his generals. Yet the vast majority of those who died in the Great Terror were killed not as individuals but because they belonged to a particular category of people. *Kulaks* (property-owning peasants) and national minorities were shot or deported in numbers so vast it is hard to comprehend.

The very first of the national operations in 1937 was mounted against a tiny minority within the Soviet Union, 600,000 of them, less than 0.4% of the total population: Soviet Poles. Originally conceived by NKVD chief Nikolai Yezhov as a means of eliminating Polish 'spies' (a threat that existed largely in Yezhov's imagination but which found a receptive audience in Stalin), the Polish operation provided an excuse for the NKVD to arrest 143,810 people on the basis of little more than being in possession of a Polish surname or a Catholic rosary, accusing them of espionage, sabotage, or terrorism. Of those arrested, 111,091 were shot; the rest were deported to the Gulag. Where was the greatest concentration of ethnic Poles to be found? In Soviet Ukraine and Belorussia, the countries adjoining the eastern Polish borderlands that Stalin coveted and that had been lost to Russia in the Treaty of Versailles. The Polish operation provided a template for further persecutions of other national minorities in the Soviet Union, but it remained the largest, second only to the *kulak* operation (in which Poles were also disproportionately targeted). When Yezhov reported back to Stalin on the excellent progress he was making, Stalin responded: 'Keep on digging up and cleaning out this Polish filth. Eliminate it in the interests of the Soviet Union.'[2]

Although Stalin put an end to the mass killings at the end of 1938, replacing Yezhov with Lavrenty Beria and blaming the excesses of the operations on an over-zealous NKVD (and in the familiar merry-go-round of Stalinist up-and-down executing many top NKVD officers 'guilty' of such enthusiasm), he had established a precedent for mass murder by shooting. The fact that few people outside the Soviet Union were aware of this goes some way to explaining why the idea that their missing officers might have been murdered simply did not enter the heads of the Polish authorities. Only General Anders was willing to contemplate such a ghastly idea.[3] The discovery by the Germans of mass graves at Vinnytsia in Ukraine in 1943 illustrates the Great Terror's role in providing a template that Katyń would follow: over 9,000 mainly Ukrainian citizens, killed in 1937–38, were found in mass burial pits hidden underneath a recreational park. They had been shot in the back of the head, their hands bound.

In this context, the murder of 22,000 Polish prisoners of war in 1940 – be they officers, the elite of a nation or otherwise – along with the deportation of hundreds of thousands of Polish citizens in 1940–41, including the families of the prisoners (another 'tradition' established during the Terror) – is simply an extension of the policy of the Great Terror. Stalin eliminated Soviet Poles ostensibly for being a threat to the Soviet Union as spies, but in reality because they belonged to a culture that was in and of itself hostile to the values of the Soviet Union. He wanted to absorb the eastern territories of Poland and impose Soviet rule on Poland itself. It was therefore in his interests to eliminate those who might offer resistance. The execution by shooting of 22,000 'hardened, irremediable enemies of Soviet power' represented nothing novel, nor were the men targeted as individuals. Rather, Stalin and Beria were reverting to the methods of the Terror.[4]

The 'complex' approach to Katyń examines the crime in the context of wartime, seeking detailed explanations for specific elements of the decision. This is the area most probed by academics and scholars. In the context of the Terror, the Katyń Massacre follows a kind of brutal logic. In the context of wartime it presents several puzzling questions: why were the men executed at this precise moment in time? Whose decision was it – Stalin's or Beria's? Why these men and not others? Why death and not the Gulag? What is the significance of the 'big mistake'?

There has been some speculation that the three camps were cleared out in expectation of receiving Finnish prisoners of war following the end of the Soviet campaign against Finland in mid-March 1940. There is no direct evidence of this. What is known, however, is that the decision to kill the men came relatively late: until the end of February 1940 discussions were ongoing between Soprunenko, Merkulov and Beria about sending certain categories of prisoner back home or to internal NKVD prisons; similarly, the prisoners were required to fill in a second set of questionnaires in late

February. So what was it that prompted the Politburo to order their liquidation on 5 March 1940?

The short answer is that, in the absence of the relevant documents recording the Soviet decision-making process, nobody knows. There are several
plausible theories, most of them centring on the usefulness of the prisoners to Stalin, suggesting that he kept them alive for as long as they could
potentially serve as a bargaining chip in putative future negotiations with
Sikorski's government about Poland's eastern borders. According to such
theories, he shot them as soon as it was clear they were of no further use.[5]

When Stanisław Swianiewicz was working on his report in Tehran in
1942 he studied the documents given to him by Ambassador Kot. Puzzling
over the absence of the missing men, he noticed contradictions which made
no sense to him. Among the officers taken to Griazovets who later joined
Anders' Army were a number who were exceptionally antagonistic towards
the Soviet Union, men like General Wołkowicki, Colonel Künstler, Ludwik
Domoń, Józef Lis, Tadeusz Felsztyn. Among those who had disappeared,
however, was a much lower percentage of officers of this type. It was not
just the political profile of the survivors that troubled Swianiewicz: the
missing officers represented thousands of professionals, specialists whose
skills could have enormously benefited the Soviet economy and the war
effort. All the hospital staff who had been swept up in the Soviet advance
of 1939; all the skilled tacticians, experts, engineers... Why murder these
men rather than put them to some use?

Lavrenty Beria was known for his ruthless efficiency. When faced with a
decision it was not ideology that triumphed but calculation. His son Sergo
later claimed that Beria argued against murdering the Poles because they
might be useful later.[6] There is no evidence to support this assertion, but
it echoes Stanisław Swianiewicz's question. The complexity involved in
killing such a large number of men in the utmost secrecy was considerable,
eating up valuable NKVD time and resources. The possible ramifications
later down the line if word got out were significant: these were not Soviet
citizens but foreign nationals, not criminals but prisoners of war captured
on the field of battle. Why go to all that trouble when they could have
simply been shipped off to Kolyma – as Czapski and his compatriots so
long believed – and left to work themselves to death? The only clue we have,
the order of execution of 5 March 1940, is addressed to Stalin from Beria,

as if it is Beria's recommendation. But the documents we lack are those that might offer some insight into the debates preceding this decision. It is perfectly feasible to suggest that Beria proposed keeping the men alive on the grounds of their potential future usefulness but was overruled by Stalin who simply, vindictively, chose to eliminate them. After all, what possible disadvantage could there be for Stalin in ridding himself of a few more Poles while the rest of the world's attention was focused on Hitler? It is equally possible Beria made the suggestion to kill them. In March 1940 the NKVD did not anticipate the threat of a Nazi invasion.

Perhaps an element of truth can be found in Beria's own words: *my zdjielali bolshuyu oshibku*. We made a big mistake. Or at least a partial one. In March 1940 the NKVD considered the Polish officers to be of no use, deeming them a hindrance to the future establishment of Soviet rule in post-war Poland. So they liquidated them, just as they liquidated many hundreds of thousands of their own citizens as 'hardened, irremediable enemies of Soviet power'. Only later did relations with the Nazis begin to cool and the priorities of the NKVD shifted accordingly, as demonstrated by the Villa of Bliss episode of October 1940. This is not to suggest that if the decision had been delayed by six months those men would still have been alive, but it is worth noting that the NKVD did not execute the Polish officers who arrived in their camps from Lithuania and Latvia in the summer of 1940 (many of whom later ended up in Griazovets in July 1941). If we view Lavrenty Beria as a proponent of pragmatism rather than ideology, it is quite possible that from the perspective of October 1940 he viewed Katyń, retrospectively, as a 'big mistake'. The changed circumstances meant they had 'wasted' men who could have proved useful to the war effort.

It is also arguable that Beria might have viewed Katyń as a mistake in terms of its consequences for the NKVD. In carrying out the mass execution of 22,000 foreign nationals captured on the field of battle the NKVD had stepped beyond the readily-controllable environment of Soviet crimes committed against Soviet citizens on Soviet soil. The elaborate measures taken to conceal the executions already point to an awareness of the possible repercussions should news get out that the Soviets had murdered foreign prisoners of war. It was one thing to bump off individuals like Ehrlich and Alter, or assassinate enemies abroad (Leon Trotsky), or dispatch thousands to the Gulag where death could be presented as the unfortunate by-product of hard work and a harsh climate. It was quite another to hide the mass execution of prisoners of war on such a scale. And after the reversal of roles brought about by the Nazi invasion of the Soviet Union, the fact that the victims belonged to an Allied country was an embarrassment neither Stalin nor Beria could possibly have foreseen.

Despite the fact that the Soviet Union recognised neither the Geneva nor the Hague Conventions, and the NKVD disregarded many international norms regarding the treatment of prisoners of war, it nevertheless remains true that their status had guaranteed these men relatively mild treatment during their captivity. They were not beaten or made to labour, they were not tortured or starved. Traditionally, to be an officer and a prisoner of war is a state simultaneously helpless and noble. The murder of such men would arouse very different feelings on the international stage to those evoked by the image of individuals tortured in a Soviet prison or toiling in a Gulag. This was a country's entire elite, thousands of distinguished professionals whose names would not be swiftly forgotten at home. And what of the thousands of Russian soldiers held in German POW camps in 1943, when the bodies were discovered? What consequences might follow for them if it came out that the Soviets had murdered their own prisoners of war? The Soviet denial of the crime is so very vehement, 'a monstrous invention' of the 'German-Fascist scoundrels'. Is it possible that there resides in these words an element – perhaps a sliver – not just of embarrassment but shame?

The effort required to cover up Katyń stretched over decades and crossed continents. In its service hundreds of employees of the NKVD, KGB, UB and SB were deployed in pursuing, suppressing and silencing anyone who would speak out. All those monuments with fake dates, all those books with fake texts. All those Polish families deported, arrested and persecuted. Such a great deal of effort for a crime which, in Soviet terms, was (numerically) relatively insignificant. And still the Poles would not keep quiet.

Having established an entire alternative narrative about Katyń while Stalin was alive, it was evidently deemed too embarrassing to admit to the truth after he was dead. Khrushchev chose not to add Katyń to the tally of Stalinist crimes that he disowned in 1956. Had he been less cautious he could potentially have cauterised the wound earlier, lessening many of the subsequent problems between the two nations. However, once he had decided not to own up there was clearly nothing to be gained by admitting it subsequently, 'with all the undesirable consequences for our country'.[7] Thus the lie stood until the collapse of the Soviet system itself made its revelation inevitable, set in stone on public monuments, written in the pages of history books, growing gradually more jaded and ridiculous as time passed and public tolerance of the 'Katyń lie' grew weak. Like an actor putting on layer after layer of make-up, at some point the mask would slide and the ugly truth be laid bare.

The unknowable version of Katyń is what is left to us when we have exhausted all other avenues. Whether or not there exist documents which could shed light on the precise reasoning behind the decision to execute these men, the chances are we will never be certain why Stalin took the decision to kill them at that specific moment in time.

The search for an 'answer' to Katyń perhaps reveals more than anything else the enormous gulf this book has attempted to explore between, on the one hand, individual Polish officers, Red Cross representatives, diplomats, politicians – 'ordinary' men – and what Dr Robel referred to as 'the most effective secret police organisation in the world', the NKVD. Between the individualist mindset of Western Europe and the Bolshevik mentality. People versus numbers. Where the Poles saw the missing (murdered) prisoners as individuals – comrades, friends, fellow soldiers – Stalin and Beria saw a mass of undesirable 'elements' to be eliminated as one would erase a mistake written in pencil. One of the best-known reasons for the triumph of the Red Army during World War II was Stalin's willingness to sacrifice thousands of lives to achieve victory. There was no sentimentality about the 'human cost'. Soviet lives were cheap. In such a vast country there were always plenty to spare. So to search for a 'motive' for Katyń as we (Westerners, Europeans, historians, Poles) understand it is perhaps to continue misinterpreting the nature of the Soviet Union under Stalin.

Chairman Madden: Would you have any opinion as to why you were saved and not murdered?

Mr Moszyński: Those of us who survived have thought about that a great deal. Looking over this group of the four hundred survivors, we have come to the conclusion, if the Russians had any particular reason for selecting us, that reason was that they wanted a complete

cross-section of all the Polish prisoners that were ever detained so
that they could subsequently say, 'Why, you have these prisoners
here.'[8]

Adam Moszyński's observation may not be an accurate interpretation of the
NKVD's motivation in sparing 395 men, but he is correct in highlighting
the diversity of the prisoners who survived. As we have seen, the survivors
of Katyń were chosen for specific reasons: because they were informers, or
had declared their willingness to cooperate with the Soviets, because they
were of German origin, or the German embassy or Lithuanian mission had
requested them. We also know that many were saved who were openly and
energetically anti-communist in a way the vast majority of the murdered
prisoners were not. These men survived either because they were known
to be talented military officers with skills which the NKVD thought could
be of use to them, or because they were deemed to be in possession of
important intelligence. Stanisław Swianiewicz himself observed that in
Kozelsk the chief interrogator, Kombrig Zarubin, was

> interested mainly in those prisoners who had distinguished themselves on
> a higher level than the average person in pre-war life. He had directed his
> curiosity towards the staff officers, not so much towards the generals as
> toward the colonels and lieutenant colonels who had completed the higher
> military academies.[9]

The survival of officers such as General Wołkowicki, Lieutenant Colonel
Felsztyn, Major Domoń, Major Lis or Lieutenant Mintowt-Czyż might be
attributed to this fact. Nevertheless, that such a small number were saved
when so many men with similar talents or skills were sent to their deaths
remains a painful mystery. Ambassador Kot mourned the loss of hundreds of
Poland's leading cultural and scientific figures in Soviet labour camps, many
of whom disappeared without trace. Every victim of Katyń has a name. We
know the loss it represents to the Polish nation: an entire generation of skilled
professionals from every walk of life. Some – like the avant-garde poet Lech
Piwowar or the graphic designer Edward Manteuffel – in the early stages
of their careers; others – like Dr Henryk Levittoux, Major Adam Sołtan
or the eleven generals – at the height or even end of theirs. An analysis of

the professions of the Griazovets prisoners reveals that a proportionately greater number of doctors and medical staff survived (over thirty, chosen from a total of around eight hundred). It is not clear why these men were saved when so many other doctors were sent to their deaths, except that the survivors were on average younger men. Without the NKVD documents to shed light on the thinking behind each individual decision, the logic in choosing survivors can appear as random as the lists of names called out during 'parrot hour' in April 1940.

What does it mean to survive Katyń? It is both a physical and a metaphorical state.

For Bronisław Młynarski and Józef Czapski, both sensitive, deeply humanistic individuals, the seven months they spent in Starobelsk was a period of intense comradeship. For the rest of their lives they were haunted by the twin mystery of their own survival and the ultimate fate of their friends. According to Doris Kenyon-Młynarski, when her husband was working on his memoir of Starobelsk, 'Every time he talked or wrote of his massacred friends he would scream in his sleep at night.'[10] His translator, Kazimierz Zdziechowski, remarked that during their many conversations Młynarski would generally avoid the subject of his wartime captivity, but

> he would always leave me with a feeling that he never really got over the fact of having survived himself while his dearest friends had to perish. The ever-nagging question why it was so, to what mysterious cause, eluding any rational explanation, did he owe his life, must never have left his conscience.[11]

Czapski's short memoir of Starobelsk, likewise, is an eloquent and melancholy elegy to those friends and comrades who disappeared in April 1940. We know now that men like Czapski and Młynarski did not survive because they were of interest to the NKVD. They possessed no useful intelligence or military skills. Somebody intervened on their behalf and their names went on a list. Mutual incomprehension permeates their encounters with their captors: think of Bronisław Młynarski attempting to explain his love of music to his bemused interrogator, or Czapski wandering hopelessly around Moscow waiting for a call from Major Raikhman. It is perhaps ironic that it is these men, so far removed in mindset from the NKVD, who have provided us with the most vivid portraits of camp existence, painting a human face on an inhuman crime.

For the people who took part in the investigations of Katyń in 1943 – the Red Cross delegations, writers, scientists, doctors and others – surviving Katyń meant avoiding arrest, imprisonment, deportation or death. For many of them it meant, as it did for the survivors, living out the remainder of their lives in exile. Those who went to Katyń were placed in an impossible situation: forced to choose whether to accept the burden of bearing witness and risk being accused as a Nazi collaborator, or refuse and leave the dead unnamed, uninvestigated, without a proper burial. Those who accepted the burden paid a high price for the risk they took.

When the news about Katyń was announced in April 1943 Stanisław Swianiewicz was stationed in Jerusalem as head of the Bureau of Studies attached to the Polish Centre of Information in the Near East. He immediately sent a coded message to Ambassador Kot, then head of the ministry of information in the Polish government in London, confirming that the German revelations agreed with the report he had submitted to the Polish embassy in Kuybyshev.

The revelations also brought Swianiewicz to a personal realisation: throughout his imprisonment in the Soviet Union he had, despite everything, retained a somewhat optimistic view of the 'moral' essence of the Soviet state:

> I had still believed that somewhere in the upper regions of the Soviet authorities there existed some remnants of respect for human life and human dignity as well as for the moral principles generally accepted in the civilised world. I had remained under the influence of stories told to me by my fellow prisoners in Lubyanka who maintained that – after the removal of Yezhov and the ascendance of Beria – there was, to a certain degree, a humanisation of the Soviet Security Services.[12]

Of all the survivors, it was Swianiewicz who understood best the gulf between 'the civilised world' and the world of Stalin and the NKVD. Where Czapski and Młynarski sought (and failed) to understand their captors in purely human, individualistic terms, Swianiewicz applied himself to understanding the rules of the system that produced such brutality. And yet even his analysis had fallen short, unable to grasp the cruel logic of Stalin's baffling, crazy, murderous world.

There are still men and women alive today who possess a vague childhood memory of a father who never came home, a tall man in shiny leather boots, perhaps, with a whiskery moustache that tickled when he embraced his son or daughter for the last time. And, in the collective memory of Poland, the loss of a generation's 'elite' is a wound that remains disturbingly fresh. But why should Katyń matter to us, in the West, and why now?

The ruthless dedication exhibited by the NKVD and its successor, the KGB, to the fabrication and maintenance of a complex narrative, complete with dates and documents, monuments and memories, strikes a chilling chord in a modern world where truth seems an expendable and ever-more-malleable commodity. In an era of fake news and political manipulation, the false narrative of Katyń does not appear so much an exception as part of a continuum in keeping with a tradition of elaborate state-sponsored deceit that can, at times, seem almost absurd. These parallels with the past may well be a good reason for telling this story now. Yet the most important thing I have attempted to do in this book is to illuminate for a modern reader just what it might be like to find oneself caught up in the centre of this spider's web. To survive Katyń is not just to live when others died: it is to bear witness, as men like Józef Czapski, Bronisław Młynarski, Stanisław Swianiewicz or Dr Marian Wodziński did, to gaze into the unfathomable darkness and somehow retain the will to make sense of what you have seen, and to speak of it to others.

Acknowledgements

FOR THEIR ADVICE, ENCOURAGEMENT AND EDITORIAL INSIGHTS I would like to thank my agent, Andrew Gordon, and editor, Sam Carter. Thank you to Rida Vaquas, Juliana Pars, Laura McFarlane, Paul Nash and all the team at Oneworld for their hard work. For translations, explanations, suggestions and connections my sincere thanks to Magda Koziej, Barbara Borsuk, Larissa Kouznetsova, Dr Stanley Bill, Eugenia Maresch, Antonia Lloyd-Jones, Dagmara Grabska and many others. To staff at the Sikorski Institute, the Piłsudski Institute and the Archiwum Akt Nowych for helping me locate the documents and pictures I needed. Also to the Wodziński family, Maria Swianiewicz-Nagięć, Lech and Witek Mintowt-Czyż, and Eva Rubinstein for their kind cooperation. I am incredibly grateful to the Society of Authors for an Authors' Foundation Grant which enabled me to travel to Warsaw and complete my research on the book. And to Alex and Hal, who have endured my obsession with this difficult subject so patiently and for so long.

Note on translations and references

WHERE AN ENGLISH-LANGUAGE VERSION OF A TEXT HAS BEEN published I have referred to this rather than the original Polish version. Where there is no published version in English any direct quotations are my own translations. A selection of the original Russian NKVD documents relating to Katyń has been translated into English, appearing in *Katyń: A Crime Without Punishment* by Anna M. Cienciala, Natalia S. Lebedeva and Wojciech Materski. The rest of these documents can be found in Polish in the four-volume work edited by Wojciech Materski, *Katyń: Dokumenty Zbrodni*. Where an NKVD document exists in English I have referred to *Katyń: A Crime*. Where it does not I have translated it and given a reference to the Materski volumes.

Notes

INTRODUCTION: CAPTURE

1   Edward Raczyński, *In Allied London*, 34.
2   Timothy Snyder, *Bloodlands, Europe Between Hitler and Stalin*, 116.
3   Władysław Anders, *Mémoires* (French edition), 26.
4   Anna M. Cienciala, Natalia S. Lebedeva, Wojciech Materski, *Katyń: A Crime Without Punishment*, 44.
5   Snyder, *Bloodlands*, 89–104.
6   Bronisław Młynarski, *The 79th Survivor*, 36.
7   Ibid., 37.
8   Ibid., 55.
9   Ibid., 58.
10 Ibid., 59.
11 Ibid., 60.
12 Not to be confused with General Władysław Sikorski, Poland's prime minister and commander-in-chief from 1939–43.
13 General Langner himself was taken to Moscow, then later allowed to return to Lwów whence he somehow managed to escape to France via Romania, ending up in Scotland.
14 Młynarski, *The 79th Survivor*, 62.
15 Polish Cultural Foundation, *The Crime of Katyń, Facts & Documents*, 12.
16 Józef Czapski, *Wspomnienia starobielskie*, 7.
17 Młynarski, *79th Survivor*, 81.

CHAPTER I: MONASTERIES

1   Młynarski, *79th Survivor*, 101.
2   Cienciala et al., *Katyń: A Crime*, 267.
3   Wojciech Materski, ed., *Katyń: Dokumenty zbrodni*, vol 1: *Jeńcy nie wypowiedzianej wojny, sierpień 1939 – marzec 1940*, doc 185, 414–21.
4   Polish Cultural Foundation, *The Crime of Katyń*, 41, and Jan Bober, *Za drutami obozów sowieckich – Wspomnienia*, 90.
5   Materski, *Katyń: Dokumenty zbrodni*, vol 1, doc 112, 270.

6   Dr Zbigniew Godlewski, *Przeżyłem Starobielsk*, Przegląd Historyczny 38 (1993), nr. 2.
7   Młynarski, *79th Survivor*, 101.
8   Godlewski, *Przeżyłem Starobielsk*.
9   A ninth general, Jarnuszkiewicz, was taken to the Lubyanka in November 1939.
10 Cienciala et al., *Katyń: A Crime*, Table 2A and 2C, 379 and 381. I have used numbers from 1 April 1940, the last date on which these statistics were recorded before the camps were emptied.
11 Młynarski, *79th Survivor*, 201–2.
12 This detail was later to prove significant during the 1943–44 investigations in the Katyń Forest. The survivors spent a total of two years without a change of uniform.
13 Tadeusz Felsztyn, *Druga strona Kozielska*, Wiadomości, 23 May 1948.
14 Wojciech Materski (cited in *Katyń: A Crime*, 473) states that 96 colonels and lieutenant colonels were held here. Zygmunt Berling also mentions that there were 'about 100' of them (Zygmunt Berling, *Wspomnienia*, 45) but camp statistics list 181 men of this rank. It is possible that the rest of them were held within the main camp.
15 Zygmunt Berling, *Wspomnienia*, vol 1, *z łagrów do Andersa*, 39–40.
16 Jan Bober, *Za drutami obozów sowieckich*, 97.
17 Czapski, *Wspomnienia starobielskie*, 12.
18 Młynarski, *79th Survivor*, 109.

CHAPTER 2: NAMES

1   Młynarski, *79th Survivor*, 110.
2   Stanisław Swianiewicz, *In the Shadow of Katyń, Stalin's Terror*, 64.
3   Cienciala et al., *Katyń: A Crime*, 55.
4   First on the list in section c, 'participants in fascist military nationalistic organisations of former Poland' was the Polish Military Organisation (*Polska Organizacja Wojskowa* – POW). This was primarily a military intelligence and sabotage group founded by Józef Piłsudski in 1914 and active initially in Russian-controlled Poland and Russia itself during the fight for Polish independence, subsequently in Ukraine, Lithuania and Russia until it was disbanded in 1921. Timothy Snyder adds a fascinating element to this story which sheds light on the NKVD's interest in the POW so many years after it ceased operating. In the 1930s the then head of the NKVD, Nikolai Yezhov, identified the POW as an espionage group in Ukraine, blaming them for the Ukrainian famine. It was an imaginary threat. Yezhov was obsessed by Poles, believing them to possess almost superhuman powers in matters of intelligence – 'they know everything'.

By 1937 Yezhov had created such an effective fiction for the non-existent group that he persuaded not only himself but Stalin that the organisation had penetrated the Red Army, the Communist Party and the NKVD itself. He used it as an excuse to purge the NKVD of its legacy of Polish officers in 1937. (The first Soviet secret police force, the Cheka, was founded by a Pole, Feliks Dzierżyński. He led the NKVD from 1919. Many of the NKVD's prominent early officers were Polish.) Then, in August 1937, Yezhov issued order 00485, which initiated the Polish operation, the first national operation of the Great Terror of 1937–38. The order authorised the NKVD to eliminate the Polish 'network of spies'. In reality, it was used as a means of liquidating large numbers of Soviet Poles. See Snyder, *Bloodlands*, 89–94.

5 Cienciala et al., *Katyń: A Crime*, 64–7.

6 Materski, *Katyń: Dokumenty zbrodni*, vol 1, doc 128, 307.

7 Ibid., doc 116, 279.

8 Bober, *Za drutami obozów sowieckich*, introduction by Krzysztof Halicki, 38–41.

9 Ibid., 118. None of these photographs survived. An order to wash out the emulsion on 4,398 photographic plates in Starobelsk was sent to Commander Berezhkov in June 1940.

10 Swianiewicz, *In the Shadow of Katyń*, 63.

11 Materski, *Katyń: Dokumenty zbrodni*, vol 1, 10 Nov 1939 doc 103.

12 Bober, *Za drutami obozów sowieckich*, 102–3.

13 Salomon W. Słowes, *The Road to Katyń*, 58.

14 Młynarski, *79th Survivor*, 128.

15 Polish Cultural Foundation, *The Crime of Katyń*, 43, and Bober, *Za drutami obozów sowieckich*, 105.

16 Młynarski, *79th Survivor*, 82.

17 Ibid., 33.

18 Godlewski, *Przeżyłem Starobielsk*.

19 Ibid.

20 Ibid.

21 Czapski, *Wspomnienia starobielskie*, 18.

22 Zdzisław Peszkowski, *Wspomnienia jeńca z Kozielska*, 20.

23 Polish Cultural Foundation, *The Crime of Katyń*, 29.

24 Czapski, *Wspomnienia starobielskie*, 15.

25 Cienciala et al., *Katyń: A Crime*, doc 32, 89–99. Also see Chapter 4, pages 53–5, regarding rumours that an international commission was coming to the camp.

26 Although a handwritten note on the report suggests that banning religious expression was a mistake. See Cienciala et al., *Katyń: A Crime*, 95.

27 Młynarski, *79th Survivor*, 148, and Godlewski, *Przeżyłem Starobielsk*. Młynarski places this event on 11 November, Dr Godlewski the following day.

28 Materski, *Katyń: Dokumenty zbrodni*, vol 1, doc 117, 281.

29 Młynarski, *79th Survivor*, 142. See also Chapter 4, pages 42–3.
30 Ibid., 136.

CHAPTER 3: QUESTIONS

1 Czapski, *Wspomnienia starobielskie*, 26.
2 Stanisław Swianiewicz in Polish Cultural Foundation, *The Crime of Katyń*, 31–2.
3 Polish Institute and Sikorski Museum, London (henceforth PISM) Kol 12/3/16 Tadeusz Felsztyn statement, Foxley, 03 April 1948.
4 Ibid.
5 Materski, *Katyń: Dokumenty zbrodni*, vol 1, doc 149, 337.
6 Peszkowski, *Wspomnienia*, 14.
7 See Chapter 2, note 4.
8 See Chapter 7.
9 Czapski, *Wspomnienia starobielskie*, 26.
10 All extracts quoted in this chapter appear in Młynarski, *79th Survivor*, 187–91.
11 Berling, *Wspomnienia*, vol 1, 44.
12 Archiwum Akt Nowych (henceforth AAN) R-156, Kazimierz Rosen-Zawadzki recorded 9 March 1965.
13 See Chapter 2, pages 16–17.
14 AAN R-156, Roman Imach, 30 November 1964.
15 AAN R-156, Stanisław Szczypiorski, 30 November 1964 and 20 October 1964.
16 Mintowt-Czyż family correspondence with the author, June 2019.
17 See Chapter 24, pages 286–8.

CHAPTER 4: LECTURES

1 Cienciala et al., *Katyń: A Crime*, doc 30, 87.
2 The term used by the NKVD to refer to World War II until June 1941, when it became 'the Great Patriotic War'. See Chapter 4, page 55.
3 Bronisław Młynarski places this meeting shortly after the events of 11 November, see Chapter 2, page 28.
4 Cienciala et al., *Katyń: A Crime*, doc 32, 91–3.
5 Materski, *Katyń: Dokumenty zbrodni*, vol 1, doc 181, 397.
6 Ibid., doc 154, 344.
7 Bober, *Za drutami obozów sowieckich*, 112.
8 Materski, *Katyń: Dokumenty zbrodni*, vol 1, doc 154, 344.
9 Berling, *Wspomnienia*, vol 1, 45.

10 Czapski, *Wspomnienia starobielskie*, 16.

11 Peszkowski, *Wspomnienia*, 16–17.

12 Czapski, *Wspomnienia starobielskie*, 21.

13 Słowes, *The Road to Katyń*, 65–6.

14 Bober, *Za drutami obozów sowieckich*, 111.

15 Lech Maligranda, *Józef Marcinkiewicz (1910–1940) – On the Centenary of His Birth.*

16 Godlewski, *Przeżyłem Starobielsk.*

17 Materski, *Katyń: Dokumenty zbrodni*, vol 1, doc 154, 344.

18 Ibid., doc 181, 397.

19 Julian Ginsbert, witness statement, London 9 June 1943, PISM Kol 12/5.

20 Młynarski, *79th Survivor*, 195.

21 Ibid., 159–70, and Peszkowski, *Wspomnienia*, 17–18.

22 Cienciala et al., *Katyń: A Crime*, 87. See also Młynarski, *79th Survivor*, Chapter 14: 'Roubles'.

23 Materski, *Katyń: Dokumenty zbrodni*, vol 1, doc 116, 278.

24 Godlewski, *Przeżyłem Starobielsk.*

25 Stanisław Lubodziecki, *Wiadomości*, nr 12, London, 21 March 1948.

26 AAN, R-156, Kazimierz Rosen-Zawadzki, 9 March 1965.

27 Bober, *Za drutami obozów sowieckich*, 93.

28 Ignacy Daszyński (1866–1936) briefly served as independent Poland's first prime minister in 1918 then, later, as deputy prime minister and Marshal of the Sejm.

29 Młynarski, *79th Survivor*, 184. Feliks Daszyński's name appears on the Katyń list as having been killed at Kharkov along with the other prisoners from Starobelsk.

CHAPTER 5: LETTERS

1 Bober, *Za drutami obozów sowieckich*, 113.

2 *Pamiętniki znalezione w Katyniu*, 209.

3 AAN, R-156, Kazimierz Rosen-Zawadzki, 9 March 1965.

4 Swianiewicz, *In the Shadow of Katyń*, 65.

5 Stalin's birthday was 18 December.

6 Młynarski, *79th Survivor*, 205.

7 Andrzej Przewoźnik, *Katyń. Zbrodnia, prawda, pamięć*, 101–2.

8 Materski, *Katyń: Dokumenty zbrodni*, vol 3, doc 93, 241. In December 1940 Kantak wrote to the NKVD requesting his removal from the list of prisoners from the Soviet zone of occupation on the grounds that he was a citizen of Gdańsk, with a Gdańsk passport. His request was accepted, as was a similar request for removal from the Soviet-zone list by Captain Adam Moszyński.

9 Berling, *Wspomnienia*, vol 1, 50.

10 Only one suicide was officially recorded in all three camps, that of an ensign named Bazyli Zacharski from Grodno, a resident of the 'skit' in Kozelsk who hanged himself in early December. His death is noted in the diary of Kazimierz Szczekowski (*Pamiętniki znalezione w Katyniu*, 106–26) and in an NKVD report from Kozelsk dated 1 December 1939 (Cienciala et al., *Katyń: A Crime*, 87).

11 Godlewski, *Przeżyłem Starobielsk*, and Młynarski, *79th Survivor*, 175–6.

12 Czapski, *Wspomnienia starobielskie*, 24–5.

13 Ibid., 13. For Kuczyński see Chapter 8, note 25.

14 Młynarski, *79th Survivor*, 217.

15 Czapski, *Wspomnienia starobielskie*, 27.

16 Młynarski, *79th Survivor*, 218–19.

CHAPTER 6: PARROT HOUR

1 Materski, *Katyń: Dokumenty zbrodni*, vol 2, doc 56, 124.

2 Swianiewicz, *In the Shadow of Katyń*, 69.

3 Słowes, *The Road to Katyń*, 68. At this time Lithuania had not yet been annexed to the Soviet Union so its residents were not yet considered Soviet subjects as those who lived in parts of eastern Poland, now incorporated as Western Ukraine and Western Belorussia, were.

4 Materski, *Katyń: Dokumenty zbrodni*, vol 1, doc 157, 358 and doc 196, 442.

5 Berling,*Wspomnienia*, vol 1, 53.

6 Tadeusz Felsztyn, *Wiadomości* nr 21, 23 May 1948.

7 AAN, R-156, recordings made on 08 October 1964, 30 November 1964, 09 March 1965.

8 Bober, *Za drutami obozów sowieckich*, 120.

9 Ibid., 121.

10 See Conclusion for a brief discussion of this theory.

11 Diary of Major Kazimierz Szczekowski, *Pamiętniki znalezione w Katyniu*, 106–26.

12 Wacław Komarnicki statement of 21 May 1943, reproduced in *Hearings Before the Select Committee to Conduct an Investigation of the Facts, Evidence and Circumstances of the Katyń Forest Massacre*, henceforth *Madden Committee Hearings*, vol 4, 16–19 April 1952, 801–7.

13 Materski, *Katyń: Dokumenty zbrodni*, vol 2, doc 44, 100.

14 Godlewski, *Przeżyłem Starobielsk*.

15 Czapski, *Wspomnienia starobielskie*, 28.

16 Komarnicki statement of 21 May 1943, *Madden Committee Hearings*, vol 4, 801–7.

17 *Pamiętniki znalezione w Katyniu*, 60.
18 Godlewski, *Przeżyłem Starobielsk*.
19 Czapski, *Wspomnienia starobielskie*, 28.
20 Peszkowski, *Wspomnienia*, 24–5.
21 Godlewski, *Przeżyłem Starobielsk*.
22 Swianiewicz, *In the Shadow of Katyń*, 71.
23 Czapski, *Wspomnienia starobielskie*, 29.

CHAPTER 7: PAVLISHCHEV BOR

1 After the Russian prime minister, Pyotr Stolypin, who first introduced the prisoner car after the 1905 insurrection to carry revolutionaries to exile in Siberia.
2 Godlewski, *Przeżyłem Starobielsk*.
3 Czapski, *Wspomnienia starobielskie*, 29.
4 Słowes, *The Road to Katyń*, 77.
5 Ibid., 77–8.
6 Polish Cultural Foundation, *The Crime of Katyń*, 73.
7 Cienciala et al., *Katyń: A Crime*, doc 86, 265. As of 1 July it was 394, possibly because a young aristocrat, Prince Jan Lubomirski (b.1913) was freed sometime in July 1940 after foreign intervention.
8 Jan Bober worked closely with former Starobelsk prisoner Adam Moszyński when compiling information on Griazovets. Moszyński was the author of the 'Katyń List' of murdered prisoners, *Lista Katyńska*, Wydawnicza Gryf, London, 1949, based on *Amtliches Material zum Massenmord von Katyń*, Berlin 1943. He sent Bober many precise details about the various arrivals and departures of prisoners of Griazovets. General Wołkowicki produces similar figures, as does Zdzisław Peszkowski, who worked on a list with a former Kozelsk prisoner, Jerzy Turski.
9 Materski, *Katyń: Dokumenty zbrodni*, vol 2, doc 229, 368, and Słowes, *The Road to Katyń*, 91.
10 Cienciala et al., *Katyń: A Crime*, doc 85, 264.
11 Materski, *Katyń: Dokumenty zbrodni*, vol 2, doc 43, 98–100.
12 In October 1939 Lithuania signed a mutual assistance pact with the Soviet Union that allowed Soviet troops to be based on its territory. Similar agreements were made with Estonia and Latvia. In June 1940 the Soviets occupied all three countries, holding sham elections just as they had in the eastern territories of Poland before declaring that they had 'chosen' to join the Soviet Union.
13 A second member of the Polish aristocracy, Edmund Ferdynand Radziwiłł, had already been released from Kozelsk in December 1939 following a request

from members of the Italian royal family. He returned to Nazi-occupied Poland, where he engaged in resistance activities.

14 Czesław Madajczyk, *Dramat katyński*, 93. The wording of the request suggests that du Chastel de la Howarderie did not know Czapski personally and had been asked by someone else to intervene. Certainly Czapski himself, when informed many years later by the Russian historian Natalia Lebedeva that the diplomat had intervened on his behalf, did not recognise the name (Eric Karpeles, *Almost Nothing*, 442). Von Plessen duly sent the request to Count Gottfried von Bismarck, another fellow aristocrat and high-ranking SS officer, and received a reply. Their brief correspondence reveals that the Germans were able to obtain little information about POWs held in the USSR, but a prisoner exchange was clearly envisaged at that time and the German response was that if Czapski lived in the German zone of occupation they would be happy to accept him as a prisoner of war in any such exchange. A further detail reveals that the Germans were aware that from a legal standpoint they could do nothing to intervene on behalf of a Polish national captured on Soviet soil.

15 Materski, *Katyń: Dokumenty zbrodni*, vol 2, doc 79, 159.

16 See Chapter 16.

17 Cienciala et al., *Katyń: A Crime*, note 147, 511.

18 Ibid., note 148, 511.

19 Komarnicki statement, *Madden Committee Hearings*, vol 4, 806.

20 Bober, *Za drutami obozów sowieckich*, 134.

CHAPTER 8: GRIAZOVETS

1 Peszkowski, *Wspomnienia*, 32.

2 Słowes, *The Road to Katyń*, 88–9.

3 Materski, *Katyń: Dokumenty zbrodni*, vol 2, doc 124, 217–18.

4 Bober, *Za drutami obozów sowieckich*, 162.

5 Młynarski, *79th Survivor*, 230 (Epilogue by Witold Kaczkowski).

6 This was certainly the opinion of some of the pro-Soviet prisoners. AAN, R-156 Józef Lipski, recorded 08 October 1964.

7 See Chapter 11, page 123.

8 Jerzy Wołkowicki, PISM, Kol 212/3.

9 Bober, *Za drutami obozów sowieckich*, 164.

10 Młynarski, *79th Survivor*, 230 (Epilogue by Witold Kaczkowski).

11 Wołkowicki, PISM, Kol 212/3.

12 Ibid.

13 AAN, R-156 Stanisław Szczypiorski, 30 November 1964 and 20 October 1964.

14 Stalin's 'Short Course on the History of the Communist Party of the Soviet Union' was the textbook for these lectures.

15 Cienciala et al., *Katyń: A Crime*, doc 89, 269–71.

16 Peszkowski, *Wspomnienia*, 43–4.

17 These were later published as a short book, *Proust contre la Déchéance: Conférences au camp de Griazovets*. Later translated as *Lost Time – Lectures on Proust in a Soviet Prison Camp*.

18 Berling, *Wspomnienia*, 63.

19 Materski, *Katyń: Dokumenty zbrodni*, vol 3, doc 20, 88.

20 Słowes, *The Road to Katyń*, 94.

21 See Chapter 11.

22 Berling, *Wspomnienia*, vol 1, 70.

23 Materski, *Katyń: Dokumenty zbrodni*, vol 3, 196.

24 See Chapter 9.

25 One of Anders' most loyal officers was Captain Stanisław Kuczyński-Iskander Bej, who refused to abandon his seriously-wounded commander and, along with a lancer named Tomczycki, helped Anders to a nearby village, where they were all captured. While Anders was taken to hospital in Lwów, Kuczyński was taken to Starobelsk. Anders later reflected that it was his injury that saved him from sharing Kuczyński's fate. See Chapter 5.

26 Anders, *An Army in Exile*, 30.

27 Anders, *Bez ostatniego rozdziału*, 26, 49. According to Anders, General Boruta-Śpiechowicz confessed to him later that, unable to withstand physical beatings, he told the NKVD about a secret meeting with Anders in Lwów in October 1939 during which Anders had shared his plan to escape to the West. Anders attributes his harsh treatment to this confession.

28 Peszkowski, *Wspomnienia*, 37.

29 Tadeusz Felsztyn, PISM 12/3/16.

30 Ibid.

CHAPTER 9: 'GUESTS'

1 Berling, *Wspomnienia*, vol 1, 71 and AAN R-156, Leon Bukojemski.

2 Berling, *Wspomnienia*, vol 1, 71.

3 Józef Lis, 23 December 1945 statement to Polish military authorities in the field, PISM Kol 12/3/44. Also in *Madden Committee Hearings*, vol 4, 570–1.

4 Berling, *Wspomnienia*, vol 1, 77.

5 Ibid., 84.

6 Lis, PISM Kol 12/3/44 and *Madden Committee Hearings*, vol 4, 570–1.

7 Lis testimony at *Madden Committee Hearings*, vol 4, 554.

8 Polish Cultural Foundation, *The Crime of Katyń*, 97.

9 Narcyz Łopianowski, 14 May 1943 statement to Polish military authorities, reproduced in *Madden Committee Hearings*, vol 4, 822.

10 Berling, *Wspomnienia*, vol 1, 95.

11 Ibid., 87–8.

12 This re-use of Kozelsk camp was later to lead to some confusion during the search for the missing officers because reports of officers who had been imprisoned in Kozelsk and Starobelsk momentarily raised the hopes of those who were searching for their comrades. Once the facts had been established Józef Czapski and his staff began referring to the later iterations of the camps as Kozelsk 2 and Starobelsk 2.

13 Wacław Przeździecki, Piłsudski Institute, London, Kol 71, syg 4–11.

14 Ibid.

15 Łopianowski, 13 October 1942 statement to Polish military authorities, PISM Kol, 12/3/45.

16 Narcyz Łopianowski, *Rozmowy z NKWD*, 33.

17 Edmund Tacik, PISM A.V.96/50/30.

CHAPTER 10: 'VILLA OF BLISS'

1 Łopianowski, *Rozmowy z NKWD*, 48.

2 A brief reference is made to Morawski's letter in an NKVD communication from Pyotr Soprunenko to Sergei Kruglov dated 3 June 1941 concerning a second letter addressed by Morawski to Beria on 26 May 1941 entitled 'The Current International Situation and the Future of Poland'. The letter contains an obsessively detailed and somewhat eccentric analysis of Poland's past mistakes and future as a socialist country, including point by point instructions for Beria concerning the necessary conditions for the victory of the proletariat: 'Unite all conscious revolutionary elements in Poland, France, Germany and other countries on the basis of a pan-European revolution, specifically: FREEDOM AND EQUALITY FOR ALL NATIONS! PEACE WITHOUT VICTOR OR LOSERS! SOCIALIST STATES IN SOCIALIST EUROPE! ONLY A UNION OF SOCIALIST EUROPE CAN BEAT WAR!' (Materski, *Katyń: Dokumenty zbrodni*, vol 3, doc 152, 358). Although he later returned to Griazovets and fought in Anders' Army, Morawski died in Egypt in 1945 in circumstances that remain unclear. A suggestion that he committed suicide (Bober, 248) almost certainly confuses Morawski with his son Zygmunt, who killed himself in 1943 (PISM A.XII.1.9). Another resident of the villa, Franciszek Kukuliński, claims that Morawski was poisoned by the Polish Intelligence Services in Egypt (AAN, R-156 Franciszek Kukuliński 08 October 1964), while

a third source contends that Morawski was arrested by the Polish military authorities in Palestine and died on release from prison in 1945 (Bober, 138, footnote by Krzysztof Halicki) and a fourth that Morawski was arrested during the evacuation of the Polish army from the USSR by Polish military counter-intelligence (Materski, *Katyń: Dokumenty zbrodni*, vol 3, footnote to doc 152, 358).

3 The sixteenth republic, the Karelo-Finnish Soviet Socialist Republic, was established by the Soviet government on 31 March 1940 following the conclusion of the Winter War. In 1956 it was merged into the Russian Soviet Federative Socialist Republic, reducing the total number of Soviet republics to fifteen.

4 AAN, R-156 Group interview recorded 09 March 1965. See also Adam Zamoyski, *Warsaw 1920*, 133.

5 Łopianowski, PISM Kol 12/3/45 and *Madden Committee Hearings*, vol 4, 816–17.

6 Łopianowski statement 19 November 1941, Piłsudski Institute, London, Kol 71 syg 7.

7 Lis, PISM Kol 12/3/44 and *Madden Committee Hearings*, vol 4, 563–5 and 570–1.

8 AAN, R-156, Leon Bukojemski.

9 Łopianowski, PISM Kol 12/3/45 and *Madden Committee Hearings*, vol 4, 816–17. Some versions of these events claim that Captain Łopianowski had been instructed by General Przeździecki to act as a spy in the villa. Although Łopianowski reported to Przeździecki as soon as he saw the general again it seems unlikely that Przeździecki gave him such an instruction since they were separated on 23 December 1940, before Łopianowski even met Berling and Gorczyński. Łopianowski himself makes no mention in his memoir, *Rozmowy z NKWD*, of any such order.

10 Lis, *Madden Committee Hearings*, vol 4, 563–5.

11 Łopianowski, PISM Kol 12/3/45, and *Madden Committee Hearings*, vol 4, 816–17.

12 Łopianowski claims that Lis too signed the document; Lis states that he did not. The disagreement may be a result of the fact that there were two versions of the declaration: in the second, the most fervently pro-communist members of the group decided that the Soviets might be offended by the men referring to themselves as 'officers of the Polish army', amending the phrase to read 'officers of the late Polish army'. This final version was not signed by Łopianowski, Gorczyński or Lis.

13 See Chapters 12 and 13 for events following the German invasion of the Soviet Union, and Chapter 19 for the breakdown of Polish–Soviet relations in May 1943 and the formation of the Kościuszko Division.

14 Łopianowski, PISM Kol 12/3/45 and *Madden Committee Hearings*, vol 4, 816–17.

CHAPTER 11: FACTIONS

1   Jan Mintowt-Czyż, statement 10 May 1943, RAF Hucknall, PISM Kol 12/5.
2   Mintowt-Czyż family correspondence with the author, June 2019.
3   Mintowt-Czyż, PISM Kol 12/5.
4   Materski, *Katyń: Dokumenty zbrodni*, vol 3, doc 116, 283.
5   Ibid., doc 55, 160.
6   Ibid., doc 64, 180. His plea draws attention to a surprising fact: that Moscow, in retaining all the personal records from the previous three camps, did not share their contents with the team at Griazovets. This suggests that Merkulov did not require additional intelligence on these men since he had what he needed in the existing files.
7   Felsztyn, PISM Kol 12/3/16.
8   Wołkowicki, PISM Kol 212/3.
9   Materski, *Katyń: Dokumenty zbrodni*, vol 3, doc 92, 236.
10   Ibid.
11   Ibid., doc 55, 160.
12   The lack of correspondence rights was a source of such anxiety to the prisoners that in order to calm them down Major Elman had given them permission to write in June and July 1940 but held back their letters. In September he complained to Moscow that the prisoners were continually harassing camp staff asking why they had received no replies, adding that he was also holding back nearly 200 letters addressed to POWs sent on from other camps from relatives living in German-occupied territory. Clearly frustrated, he awaited Moscow's response. (Materski, *Katyń: Dokumenty zbrodni*, vol 3, doc 38, 123.) General Wołkowicki wrote several times to Moscow to protest at the refusal to permit correspondence, the lack of pay and the absence of any provision for suitable clothing to survive a second winter in captivity (Wołkowicki, PISM Kol 212/3, and Materski, *Katyń: Dokumenty zbrodni*, vol 3, doc 40, 127 and doc 49, 147). Meanwhile, letters continued to arrive in Starobelsk from wives asking for news of their husbands. On 5 June 1940 a telegram was sent in response: 'Your husband has gone away. We do not know the address.' The women were told to ask for information from the Department of Prisoner of War Affairs at NKVD headquarters in Moscow (Materski, *Katyń: Dokumenty zbrodni*, vol 1, doc 226, 362). On 23 July 1940 the NKVD issued a protocol ordering the destruction of all incoming correspondence addressed to the prisoners previously held in Starobelsk.
13   Julian Ginsbert, witness statement, London 9 June 1943, PISM Kol 12/5.
14   Wołkowicki, *Madden Committee Hearings*, vol 4, 641.
15   Materski, *Katyń: Dokumenty zbrodni*, vol 3, doc 116, 283. An order was sent by

Merkulov on 6 April 1940 issuing instructions that the wives of specific officers were not to be deported along with the rest. The names on the list included the wives of Major Domoń, Lieutenant Colonel Morawski, General Wołkowicki and Lieutenant Colonel Bukojemski. (Materski, *Katyń: Dokumenty zbrodni*, vol 2, doc 66, 136–7.)

16 Bober, *Za drutami obozów sowieckich*, 200.
17 Młynarski, *79th Survivor*, 235.
18 Bober, *Za drutami obozów sowieckich*, 201.

CHAPTER 12: WAR!

1 Kamil Kantak, *Wybuch wojny w Griazowcu*, Wiadomości, London 1950, nr 52.
2 Timothy Snyder, *Bloodlands*, and Simon Sebag Montefiore, *Stalin – The Court of the Red Tsar.*
3 Młynarski, *79th Survivor*, 239.
4 Komarnicki statement, *Madden Committee Hearings*, vol 4, 801–7.
5 Kantak, *Wybuch wojny w Griazowcu*, Wiadomości.
6 Mintowt-Czyż, PISM Kol 12/5.
7 Materski, *Katyń: Dokumenty zbrodni*, vol 3, doc 176, 399.
8 Ibid., doc 185, 415.
9 Ibid., doc 176, 399.
10 Ibid., doc 188, 423.
11 Ibid., doc 178, 399. For the British prisoners see Stanisław Jaczyński, *Losy oficerów polskich ocalałych z zagłady na Wschodzie po wybuchu wojny niemiecko-radzieckiej, czerwiec-sierpień 1941 roku*, Przegląd Historyczno-Wojskowy 13 (64)/1 (239), 29–60, 2012, and Dr Kazimierz Strączyński, PISM Kol 372/6.
12 Materski, *Katyń: Dokumenty zbrodni*, vol 3, doc 178, 400.
13 Ibid., doc 178, 400.
14 Ibid. According to Polish accounts the French left the camp shortly afterwards as a result of intervention by the French authorities, seen off by the Poles with enthusiastic cries of 'Long live free France, long live General de Gaulle' and mass renditions of the Marseillaise – to which they replied with cries of '*Vives les braves camarades*', '*Vive la Pologne*' and so on (Strączyński, PISM Kol 372/6).
15 Strączyński, PISM Kol 372/6.
16 Ibid.
17 Ibid.
18 Materski, *Katyń: Dokumenty zbrodni*, vol 3, doc 195, 434.

19 Ibid., doc 195, 438. A reference to soldiers who fought in Józef Piłsudski's Polish legions during World War I.

20 Swianiewicz, *In the Shadow of Katyń*, 65, also Stanisław Kilian, ed. *Wacław Komarnicki o ustroju państwa i konstytucji.*

21 Anders, *An Army in Exile*, 44.

22 Ibid., 48–9.

23 Not to be confused with his more famous namesake, who was chief of staff of the Red Army.

24 Słowes, *The Road to Katyń*, 215.

25 Peszkowski, *Wspomnienia*, 56.

26 Anders, *An Army in Exile*, 58.

27 Młynarski, *79th Survivor*, 243.

28 Bober, *Za drutami obozów sowieckich*, 216.

29 PISM, A. 12/5 'Uniwersytet' w Griazowcu, k. 1–11.

30 Materski, *Katyń: Dokumenty zbrodni*, vol 3, doc 206, 458–63. According to Dr Salomon Słowes, the men who chose to remain behind as Soviet citizens were left to fend for themselves by the Russians; eventually some were permitted to join Anders' Army after intervention from friends on their behalf; others volunteered for the pro-Soviet Kościuszko division, formed in 1943 under Berling's leadership (Słowes, *The Road to Katyń*, 115).

31 Czapski, *The Inhuman Land*, 8.

32 Peszkowski, *Wspomnienia*, 58.

CHAPTER 13: THE NEW POLISH ARMY

1 Czapski, *The Inhuman Land*, 13.

2 Ibid., 12.

3 Keith Sword, *Deportation and Exile*, 5–6.

4 Anders, *An Army in Exile*, 66.

5 Halik Kochański, *The Eagle Unbowed*, 138.

6 Sword, *Deportation and Exile*, 25–7.

7 Cienciala et al., *Katyń: A Crime*, 139.

8 For a detailed discussion of this subject see Sword, 25–7, Kochanski, 137–8, also Cienciala et al., 138–79 and note 34 to these pages.

9 Anne Applebaum, *Gulag, A History*, 402.

10 Czapski, *The Inhuman Land*, 23.

11 Anders, *An Army in Exile*, 54.

12 Ibid., 64.

13 General Przeździecki was initially appointed leader of the Emergency Army Centre (*Ośrodek Zapasowy Armii*) but was suspended from the position after Soviet

accusations that he criticised their government after the signing of the Sikorski–Maisky agreement. He spent much of the rest of the war a reluctant retiree from front-line action, penning letters from Palestine to the military authorities begging to be allowed to return to active service (Piłsudski Institute, Kol 71, syg 4). After the war he lived in exile, working as a carpenter and radio technician before retiring to the Penley Polish Hospital near Wrexham in Wales, where he died in 1964.

14 Zygmunt Bohusz-Szyszko, *Berling i jego towarzysze*. Notatnik wojenny, cz 10, 'Orzel Biały', London 1975, no. 9, 10–12.

15 Anders, *An Army in Exile*, 52, and *Madden Committee Hearings*, vol 4, 939, referring to *Pravda*. Also *Red Star* (newspaper of the Red Army) No 218/4667, 17 September 1940.

16 General Januszajtis-Żegota, who had been one of the NKVD's potential 'candidates' to lead a Polish division in the Red Army, was transferred to the UK in August to serve in the Polish military administration.

17 Bohusz-Szyszko, *Madden Committee Hearings*, vol 4, 659.

18 Raczyński, *In Allied London*, 114.

19 Polish Cultural Foundation, *The Crime of Katyń*, 80.

20 Stanisław Kot, *Conversations with the Kremlin*, 74.

21 Ibid., 86.

22 Ibid., 105.

23 Polish Cultural Foundation, *The Crime of Katyń*, 86.

24 Later, once Czapski left for Moscow, Jan Kaczkowski headed the bureau, assisted by Roman Voit and Tadeusz Felsztyn.

25 Swianiewicz, *In the Shadow of Katyń*, 218.

26 Czapski, *The Inhuman Land*, 39.

27 Bohusz-Szyszko, *Madden Committee Hearings*, vol 4, 662.

28 Polish Cultural Foundation, *The Crime of Katyń*, 86.

29 Kot, *Conversations with the Kremlin*, 142.

CHAPTER 14: CZAPSKI'S QUEST

1 Czapski's account of his efforts to obtain information about the missing officers is the subject of his memoir, *The Inhuman Land*. This chapter refers mainly to events related in pages 84–8, 98–129 and 163–4 of the 1987 English edition published by the Polish Cultural Foundation. For ease of reading I have not provided multiple references.

2 See also Swianiewicz, *In the Shadow of Katyń*, 162–3.

3 Czapski, *Madden Committee Hearings*, vol 4, 949.

4 The National Archives (TNA), WO 208/1735 – cited in Eugenia Maresch, *Katyń 1940*, 19.

5 TNA WO 32/15548, cited in Maresch, *Katyń 1940*, 12.
6 Raikhman was in fact a major when Czapski met him. He was promoted to general in 1945.

CHAPTER 15: EVACUATION

1 Sword, *Deportation and Exile*, 57.
2 Ibid., 62, and Norman Davies, *Trail of Hope*, 125.
3 Davies, *Trail of Hope*, 126. Between August and September 1941 the British and the Soviets undertook a joint military action to prevent oil-rich Iran from falling into the German sphere of influence, the result of which was the establishment of an Anglo-Soviet protectorate.
4 Polish Cultural Foundation, *The Crime of Katyń*, 92–3.
5 Davies, *Trail of Hope*, 177.
6 Sword, *Deportation and Exile*, 67.
7 Ibid., 84.
8 Ibid., 74–5.
9 Davies, *Trail of Hope*, 177.
10 Peszkowski, *Wspomnienia*, 64–5.
11 See Chapter 23, pages 279–82 for a discussion of the further fate of Berling and other pro-Soviet officers.
12 Czapski, *The Inhuman Land*, 281–2.

CHAPTER 16: THE WITNESS

1 Swianiewicz's account of his journey from Kozelsk to Smolensk, Moscow and Kotlas is covered in pages 71–128 of his memoir, *In the Shadow of Katyń*. For ease of reading I have not provided multiple references.
2 See Chapter 6, page 66.
3 Michał Romm was reprieved on the morning he was due to leave Ostashkov, spared because he was the nephew of a prominent Soviet film director, his namesake Mikhail Romm. He remained in the Soviet Union, taking Soviet citizenship (Cienciala et al., *Katyń: A Crime*, 126).
4 Main Administration for State Security, the 'secret political' section responsible for surveillance of the Communist Party, the intelligentsia, religious and other groups (Cienciala et al., *Katyń: A Crime*, 490, note 115).
5 Materski, *Katyń: Dokumenty zbrodni*, vol 2, doc 149, 246, translation from Cienciala et al., *Katyń: A Crime*, 185.
6 See Chapter 2, note 4.

7   AAN, R–156 Kazimierz Rosen-Zawadzki, 09 March 1965.

CHAPTER 17: ESCAPE

1   The second stage of Swianiewicz's account of his journey from Kotlas to Tehran is covered in pages 129–223 of his memoir, *In the Shadow of Katyń*. For ease of reading I have not provided multiple references.
2   Kot, *Conversations with the Kremlin*, 74.
3   Tadeusz Romer is known best for his actions as Poland's ambassador to Tokyo. Between 1940–41 he was responsible for helping around 6,000 Polish and Lithuanian Jewish refugees to obtain transit visas to Japan and further papers to safe countries, thus enabling them to escape the Holocaust.
4   Kot, *Conversations with the Kremlin*, 267.
5   Ibid., 268.
6   Raczyński, *In Allied London*, 116.

CHAPTER 18: BODIES

1   Louis Paul Lochner, ed., *The Goebbels Diaries*, 245.
2   Soviet War News, no. 541, 17 April 1943, cited in Polish Cultural Foundation, *The Crime of Katyń*, 102.
3   Cienciala et al., *Katyń: A Crime*, 215.
4   Ferdynand Goetel, *Czasy wojny*, 67.
5   Ibid., 69.
6   Ibid., 68.
7   Ibid., 71.
8   Professor Buhtz was the author of the German 'white book' on Katyń, *Amtliches Material zum Massenmord von Katyń*, which includes all the material amassed by the Germans on the subject of Katyń, including the findings of the International Medical Commission.
9   Goetel, *Czasy wojny*, 71.
10 Ibid., 71.
11 *Nowy Kurier Warszawski*, 17–18 April 1943, cited in Stanisław Jankowski, Ryszard Kotarba, *Literaci a sprawa katyńska – 1945*.
12 Janina Kremka, widow of Reserve 2nd Lieutenant Edward Kremka, in *Pisane miłością: losy wdów katyńskich*, vol 1, 313.
13 Kazimierz Skarżyński, *Madden Committee Hearings*, vol 3, 397.
14 Ibid., 394.

CHAPTER 19: POLITICS

1 Raczyński, *In Allied London*, 141, and *The Diaries of Sir Alexander Cadogan, 1938–45*, 520–1.
2 *The Goebbels Diaries*, 258.
3 The Poles were extremely popular in the early stages of the war but, once the Soviet Union became allied to the British and Americans, attitudes changed. For the sake of the war effort Stalin was routinely portrayed in the press as genial 'Uncle Joe', the saviour of the Western alliance; the enormous sacrifices of the Russian people were constantly emphasised. Polish hostility towards the Soviet government was viewed with displeasure. Some British newspapers even accused the Poles of conducting an irresponsible private war from British soil. Throughout the war the US and British governments routinely suppressed any suggestion that the Soviets were responsible for the crime of Katyń.
4 Cienciala et al., *Katyń: A Crime*, 214.
5 *The Goebbels Diaries*, 270.
6 TNA FO 371/34577 C6160/258/55.
7 Ibid.

CHAPTER 20: IN THE FOREST

1 In a striking parallel, shortly after the public announcement about Katyń the Germans discovered similar mass graves in the Ukrainian city of Vinnytsia, where over 9,000 (mainly) Ukrainian citizens were massacred by the NKVD during the Great Terror of 1937–38. They were shot in the back of the head, their hands bound, their bodies buried under a recreational park. Just as they did at Katyń, the Nazis sought to use the discovery for propaganda purposes, inviting journalists and other visitors to inspect the site. They also brought an international medical commission to investigate the graves, including two forensic specialists (Professor Orsós of Hungary and Professor Birkle of Romania) who had only just finished working at Katyń. (*Remembering Katyń*, Alexander Etkind, Rory Finnin et al., 62.)
2 Dr Wodziński's account of the five weeks he spent in Katyń can be found in Polish and English at PISM 12/4/37. It is also reproduced in English in Polish Cultural Foundation, *The Crime of Katyń*, 191–228. For ease of reading I have not given multiple references.
3 PISM Kol 12/3/37.
4 Colonel Jerzy Grobicki, *Facts About Katyń, Lwów and Wilno*, Nr 47, 1947.
5 Polish Cultural Foundation, *The Crime of Katyń*, 285.

6   See Chapter 26.
7   Captain Gilder's report, PISM Kol 12/30F/38.
8   See Chapter 24, note 2.
9   *Madden Committee Hearings*, vol 1, 15.
10 Dr Robel was arrested by the Nazis in November 1939 as part of the Sonderaktion Krakau, when 183 Polish academics were arrested by the Gestapo and sent to concentration camps. He was released in February 1940 and allowed to return to his post.
11 This happened briefly to survivor Zdzisław Peszkowski. In a terrible irony, in February 1940 Peszkowski had given his blanket to a close friend from school, Juliusz Bakoń, who had no coat and was wearing light summer boots. When the bodies of the Kozelsk prisoners were found at Katyń in 1943 the blanket was discovered with Peszkowski's name on it, causing him to be placed temporarily on the list of the dead.
12 Andrzej Przewoźnik, *Katyń. Zbrodnia, prawda, pamięć*, 308–9.
13 *Pamiętniki znalezione w Katyniu*, 105.
14 *Madden Committee Hearings*, vol 5, 1511–18.
15 Allen Paul, *Katyń*, 281.
16 *Madden Committee Hearings*, vol 5, 1511–18.
17 Jankowski, Kotarba, *Literaci a sprawa katyńska*, 105–6.
18 *Katyń i Czerwony Krzyż*, 'Kultura', Paris, May 1955.
19 J.K. Zawodny, *Katyń*, 272.

CHAPTER 21: BURDENKO

1   *The Goebbels Diaries*, 395.
2   *Amtliches Material zum Massenmord von Katyń*, Berlin 1943.
3   The details of this NKVD preparatory work only became public after 1990 (Cienciala et al., *Katyń: A Crime*, 226–9). The work of the Burdenko Commission has been analysed principally by Russian researchers, notably Natalia Lebedeva and Professor Inessa Jażborowska.
4   Natalia Lebedeva, *Komisja specjalna i jej przewodniczacy Burdenko*, 'Zeszyty Katyńskie' nr 23 (2008), 62, cited in Przewoźnik, *Katyń. Zbrodnia, prawda, pamięć*, 358.
5   See Chapter 22, page 265.
6   The Orthodox equivalent of a bishop or archbishop.
7   Alexander Werth and Nicholas Werth, *Russia at War 1941–1945*, 661–2.
8   Ibid., 662.
9   W.H. Lawrence, *New York Times*, 27 January 1944.
10 Werth, *Russia at War*, 663.

11 Ibid., 665.

12 Ibid., 663–4.

13 See Chapter 20, note 1.

14 *Madden Committee Hearings*, vol 7, 2124.

15 Ibid., 2132–49.

16 Ibid., 2136.

17 W.L. White, *Report on the Russians*, 110.

18 Werth, *Russia at War*, 666.

19 See Chapters 15 and 19.

20 White, *Report on the Russians*, 109.

21 TNA FO 371/39390 C2099/8/55G dispatch 25.

22 Ibid.

23 Ibid.

24 TNA FO 371/39390 C2096/8/55G.

25 TNA FO 371/39390 C2096. Such a test was made during the Madden hearings when a forester, Fritz von Herff, was asked his opinion regarding the age of the trees (*Madden Committee Hearings*, vol 5, 1493–4).

26 TNA FO 371/39393 C 2957/8/55G, cited in Maresch, *Katyń 1940*, 178.

27 Maresch, *Katyń 1940*, 184.

28 TNA FO 371/39393 C 2957/8/55G, cited in Maresch, *Katyń 1940*, 185.

29 Berling, *Wspomnienia*, vol 1, 26.

30 *Wolna Polska*, ed. 4, 11 Feb 1944.

31 J.K. Zawodny, *Death in the Forest*, 158. Zawodny cites a letter from Olshansky to a Russian-language journal published in the US in June 1950 making the same claim. See also *Madden Committee Hearings*, vol 7, 1941. Burdenko's daughter-in-law allegedly confirmed this statement to Yuri Zoria, son of the Soviet deputy prosecutor at the Nuremberg trials (Cienciala et al., *Katyń: A Crime*, 228).

CHAPTER 22: PURSUIT

1 PISM Kol 12/3/9, statement by Stefania Wanda Cioch, 29Mar46.

2 Ibid.

3 Specifically, the NKGB, from 1943 the section of the NKVD responsible for foreign intelligence and counter-intelligence, headed by Vsevolod Merkulov.

4 See Stanisław Jankowski, Ryszard Kotarba, *Literaci a sprawa katyńska – 1945*, from 81 on, *Śledztwo czy mistyfikacja?*

5 PISM Kol 12/4/37, and Przewoźnik, *Katyń. Zbrodnia, prawda, pamięć*, 372.

6 PISM Kol 12/3/9.

7 *Madden Committee Hearings*, vol 4, 768.

8 The case of Józef Mackiewicz bears some resemblance to that of Goetel. Mackiewicz, a resident of the city of Wilno, took part in the second Polish delegation to Katyń. On his return he wrote a report for a German-sponsored publication, *Goniec Codzienny*. Despite the fact that Mackiewicz had the approval of the Polish Underground both for the visit and the report, he was accused of collaboration with the Germans first by his fellow Poles and then, after the war, by the communist authorities. He fled Poland in 1946, travelling to Italy, where he joined the Polish II Corps and met Krivovertsov, whom he had first encountered at Katyń, taking a statement from him as Goetel did. Mackiewicz later settled in London and in 1954 moved to Germany. Immediately after the war he was asked to write and edit the official publication of the Polish government in exile, *Zbrodnia Katyńska* (*The Crime of Katyń, Facts & Documents*, 1948) but because of the accusation of collaboration he could not be acknowledged as its author. He later published another book, *The Katyń Wood Murders* (1951) and gave evidence at the Madden Committee hearings in 1952.

9 PISM Kol 12/3/37c and Mackiewicz in *Wiadomości* nr 15–16, London, 20 April 1952.

10 See Jankowski, Kotarba, *Literaci a sprawa katyńska*, from 81 on, *Śledztwo czy mistyfikacja?*

11 Materski, *Katyń: Dokumenty zbrodni*, vol 4, 343–4.

12 Cienciala et al., *Katyń: A Crime*, 233–4.

13 PISM Kol 12/3/9.

14 Wodziński family correspondence with Bogusław Hynek, 10 June 2009.

15 Dr Adam Schebesta (Szebesta), PCK Kraków, http://pck.malopolska.pl/dr-adam-schebesta-szebesta, accessed 12 August 2020.

16 Przewoźnik, *Katyń. Zbrodnia, prawda, pamięć*, 386.

17 PISM Kol 12/3/9.

18 Przewoźnik, *Katyń. Zbrodnia, prawda, pamięć*, 377.

19 Teresa Kaczorowska, *Children of the Katyń Massacre*, 139.

20 Ibid., 45.

21 See Cienciala et al., *Katyń: A Crime*, 229–35.

CHAPTER 23: THE SURVIVORS

1 Raczyński, *In Allied London*, 277.

2 Bober, *Za drutami obozów sowieckich*, 236–7, and Materski, *Katyń: Dokumenty zbrodni*, vol 3, doc 206, 458–63.

3 Poland was compensated for the loss of its eastern regions with additional territory in the west.

4   Sixteen prominent members of the Polish underground were invited to Moscow on the pretext of a conference about their future involvement with the new Polish government. Instead they were kidnapped by the NKVD and subjected to a show trial at which they were accused of anti-Soviet activities. Amongst them was General Okulicki, whom Józef Czapski met in 1941. He died in prison.

5   Owen O'Malley, *Phantom Caravan*, 228, 232.

6   *Człowiek, który uniknął Katynia*, Gazeta Wyborcza, 06 April 2012.

7   Polish historian Krzysztof Halicki edited and published Bober's manuscript.

8   Kaczorowska, *Children of the Katyń Massacre*, Chapter 16, 201–20.

9   See Bober, *Za drutami obozów sowieckich*, 233–55. Adam Moszyński's invaluable work on compiling the so-called 'Katyń List' of names of victims took up many years of his exile in the UK. Less well known is the fact that he also put together a list of 'the saved' – the men from the three camps who ended up at Griazovets. He sent this to Bober, offering it as an addition to Bober's manuscript. This list appears in the published book of Bober's memoir, along with detailed notes about groups and individuals who left Griazovets and the dates when they left and/or returned.

10 Jolanta Zaręba-Wronkowska, Okręgowa Izba Lekarska w Kielce, http://www.oil.org.pl/xml/oil/oil56/gazeta/numery/n2004/n200407/n20040717, accessed 12 August 2020, and obituary of Dr Zofia Godlewska z Pamfiłowskich by Jolanta Zaręba-Wronkowska, *Gazeta Wyborcza*, 21 December 2010.

11 Materski, *Katyń: Dokumenty zbrodni*, vol 3, doc 16, 81 and AAN R-156 Roman Imach 30 November 1964.

12 Godlewski, *Przeżyłem Starobielsk*.

13 Materski, *Katyń: Dokumenty zbrodni*, vol 4, 544.

14 AAN, R–156 Kazimierz Rosen-Zawadzki 09 March 1965, Roman Imach 30 November 1964, Franciszek Kukuliński 08 October 1964, Stanisław Szczypiorski 30 November 1964 and 20 October 1964. Lieutenant Colonel Bukojemski had already been arrested by the Polish military authorities in March 1942. He was put on trial, accused of 'cooperation with the enemy', and sentenced to 15 years in prison. After a short spell in prison in Tashkent, Bukojemski received a tip-off that he was going to be evacuated along with everyone else, so he adopted the ploy suggested by the NKVD and pretended to be suffering from typhus, thus remaining behind and deserting from the Polish army. He was taken to Moscow, where he was met by Berling. In May 1943 they began organising the Polish 1st Division (AAN, R-156 Leon Bukojemski).

15 Ibid.

CHAPTER 24: COLD WAR

1   See *Madden Committee Hearings*, vol 4.
2   Captain Gilder and Colonel Van Vliet filed reports to their respective military authorities in 1945, shortly after the end of the war. These reports later acquired some significance when it transpired that, despite the fact that they were both supposed to have been transmitted in August 1945 to the Office of Controls of the US Department of State by Major General Clayton Bissell, they had disappeared. Van Vliet also had a personal conversation with Bissell about the case on 22 May 1945, after which Van Vliet dictated his report and Bissell, having marked it as 'Top Secret', asked Van Vliet to sign a document committing him not to speak publicly of the matter (PISM Kol 12/30F/38). When press interest in Katyń rose again in 1949–50 the chief of information of the Department of the Army, Major General Parks, asked Van Vliet to submit a second memorandum about his visit to Katyń, which he did in May 1950 while still on active service in the Far East. Gilder's report was declassified by the British authorities and sent to accompany it.
3   Cienciala et al., *Katyń: A Crime*, 334–5.
4   Ibid., 336–7.
5   Ibid., 332–3.
6   Researchers are still working to identify the names of these victims, to date with only partial success, particularly in the case of the victims shot in Belorussia (Belarus).
7   The SB replaced the UB in 1956 as the state security service in Poland, just as the KGB replaced the NKVD in the Soviet Union in 1954.
8   Since the Katyń Massacre took place on multiple dates in multiple sites there is no single day on which it can be commemorated. 13 April was the date Radio Berlin first broadcast news of the discovery of the graves by the Germans in 1943.
9   Przewoźnik, *Katyń. Zbrodnia, prawda, pamięć*, 423.

CHAPTER 25: REVELATIONS

1   I am indebted to two works in particular for the clarity and detail of their accounts of this complex period: Cienciala et al., *Katyń: A Crime* and Andrzej Przewoźnik, *Katyń. Zbrodnia, prawda, pamięć*.
2   Cienciala et al., *Katyń: A Crime*, 338–9.
3   Ibid., 343.
4   Ibid., 345.
5   Ibid., 118.

CHAPTER 26: DEATH

1 Maria Skrzyńska-Pławińska, *Indeks represjonowanych*, vol 2. *Rozstrzelani w Charkowie*.
2 Stanisław Mikke, *Śpij, mężny w Katyniu, Charkowie i Miednoje*, 27.
3 Przewoźnik, *Katyń. Zbrodnia, prawda, pamięć*, 454.
4 Skrzyńska-Pławińska, *Indeks represjonowanych*, vol 3. *Rozstrzelani w Twerze*.
5 Ibid., vol 1. *Rozstrzelani w Katyniu*.
6 Cienciala et al., *Katyń: A Crime*, 136.
7 Kaczorowska, *Children of the Katyń Massacre*, 36–7.
8 *Pisane miłością*, 137–42.

CHAPTER 27: SMOLENSK

1 Przewoźnik, *Katyń. Zbrodnia, prawda, pamięć*, 572.
2 Gazeta Wyborcza, nr 90, 17–18 April 2010, *Serce Rosjan i wielka szansa*. Marcin Wojciechowski rozmawia z Adamem Danielem Rotfeldem. Cited in Przewoźnik, *Katyń. Zbrodnia, prawda, pamięć*, 596.
3 Przewoźnik, *Katyń. Zbrodnia, prawda, pamięć*, 572.
4 Cienciala et al., *Katyń: A Crime*, 261–2.
5 Andrzej Przewoźnik, cited in Przewoźnik, *Katyń. Zbrodnia, prawda, pamięć*, 587.
6 Ibid., 590.
7 Speech by Vladimir Putin, cited in Przewoźnik, *Katyń. Zbrodnia, prawda, pamięć*, 631.
8 Russian Parliament Condemns Stalin for Katyń Massacre, BBC News website, 26 November 2010, https://www.bbc.co.uk/news/world-europe-11845315, accessed 12 August 2020.
9 Snyder, *Bloodlands*, 406.
10 'Russians Remove Memorial to Poles Killed by Stalin', *The Times*, 11 May 2020.

CONCLUSION: SURVIVING KATYŃ

1 Polish premier Jerzy Buzek at the opening of the Polish War Cemetery at Katyń in 2000, cited in Cienciala et al., *Katyń: A Crime*, 351.
2 Snyder, *Bloodlands*, 89–104.
3 Czapski, *The Inhuman Land*, 164.
4 The Nazis followed a similar policy in Poland during the war, aimed at

'decapitating' the country by destroying its intellectual, spiritual and political leaders. Although there is no evidence of direct Nazi–Soviet collaboration in this respect there is an uncanny echo in the fact that the infamous AB Aktion, in which governor of Poland Hans Frank ordered the elimination of Poles on the basis of their education, religious convictions or political persuasions, was conceived and carried out in March 1940, just as Stalin was signing off Beria's execution order.

5 For a detailed examination of this question, see Cienciala et al., *Katyń: A Crime*, 141–8.

6 Sebag Montefiore, *Stalin*, 341.

7 Aleksandr Shelepin, 1959, referring to the dangers of the operation being revealed. See Chapter 24, pages 286–8.

8 *Madden Committee Hearings*, vol 4, 653.

9 Swianiewicz, *In the Shadow of Katyń*, 122.

10 Młynarski, *The 79th Survivor*, 9.

11 Ibid.

12 Swianiewicz, *In the Shadow of Katyń*, 222.

Select Bibliography

While Polish spelling is used throughout this text and its notes, in the Bibliography we have honoured the anglicised spellings of the original publication.

ARCHIVES

Archiwum Akt Nowych, Warsaw
Centralne Archiwum Wojskowe, Wojskowe Biuro Historyczne, Warsaw
The Polish Institute and Sikorski Museum, London
Joseph Piłsudski Institute, London
The National Archives, Kew

PUBLISHED SOURCES

Amtliches Material zum Massenmord von Katyn (Berlin: Zentralverl. der NSDAP F. Eher, 1943)

Anders, Władysław, *An Army in Exile* (London: Macmillan, 1949)

— *Bez ostatniego rozdziału* (London: Gryf, 1959)

Applebaum, Anne, *Gulag* (London: Allen Lane, 2003)

— *Iron Curtain* (London: Allen Lane, 2012)

Ascherson, Neal, *The Struggles for Poland* (New York: Random House, 1987)

Berling, Zygmunt, *Wspomnienia*, vol 1: *Z łagrów do Andersa* (Warszawa: Polski Dom Wydawniczy, 1990)

Bliss Lane, Arthur, *I Saw Freedom Betrayed* (London: Regency Publications, 1949)

Bober, Jan, and Krzysztof Halicki (ed), *Za drutami obozów sowieckich: wspomnienia* (Łódź: Księży Młyn Dom Wydawniczy Michał Koliński, 2016)

Bór-Komorowski, Tadeusz, *The Secret Army* (Havertown: Frontline Books, 2011)

Cadogan, Alexander, and David Dilks (ed), *The Diaries of Sir Alexander Cadogan, O.M., 1938–1945* (London: Cassell, 1971)

Carton de Wiart, Adrian, *Happy Odyssey* (Havertown: Pen and Sword, 2007)

Cienciala, Anna M., Natalia S. Lebedeva, and Wojciech Materski, *Katyń: A Crime Without Punishment (Annals of Communism)* (New Haven, CT: Yale University Press, 2007)

Czapski, Józef, *Wspomnienia starobielskie* (Lublin: Spotkania, 1985)

— and Gerard Hopkins, *The Inhuman Land* (London: Polish Cultural Institute, 1987)

— and Antonia Lloyd-Jones, *Inhuman Land: Searching for the Truth in Soviet Russia 1941–1942* (New York: New York Review of Books, 2018)

— and Eric Karpeles, *Lost Time* (New York: New York Review of Books, 2018)

Davies, Norman, *God's Playground, Vol. 2, 1795 to the Present* (Oxford: Clarendon Press, 1983)

— *Heart of Europe* (Oxford: Oxford University Press, 2001)

— *Trail of Hope* (Oxford: Osprey Publishing, 2015)

Etkind, Alexander, Rory Finnin, Uilleam Blacker et al., *Remembering Katyń* (Cambridge: Polity Press, 2012)

Fitzgibbon, Louis, *Katyń: a Crime Without Parallel* (London: Tom Stacey, 1971)

— *The Katyń Cover-up* (London: Tom Stacey, 1972)

Godlewski, Zbigniew, 'Przeżyłem Starobielsk', *Wojskowy Przegląd Historyczny*, 1993, 306–31

Goetel, Ferdynand, *Czasy wojny* (London: Nakładem Katolickiego Ośrodka Wydawniczego 'Veritas', 1955)

Gruner-Żarnoch, Ewa, *Starobielsk w oczach ocalałych jeńców* (Warszawa: Tow. Opieki nad Archiwum Instytutu Literackiego w Paryżu, 2008)

— and Maria Danuta Wołągiewicz, *Słowa tęsknoty* (Szczecin: Stowarzyszenie Katyń, 1996)

Hearings, United States Congress, House of Representatives. Select Committee to Conduct an Investigation of the Facts, Evidence and Circumstances of the Katyn Forest Massacre (Washington: US Government Printing Office, 1952)

Herling, Gustaw, and Andrzej Ciołkosz, *A World Apart* (London: Joseph Heinemann, 1951)

Jaczyński, Stanisław, 'Losy oficerów polskich ocalałych z zagłady na wschodzie po wybuchu wojny niemiecko-radzieckiej, czerwiec-sierpień 1941 roku', *Przegląd Historyczno-Wojskowy*, 13 (2012), 29–60

— 'Polscy jeńcy wojenni obozu NKWD w Griazowcu wobec radzieckiej indoktrynacji i penetracji wywiadowczej', *Przegląd Historyczno-Wojskowy*, 13 (2012), 19–42

— '"Willa Szczęścia" w Małachówce. Próby pozyskania przez NKWD oficerów polskich do współpracy politycznej i wojskowej (1940–1941)', *Przegląd Historyczno-Wojskowy*, 12 (2011), 57–82

Jankowski, Stanisław M., and Ryszard Kotarba, *Literaci a sprawa katyńska – 1945* (Kraków: Wydawn. Tow. Naukowego 'Societas Vistulana', 2003)

Jażborowska, Inessa, Anatolij Jabłokow, and Jurij Zoria, *Katyń. Zbrodnia chroniona tajemnicą państwową* (Warszawa: Książka i Wiedza, 1998)

Kaczorowska, Teresa, *Children of the Katyn Massacre* (Jefferson, NC: McFarland, 2006)

Karski, Jan, *Story of a Secret State* (London: Penguin, 2011)

Kemp-Welch, A., *Poland Under Communism: A Cold War History* (Cambridge: Cambridge University Press, 2008)

Kilian, Stanisław, *Wacław Komarnicki o ustroju państwa i konstytucji* (Warszawa: Wydawnictro Sejmowe, 2000)

Kisielewski, Tadeusz A., *Katyń: Zbrodnia i kłamstwo* (Poznań: Dom Wydawniczy Rebis, 2010)

Kochanski, Halik, *The Eagle Unbowed: Poland and the Poles in the Second World War* (London: Allen Lane, 2012)

Kot, Stanislaw, *Conversations with the Kremlin and Dispatches from Russia* (London: Oxford University Press, 1963)

Lochner, Louis Paul, ed., *The Goebbels Diaries* (London: Hamish Hamilton, 1948)

Łopianowski, Narcyz, *Rozmowy z NKWD 1940–1941* (Warszawa: Instytut Wydawniczy Pax, 1990)

Mackiewicz, Joseph, *Katyn Wood Murders* (London: Hollis & Carter, 1951)

Madajczyk, Czesław, *Dramat katyński* (Warszawa: Książka i Wiedza, 1989)

Maisky, Ivan, and Gabriel Gorodetsky, *The Maisky Diaries: Red Ambassador to the Court of St James's 1932–1943* (London: Yale University Press, 2016)

Maligranda, Lech, 'Józef Marcinkiewicz (1910–1940) – On the Centenary of his Birth', *Banach Center Publications*, 95 (2011), 133–234

Maresch, Eugenia, *Katyń 1940, The Documentary Evidence of the West's Betrayal* (Stroud: Spellmount, 2010)

Materski, Wojciech, *Katyń: Dokumenty zbrodni*, vol. 1: *Jeńcy nie wypowiedzianej wojny, sierpień 1939 – marzec 1940* (Warszawa: Wydawnictwo TRIO, 1995)

— *Katyń: Dokumenty zbrodni*, vol 2: *Zagłada, marzec – czerwiec 1940* (Warszawa: Wydawnictwo TRIO, 1998)

— *Katyń: Dokumenty zbrodni*, vol. 3: *Losy ocalałych, lipiec 1940 – marzec 1943* (Warszawa: Wydawnictwo TRIO, 2001)

— *Katyń: Dokumenty zbrodni*, vol. 4: *Echa Katynia, kwiecień 1943 – marzec 2005* (Warszawa: Wydawnictwo TRIO, 2005)

Mikke, Stanisław, *Śpij, mężny w Katyniu, Charkowie i Miednoje* (Warszawa: Wydawnictwo LTW, 2011)

Młynarski, Bronisław, *The 79th Survivor* (London: Bachman and Turner, 1976)

Moorhouse, Roger, *First to Fight: The Polish War 1939* (London: The Bodley Head, 2019)

Moszyński, Adam, *Katyń. Wybór publicystyki 1943–1988 i 'Lista Katyńska'* (London: Polonia, 1988)

O'Malley, Owen St. Clair, *The Phantom Caravan* (John Murray: London, 1954)

Overy, Richard, *1939: Countdown to War* (New York: Viking, 2010)

Paczkowski, Andrzej, and Jane Cave, *The Spring Will Be Ours* (University Park, PA: Pennsylvania State University Press, 2003)

Paul, Allen, *Katyń* (DeKalb, IL: Northern Illinois University Press, 2010)

Peszkowski, Zdzisław, *Wspomnienia jeńca z Kozielska* (Warszawa: Wydawnictwo Archidiecezji Warszawskiej, 1989)

Pieńkowski, Tadeusz, *Droga polskich żołnierzy do Katynia, Miednoje, Piatichotek i …?* (Warszawa: MAG, 2000)

Porter, Brian, *Poland in the Modern World* (Chichester: Wiley Blackwell, 2014)

Przewoźnik, Andrzej, *Katyń. Zbrodnia, prawda, pamięć* (Warszawa: Świat Książki, 2010)

Raczyński, Edward, *In Allied London* (London: Weidenfeld & Nicolson, 1963)

Roliński, Adam, and Andrzej Rybicki, *Kłamstwo katyńskie* (Kraków: Księgarnia Akademicka, 2000)

Rutkowski, Tadeusz P., 'Żołnierz, renegat, więzień, historyk. O biografii Kazimierza Rosen-Zawadzkiego', *KLIO POLSKA, Studia i materiały z dziejów historiografii polskiej XIX-XX wieku*, 6 (2012), 101–40

Sanford, George, *Katyn and the Soviet Massacre of 1940* (Abingdon: Routledge, 2005)

Sarner, Harvey, *General Anders and the Soldiers of the Second Polish Corps* (Cathedral City, CA: Brunswick Press, 1997)

Sebag Montefiore, Simon, *Stalin: The Court of the Red Tsar* (London: Weidenfeld and Nicholson, 2003)

Shalamov, Varlam, *Kolyma Tales* (London: Penguin, 1994)

Skarżyński, Kazimierz, *Katyń: Raport Polskiego Czerwonego Krzyża* (Warszawa: Oficyna Wydawnicza 'Pokolenie', 1989)

Skrzyńska-Pławińska, Maria, *Rozstrzelani w Charkowie* (Warszawa: Ośrodek KARTA, 1996)

— *Rozstrzelani w Katyniu* (Warszawa: Ośrodek KARTA, 1995)

— *Rozstrzelani w Twerze* (Warszawa: Ośrodek KARTA, 1997)

Słowes, Salomon W., *The Road to Katyn* (Oxford: Blackwell Publishers in association with the Institute for Polish-Jewish Studies, 1992)

Snyder, Timothy, *Bloodlands, Europe between Hitler and Stalin* (London: Vintage, 2011)

— *The Reconstruction of Nations* (New Haven and London: Yale University Press, 2008)

Solzhenitsyn, Alexander, *The Gulag Archipelago 1918–1956* (London: Collins & Harvall, 1974)

Spanily, Andrzej, *Pisane miłością: losy wdów katyńskich* (Gdynia: ASP Rymsza Gdyńska Oficyna Wydawnicza, 2003)

Swianiewicz, Stanisław, *In the Shadow of Katyn: Stalin's Terror* (Pender Island: Borealis, 2002)

Sword, Keith, *Deportation and Exile* (Basingstoke: Macmillan in association with the School of Slavonic and East European Studies, University of London, 1994)

— *The Formation of the Polish Community in Great Britain 1939–1950* (London: School of Slavonic and East European Studies, University of London, 1989)

Szcześniak, Andrzej Leszek, *Katyń. Relacje, wspomnienia, publicystyka* (Warszawa: Wydawnictwo Alfa, 1989)

The Crime of Katyn, Facts & Documents (London: Polish Cultural Foundation, 1965)

Tucholski, Jędrzej, *Mord w Katyniu* (Warszawa: Instytut Wydawniczy PAX, 1991)

Werth, Alexander, and Nicolas Werth, *Russia at War 1941–1945* (New York: Skyhorse Publishing, 1964)

White, W.L, *Report on the Russians* (London: Eyre & Spottiswoode, 1945)

Wittlin, Thaddeus, *Time Stopped at 6:30: The Untold Story of the Katyn Massacre* (Indianapolis: The Bobbs-Merrill Company, 1965)

Wójcicki, Bolesław, *Prawda o Katyniu* (Warszawa: Czytelnik, 1953)

Zamoyski, Adam, *Lenin's Failed Conquest of Europe* (London: HarperPress, 2008)

— *The Polish Way* (London: John Murray, 1987)

Zawodny, J.K., *Katyń* (Paris: Editions Spotkania, 1989)

— *Death in the Forest* (Illinois: University of Notre Dame Press, 1962)

— ed. *Pamiętniki znalezione w Katyniu* (Paris: Editions Spotkania, 1990)

Index

References to images are in *italics*; references to notes are indicted by n.